Auto–Identification and Ubiquitous Computing Applications:
RFID and Smart Technologies for Information Convergence

Judith Symonds
AUT University, New Zealand

John Ayoade
American University of Nigeria, Nigeria

David Parry
AUT University, New Zealand

INFORMATION SCIENCE REFERENCE

Hershey · New York

Director of Editorial Content:	Kristin Klinger
Senior Managing Editor:	Jamie Snavely
Managing Editor:	Jeff Ash
Assistant Managing Editor:	Carole Coulson
Typesetter:	Chris Hrobak
Cover Design:	Lisa Tosheff
Printed at:	Yurchak Printing Inc.

Published in the United States of America by
Information Science Reference (an imprint of IGI Global)
701 E. Chocolate Avenue, Suite 200
Hershey PA 17033
Tel: 717-533-8845
Fax: 717-533-8661
E-mail: cust@igi-global.com
Web site: http://www.igi-global.com/reference

and in the United Kingdom by
Information Science Reference (an imprint of IGI Global)
3 Henrietta Street
Covent Garden
London WC2E 8LU
Tel: 44 20 7240 0856
Fax: 44 20 7379 0609
Web site: http://www.eurospanbookstore.com

Library of Congress Cataloging-in-Publication Data

Auto-identification and ubiquitous computing applications : RFID and smart technologies for information convergence / Judith Symonds, John Ayoade and Dave Parry, editor.

p. cm.

Includes bibliographical references and index.

Summary: "This book reports on practical problems and underlying theory related to the use of primary RFID technologies"--Provided by publisher.

ISBN 978-1-60566-298-5 (hbk.) -- ISBN 978-1-60566-299-2 (ebook)

1. Radio frequency identification systems--Industrial applications. I. Symonds, Judith, 1972- II. Ayoade, John, 1970- III. Parry, Dave, 1963 July 11-

TK6570.I34A98 2009

658.4'038--dc22

2008037980

British Cataloguing in Publication Data
A Cataloguing in Publication record for this book is available from the British Library.

All work contributed to this book is new, previously-unpublished material. The views expressed in this book are those of the authors, but not necessarily of the publisher.

Table of Contents

Section I
Setting the Scene

Section II
Smart Identification

Section III
Smart Health

Section IV
Smart Data & Convergence

Section V
Selected Readings

Detailed Table of Contents

Section I
Setting the Scene

Chapter I

Chin Boo Soon, The University of Auckland, New Zealand

Chin Boo Soon is an information systems supply chain specialist. The author was invited to write this introductory chapter based on his unique view of RFID technology. This chapter provides an overview of RFID development including a timeline critical RFID achievements and discussion of how auto-identification fits with this. In addition to this very knowledgeable view of RFID history, Chin Boo has also conducted a comprehensive survey of RFID uptake in New Zealand and although his study is reported elsewhere, this unique insight informs this chapter.

Section II
Smart Identification

Chapter II

John Garofalakis, University of Patras, Greece
Christos Mettouris, University of Patras, Greece

John Garofalakis and Christos Mettouris describe a prototype intelligent M-Commerce application designed for use in retail to identify customers wirelessly. Whilst they consider the use of RFID, they find wireless Blluetooth technology to be much more useful for their application. The development of such information location systems will lead a new generation of mobile enabled marketing customization.

Chapter III

John Ayoade, American University of Nigeria, Nigeria
Judith Symonds, Auckland University of Technology, New Zealand

In M-Commerce applications, such as in Chapter II, security of data held locally will be both the business value as well as main security concern. John Ayoade and Judith Symonds report on a prototype developed to explore security issues related to storing information on mobile devices such as RFID tags. The proposed system allows for quick identification of items and utilises the RFID authentication framework proposed as part of John Ayoade's research work at the National Institute of Information and Communications Technology, Tokyo, Japan.

Chapter IV

Filippo Gandino, Politecnico di Torino, Italy
Erwing Ricardo Sanchez, Politecnico di Torino, Italy
Bartolomeo Montrucchio, Politecnico di Torino, Italy
Maurizio Rebaudengo, Politecnico di Torino, Italy

The work of Filippo Gandino and his research team in Italy has provided valuable insight into the intricate requirements for agri-food traceability. Particularly as consumers become more mindful of the origins of food related to rising transport costs and the threat of diseases that are faced by our beef producers; the ability to consumers to access information about the origins of food products becomes more important. Additionally, many more consumers live with food intolerances and allergies that make it vital for them to be able to access and understand processing and ingredient information.

Section III
Smart Health

Chapter V

Lena Mamykina, GVU Center, Georgia Institute of Technology, USA
Elizabeth D. Mynatt, GVU Center, Georgia Institute of Technology, USA

Smart technologies including RFID and sensors produce vast amounts of complicated, low level data. Such data can be collected and stored, but until it is transformed into information that is useful and comprehendible, there is very little gain. Colleagues Lena Mamykina and Elizabeth Mynatt of Georgia in the United States of America present ground breaking work in the presentation of health related data that can be comprehended and understood by a lay person. This work is fascinating reading and is also a good introduction to the many very valuable contributions yet to be made to the field of health informatics.

Chapter VI

Bryan Houliston, Auckland University of Technology, New Zealand

RFID in hospitals is a very topical discussion as it is very difficult to get agreement on whether the technology is compatible with other highly technical operating theatre equipment. The safety of RFID is also not agreed. One first crucial step in getting agreement is in getting the stakeholders talking. Bryan Houliston reports the results of a number of interviews completed in New Zealand that helps to start the discussion in this area and to at least outline the critical issues.

Some of what allowed the editors to drawn in interested authors in their call for chapters for this book was their own project in health informatics that uses RFID to identify objects and landmarks is a unique low infrastructure approach to finding losable objects around the domestic house. Two of the editors include their work in this chapter .This chapter describes a project in health informatics that uses RFID to identify objects and landmarks in an unique low infrastructure approach to finding losable objects around the home.

Ashir and Ly-Fie present a framework to help with the use of RFID for authentication and management in emergency management. They consolidate much of the literature in the area and they draw together work on several different natural disaster areas that will provide researchers with a good background that will benefit both postgraduate students and researchers with an interest in the area.

Section IV
Smart Data & Convergence

Many so called "smart systems" capture video data. However, the captured data still needs human intervention to convert it into knowledge. Bin and Yu-Jin cover very relevant work on approaches to analyse video data to track the movement of objects. This has applications in security systems that use closed circuit TV as well as applications in the health field from activity management for frail elderly people through to sports science performance enhancement projects.

Chapter X

John Ayoade, American University of Nigeria, Nigeria

In this chapter John Ayoade investigates the challenges ahead in negotiating convergence between fixed and mobile networks. Although there is much work on enabling mobile phones for example to access a fixed network while within the home or office and to seamlessly search for a suitable mobile network while outside the home, this is the first work to our knowledge that proposed a framework.

Chapter XI

Sarita Pais, Whitireia Polytechnic, New Zealand
Judith Symonds, Auckland University of Technology, New Zealand

One approach to storing data on tags is simply to link the unique identification number on the tag to a record in a centralised database. Whilst this does ensure responsibility and accountability for the data, it also means that large ubiquitous networks are reliant on accessing a primary data warehouse. Another approach that is gaining some tracking is to store more data locally on the tag. Sarita and Judith explore the concept of storing data on tags looking at some of the implications for memory and read/write requirements on the tag as well as new modelling capabilities.

Section V
Selected Readings

Chapter XII

Maryam Purvis, University of Otago, New Zealand
Toktam Ebadi, University of Otago, New Zealand
Bastin Tony Roy Savarimuthu, University of Otago, New Zealand

The objective of this research is to describe a mechanism to provide an improved library management system using RFID and agent technologies. One of the major issues in large libraries is to track misplaced items. By moving from conventional technologies such as barcode-based systems to RFID-based systems and using software agents that continuously monitor and track the items in the library, the authors believe an effective library system can be designed. Due to constant monitoring, the up-to-date location information of the library items can be easily obtained.

Chapter XIII

Tommaso Di Noia, Politecnico di Bari, Italy
Eugenio Di Sciascio, Politecnico di Bari, Italy
Francesco Maria Donini, Università della Tuscia, Italy
Michele Ruta, Politecnico di Bari, Italy
Floriano Scioscia, Politecnico di Bari, Italy
Eufemia Tinelli, Politecnico di Bari and Università degli Studi di Bari, Italy

This chapter proposes a novel object discovery framework integrating the application layer of Bluetooth and RFID standards. The approach is motivated and illustrated in an innovative U-Commerce setting. Given a request, it allows an advanced discovery process, exploiting semantically annotated descriptions of goods available in the U-Marketplace. The RFID data exchange protocol and the Bluetooth Service Discovery Protocol have been modified and enhanced, to enable support for such semantic annotation of products. Modifications to the standards have been conceived to be backward compatible, thus allowing the smooth coexistence of the legacy discovery and/or identification features. Also noteworthy is the introduction of a dedicated compression tool to reduce storage/transmission problems due to the verbosity of XML-based semantic languages.

Chapter XIV

Indranil Bose, University of Hong Kong, Hong Kong
Chun Wai Lam, University of Hong Kong, Hong Kong

Radio-frequency identification (RFID) has generated vast amounts of interest in the supply chain, logistics and manufacturing area. RFID can be used to significantly improve the efficiency of business processes by providing automatic data identification and capture. Enormous data would be collected as items leave a trail of data while moving through different locations. Some important challenges such as false read, data overload, and real time acquisition of data, data security and privacy must be dealt with. Good quality data is needed because business decisions depend on these data. Other important issues are that business processes have to change drastically as a result of implementing RFID and data has to be shared between suppliers and retailers. The main objective of this paper is focused on data management challenges of RFID and it provides potential solutions for each identified risk.

Chapter XV

Masoud Mohammadian, University of Canberra, Australia
Ric Jentzsch, Compucat Research Pty Limited, Australia

The cost of health care continues to be a world wide issue. Research continues into how the utilization of evolving technologies can be applied to reduce costs, improve patient care, while maintaining patient's life. To achieve these needs requires accurate, near real time data acquisition and analysis. At the same time there exists a need to acquire a profile on a patient and update that profile as fast and as possible. All types of confidentiality need to be addressed no matter which technology and application is used. One possible way to achieve this is to use a passive detection system that employs wireless radio frequency identification (RFID) technology. This detection system can integrate wireless networks for fast data acquisition and transmission, while maintaining the privacy issue. Once this data is obtained then up to date profiling can be integrated into the patient care system. This chapter discusses the use and need for a passive RFID system for patient data acquisition in health care facilities such as a hospital. The development of profile data is assisted by a profiling intelligent software agent that is responsible for processing the raw data obtained through RFID and database and invoking the creation and update of the patient profile.

Chapter XVI

When dealing with human lives the need to utilize and apply the latest technology to help in saving and maintaining patient's lives is quite important and requires accurate, near real-time data acquisition and evaluation. At the same time the delivery of patient's medical data need to be as fast and as secure as possible. One possible way to achieve this is to use a wireless framework based on radio frequency identification (RFID). This framework can integrate wireless networks for fast data acquisition and transmission, while maintaining the privacy issue. This chapter discusses the development of an agent framework in which RFID can be used for patient data collection. The chapter presents a framework for the knowledge acquisition of patient and doctor profiling in a hospital. The acquisition of profile data is assisted by a profiling agent that is responsible for processing the raw data obtained through RFID and database of doctors and patients.

We are in the midst of what may become one of the true technological transformations of our time. RFID – radio frequency identification – is by no means new a "new" technology. RFID is fundamentally based on the study of electromagnetic waves and radio, pioneered in the 19th Century work of Faraday, Maxwell, and Marconi. The idea of using radio frequencies to reflect waves from objects dates back as far as 1886 to experiments conducted by Hertz. Radar was invented in 1922, and its practical applications date back to World War II. However, it would take decades of development before RFID technology would become a reality. Since 2000, significant improvements in functionality, decreases in both size and costs, and agreements on communication standards have combined to make RFID technology viable for commercial and governmental purposes. Today, RFID is positioned as an alternative way to identify objects to the ubiquitous bar code.

Foreword

RFID has come of age. Recent years have seen a proliferation of RFID technologies and, more importantly, novel applications in areas ranging from fine arts to manufacturing. Inventory tracking through RIFID in a factory is now quite common, and who hasn't used an RFID swipe card to unlock the door to their building? It is also beginning to be seen in health applications such as patient tracking and medication monitoring in hospitals. A quick scan of currently existing RFID solutions and implementations reveals applications including, just to name a few, pigeon flight monitoring, beer barrel stock control, pet identification, toxic waste monitoring, person identification, food production control, blood analysis identification, timber grade monitoring, vehicle parking monitoring, valuable objects insurance identification, asset management, and stolen vehicle identification.

Though the cost of the RFID tags has always been relatively low, it is reductions in the prices of RFID scanners (and in their sizes) that is beginning to see an increase in the number of new applications being found for these technologies. Contemporary artists are now seizing the potential of RFID to create interactive artworks that react to the users RFID tags as they move around the artwork or environment. These cost reductions have also seen RFID beginning to be used to create ubiquitous computing networks. A ubiquitous network is one that is present everywhere throughout an environment and has the ability to detect where users are within the network and based on that information meet their needs or serve them information. A simplistic example of the use of a ubiquitous network could be that of a user working on a document on a computer, and then moving to a different part of the building to another computer and having the document automatically follow them to that computer allowing them to seamlessly continue their work.

Tokyo, as well as many other Japanese cities, is a city without street names. This can cause great difficulties to business and tourism. The Japanese (especially trainee post workers) and bewildered visitors spend countless hours lost in Tokyo's labyrinth of streets with no names. This, in the 1980s led to improvements and miniaturization of the fax machine so that people could send maps and directions to each other. This problem has also led to the Tokyo Ubiquitous Network Project, in which scientists are planning an RFID and computer infrastructure that will fill such information gaps for good and create a true ubiquitous network. Streets, and any other structures or points of interest, will be tagged with RFID tags allowing low cost readers to be installed in a variety of devices and allowing users to know not only where they are, but also to receive other information that could be of use or interest to them on their mobile phones.

RFID has now become a truly convergent technology that allows a number of sensing, communication and computing technologies to be transformed into useful applications. RFID is the communication medium through which devices can talk to each other when within range and, when used to its full potential, allows for a truly seamless integration of people, devices, and software.

This book presents a number of leading examples of RFID research being developed for part identification, health systems and on the data convergence required for the technology to be used effectively. It presents how RFID is being used as a point of convergence for a number of disciplines and how the technology can be used in new and innovative ways.

Professor Olaf Diegel
Director, Creative Industries Research Institute
Auckland University of Technology

Preface

OVERVIEW

This edited book project began when our colleague, Dr. John Ayoade visited us from what was then his post at the University of the South Pacific. Both Auckland University of Technology and the University of the South Pacific have growing postgraduate research degrees in Information Science and both Universities offer a course in contemporary issues and ubiquitous computing. There are many conference formats such as the annual ubicomp conference that attracts an international body of researchers. However, we had found a lack of information on applications of RFID.

At the time of inception of this project, RFID was beginning to return from a cycle of ridicule caused by over hyping and overselling the capabilities of RFID during 2004 and 2005. Therefore, we felt it was timely to draw on the advances made in the RFID hardware development field and to showcase some of the very important work in the field.

We edited this book with our postgraduate research students in mind, to demonstrate some of the applications of RFID technology and to show that it is not just a glorified barcode that will eventually hold the universal product code of every item in the supermarket. Whenever we socialised the concept of RFID with our students, they fairly quickly came up with the concept of being able to walk a trolley of groceries through a portal at the supermarket and have the technology tally and total the order in a matter of seconds. As favourable as this may seam, RFID has far more potential than this, and will reach much further than Wal-Mart and will have more profound effects on the economy other than simply helping Gillette have less stock shrinkage.

This book is essentially about applications of RFID and smart technologies which has arisen out of our own fruitless search for published applications of RFID. In our work since 2005 we have worked with many different RFID hardware and tag suppliers and we have noticed that as researchers and industry have developed more applications that push the edge of RFID capability, more innovative, portable and multi-function versions of RFID hardware have emerged. In our research with assisted living, our first prototypes struggled with readers that simply did not have the read range or power capacity to do what we wanted. We then moved to more powerful readers, but these were too large, heavy and too hard to supply power to. Only now are we finding more portable equipment. However, we regard this as an important cycle of application development feeding back into the hardware development and design. Therefore, through encouraging authors to publish their work on RFID application development we hope to help hardware developers to fine-tune their designs further to meet the application needs better.

WHERE THE TOPIC FITS IN THE WORLD TODAY

In the information age, consumers have access to instant, detailed information about the products and services that they purchase. There is so much more information available about our individual health. Also, our world seems to be under threat from animal and human diseases, the cost of fossil fuel and the effects of global warming. Consumers want to know more about the status of their own health so that they can seek alternative treatments. Consumers want to know where their food comes from so that they can made informed decisions about buying local and buying disease free food. Consumers also have more reactions to processed food and therefore want to know more about the contents of the foods that they eat. The world today is demanding more information than can fit on a label. Hence, there is a place for RFID and other smart technologies to provide more local information. Imagine, for example, being able to verify the geographic area where your T-bone steak originated from or if you could have your own personal health heart tick on your personal digital assistant that will quickly guide you on what food to purchase in order to live better as you browse the supermarket shelves.

The developed world is heading down the carbon neutral path. Australia and New Zealand already have voluntary carbon emissions trading schemes that are listed on the stock exchange. In 2010, tracking carbon emissions will begin to become compulsory. Information that can be stored in central databases can be difficult to access and might be bared by stakeholders or may not be accessible do to incongruent data standards. Because products cross many of the natural boundaries in our world such as companies and countries, the probability that one countries data will not be accessible by other countries is high. On the face of it, carbon emissions trading schemes appear to allow dirty companies to simply pay for their emissions and continue on their way without addressing it. However, market competition will place pressure on companies and countries with high emissions as they will need to lower their costs in order to compete with other cleaner competitors.

Storing data on tags or other low cost solid state storage alternatives so that it can be read easily be each company in the supply chain will allow statistics about the product including carbon emissions data to travel with the product. Therefore, possession of the product will also mean possession of the data. Having the tags travel with the product will also enforce standards and require the installation of RFID readers that can read many different types of tag. RFID tags have the advantage of being about to communicate their data wirelessly and without line of sight. The can also potentially hold much more data than can be coded into a barcode or magnet strip.

THE CHAPTER SUBMISSIONS

Chapter I starts by setting the scene for the rest of the book by giving a information-oriented view of the development of RFID. This work is covered by Chin Boo Soon from The University of Auckland in New Zealand. Chin Boo's interest in supply chain management shows through in this first chapter and readers are treated to a thorough and intelligent summary of automatic identification technology and the development of RFID. Although we don't focus blindly on RFID, most of the chapters are concerned with it, and so by setting the scene up front we managed to avoid unwanted repetition throughout the book and we also provide a very valuable introduction to the topic area for postgraduate students who might be considering several research areas before making a final choice for their dissertation topic. Course leaders might also use some of the material from this chapter in their introductory sessions with students.

Around 2004, Nokia released a mobile phone with a RFID reader. They developed in-car kits that could allow the user to swipe certain tags to perform a set of activities on their phone. It was envisaged that maybe bill posters could also include RFID tags with URL information that the consumer could download to their phones and access later. Alas, Nokias mobile phone RFID reader was before its time and they discontinued the line as it was a technology looking for an application. However, that time for RFID readers and near field communications enabled phones may be approaching as John Garofalakis and Christos Mettouris demonstrate a wireless system that could be used in supermarkets to push information to users based on their position within the store.

There is a wide range in size of tags ranging from large battery powered tags that are approximately the size of a cigarette packet down to small passive tags that rely on the reader unit for power that can be as small as a grain of sand. Small tags could be embedded in high value personal belongings such as cell phones, plasma TVs and garden equipment which could allow the owners details to be stored with each item. As we discuss in our chapter, finding and verifying the owners of recovered stolen or lost items can be time consuming and difficult. In addition, potential identification of items using very small tags may actually act as a deterrent for would-be thieves. Equally, if the information on the tags is completely open to be read with any reader that uses the corresponding standard may be dangerous if it falls into the wrong hands. We draw particularly on John's framework for encryption and authentication for readers to address this problem.

Experts tell us that by 2020, the world will have difficulty producing enough food for earth's population, as the current cropping methods become less efficient against global warming and the current fields become less fertile. There is also the added threat of diseases. Honey bees can be attacked by mites and other vegetable and fruit crops can be attacked by mould, but perhaps the most serious threats are posed by diseases in animals such as mad cow and foot and mouth. In an outbreak, the movements of stock must be traced over the incubation timeframe and in the current environment were permits to move stock are not necessarily enforced and are either paper-based or stored in separate databases, marshalling such a wide-range of data with any certainty can be so impossible that the only option is for officials to order the mass slaughter and destruction of animals within a "hot zone". A technology such as RFID could alleviate this problem by automatically tracking the movement of stock. Filippo Gandino and colleagues consider the European challenges for management of data that might be collected electronically and then used to trace stock movements in the case of a disease outbreak.

There is something about an aquarium that is soothing and comforting. Many high stress environments use an aquarium to providing a calming environment. The dentist office in the movie "Finding Nemo" is a good example. Lena Mamykina and Elizabeth Mynatt are our only contributors from the United States and interestingly, they use a type of aquarium screen saver idea to convey complex medical data to lay people. Although not about RFID specifically, their work is about interpreting large amounts of complex data in a very meaningful way and in this way, the authors are able to make a fascinating contribution that will be readers interested in design.

RFID is already a major enabling technology for smart buildings and has replaced keyed office buildings to some extent because unlike a key, a RFID badge can be enabled and disabled through a central management system. Instead of needing to rekey a whole office floor in the case of a lost key, administrators can simply disable the lost badge. However, many industries including manufacturing environments and hospitals would like to implement RFID enabled time cards. Time cards would speed clocking on and clocking off and could give management an idea of how many people are on the factory floor and whether they are dispersed correctly, however, some workers unions fear that detailed information about the specific location of employees whilst at work could invade individual privacy. By way of indepth interviews, Bryan Houliston explores some of the perceptions of using RFID in the healthcare workforce. Health is renowned for its lack of technology update and Bryan's interview data certainly sheds some light on the perceptions of healthcare workers on RFID.

Many of our hospitals are being pushed to breaking point. As changes in healthcare enhance our quality of life and help us to live longer, more people are living for longer and therefore we have an increase in the number of frail elderly people in our community. These are people who want to remain in their own homes and assisted living systems can help. In our article we look at different ways to interpret information from RFID tags and readers to better understand placement of objects within a map of landmarks within the home. Our initial work was with a much larger "industrial sized" reader and passive HF tags (the reader is 1.6kg) and required a large batter pack for portable power supply. Our more recent work involves a smaller UHF reader with a more portable design.

RFID tags themselves are quite robust. The antenna and microprocessor can be encapsulated with plastic or glass. Tags are made to withstand commercial laundry processes as well as being inserted into flesh. That is why Ashir and Ly-Fie consider RFID in their work in emergency management which covers response to all kinds of natural disasters including some of the most destruction forces of fire (in a bush or wild fire for example) and water (in a tsunami for example).

Video surveillance data is collected in case it is needed. When needed, humans sift back through it to find significant data. Imagine what might be possible if real-time online tracking of video data were possible. Bin Shen and Yu-Jin Zhang work on this problem and provide details of a prototype system that is unique in the way it samples video frames, thus cutting down on the overhead required to track objects in real-time data.

In our anecdotal experience, "land-line" infrastructure in homes is being overtaken by mobile cell networks and voice-over-IP. Technologies that rely on telecommunications infrastructure in the home now need to cater for both the possibility of a mobile telecommunications link as an alternative to a fixed telecommunications link. This signifies the beginning of a need to develop frameworks and approaches for fixed-mobile convergence. John Ayoade begins very important work in canvassing the existing work in the literature.

The final chapter reports on important work being undertaken at AUT around the new challenges with data management. Smart technology at the local site can allow more manipulation of the data to be undertaken and more consolidated, useful information can be made available. Also, storing data locally allows critical data to travel with the object it describes and so access to that data is not reliant on access to a communications network and central data repository. However, this ability to store and manipulate data locally also presents challenges in terms of data manipulation of time sensitive data and tools needed to model and develop. This chapter explores these challenges, consolidating existing work completed in the area and recommending future work.

In the final section, we have assembled a selection of six readings that will provide further information on RFID applications. These applications include examples from library management systems.

Much of the work in object location systems has relevance to library information systems. Although RFID is considered a candidate to replace barcodes in borrower systems, there is far greater application for keeping track of tangible resources (books, CDs and so on) that become misplaced in the building and are not recoverable. Maryam Purvis, Toktam Ebadi, and Bastin Savarimuthu of University of Otago, New Zealand report on an Agent-based Library Management System using RFID Technology. Their prototype uses an intelligent robot that periodically scans the shelves to check the location of items.

Future applications might also apply the same sort of technology to develop smart shelving that can keep track of resources and interfaces with the borrowing records to verify if resources are on loan or still somewhere in the library. Similarly, resources that are not registered with that shelf can be identified and flagged for reshelving.

As the capability to read, store, and use data from sensors in the environment, so does the information overload. Indranil Bose and Chun Lam of The University of Hong Kong, Hong Kong, address the issues of this overload in their chapter "Facing the Challenges of RFID Data Management". They provide a thorough discussion of the challenges such as false read, data overload, and real time acquisition of data, data security and privacy for readers considering working in this area.

RFID tags are increasingly being used for identification of users in systems. At the time of writing, the Auckland domestic airport in New Zealand has issued adhesive RFID chips to frequent fliers. The chip provides for fast processing of passenger details at automated check-in desks and flight gates. However, the security of such information needs to be ensured as some RFID tags can be effectively skimmed by modern day pick pockets with mobile RFID readers. Masoud Mohammadian of University of Canberra, Australia, and Ric Jentzsch of Compucat Research, Australia, consider the privacy problem where RFID tags are used to store patient details. They argue that the best way to address this problem is to employ a Passive RFID Detection System and they present a research framework based on their work.

The final reading covers much of the history of radio frequency development and considers RFID as a replacement for the ubiquitous barcode. The work by David Wyld, Southeastern Louisiana University, USA, serves as a valuable overview of the technology and along with our introductory chapter, is excellent background reading. However, readers should remember that the replacement of barcodes with RFID tags is just one application of RFID technology and is a specialised research field in its own right.

CONCLUSION

Almost every student knows of what Wal-Mart and Gillette achieved with RFID. But so much more is possible with RFID in that initial uptake has been to use the technology in much the same way as a barcode. New applications of RFID technology are looking at using it in new ways that take advantage of the strengths of the technology. In this edited book we set out to showcase some of the more novel and innovative applications of RFID and smart technologies to show how the technology could add value to business. We believe that we have achieved this. We have attracted authors from an international stage and from varied backgrounds and have brought them together into one book for the benefit of postgraduate students and researchers who want to learn more about RFID worldwide.

Acknowledgment

This edited book is the culmination of a collaborative relationship between three researchers that was born from an interest in teaching ubiquitous computing to students of a postgraduate research degree. However, no matter how enthusiastic and keen, we still had to convince others of our convictions. Looking back over this year-long project, it is astonishing that we managed to achieve so much. In this brief section we acknowledge the help of all involved in the collation and review process of the edited book, without whose support the project could not have been satisfactorily completed.

Most of the authors of chapters included in this handbook also served as referees for chapters written by other authors. Thanks go to all those who provided constructive and comprehensive reviews. However, some of the reviewers must be mentioned as their reviews set the benchmark. Reviewers who provided the most comprehensive, critical and constructive comments include: Wendi Heinzelman of Rochester University, New York, Nural Sakar, Brian Houliston and Jim Buchan of Auckland University of Technology and Rosemary Stockdale, Massey University. Support of the School of Computing and Mathematical Sciences at AUT University, Auckland, New Zealand is acknowledged for archival server space utilized in the review process.

Special thanks also go to the publishing team at IGI Global, whose wise guidance throughout the whole process from inception of the initial idea to final publication has been invaluable. In particular to Jan Travers and Julia Mosemann at IGI Global, for their assistance with development of the proposals and plans and who carefully and gently reminded us that our project milestones were due. We also wish to thank Mehdi Khosrow-Pour, whose enthusiasm motivated us to initially accept his invitation for taking on this project.

Special thanks go to our mentor, Dr. Aileen Cater-Steel, who has completed two edited book chapter projects with IGI Global herself and who provided insights and helpful approaches from her own experience. And last but not least, our families, who have provided support and encouragement to carry on.

In closing, we wish to thank all of the authors for their insights and excellent contributions to this handbook. In drafting our call for chapters, we had no idea that reports from research would come from all four corners of the world to inform, inspire and ignite passion in our students.

Judith Symonds, John Ayoade, and Dave Parry

September 2008

Section I
Setting the Scene

Chapter I
Radio Frequency Identification History and Development

Chin-Boo Soon
The University of Auckland, New Zealand

ABSTRACT

This chapter describes the history and development of Radio Frequency Identification (RFID). Key information on RFID such as the ratification of the RFID standards and important regulations on frequency usage is presented. As businesses move towards the convergence of information, RFID technology provides a step closer to the reality of connecting the real world and the digital world seamlessly. This is possible as RFID communication does not require the line of sight as barcodes do. Thus, is the continued existence of the barcodes technology under threat? Before RFID makes its way into the mainstream, there are teething issues to be sorted out. The immediate attention for a global uptake of RFID is the adoption of a frequency standard that is accepted internationally. This chapter provides an understanding of the RFID technology, its background and its origin.

INTRODUCTION

Radio Frequency Identification (RFID) is an Automatic Identification and Data Capture (AIDC) technology. Its application can be found in most industries, offices and even homes. The application ranges from electronic article surveillance (EAS) in retails, electronic toll collection in transportations, to building access control in offices. RFID is fundamentally a radio technology and its history can be traced back to the 1930s (Bhuptani & Moradpour, 2005). The underlying principle of

RFID is the transmitting and receiving of data in a form of electromagnetic energy. The primary components are tags and readers. Together these components form a coupling relationship where communication becomes possible. This chapter revisits the history of RFID development and looks at other forms of AIDC. This helps to form an epistemology of what RFID is and its origin, so that we could relate to the various aspects of RFID characteristics when planning on a RFID project. The emergence of RFID has raised the question of barcodes' continued existence (Allen,

1991; Atkinson, 2004). It is therefore inevitable to know the characteristics of RFID and barcodes, and examine their future existence, particularly in the supply chain.

The discussion in this chapter is motivated by the activities of RFID surrounding supply chain management. The suppliers' mandates to use RFID in the supply chains have significant impact on businesses (C. B. Soon & J. A. Gutierrez, 2008). This has created interest in RFID by businesses around the world. It is thus an appropriate topic to introduce RFID. Although this chapter is focused on RFID applications in the supply chains, the technical aspects are common across application areas.

This chapter is arranged as follows. First, the development of RFID is summarised with key events identified from the history of RFID. Second, the various concepts of AIDC are discussed. Third, the RFID system is discussed with particular attention to the tag classification and frequency allocation. Fourth, a comparison between RFID and barcodes is made. The continued existence of barcodes and the future of RFID are discussed in the conclusion.

HISTORY: THE DEVELOPMENT OF RFID

Electromagnetic theory was developed in the 1800s. Michael Faraday discovered that light and radio waves are part of electromagnetic energy and James Clerk Maxwell demonstrated that electric and magnetic energy travel at the speed of light in transverse waves (Landt, 2001). The discovery led to consequential experiments. In 1896, Guglielmo Marconi successfully transmitted radio waves across the Atlantic (Landt, 2001). Marconi's demonstration was followed by more innovations. In 1922, radar was developed. The transponder (or tag) and interrogator (or reader) were then bulky and heavy. Radar was extensively used by the Allies during World War II to iden-

tify friendly military aircraft. Radar was further developed into a commercial air traffic control system in the late 1950s following the invention of integrated circuits (IC), which greatly reduced the size of RFID components. The 1960s marked the start of RFID development as scientists and commercial businesses started to show interest in the technology. The first concept of RFID for commercial use was probably thought of by Mario Cardullo in 1969 when he worked with an IBM engineer on a car tracking system using barcodes for the railroad industry (Shepard, 2005).

Most RFID applications were identified in the 1970s. The use of RFID for EAS began in early 1970s (Bhuptani & Moradpour, 2005). EAS is a simple anti-theft measure for use in retail stores. It is the first and most widely used RFID application commercially (Landt, 2001). Further interest in the adoption of RFID extended to areas such as vehicle tracking, access control, animal tagging, and factory automation. The use of RFID cards for controlling access to office building by Westinghouse (Mullen & Moore, 2005) is an example of access control. Further development improved the reading speed and enabled a longer read range. The advanced RFID systems were utilised to identify railroad cars and track animals in the 1980s, and for electronic toll collection in the 1990s (Bhuptani & Moradpour, 2005).

RFID applications became more widespread in the 1990s. The success of electronic toll collection kicked off large scale deployments throughout the United States, Europe and Asia (Landt, 2001). There are two basic systems employed in road toll collection. One uses a contactless card or proximity card and the other uses a transponder fitted into the vehicle. The latter does not require the vehicle to halt at a barrier unlike the proximity card model where, the driver has to stop and hold the proximity card close to a reader at the barrier or toll plaza. Standards for contactless smart cards were developed between 1992 and 1995. Contactless smart cards are now widely used in retail electronic payment, access control, transport fare payment, and airlines ticketing.

It is not until late 1999 that RFID made its way into supply chains. Sanjay Sarma, a professor at MIT, started a project called the Distributed Intelligent Systems Center to work on ubiquitous object identification (Sarma, 2005). The centre also developed Electronic Product Code (EPC), Object Naming Service (ONS), Physical Markup Language (PML), and the Savant system. Together these components form the fundamental mechanism in the RFID system known as the EPC network.

Sarma and his team developed a microwave prototype installed with a RFID reader. The reader read the tag information on a packet food, retrieved the cooking instructions from a server using the tag identity or EPC, and started cooking with the downloaded instructions. Having successfully demonstrated the EPC concept using the microwave prototype, Sarma and his team were eager to secure commercial support as well as sponsorships to further develop the technology. After some convincing selling, they finally launched the Auto-ID Center with sponsorship from Gillette and Procter & Gamble on September 30, 1999 (Sarma, 2005). The Center continued its research work, and by 2003 there were six laboratories and more than a hundred

sponsors. The increasing demand and interest triggered the Auto-ID Center to spin-out and hence EPCglobal was formed. EPCglobal is a not-for-profit organization jointly administered by Uniform Code Council (UCC) and European Article Numbering (EAN) International, or GS1[1]. Under the GS1 umbrella, EPCglobal's membership now reaches the entire globe with more than 100 member organizations (Smucker, 2006).

A turning point for RFID in supply chain (RFID/SC) widespread use came when Wal-Mart joined the Auto-ID Center in 2001 (Sarma, 2005). A major field trial was conducted which involved forty companies across eight states and ten cities in the United States. The trial was not only successful, it demonstrated the practicality of RFID/SC and its economic benefits. This prompted Gillette to order 500 million tags in late 2002 and Wal-Mart to announce the mandate for its suppliers in 2003. Both events proved to be the catalysts of RFID/SC adoption. Figure 1 shows the development of RFID described above in a time chart.

Other recent RFID applications are location sensing or real-time locating systems (RTLS), content management, electronic pedigree (e-pedigree), and in the sports for time tracking.

Figure 1. The history of RFID

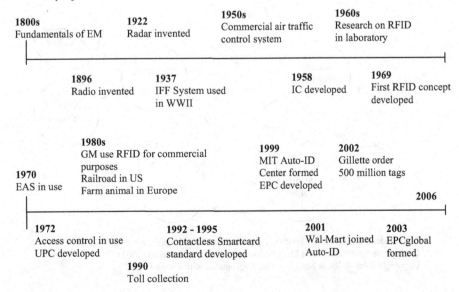

The use of RFID for location sensing applications has some successful implementation such as the WhereNet RTLS infrastructure used to track shipping containers at APL terminals (Violino, 2006). Other location sensing innovation using radios includes LANDMARC (Ni, Liu, Lau, & Patil, 2004), RADAR (Bahl & Padmanabhan, 2000), and SpotON (Hightower, Vakili, Borriello, & Want, 2001). The use of RFID for content management includes authenticating and monitoring the content of a desired inventory. Examples of such applications are the e-pedigree used in the healthcare industry (Swedberg, 2008b) and tanker monitoring systems used by petroleum company to ensure the correct type of oil is delivered (Swedberg, 2008a). The use of RFID in the sport arena has several applications such as ticketing and recording the lap time of the NASCAR races (Edwards, 2008).

AUTOMATIC IDENTIFICATION AND DATA CAPTURE (AIDC)

This section describes the various concepts of AIDC and traces the historical context of these technologies in the attempt to draw comparisons to RFID and put in perspective the development of RFID technology. AIDC is a collective of technologies that capture or collect data using automated mechanism without the need for manual input. Finkenzeller (2003) highlights five types of AIDC systems; (1) Barcode, (2) Optical Character Recognition, (3) Biometric, (4) Smart Card, and (5) RFID. Figure 2 illustrates his AIDC diagram. Magnetic Stripe and Magnetic Ink Character Recognition (Mullen & Moore, 2005) has been added to the diagram to illustrate AIDC more fully.

The barcode, magnetic stripe, and RFID technologies emerged between the 1930s and the 1940s. Barcode was first patented in 1949 to Norman Woodland and Bernard Silver (Shepard, 2005). Woodland used ancient movie soundtrack encoding schemes and the dot and dash patterns in Morse code to create the first barcode. He extended the dots and dashes vertically to form linear pattern of thick and thin lines. He later realised that the linear pattern had to be scanned from a particular direction. Woodland replaced the linear pattern with a circular centric pattern resembling a bull's-eye. This design could be

Figure 2. Overview of AIDC

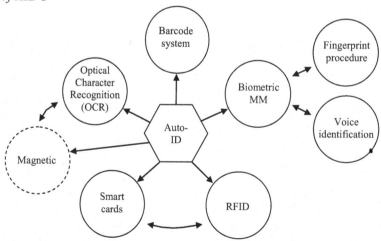

Figure adapted from RFID Handbook – Fundamentals and Applications in Contactless Smart Cards and Identification (2nd Ed.), Finkenzeller (2003). Copyright John Wiley & Sons Limited. Reproduced with Permission.

read generally from any direction. However, the machine he designed to read the barcode was huge and therefore was not suitable for grocery checkout as it was originally intended. Nevertheless, it did find its way to tracking rail cars on the United States national railroad system in the late 1960s after some modification to the barcode pattern. Meanwhile, barcodes continued to evolve around the grocery industry in the United States. The bull's-eye system was eventually replaced by the Universal Product Code (UPC) due to the difficulty of printing concentric circles on products. As such, linear barcode was adopted as it was easily printed, and with advanced scanner using laser technology, the linear barcode can be read from different angles. UPC was adopted on April 3, 1973 (Shepard, 2005), and was first scanned in commercial transactions in 1974 (Jilovec, 2004). As its popularity increased, international bodies started to ratify their own standards. EAN International and Japanese Article Numbering (JAN) are the other widely adopted systems. Barcodes became globally adopted in manufacturing, production, and distribution. There are now advanced barcodes with more data storage capacity such as the two-dimensional (2D) barcodes introduced in 1988 (Anonymous, 2006; Man, 2007). The 2D barcodes use the matrix symbol technology to achieve higher data density than the linear barcode while utilising lesser space. Barcode, as referred to in this chapter, is the one-dimensional, linear barcode widely used in retail, manufacturing, and supply chain.

Magnetic stripe is another AIDC widely used in the banking industry. Its standard was established in 1970 (Anonymous, 2007a). It is commonly used on credit and debit cards, and access control cards. The magnetic stripe when run past a reader produces an electromagnetic signal recordable by the reader. Another version of magnetic AIDC is the Magnetic Ink Character Recognition (MICR). Similarly, MICR is widely used in the banking industry. It is being used for bank cheque authentication. Both technologies

were adopted by the American Banking Association (Mullen & Moore, 2005) and banks around the world.

Optical Character Recognition (OCR) was introduced in the 1960s, almost twenty years after barcode's emergence. Like the MICR, special characters that are legible to both humans and machines are used to present a series of unique codes. OCR is also used in the banking industry, production, and service and administrative fields (Finkenzeller, 2003).

More recently, biometric and smart cards have attracted interest. There are two main forms of biometric identification, one is voice recognition and the other is fingerprinting. A highly sophisticated system converts voice into digital signals to process the authentication of a subject. Voice identification is now being implemented in supply chain management to aid in picking orders (Allen, 1991; Kondratova, 2003). Fingerprinting recognises the unique finger patterns of individuals. As such, its application is commonplace around security and access control. A common application of fingerprinting is the employee time tracking system.

Smart cards first gained publicity as a pre-paid telephone card launched in 1984. By 1995, 600 million smart cards were issued (Finkenzeller, 2003). Smart card is a secured data storage device widely used in Global System for Mobile communications (GSM) devices and as cash cards for micro-payments. It has a galvanised input/output connection with processing capability. An external power source is required to operate the smart card. The card needs to be placed in contact with a reader in order to transfer data. Wear and tear to the smart card processor is inevitable with frequent usage and contact. Another version of the smart card, known as the contactless smart card, uses radio frequency (RF) technology. Data can be transferred without the need to slot the card into a reader, thus no contact with the reader is necessary. The International Organization for Standardisation (ISO) standard for contactless smart card was developed between 1992 and 1995 (Finkenzeller, 2003). A contactless smart card works in close proximity to a reader. It is thus suitable for applications where masses flow, such as, a high traffic channel. Contactless smart cards are for that reason widely used in public transport ticketing, allowing a quicker, smoother commuter flow through train station barriers or buses doors (Finkenzeller, 2003).

The above section shows that AIDC has evolved into a well-received technology for use in electronic payment, access control, production, and distribution. Barcodes and RFID are the two AIDC technologies utilised in supply chains where products are being identified at different stages. The rest of the AIDC technologies are primarily used in security, banking, and public transportation domains. Figure 3 shows the development of AIDC in a time chart.

RFID SYSTEM

A RFID system is made up of two main hardware components: tags and readers (Grasso, 2004). The tags or transponders consist of a memory chip and have a built-in antenna. The memory, depending on its size, can store up to 64K of data. The antenna receives and transmits data using radio waves. There are three basic forms of tag: passive, active, and hybrid or semi-passive. A passive tag does not have an internal power source to process nor transmit signals. An active tag has an integrated battery as the power source. An active tag can broadcast signals and transmit at a longer range than a passive tag. In contrast, a passive tag is only operational when it receives RF signals from an authenticated reader or source. The tag uses the RF as a source of power to transmit data back to the reader, a process called inductive coupling (Weinstein, 2005). A semi-passive tag has an on-board power source and yet behaves like a passive tag. It has a switch that turns on the internal power source when it receives RF signals from a reader. A semi-passive tag overcomes the short range limitation of a passive tag and the complexity of an active tag response method (Jones et al., 2006).

Tags can be read only, write once and read many times, or read and write many times. There are six classes of tags: Class 0 to Class 5. A Class 0 tag is a factory programmed read-only passive tag. Once programmed, the data in the tag cannot be altered. A Class 1 tag is similar to a Class 0 tag except that it can be programmed by the user. It contains minimum features to keep the cost low. A Class 2 tag is a read-write passive tag with a longer communication range than a Class 1 tag.

Figure 3. The development of AIDC

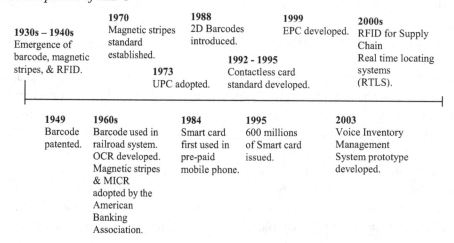

It has extended memory and authenticated access control features not available in Class 1 tags. A Class 3 tag is a semi-passive read-write tag. It has an on-board power source and thus has a longer communication range and higher transmission reliability than Class 2 tags. A Class 4 tag is an active ad-hoc read-write tag with the functionalities of a Class 3 tag. It is capable of communicating with other Class 4 tags within range of its ad-hoc network. A Class 5 tag is an autonomous active read-write reader tag. It has the features of a Class 4 tag and is capable of communicating with all classes within its subsets. As you see, each successive class "is a superset of the functionality contained within, the previous class, resulting in a layered functional classification structure" (Engels & Sarma, 2005, p. 3). Figure 4 shows the layered classification structure of tags. Class 0 is not shown in the figure as it could be classified as Class 1 due to their similar features. Class 1 is established as the foundation of the RFID class structure (Engels & Sarma, 2005).

Besides the classes of tag, the use of a tag is controlled by the radio frequency spectrum. RFID utilises the Industrial, Scientific, and Medical (ISM) band available worldwide. There are four categories of spectra available for commercial use: 125 to 134 KHz in the low frequency category, 13.56 MHz in the high frequency category, 433 MHz and 868 to 928 MHz in the ultra high frequency (UHF) category, and 2.45 GHz in the

microwave category (Walker, 2003). There may be some variation in the classification of spectra due to the different regulatory on the use of ISM band in different parts of the world. In the effort to ensure global interoperability of RFID tags for global roaming applications, EPCglobal has been advocating the use of RFID in the 860 to 960 MHz spectrum. This is the spectrum used in the EPC Class 1 Generation 2 tags that aims at covering a wide group of countries that can use the same tags. As of September 2007, there are a total of 54 countries with regulations in place for the use of RFID within the 860 to 960 MHz spectrum (Barthel, 2007). These countries represent about 92 per cent of the world gross national income. Table 1 shows the allocated frequencies for RFID use in the UHF spectrum by countries.

The other component of a RFID system is the reader. A reader sends and receives RF signals. It may be portable or fixed in a position and is linked to a computer. In a proprietary system, readers usually read only proprietary tags. The readers and tags must be programmed within the same range of a spectrum to communicate. Thus, one of the biggest challenges is harmonising the frequency for RFID use in the UHF spectrum, particularly, in Europe where available UHF spectrum is limited (Wasserman, 2007). For example, France, Italy, Spain, and Turkey were using the UHF spectrum for military equipment before the ratification of RFID use in the UHF

Figure 4. Auto-ID center RFID class structure – layered hierarchy

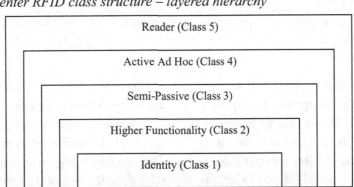

Source: ©2005 Engels & Sarma. Reproduced with Permission.

Table 1. Frequency Allocation for RFID in the UHF Spectrum

Country	Frequency (MHz)	Technique	Regulator Website
Australia	920 to 926	NA	www.acma.govt.au
Brazil	902 to 907.5	FHSS	www.anatel.gov.br
China	840.5 to 844.5 920.5 to 924.5	FHSS	www.mii.gov.cn
Finland	865.6 to 867.6	LBT	www.ficora.fi
France	865.6 to 867.6	LBT	www.arcep.fr
Germany	865.6 to 867.6	LBT	www.bundesnetzagentur.de
Hong Kong	865 to 868 920 to 925	NA	NA
India	865 to 867	NA	www.trai.gov.in
Italy	865.6 to 867.6	LBT	www.agcom.it
Japan	952 to 954	LBT	www.soumu.go.jp
Korea, Rep.	908.5 to 910 910 to 914	LBT FHSS	www.kcc.go.kr
Malaysia	866 to 869	NA	www.cmc.gov.my
New Zealand	864 to 868	NA	www.med.govt.nz
Singapore	866 to 869 920 to 925	NA	www.ida.gov.sg
South Africa	865.5 to 867.6 917 to 921	LBT FHSS	www.icasa.org.za
Spain	865.6 to 867.6	LBT	www.mityc.es
Sweden	865.6 to 867.6	LBT	www.pts.se
Switzerland	865.6 to 867.6	LBT	www.bakom.ch
Taiwan	922 to 928	FHSS	NA
Thailand	920 to 925	FHSS	www.ntc.or.th
Turkey	865.6 to 867.6	LBT	www.tk.gov.tr
United Kingdom	865.6 to 867.6	LBT	www.ofcom.org.uk
United States	902 to 928	FHSS	www.fcc.gov
Vietnam	866 to 869	NA	www.mpt.gov.vn

Source: ©2007 Barthel. (FHSS – Frequency Hopping Spread Spectrum, LBT – Listen Before Talk). Reproduced with Permission.

spectrum (Barthel, 2006). The UHF spectra shown in Table 1 are the approved frequency slots for RFID use in the respective countries. This means that a RFID reader has to be tuned to the approved frequency slots for operation in that country. Therefore, the EPC Class 1 Generation 2 tags can roam internationally among these countries thus allowing a worldwide supply chain visibility in these countries.

A reader broadcast its signal within a specific spectrum depending on its power and frequency. The distance a tag and a reader can transmit is relative to the size of the antenna. In a same-frequency band, the larger the antenna, the longer the transmission range is. The orientation or shape of the antenna is equally important in its role of picking up electromagnetic signals, particularly, when the tag is used on a material that attenuates the electromagnetic signals. Thus the "surface area and the shape of the tag antenna have to be optimised for not only backscattering the modulated electromagnetic wave but also harvesting energy for the microchip to function" (Ukkonen, Schaffrath, Kataja, Sydanheimo, & Kivikoski, 2006, p. 111). There are now many shape and sizes of antennas designed for use on different materials and environments.

There are also various transmission methods. The frequency hopping spread spectrum (FHSS) method switches channels at a sequence for a more reliable transmission. The FHSS method allows the efficient use of the bandwidth. The other method used mostly in Europe is the listen before talk (LBT) method. In the LBT, a reader has to listen for other transmitters using the same channel before communicating with the tags through an unused channel (Eeden, 2004). This method is derived due to the restriction on the amount of energy emission in Europe set by the European Telecommunications Standards Institute (ETSI). A LBT reader is allowed to transmit signals for a period of four seconds and then stop the transmission for a least 0.1 second (Anonymous, 2007b; Roberti, 2004). The disadvantage of the LBT method is the slower data transfer rate, which is about thirty percent of the FHSS data rate (Roberti, 2004).

BARCODES AND RFID

RFID is generally thought of as a replacement for barcodes (Atkinson, 2004; Lazar & Moss, 2005; Sheffi, 2004). Barcodes have been around since 1949 when they were first patented. It took almost thirty to forty years for barcodes to gain wide adoption. This is evident in the late 1980s to early 1990s when there were numerous articles on

the application and implementation of barcodes; Walter (1988), Carter (1991), Lacharite (1991), Ekman (1992), and Burkett (1993) are examples of barcodes application in the various industries, to name a few. By the 2000s, the barcode is already an established technology. This is also evident in articles claiming barcode is still "alive" amidst the emergence of RFID (Katz, 2006) and proclaiming success stories of barcode implementations (Heinen, Coyle, & Hamilton, 2003; May, 2003). The announcement by the Food and Drug Administration (FDA) in the United States about the use of barcodes for the labeling of medications further strengthen the barcode's position in the industry (Heinen, Coyle, & Hamilton, 2003). A recent survey by Venture Development Corporation shows that the demand for barcode scanners is strong (Mason, 2005). Therefore the general preconception of RFID replacing barcode needs to be refined. It is important to understand the difference between RFID and barcodes in order to successfully implement a RFID system especially in a barcode dominant environment.

Table adapted from RFID Handbook – Fundamentals and Applications in Contactless Smart Cards and Identification (2nd Ed.), Finkenzeller (2003). Copyright John Wiley & Sons Limited. Reproduced with Permission.

Undoubtedly, RFID has far more capability offering more advantages than barcodes. Table 2 shows the differences between the two technologies. Barcode readers use optical technology to capture the patterns of a barcode label. It therefore requires a line of sight within a short distance to read the label. This inevitably calls for the need to locate a barcode label by either pointing a scanner directly at the label or by positioning the label such that it can be read by a fixed scanner. Either way involves labour. By contrast, RFID uses RF or electromagnetic waves as a means of data collection. RF works in omni-direction ally up to a few yards. This attribute enables a RFID reader to communicate with a tag without the need to be in the line of sight, which has an

Table 2. RFID and barcode comparison

System parameters	Barcode	RFID
Typical data quantity (bytes)	1-100	16-64k
Content	Specific (SKU level)	Dynamic
Machine readability	Good	Good
Readability of people	Limited	Impossible
Line of sight requirement	Yes	No
Influence of dirt	Very high	No influence
Influence of covering	Total failure	No influence
Influence of direction and position	Low	No influence
Influence of metal and liquid	Very low	High
Degradation/wear	Limited	No influence
Reading speed	Low (one label at a time)	Very fast (multiple tag)
Reading distance	0-50cm	0-5m (microwave)
Cost of label/tag	Inexpensive	Expensive
Standards	Defined	Being defined
Stage of maturity	Mature	Evolving

Table adapted from RFID Handbook - Fundamentals and Applications in Contactless Smart Cards and Identification (2nd Ed.), Finkenzeller (2003). Copyright John Wiley & Sons Limited. Reproduced with permission.

added advantage of having a reader reading multiple tags simultaneously. This feature of RFID presents the reality of connecting the real world "with its representation in information systems" (Strassner & Schoch, 2002, p. 1). Strassner & Schoch (2002) suggest that the media break, a break between physical and its information, can be avoided with automation, awareness of smart objects, and mobility. Figure 5 shows the progress towards the convergence with the use of RFID (Fleisch, 2001).

The capability of reading multiple tags at a given time increases the throughput to a level that barcode cannot achieve. This also eases the bottleneck of scanning each item at a time with a faster reading speed. However, this capability has its downside. The fact that, in a RFID system, tags within range are read almost simultaneously also means that the exact sequence of the cartons is not picked up by the reader (Bednarz, 2004). In a conveyor setup, cartons are often required to be routed to different locations. It is therefore important to know the order of the cartons in or-

der to direct them to the right locations. Barcode systems have been successful in such scenario. A "bar-code-based system knows more about the order of packages moving along a belt" (Bednarz, 2004, p. 8).

An advantage of RF is the ability to communicate in a harsh environment where the barcode label is worn or covered by dust. RF is able to penetrate most types of material. However, the signal is vulnerable to metal, liquid or material with high moisture content, particularly the high frequency range. More energy or power is needed to mitigate the loss of RF propagation through those materials. There are on-going projects to overcome this drawback (Collins, 2004).

At a mature stage of development, barcode is relatively inexpensive to implement for a cost-effective solution (Anonymous, 1993; Ekman, 1992). A record storage warehouse of 30,000 sq ft uses only two computers and two wand scanners to keep track of thousands of boxes of record files (Anonymous, 1993). Conversely, RFID technology is evolving steadily particularly in the supply

Figure 5. Avoidance of media breaks

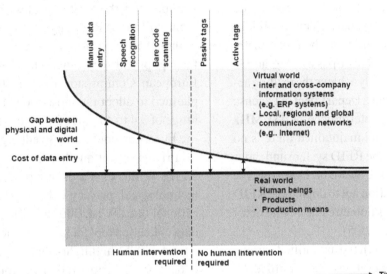

Source: ©2001 Fleisch. Reproduced with Permission.

chain industry. Setting up an RFID infrastructure is expensive and hence requires careful study on systems integration with existing business information systems. The RFID tags make up the main outlay. Each tag costs US$5 in early 2000 down to between US$1 to 50 cents in 2004 as reported by Atkinson (2004). The cost of a tag continues to drop and each tag is expected to cost no more than five cents per tag for mass adoption to take place. In 2006, the five cents per tag benchmark has been achieved at an order of 100 million pieces (Roberti, 2006). The self-regulating market forces necessitate that should prices fall to five cents a tag, the demand for tags will increase. This in turn may create a supply issue with production capacity lacking behind demand (Sarma, 2001). It may push prices back up, thus dwindling the prospect of an earlier mass adoption of RFID technology.

Another drawback of RFID is the lack of a harmonised standard across this system. Barcode has clearly defined standards and the different standards are globally accepted. In terms of a unique numbering system for item identification, EPC is one of the standards for RFID. The use of

RF is posing a challenge to a globally accepted standard. This is largely due to the different frequency allocation by the local governments. At present, different standards are adopted across different RFID systems complying with the local regulations. Manufacturers, importers and businesses are concerned that their products cannot be tracked across countries' borders because of different regulations. This would warrant them to use different systems to cater for customers in different parts of the world (Atkinson, 2004).

The 13.56 MHz spectrum is commonly used for RFID applications such as proximity access cards to premises, and smart cards. The 433 MHz spectrum is commonly reserved for supply chain use in most countries making it a suitable candidate for global supply chains. It was also considered the industry standard for supply chains (Li, Visich, Khumawala, & Zhang, 2006). The China State Radio Regulation Committee on 9th November 2006 approved the use of 433 MHz for RFID devices compatible with the ISO standard. This seems to solidify the 433 MHz spectrum as an international standard (Swedberg, 2006). New Zealand has also assigned the 433 MHz spectrum for RFID and other short range devices. Unfortunately, frequencies in this spectrum do not work reliably under supply chain conditions due to the short wavelength of about one metre (Anonymous, 2004). Thus a passive tag at 433 MHz might not adequately achieve the reading accuracy. The United States Department of Defense (DOD) has tested the interference of 433 MHz active RFID system and maintained there is no interference between the RFID system and radar equipments that they are aware of. However, the DOD is taking precaution not to deploy the RFID systems within forty kilometres of any military radar system (Collins, 2005).

EPCglobal on the one hand has ratified various standards for RFID operations. It has ratified the Generation 1 tag in 13.56 MHz, 860 to 930 MHz, and 900 MHz. The latter is factory programmed tag or Class 0 while the others are writeable or Class 1. A notable improved standard of EPCglobal is the Class 1 Generation 2 UHF tags (Wessel, 2007). This standard allows interoperability across the 860 to 960 MHz spectrum making this standard more scalable and raising its tolerance to interference in a dense RF environment. The United States has adopted the 915 MHz frequency as the national standard for passive RFID systems (Porter, Billo, & Mickle, 2006) which is within the EPCglobal defined range for UHF tags. The Australian Communications and Media Authority has issued a license to GS1 for the use of 920 to 926 MHz in Australia. The New Zealand Government has allocated two short range device slots in the 902 to 928 MHz range for RFID experiments. Besides assigning the 864 to 868 MHz spectrum for RFID, the New Zealand Government has plans to freeze any further issuance of licenses in the band of 915 to 921 MHz to cater for future RFID uses (Anonymous, 2007c). The New Zealand Government is adopting generic frequency standards across the ISM spectrum as a strategy for keeping the use of RFID devices and licensing open. The Government is actively discussing and harmonising the frequency arrangements with key trading partners such as the Australia, Europe, and the United States. Such arrangement will make RF equipments easily available without incurring additional cost for modifying the equipment according to local standards. The European Commission on the other hand has planned to adopt the ultra-wide band frequency range of 3.4 to 4.8 GHz and 6 to 8.5 GHz among the European countries (Swedberg, 2007).

Privacy is yet another issue with the use of RFID. While standards and costs are primarily technological, privacy is believed to be an educational one (Twist, 2005). RFID is just another data collection tool for keeping track of products. Sarma (2005) highlights that the electronic toll collection, a form of RFID applications with longer read range than the cheaper RFID/EPC tag, is already in use in many countries. The information in a RFID/EPC tag is encoded and does not contain information about the consumers. It adopts the Internet technology where the information in the tag is used as an address to more information about the content. The access to such further information is secured and authenticated. Another similar application widely used is the credit card.

CONCLUSION

RFID has been in commercial use since the 1970s. As an AIDC technology using wireless communication, RFID enables simultaneous collection of objects data with no or little human intervention. Thus RFID is an important technology from the point of view of ubiquitous computing. RFID is also an emerging technology that performs better than barcodes in most aspects. Of note, RFID's unique characteristics offer more utilities than barcodes. An example is the tracking of items without the need for line of sight. Tagging at item level enhances supply chain visibility and security. Manufacturers and retailers can have tighter control over their products from unwanted spoilage to out-of-stock with more accurate and timely data capturing. Although efforts to improve the performance are evident, the impediment to RFID implementation is the lack of standards, the relatively high cost of tag per unit, and privacy (ABIResearch, 2006; C. B. Soon & J. Gutierrez, 2008; Vijayaraman & Osyk, 2006). By far, these are the three main hurdles, among a number of secondary obstacles such as frequency interference, which need to be resolved before the technology can be widely adopted. Unless solutions are found for the three hurdles, barcode is still the cheaper and easier option although the benefits are not as extensive as what RFID can yield. With this stance, it is not to say that RFID will totally replace barcode, at least not in the next twenty to thirty years until a RFID tag is possibly as cheap as a barcode label and when the technology has matured. This projection is in line with what Bhuptani (2005) has noted, namely, that a new technology typically takes twenty to thirty years to become commercialised and forty to fifty years to become fully mature. And so accordingly, RFID has just reached the commercial stage since its inception in the supply chain and thus has another twenty to thirty years before reaching its maturity. Blau (2006) suggests that it will take fifteen years before RFID replaces barcodes and be used to identify products at item level.

RFID and barcodes may in fact be complementary to each other having merits in their respective applications. Woolworths has tested out the tracking of dollies and items using both RFID and barcode systems (Alexandra, 2003). It overcame the cost factor of tagging each item with RFID tags by utilising a barcode system and tagging only the dollies that hold the items with RFID tags. Woolworths reported full item-level visibility without the cost of item-level tagging. From a worst case scenario perspective, Jilovec (2004) suggests barcode as a backup for RFID in case of failure. This is sensible since most companies would already have implemented barcode systems.

The use of RFID at the UHF 860 to 960 MHz spectrums is now an internationally accepted standard. With the ratification of this standard, there will be more hardware available for the uptake of RFID in supply chains. The remaining challenges would be to enhance the data transfer rate, enable communication in a dense environment, and educate users on privacy concerns. As the technology matures, the investment and operating costs should gradually reduce.

RFID is becoming widespread not only in the supply chain, but also in other industries. The advancement of the technology has introduced RFID to many fields as innovators continue to explore the characteristics of RFID. It will continue to find innovation in the field of real time locating system, positioning system, product authentication, and in the sport arena. Like barcodes, RFID is an enabling tool for data capturing and identification. RFID is thus a smart technology that enables the convergence of information with its speedy event's data capture. It closes up the gap between the physical world and its representation in information systems. The next phase in the field of RFID is to explore the adoption and diffusion of the technology as a business case.

REFERENCES

ABIResearch. (2006). RFID End-User Survey. *ABIResearch*. Retrieved November 13, 2007, from http://www.abiresearch.com

Alexandra, D. (2003). Woolworths counts on RFID for security's sake. *Logistics Management, 42*(9), 61.

Allen, L. G. (1991). Automatic Identification: How Do You Choose It & Where Do You Use It? *Automation, 38*(7), 30-33.

Anonymous. (1993). Bar code technology increases efficiency for off-site records storage firm. *Managing Office Technology, 38*(11), 65-67.

Anonymous. (2004). Active RFID System Frequencies. Retrieved December 21, 2007, from http://www.idtechex.com

Anonymous. (2006). How do 2D barcodes work? *Who, What, Why?* Retrieved April 20, 2008, from http://news.bbc.co.uk/

Anonymous. (2007a). Automatic Identification and Data Capture Technologies - An overview. Retrieved January, 29, 2007, from http://www.aimglobal.org/technologies/aidc_overview.asp

Anonymous. (2007b). *Electromagnetic compatibility and Radio spectrum Matters (ERM)*: European Telecommunications Standards Institution.

Anonymous. (2007c). *An Engineering Discussion Paper on Spectrum Allocations for Short Range Devices*: New Zealand Ministry of Economic Development.

Atkinson, W. (2004). Web-Based RFID: Hype or Glimpse of the Future? *Apparel, 45*(6), 24-28.

Bahl, P., & Padmanabhan, V. N. (2000). *RADAR: An in-building user location and tracking system.* Paper presented at the Proceedings of the IEEE Infocom 2000.

Barthel, H. (2006). *Regulatory Status for Using RFID in the UHF Spectrum*. Brussels: GS1.

Barthel, H. (2007). *Regulatory Status for Using RFID in the UHF Spectrum*. Brussels: GS1.

Bednarz, A. (2004). RFID joins wireless lineup at UPS. *Network World, 21*(38), 8.

Bhuptani, M., & Moradpour, S. (2005). *RFID Field Guide - Deploying Radio Frequency Identification Systems*. NJ: Prentice Hall.

Blau, J. (2006). RFID on all goods is 15 years away, says Metro. *Computerworld* Retrieved November 16, 2006, from http://www.computerworld.co.nz

Burkett, T. (1993). Bar code implementation. *Quality, 32*(3), 28.

Carter, J. R., & Ragatz, G. L. (1991). Supplier Bar Codes: Closing the EDI Loop. *International Journal of Purchasing and Materials Management, 27*(3), 19.

Collins, J. (2004). New Two-Frequency RFID System. *RFID Journal*. Retrieved April 2, 2007, from http://www.rfidjournal.com

Collins, J. (2005). Test Detect RFID-Radar Interference. Retrieved December 21, 2007, from http://www.rfidjournal.com

Edwards, J. (2008). RFID Is a Winner in the Sports Arena. *RFID Journal*. Retrieved April 26, 2008, from http://www.rfidjournal.com

Eeden, H. v. (2004). Europe Needs New RFID Regulations. *RFID Journal* Retrieved December 21, 2007, from http://www.rfidjournal.com

Ekman, S. (1992). Bar Coding Fixed Asset Inventories. *Management Accounting, 74*(6), 58.

Engels, D. W., & Sarma, S. E. (2005). *Standardization Requirements within the RFID Class Structure Framework*. MA: Auto-ID Labs.

Finkenzeller, K. (2003). *RFID Handbook - Fundamentals and Applications in Contactless Smart Cards and Identification* (2nd ed.). Chichester: Wiley.

Fleisch, E. (2001). *Business Perspectives on Ubiquitous Computing* (M-Lab Working Paper No. 4). St Gallen: University of St Gallen.

Grasso, J. (2004). The EPCglobal Network. *EPCglobal* Retrieved December 21, 2007, from http://www.epcglobalus.org

Heinen, M. G., Coyle, G. A., & Hamilton, A. V. (2003). Barcoding makes its mark on daily practice. *Nursing Management, Oct 2003*, 18-20.

Hightower, J., Vakili, C., Borriello, G., & Want, R. (2001). Design and Calibration of the SpotON Ad-Hoc Location Sensing System. *University of Washington* Retrieved April 26, 2008, from http://seattle.intel-research.net/people/jhightower//pubs/hightower2001design/hightower2001design.pdf

Jilovec, N. (2004). *EDI, UCCnet & RFID - Synchronizing the Supply Chain.* Colorado: 29th Street Press.

Jones, A. K., Dontharaju, S., Tung, S., Hawrylak, P. J., Mats, L., Hoare, R., et al. (2006). Passive active radio frequency identification tags. *International journal of Radio Frequency Technology and Applications, 1*(1), 52-73.

Katz, J. (2006). Bar Codes: Alive and Well. *Industry Week, 255*(7), 14.

Kondratova, I. (2003). *Voice and multimodal access to AEC project information.* Paper presented at the The 10th ISPE International Conference on Concurrent Engineering: The Vision for Future Generations in Research and Applications, Portugal.

Lacharite, R. (1991). Rethinking Bar Coding: Turning Preconceptions into System Tools. *ARMA Records Management Quarterly, 25*(2), 3.

Landt, J. (2001). Shrouds of Time. *The history of RFID* Retrieved 19 January, 2006, from http://www.aimglobal.org/technologies/rfid/resources/shrouds_of_time.pdf

Lazar, L. D., & Moss, H. K. (2005). *Radio Frequency Identification Technology: An Introduction.* Paper presented at the Proceedings of the 2005 Southern Association for Information Systems Conference, Savannah.

Li, S., Visich, J. K., Khumawala, B. M., & Zhang, C. (2006). Radio frequency identification technology: applications, technical challenges and strategies. *Sensor Review, 26*(3).

Man, M. (2007). All About 2D Bar Codes. *Socket Communications Technology Brief.* Retrieved April 20, 2008, from http://www.socketmobile.com

Mason, B. (2005). *Bar Code Scanner Demand Remains Strong* (Press Release). Massachusetts: Venture Development Corporation.

May, E. L. (2003). The case for bar coding: Better information, better care and better business. *Healthcare Executive, 18*(5), 8-13.

Mullen, D., & Moore, B. (2005). Automatic Identification and Data Collection: What the future holds. In S. Garfinkel & B. Rosenberg (Eds.), *RFID Applications, Security, and Privacy* (pp. 3-13). NJ: Addison-Wesley.

Ni, L. M., Liu, Y. H., Lau, Y. C., & Patil, A. P. (2004). LANDMARC: Indoor Location Sensing Using Active RFID. *Wireless Networks, 10,* 701-710.

Porter, J. D., Billo, R. E., & Mickle, M. H. (2006). Effect of active interference on the performance of radio frequency identification systems. *International journal of Radio Frequency Technology and Applications, 1*(1).

Roberti, M. (2004). New ETSI RFID Rules Move Forward. *RFID Journal.* Retrieved December 21, 2007, from http://www.rfidjournal.com

Roberti, M. (2006). SmartCode Offers 5-Cent EPC Tags. *RFID Journal.* Retrieved April 26, 2008, from http://www.rfidjournal.com

Sarma, S. (2001). *Towards the 5-cent Tag.* MA: Auto-ID Labs.

Sarma, S. (2005). A History of the EPC. In S. Garfinkel & B. Rosenberg (Eds.), *RFID Applications, Security, and Privacy* (pp. 37-55). NJ: Addison-Wesley.

Sheffi, Y. (2004). RFID and the Innovation Cycle. *The International Journal of Logistics Management, 15*(1).

Shepard, S. (2005). *Radio Frequency Identification*. NY: McGraw-Hill.

Smucker, T. (2006). *Making the GS1 Vision a Reality* (Annual Report). Brussels: GS1.

Soon, C. B., & Gutierrez, J. (2008, May 18-20). *Where is New Zealand at with Radio Frequency Identification in the Supply Chain? - A Survey Result*. Paper presented at the Proceedings of 2008 International Conference on Information Resources Management, Niagara Falls, Canada.

Soon, C. B., & Gutierrez, J. A. (2008). Effects of the RFID Mandate on Supply Chain Management. *Journal of Theoretical and Applied Electronic Commerce Research, 3*(1), 81-91.

Strassner, M., & Schoch, T. (2002). *Today's Impact of Ubiquitous Computing on Business Processes*. Paper presented at the First International Conference on Pervasive Computing, Zurich, Switzerland.

Swedberg, C. (2006). China Endorses ISO 18000-7 433 MHz Standard. *RFID Journal* Retrieved July 29, 2007, from http://www.rfidjournal.com/

Swedberg, C. (2007). EC Spectrum Decision Expected to Boost UWB RFID Adoption. *RFIDJournal*. Retrieved December 29, 2007, from http://www.rfidjournal.com

Swedberg, C. (2008a). RFID Fuels Gas Tank Sercurity. *RFIDJournal*. Retrieved April 26, 2008, from http://www.rfidjournal.com

Swedberg, C. (2008b). U.S. FDA Seeks Research for Medical Device Tracking System. *RFIDJournal*. Retrieved April 26, 2008, from http://www.rfidjournal.com

Twist, D. C. (2005). The impact of radio frequency identification on supply chain facilities. *Journal of Facilities Management, 3*(3), 226-239.

Ukkonen, L., Schaffrath, M., Kataja, J., Sydanheimo, L., & Kivikoski, M. (2006). Evolutionary RFID tag antenna design for paper industry appli-cations. *International journal of Radio Frequency Technology and Applications, 1*(1), 107-122.

Vijayaraman, B. S., & Osyk, B. A. (2006). An empirical study of RFID implementation in the warehousing industry. *The International Journal of Logistics Management, 17*(1), 6-20.

Violino, B. (2006). APL Reaps Double Benefits From Real-Time Visibility [Electronic Version]. *RFIDJournal*. Retrieved December 28, 2006 from http://www.rfidjournal.com.

Walker, J. (2003). What You Need To Know About RFID in 2004. *Forrester Research*. Retrieved December 20, 2003, from http://www.forrester.com

Walter, E. J. (1988). Bar Code Boom Extending thru Industry. *Purchasing World, 32*(2), 39.

Wasserman, E. (2007). Europe Embraces EPC - Slowly. *RFIDJournal*. Retrieved December 21, 2007, from http://www.rfidjournal.com

Weinstein, R. (2005). RFID: A Technical Overview and Its Application to the Enterprise. *IT Professional Magazine, 7*(3), 27-33.

Wessel, R. (2007). European EPC Competence Center Releases UHF Tag Study. *RFIDJournal*. Retrieved July 16, 2007, from http://www.rfidjournal.com

KEY TERMS

AIDC: Automatic Identification and Data Capture.

EPC: Electronic Product Code.

EPCglobal: An international subscriber-driven organization aimed at enhancing RFID standards.

GS1: Former Uniform Code Council (UCC) and European Article Numbering (EAN) International.

ISM: Radio bands available worldwide reserved for use in the Industrial, Scientific, and Medical fields. ISM bands range from 6.765 MHz to 246 GHz.

RF: Radio Frequency.

RFID: Radio Frequency Identification.

Supply Chain Management: The managing of all movements of products and materials from source to point of consumption including storage.

Tag: A transponder with built-in memory chip and antenna encoded with an identifier. It can be passive (without battery) or active (with battery).

ENDNOTE

[1] Uniform Code Council and EAN International merged to form GS1.

Section II
Smart Identification

Chapter II
Using Bluetooth for Indoor User Positioning and Informing

John Garofalakis
University of Patras, Greece

Christos Mettouris
University of Patras, Greece

ABSTRACT

The continuous evolution of wireless technologies has made them ideal for use in many different applications, including user positioning. Until now, user positioning applications were focused mainly on providing users with exact location information. This makes them computational heavy while often demanding specialized software and hardware from mobile devices. In this chapter, we present a new user positioning application. The application is intended for use with m-commerce by sending informative and advertising messages to the users after locating their position indoors. The application is based exclusively on Bluetooth. The positioning method we use, while efficient, is nevertheless simple. The m-commerce based messages can be received without additional software or hardware installed. After discussing the available technologies and methods for implementing indoor user positioning applications, we shall focus on implementation issues, as well as the evaluation of our application after testing it. Finally, conclusions are extracted and future work is proposed.

INTRODUCTION

Wireless technologies have become a very important part of today's life. Bluetooth, Wi-Fi and Infrared are three examples of such technologies, with a variety of usages for each one of them.

Wireless technologies can be used to form wireless networks among computers themselves and among computers and mobile devices. These wireless networks can be used for many applications including data exchange and accessing the internet from mobile devices. These potentials gave ground for m-commerce to grow to a very profitable field of the business world (Xiaojun, Junichi, & Sho, 2004).

During the past few years, Bluetooth has become a very popular technology. Its low cost and low power consumption have made it ideal for use with small, low powered devices such as mobile phones and PDAs. Apart from forming wireless ad-hoc networks for sending and receiving data among Bluetooth enabled devices, wireless voice transferring, wireless printing, object exchange (such as business carts and messages) and many more applications, Bluetooth technology is also ideal for user location detection applications, mainly for two reasons: the first is that the technology itself provides ways for a variety of positioning methods to be efficiently implemented, like the triangulation and RX (Received X) power level methods (Kotanen, Hännikäinen, Leppäkoski & Hämäläinen, 2003). The second reason is that almost everyone possesses at least one Bluetooth device that can be used by a positioning application.

User positioning is the methodology used to detect the position of a user. This detection can be done according to some stationary points, which are usually called base stations. The position of a user arises when his distance from every base station becomes known. Two techniques can be followed: the first uses a central stationary point (server) that analyzes the data that come up from the base stations, resulting in the location of the user. The result is then sent to the user. The second technique, on the contrary, does not use any central stationary point. Instead, either the data that come up from the base stations are sent directly to the user's device to be processed there, or the user's device itself collects these data by detecting the base stations, and then processes them appropriately to find the desirable distances from the stations. This means that the user's device must be equipped with the necessary software to collect and process the data to find the users position, hence become software depended, something not desirable.

User positioning can be global or indoor. Global positioning is used to detect the geographic location of a user. GPS is a very well known and efficient global positioning system that uses satellite links to detect the location of a GPS device worldwide. Indoor positioning on the other hand is used to locate a user inside a building. Global positioning cannot be used for indoor positioning because the latter needs more accuracy than the former can achieve and because the building walls block the satellite signal.

In the bibliography, many positioning systems fall in an intermediate category, which may not be characterized neither as global, nor as indoor positioning. The target areas of these systems are larger than buildings and smaller than cities, for example large shopping malls, campus areas, even ancient castles. In such places, a technology that aims strictly to locate users worldwide, like GPS may not give as good results as a more general purpose technology, like Wi-Fi.

According to Xiaojun, Junichi, & Sho (2004), the development of wireless technologies and mobile network has created a challenging research and application area, mobile commerce. They note that, as an independent business area, it has its own advantages and features as opposed to traditional e-commerce and that many unique features of m-commerce like easier information access in real-time, communication that is independent of the users' location, easier data reception and having accessibility anywhere and anytime make a widespread acceptance and deployment of its applications and services. Such services can be disposed to the public using wireless technologies. In the next pages we study the use of wireless technologies in informing the users by sending them m-commerce related messages.

Xiaojun, Junichi, & Sho (2004), also state that according to the market research firm Strategy Analytics, the global market for m-commerce is expected to reach $200 billion by 2004. Burger (2007) points out that while the U.S. and European Union markets are more crowded, closely regulated and contested, their size and technological infrastructure mean that they will be important proving grounds for m-commerce. According to Burger (2007), David Chamberlain, In-Stat's principal analyst for wireless technology, told the E-Commerce Times that there could be 10 million to 20 million m-commerce users in the U.S. by 2010. Indeed, the past few years there has been much interest in a variety of different applications regarding m-commerce. Varshney (2001) has identified several important classes of m-commerce, as well as examples within each class. Apart from mobile advertising, which is a very important class of m-commerce, the set of classes includes among other Mobile Financial Applications (Applications where mobile device becomes a powerful financial medium), Product Locating and Shopping (Applications that help in finding the location of products and services), Proactive Service Management (Applications attempting to provide users information on services they may need in the very-near-future), Wireless Re engineering (Applications for improving the quality of business services using devices and wireless infrastructure), Mobile Entertainment Services and games (Applications providing the entertainment services to users on per event or subscription basis), Mobile Office (Applications providing the complete office environment to mobile users any where, any time) and Mobile Distance Education (Applications extending distance/virtual education support for mobile users everywhere). Regarding mobile advertising applications, Varshney (2001) points out some important features of such applications: 1. advertisements sent to a user can be location-sensitive and can inform a user about various on-going specials (shops, malls, and restaurants) in surrounding areas, 2. depending on interests and the personality of individual mobile users, a push or pull method may be used and 3. the messages can be sent to all users located in a certain area. The aforementioned statements concern our application as well, as we explain in another section.

In this chapter we present a User Positioning Application based on Bluetooth technology for use in m-commerce. The application utilizes the solutions that wireless technologies and more specific Bluetooth offer, in such a way that they can be used in m-commerce. The application uses exclusively the Bluetooth technology to detect the position of all nearby users and send them advertising, informative and other kind of messages related to m-commerce. At first, we talk about various known wireless technologies that are or were used for global positioning and why these technologies are ineffective for indoor positioning. After a brief introduction to Bluetooth technology, we compare it with other known wireless technologies and explain why we used Bluetooth. Next, we discuss briefly all available positioning methods that can be used with Bluetooth technology. A preview follows of the related work that has already been done regarding wireless positioning systems and how our work differentiates from them. We show that Bluetooth technology is the best technology to be used for indoor positioning and that the triangulation method gives very good results for positioning applications that don't need very high accuracy. We talk about our positioning method, which is derived from the triangulation method and the implementation issues regarding the application. A relatively low accuracy but reliable end efficient application such as the one we present in this chapter can be used with very good results for the needs of m-commerce. This is indicated by our test that shows how the application functions and what its strong and weak points are. Finally we discuss our conclusions from our work and what future work can be done for further improvements.

WIRELESS GLOBAL POSITIONING: TECHNOLOGIES

Many technologies are known that have provided very good solutions for global user positioning. In this section, we present such technologies.

The GPS is a very well known positioning system technology that uses satellite connections to locate the geographic location of the user. Developed and maintained by the U.S. government, it was initially designed for military applications. Soon, civilian users have found numerous applications using this technology (Anonymous, 2007). The way GPS works is by sending Radio signals from orbiting satellites to earth. GPS receivers on the ground can collect and convert the radio signals into position, velocity, and time information. Some GPS receivers have also the ability to store attribute information in addition to position information, such as the condition of a street sign, the name of a road, or the condition of a fire hydrant. Position and attribute information can be stored in a Geographic Information System (GIS) to help users manage their assets more efficiently (Anonymous, 2007).

The Loran (LOng RAnge Navigation) (Proc, 2006b) is a terrestrial navigation system. It uses low frequency radio transmitters. By receiving radio signals of two or more stations, it can determine the position of a ship or airplane.

The Decca navigation system (Proc, 2006a) was initially developed during World War II for helping in precise airplane landing. Next, it was used as a terrestrial navigation system, like Loran. Nowadays, this technology has been replaced by GPS.

Another system developed for military purposes was Omega (Proc, 2006c). It was used for locating ships and submarines and could cover oceans with a 4 mile precision. Like Decca, this technology has been replaced by GPS.

Despite the success of the aforementioned technologies, the need for indoor user positioning could not yet be satisfied. Using GPS to locate the position of a user inside a building will provide imprecise results, since a GPS receiver needs line-of-sight with a satellite, which is unachievable due to building walls.

WHAT IS BLUETOOTH?

Bluetooth is a low power short range wireless technology. At first it was to be used as a cable replacement technology by connecting peripheral devices to computers. Soon it became the ideal technology for connecting small, low power consumption devices by forming short range wireless networks called PANs (Personal Area Networks) at speeds up to 3 Mbit/sec (Anonymous, 2006c).

Bluetooth operates in the ISM (Industrial Scientific and Medical) frequency band, at 2.4 GHz. This band is divided into 79 channels, each 1MHz wide (2.402 GHz - 2.480GHz). To avoid interference with other devices using the 2.4GHz frequency zone, Bluetooth technology uses the fast frequency hopping technique. Thus, a Bluetooth device when transmitting data is hopping from one channel to another every 625μs. If a channel is occupied, the device will use the next free one. Due to the high frequency used, a direct line of sight is not needed between communicating Bluetooth devices (Anonymous, 2003).

There are three classes of Bluetooth radios, each of different range. Class 1 radios use more power than classes 2 and 3, ranging up to 100m. Class 1 is used by not very low power consumption devices like computers. Class 2 is used by low powered devices such as mobile phones and PDAs. Its range is up to 10m. Finally, class 3 radios can connect Bluetooth devices at distances up to 1m (Anonymous, 2006c).

A Bluetooth core system consists of a Radio-Frequency receiver (RF), the baseband and the Bluetooth Protocol stack. The RF receiver is the lowest layer of the system with the baseband being above it. The protocol stack consists of a set of protocols used to connect the layers. In the Bluetooth specification it is given a description of the Bluetooth protocol stack and the Bluetooth profiles. The profiles are being used as models to show how the applications should use the Bluetooth protocols (Anonymous, 2006c).

Figure 1. Bluetooth protocol stack

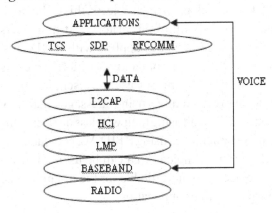

The layers of the Bluetooth protocol stack starting from the lower are shown in Figure 1. The last three layers constitute one of the two Bluetooth subsystems, the Bluetooth Controller. The rest of them constitute the other subsystem, the Bluetooth Host. For the communication of the two subsystems, a standard physical communications interface is being used.

CHOOSING THE APPROPRIATE WIRELESS TECHNOLOGY FOR IMPLEMENTING INDOOR USER POSITIONING

IrDA, 802.11b (Wi-Fi), RFID and Bluetooth are well known, mature wireless technologies. They are met in many devices and are used for many purposes like exchanging data, communicating, forming wireless networks, controlling other devices and more. In this section, we shall analyze each technology's advantages and disadvantages, as candidate technologies for use in our positioning purposes.

First, we summarise the key features of our application, that directly effect the decision for which technology to be used: 1. quick detection of all devices nearby a base station, 2. ability to detect all kinds of mobile devices used by users, especially popular devices that are being used more often and by most people, such as mobile phones, 3. no need for pre-installing any additional hardware or software to a mobile device, so that it can be used by the system and 4. the users should be able to easily receive the messages and read them.

IrDA

IrDA (Infrared) is a low cost technology used for many purposes. Most common usage of IrDA is the short distance communication of devices for exchanging data, like a TV remote control device with a TV set or two mobile phone devices exchanging files. The technology requires a line of sight between communicating devices for them to be able to exchange data. Furthermore, these devices must be relatively close to each other. According to Nilsson & Hallberg (2002), there are several sources of interference that can affect IrDA. Light can be affected by other light sources and electromagnetic fields.

In considering IrDA as a technology to be used for a user positioning application, we face several challenges. The line of sight and the short distances that IrDA need to function are the most important. Our positioning application intents to locate users by utilizing their own equipment, such as a mobile phone or a PDA. The fact that these IrDA devices require to be in line of sight and in short distances in order to communicate is very limitative to such an application. For all the aforementioned reasons, the IrDA technology is not suitable to be used by our application.

Wi-Fi

802.11b (Wi-Fi) is a wireless technology operating in the 2.4GHz zone. It is used for connecting high power devices like computers, laptops and PDAs. The connection speeds are much higher than IrDA's or Bluetooth's, as well as the range of the connection, making Wi-Fi suitable for forming large Wireless Local area Networks (WLAN) (Coursey, 2002).

Because of the aforementioned specifications, Wi-Fi may be successfully used for a user positioning application. Such an application would utilize the advantage of the long range and high connection speed to scan for Wi-Fi devices and locate them. On the other hand, the cost of having long range and high connection speed is the high power consumption. This is the main reason why Wi-Fi is not popular to mobile devices, with the exclusion of PDAs, some smartphones and some mobile phones, called Wi-Fi phones. Despite the fact that many Wi-Fi positioning systems mentioned in the bibliography function with such mobile devices, our essential need to locate all user mobile devices and not just a small portion of them, especially low power devices such as common mobile phones, forces as to reject this technology. Some innovating Wi-Fi positioning systems are described in a following section.

RFID

Despite the fact that Radio Frequency Identification (RFID) technology was not designed for location sensing systems, it has been used for such purposes in the past. The LANDMARC (Ni, Liu, Lau, & Patil, 2003), the RADAR (Bahl & Padmanabhan, 2000) and the SpotON (Hightower, Vakili, Borriello & Want, 2001) systems are such examples. A location sensing system may exploit certain advantages of the RFID technology to track objects, using RFID tags. These advantages are the no contact and non-line-of-sight nature of the RFID technology, that all RF tags can be read despite extreme environmental factors, the fact that such tags are able to work at remarkable speeds and finally that they have adequate transmission range and are cost effective (Ni, Liu, Lau, & Patil, 2003). By placing RFID tags on the objects to be located, a system may appropriately use RFID readers to locate the tags, thus the objects. One issue is the proper placing of the RFID readers, so they can locate all tags in their coverage area.

Despite the aforementioned advantages of the RFID technology to track objects, this technology doesn't satisfy all of our criteria. At first, users to be located must be supplied with RFID tags, something not feasible and cost ineffective. As set, we need to inform users by sending them informative and advertising messages that they could easily read using their wireless devices. This cannot be achieved using RFID. We conclude that RFID is a technology that can be used for locating objects, but not suitable for the m-commerce purposes of our application.

The Ideal Technology

From the aforementioned discussion we conclude that Bluetooth is the ideal technology to be used for indoor user positioning. A line of sight is not required, making it possible for the user to be able to be detected and receive messages from our application just by possessing a Bluetooth enable device and having the Bluetooth turned on. Such a device may be any common Bluetooth enabled mobile phone. Bluetooth is so popular a technology that almost all mobile phone manufacturers include it in the basic features of their phones, making it easy and cheap for anyone to possess a Bluetooth mobile device. For more information on Bluetooth technology, the reader is referred to the Specification of the Bluetooth System and Mahmoud (2003).

POSITIONING METHODS THAT CAN BE USED WITH BUETOOTH TECHNOLOGY

There are many positioning methods to be used with the Bluetooth technology (Kotanen, Hännikäinen, Leppäkoski & Hämäläinen 2003):

Angle of Arrival is based on determining the direction of a mobile device's Bluetooth signal by at least two base stations.

Cell Identity is a more simple method. The area is divided into cells. One base station corresponds to each cell. If a mobile device enters a cell, the corresponding station will trace the device, hence the location of the mobile device is considered to be that cell.

Time of Arrival and Time Difference of Arrival are two methods based on the round-trip time of the Bluetooth signal of a mobile device to reach the base station and return to the device. By estimating the round-trip time we can calculate the distance between the device and the station. This procedure must be applied to three stations so that the device's location may arise. The Time Difference of Arrival technique is an improvement of Time of Arrival regarding the synchronization. Because of this, only the latter can be used by Bluetooth Technology and only if the clocks of the Bluetooth devices improve in synchronization matters.

The RX power level method is based on measuring the strength of the signal of a particular wireless connection. In Bluetooth, this can be done by using the RSSI (Received Signal Strength Indicator) value. The RSSI value is an indicator of the signal strength of the connection between two Bluetooth devices. Each of these devices is able to receive this value and with proper calculations an estimation of their distance may arise. By using this technique, each base station is able to connect to a mobile device being in its coverage area and receive the RSSI value corresponding to this connection. By knowing the distance of a mobile devise from three base stations, we can find the exact location of the device. The RSSI is implemented in the Bluetooth module and can be received by the Host Controller Interface.

The Triangulation Method

The triangulation method uses at least three base stations to locate the position of a mobile device. For every station that detects the device, we can say that the device is somewhere on the

Figure 2. Worst case scenario (The Mobile device is shown as the big dot and the Base station as the small one)

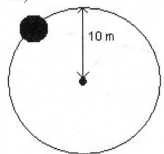

perimeter or inside the circle with the station in the centre and the range of the Bluetooth radio as the radius. The best case scenario is when the device is on the centre of the circle and the worst when it's on the perimeter of the circle, shown in Figure 2. In this case, the error is up to 10m, supposing that the range of the Bluetooth radio we are using is 10m.

By using three base stations we have three such circles. We next find the points of intersection of the three circles. There are two points (Figure 3) on each circle for every intersection with another one. These points designate six small arcs, two on each circle. By taking the vertical line in the middle of every arc, we result to three straight lines forming a triangle. This is because every intersection of two circles corresponds to two arcs but only one line (see Figures 3 and 4).

Figure 3. Forming the three straight lines in the triangulation method

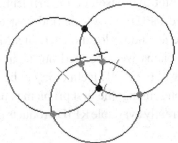

Figure 4. Finding the center of the triangle, the x point

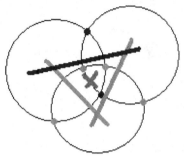

The triangulation method results in the centre of the triangle being the location of the mobile device. This is shown in Figure 4 by an x mark.

RELATED SYSTEMS

In the bibliography, there are many positioning systems based on wireless technologies. In previous sections, we have decided Bluetooth to be the ideal technology and the triangulation method to be the most suitable positioning method for our application. In this section, for completeness purposes, we present the most innovative positioning and location aware systems that use not only Bluetooth, but various wireless technologies and positioning methods.

RFID and RF Location Sensing Systems

The LANDMARC system (Ni, Liu, Lau, & Patil, 2003) uses RFID for locating the position of a user indoors. The creators of the LANDMARC system point that based on experimental analysis, active RFID is a viable and cost effective candidate for indoor location sensing. Moreover three problems were pointed out regarding the efficiency of the RFID technology in being used in location sensing: the first problem is that none of the currently available RFID products provides

the signal strength of tags directly. Instead, the reader reports "detectable" or "not detectable" in a given range, forcing the creators of LANDMARC to scan the 8 discrete power levels and to estimate the signal strength of tags. The second problem is the long time interval (7.5 seconds) of emitting two consecutive IDs from an active tag. RFID vendors should provide a mechanism to allow users to reconfigure the time interval. The third problem is the variation of the behaviour of tags. The power level detected by the same reader from two tags in an identical location may be different. According to Ni, Liu, Lau, & Patil (2003) if all the aforementioned problems can be overcome, the accuracy and latency will be greatly improved and RFID technology will be a very competitive technology in location sensing systems.

The RADAR system (Bahl & Padmanabhan, 2000) is a radio-frequency (RF) based system. It can locate a user indoors by measuring the signal strength using multiple base stations, which are placed in such a way, that are able to provide coverage for the desired area. The system combines empirical measurements of the signal strength with a simple yet efficient signal propagation model. The empirical method is proved to be more precise, but the signal propagation method makes the development easier. According to the authors, the RADAR system provides 2-3m accuracy.

The Cricket system (Priyantha, Chakraborty & Balakrishnan, 2000) uses a combination of ultrasonic pulses and radio-signals. The mobile device to be located doesn't need to transmit any data and it carries a set of radio-signal and ultrasonic pulse receivers. A set of static devices called Crickets constantly transmits radio-signals and ultrasonic pulses, allowing the mobile device's receivers to calculate it's position, in relation to the Cricket devices. The system provides accuracy but it has cost and Hardware pre-installing issues. Moreover, due to the use of radio-signals and ultrasonic pulses, the system can not function through walls or other insulating materials.

Wi-Fi Positioning Systems

Herecast (Paciga & Lutfiyya, 2005) is a location positioning system based on Wi-Fi. The system uses wireless access points that broadcast a unique identifier, which can be used to discriminate them from other access points. When a computing device receives this unique identifier, it uses it to map to location information. The location information can then be used to look up services that are specific to the location. With an access point the following information is associated: information about the location of an access point, the network that the access point is on and the services associated with an access point. Thus, a wireless device by receiving the signal of a Wi-Fi access point may locate itself as well as discover services in the area. Herecast provides such services, which are:

- Mapping services for navigating city streets by car. This service allows for the production of detailed maps for a specific area. Maps are optimized to fit on a Pocket PC screen, and can be navigated by clicking on the image.
- A friend finder service: when a user subscribes to this service, the device automatically publishes the user's location to a web page as the user moves from place to place. The web site displays the most recently seen location of each individual.
- Heresay service: users can leave a message at their current location, and see messages that have been left by other people in the same building.
- Bandwidth Advisor service: users experiencing a lack of connectivity can bring up a list of access points in the area, along with an indication of the load associated with each access point. If the device notices that the network is currently slow and congested, it can proactively advise the user to move to a location that has lower usage. This service

helps users by suggesting areas where they may obtain optimal service and helps the network by balancing network traffic.

Wang, Jia & Lee, (2003) describe a WPS (Wireless Positioning System) that uses the signal strength of WLAN transmissions from/to WLAN Access Points to determine the position of the mobile user. The system uses six 11Mbps WLAN Access Points which were installed at several locations in a building. The Access Points act as the wireless signal transmitters or base stations. The devices to be located are laptops or Pocket PCs with Wi-Fi network cards. These network cards can detect and synchronize the signal strength from the six wireless Access Points. According to the authors, the results of the experiments show that a positioning accuracy of 1-3m can be achieved while an accuracy of 0.1m level can be obtained under an idealized situation.

Singh, Gmdetto, Guainazzo, Angiati & Ragazzoni, (2004) describe a Wireless Positioning System. The system is based on a WLAN network. It uses the Signal Strength of WLAN transmissions (802.11b at 11 Mbps) between Access Points and the user's mobile device to determine the position of the mobile device. After receiving the signal strength, the system converts it to approximate distance. The system improves the positioning accuracy by mitigating multi-path and noise. It is also environment adaptive and can be applicable both indoor and outdoor.

Bluetooth Positioning Systems

The Alipes (Hallberg, Nilsson & Synnes, 2003) is a positioning platform for mobile devices. It uses stationary points called positioning servers, which provide mobile devices with positioning information. Alipes provides 3 different ways to locate a user: i) a positioning server provides a positioning service which users may use to ask for their location, ii) user's Bluetooth device's address is used by a stationary point, in order for the latter to provide the device's location after searching a Data Base and iii) a location received by Alipes is been forwarded via Bluetooth. Besides static positioning servers, the system also uses mobile positioning servers as well. These mobile servers update their current position when they change location, thus when they move. The system also uses a central server called location server, which stores all the unique addresses of the positioning servers. To any such address, a location is been assigned. The authors point out that if a mobile device is moving with the speed of a walking human, then the device may not have enough time to connect to all near positioning servers. A solution proposed is that the device, thus the user, moves slower.

The BLPA (Bluetooth Local Positioning Application) (Kotanen, Hännikäinen, Leppäkoski & Hämäläinen 2003) uses the RX power level method for detecting a user's location. As said, the RX power level method uses the RSSI value, which indicates the strength of the signal of a particular wireless Bluetooth connection. The system first measures the RSSI values for the Bluetooth connections between the static base stations and the user's mobile device. Next, a radio wave propagation model is used in order to estimate the mobile device distance from each station by using the RSSI values. Finally, a Kalman filter is been used to estimate user's position, given his approximate distance from each station. BLPA runs on mobile devices to be located.

B-MAD (Bluetooth – Mobile Advertising) (Aalto, Göthlin, Korhonen & Ojala, 2004) system uses the Cell Identity positioning method to detect mobile devices and send ad messages to them. After a mobile device is discovered by a stationary station, the latter sends via WAP (Wireless Application Protocol) the Bluetooth address of the device to a server called Ad Server. The server uses a database to match the address with the phone number of the user and to check if the user had received the ad corresponding to that location in the past. If not, the ad is sent to him

as WAP push SI (Service Indication) message. The B-MAD system requires that the stations are equipped with GPRS and the mobile devices with GPRS and XHTML browser.

The Novel Location Sensing System (Bandara, Hasegawa, Inoue, Morikawa & Aoyama, 2004) is based on Bluetooth Signal Strength. It uses a Bluetooth Access Point (AP) for the calculation of the location of mobile devices. The AP is composed of multi-antennas, which are connected to it. Each antenna is equipped with an attenuator. The strength of the attenuator may be controlled by a server. When a Bluetooth mobile device enters the coverage area of the AP, the latter initiates a connection to the mobile device by using an antenna. Then, the AP measures several times the signal strength of the connection. During the measurements, the AP often changes the antenna it uses as well as the strength of the antenna's attenuator. This increases the range of the Bluetooth signal that can be read.

The BIPS (Bluetooth Indoor Positioning Service) (Anastasi, Bandelloni, Conti, Delmastro, Gregori & Mainetto, 2003) system is an indoor user positioning system that combines the Bluetooth and Ethernet LAN technologies. The system offers a service that indicates to the user's mobile device the shortest path to another mobile device in the same building.

The aforementioned are some of the many positioning systems that effectively use the Bluetooth technology to detect the position of mobile devices. Despite the fact that most of the systems mentioned in the bibliography are positioning systems that inform the users of their location mainly by sending them location data, only one of them sends messages not related with the location itself. B-MAD sends advertising messages to the users, informing them not about their location, but about products and services. We differ from that system as well in the aspect of how the user receives the messages. We do not use technology not available to all users like GPRS and XHTML browsers on mobile devices. Instead, our approach proposes a system depending exclusively on the Bluetooth technology to detect the position of all nearby users and send them messages. Our purpose is to make it possible for any user entering our system's coverage area with a common mobile Bluetooth enabled device to be able to receive messages related to m-commerce, like ads, with the least possible effort on his behalf. User's Bluetooth mobile device does not need any specific hardware or software installed to interact with the system. The only requirement is that the device implements the Obex Object Push Profile (OPP). Obex (Object Exchange Protocol) is a protocol for exchanging objects among Bluetooth enabled devices. These objects may be files, pictures, vCarts e.t.c. The Obex OPP is implemented mainly in all new mobile phones and PDAs.

A USER POSITIONING APPLICATION

In this section we discuss the positioning method and implementation issues regarding our application. We also provide the architecture of the application schematically.

Aim of the Application

The application aims to locate and inform any user in its coverage area. Such an application may be used in a supermarket, in a museum or in any other place where people would like to be informed in real time about things nearby. In a supermarket the system will be able to locate all users in it's coverage area, estimate their position, that is find the area or section of the supermarket they currently are and send them informative messages and adds which are related to the goods sold in that area. In a museum, the application after finding users' position, it will inform them about the exhibits that are near them.

Our Positioning Method

Our positioning application is meant to be used by m-commerce. Such an application does not demand the exact location of the user. We can apply a method that provides the location of the user approximately, in respect to the stationary points.

Our approach suggests three base stations. These stations are stationary points that are placed in a way to form a triangle (white dots in Figure 5). The distances between the stations depend on the given location. Each station's coverage area should be in partial mutual coverage with the coverage area of the other two stations, so that our application comprises of more sub-areas (seven) than just three. The coverage area of the three base stations together is the coverage area of our positioning application. In Figure 5, the coverage area of the application is the entire square room, excluding the light grey area surrounding the three circles.

Our method is derived from the triangulation method and it depends on which of the three base stations will detect each mobile device. If all three stations detect a device, according to the triangulation method, the location of that device is the black centered area in Figure 5. If only two stations detect a device, then the device's location is somewhere in the area of intersection of the two circles corresponding to the two stations, excluding the area of intersection with the

Figure 5. The seven sub-areas of our application are shown in different colours

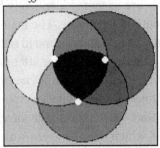

third station. Finally if only one station detects a device, the latter is located somewhere in the area formed by the circle corresponding to the station, excluding the areas of intersection with the other two circles. Figure 5 shows these areas in different colors.

Implementation Issues

Our application consists of four modules: 1. three base stations, 2. a central server, 3. a database and 4. an interface to administrate the database. The stations and the server are Java programs, the database is implemented using mySQL and the interface is written in php.

The java programs use the JSR 82 (Anonymous, 2002), also known as JABWT (Java API for Bluetooth Wireless Technology). JSR 82 is a standard used for implementing Bluetooth applications in java. It contains a set of java APIs which we used for implementing our application. We used BlueCove's implementation of JSR82 (Anonymous, 2006b) and Avetana's implementation of Obex (Anonymous, 2006a). These software packages work well with Win XP SP2 Bluetooth Protocol stack.

The application works in loops. In each loop, the stations detect mobile devices, send their addresses to the server and then the server sends the corresponding messages to the devices. The three base stations are programmed to: a) Scan the area for mobile Bluetooth devices, and retrieve their Bluetooth addresses, b) provide the central server with the Bluetooth addresses of the detected mobile devices and c) give time to the server to process the data and send the messages. These three phases are executed identically by all stations at about the same time. The main idea is to scan only for mobile devices and to retrieve their Bluetooth addresses. A station after detecting a mobile device, examines if the device implements the Obex Object Push Profile service. If it does, the station finds the channel that corresponds to that service, which must be given with the Blue-

tooth address to the server. These addresses with the given channel will be used afterwards by the server for sending the messages related to m-commerce to the corresponding mobile devices. The Obex OPP must be implemented by a Bluetooth mobile device, for the latter to be able to receive the messages from the Server. If the channel of the Obex OPP service of a device cannot be found, the station considers the channel to be number six (the channels are positive integers). That is because from our experiments, we concluded that number six is the most frequently used channel for that service. If the mobile device does not implement the Obex Object Push Profile service, its address is not send to the server.

The central server, having a mobile device's Bluetooth address, is able to send a message to that device. As said, this is done by using the Bluetooth OBEX Object Push Profile. The main work of the server is to receive data from the base stations. After receiving data from a station, the server stores them locally and waits for more connections. When all three stations provide him with their data, the server runs an algorithm which distinguishes which mobile devices were discovered by each station, by any two of them and by all three of them. In this way, the server knows how many and which stations detected each mobile device, hence where in the coverage area of the application (Figure 5) the mobile device is located. Next, the server sends to each mobile device an m-commerce message corresponding to its location.

At this point, note that neither the stations, nor the server maintain a connection with a mobile device. A station performs a simple scan, retrieving the Bluetooth addresses. The server on the other hand, having the detected Bluetooth mobile devices address list, connects to the first device in the list, forming a small network of two, sends the messages and closes the connection, before sending the next message to the next device in the list. Hence, no wireless network exists among the devices, the stations and the server. Had such a

Figure 6. Application's architecture: The four modules

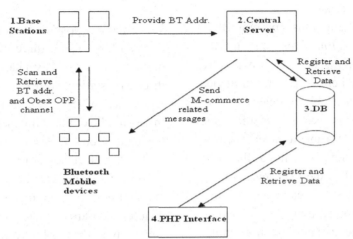

network existed, it would have limited the amount of devices connected to it, since a network among Bluetooth enabled devices, called piconet, may only have 8 members, with one of them being the master and the rest being the slaves. Moreover, this method makes the system able to deal with multiple users.

The server interacts with the database as well. It registers in it the Bluetooth addresses of the users' mobile devices discovered by the application, how many times they were discovered and which messages each device received or rejected and how many times. It also reads the messages to be sent to the users and several useful data regarding the application's operation, like how many times should a user be able to receive or reject a message, before the application stops sending that message to him.

Along with the database, we implemented an interface for the administrator to be able to supervise the operation of the application. The administrator can be informed about the Bluetooth addresses of the users detected, how many times were they detected, which messages did they receive or reject and how many times, the available messages the application is able to send to the users and about the data regarding the application's operation. He is also able to delete a user or the

messages received or rejected by him, change the context of a message or entirely delete one, create a new message and finally change the important data regarding the application's operation. Figure 6 shows the four modules of the application and how they interact.

Application's Topology

Topology is very important for the proper operation of our application. The central server must be situated in a spot so that it can communicate with all stations at any time. We positioned the server in the middle of the coverage area of the application. That position is shown in Figure 7

Figure 7. The application's topology

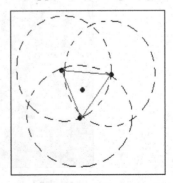

as the central dot. The other three dots forming a triangle designate the stations.

The Bluetooth range for most common Bluetooth enabled devices is 10m. This constrains the functionality of our application in a way that we are going to describe here. A Bluetooth device with a range of 100m is able to detect another mobile device within its coverage area, under the condition that the latter is able to detect the first one as well. If the second device has a Bluetooth radio of range 10m, then the two devices must be in 10m distance or less for each one to detect the other one. This forced us to use Bluetooth radios with 10m range (and not 100m) to implement our application (stations and server). This means that in Figure 5 the radiuses of the three circles are 10m. Since this positioning application is destinated to be used in real m-commerce scenarios, one may say that the sub-areas created by the application are small in comparison to the sections of a supermarket or a museum. This is just a minor drawback of our application.

EVALUATION BY TESTING

We tested our positioning application in our offices building using three offices, of which the one was surrounded by a hallway (Figure 8). The three base stations were placed on desks 1m high, one in each office. The central server was placed in the middle of the stations, in office 2, so it can reach all three stations.

For the purposes of this application test, we supposed that this area belonged to a supermarket. Figure 9 shows in different colors the seven different sub-areas in which our application was able to divide the whole coverage area. We let each sub-area of different colour be a unique section of the supermarket. As the Figure shows, we had a frozen food section, a bakery, a cosmetics section, a clothing section, a dairy section, a cleaning products section and a cigarette section.

Figures 10 to 13 show the interface of the application. By using this interface one is able to administrate the database in such a way to be suitable for use with the supermarket.

Figure 8. The building used for testing the application

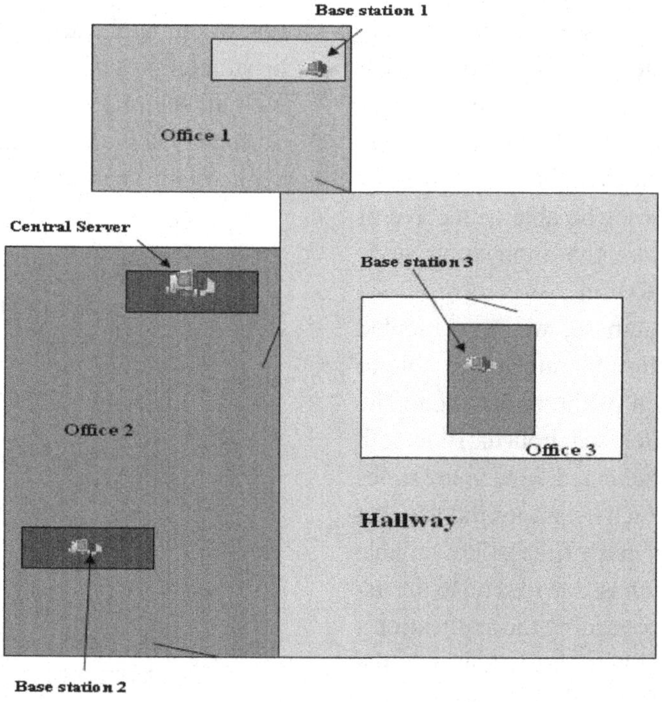

Figure 9. In different colours are shown the seven different sub-areas in which the application was able to divide the whole coverage area

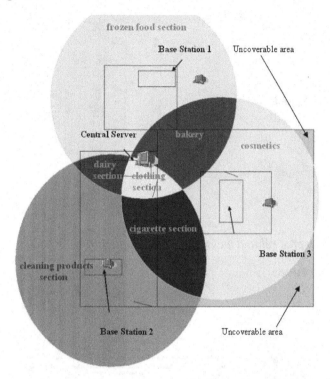

During the tests, the application could detect in which one of the seven sub-areas of Figure 9 each Bluetooth mobile device was located and send to it the corresponding messages. Having numbered these sub-areas and according to the number of the sub-area a user was located in, he received the message with the corresponding message id (a user in area 3 received the message with id=3).

Figure 10. Users detected by the application during the tests

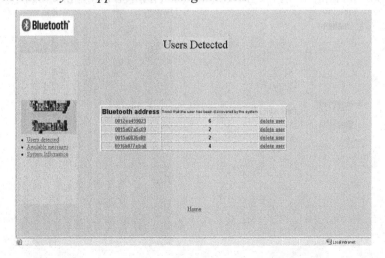

Figure 11. Messages received and rejected by a user and the number of receptions and rejections

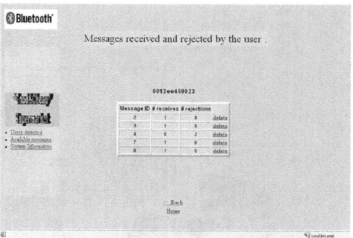

Figure 12. The m-commerce related messages of the application

Figure 13. The important data of the application may be changed by the administrator

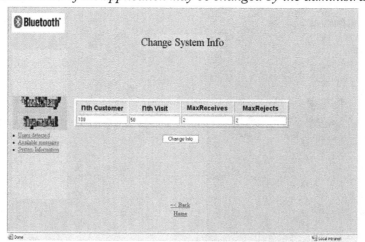

These messages are related to m-commerce and are shown in Figure 12. Such messages inform the users about product discount offers in the area they are currently located and advise them about smart purchases. The application is also provided with special messages (messages 8 and 9 in figure 12) to send to clients in special occasions like: *"Congratulations!!!! You are our 100th client!! You win 30% discount to everything you buy!! Thank you."* and *"We thank you for choosing for the 50th time our supermarket for your shopping!! We offer you 15% discount to everything you buy!!! Thank you."*. The 100th client and the 50th visit constitute parts of the important data of the application and the administrator may change them to any other numbers (Figure 13).

For the tests of the application we used relatively new Bluetooth enabled mobile phones such as Sony Ericsson V800. The application was running in a continual loop, detecting all devices and sending them messages. The messages were not sent to mobile devices not implementing the Obex OPP. Also, a mobile device could fail to receive the message, if its Bluetooth radio was busy by another connection at the same time.

Our application needs approximately 40-50 secs, according to the number of the mobile devices to be discovered, to detect these devices and send them messages, thus to finish a loop. Each base station needs 20 to 30 secs to detect all mobile devices within its coverage area, check each one for the Obex OPP service and then send their Bluetooth addresses to the server, after detecting it. If a station does not detect any devices, then it needs approximately 10 secs to scan and return 'null' to the server. The three stations function at the same time, thus in a period of 30-40 secs the server will possess their results. The central server needs very little time to send the messages to the detected devices, if the users accept them immediately. After sending a message, it waits for the user to accept it. When he does so, the server needs a second or two to send it, depending on the distance of the user. If the user does not accept the

message, the server waits for approximately 8 secs and then times out and continues its work.

The aforementioned timings suppose that the stations start simultaneously. If they don't, the application takes longer to finish a loop. Let's assume that the stations start with 20 secs of time difference from one another. The stations will have transmitted the data to the server in 20+20+40=80 secs instead of 40. As we notice, the duration of a loop has doubled.

Discussing the timing of the application, we mention that a period of 50 secs is satisfactory. Users in supermarket take quite some time for their shopping, spending several minutes in their favorite sections of the store, giving our application the time to locate them. But even if a user spends less time in a section, the application, needing only 10 secs to detect him, will locate and send him the informative message, even if he is in a different location at that time.

A user will miss a message if he passes through a section during the period of time starting when the stations finish the scanning and finishing just before the stations start scanning again. This period takes about 30 secs.

Multipath Effects

Bandara, Hasegawa, Inoue, Morikawa & Aoyama (2004), state that in indoor environments, the signal strength is affected by many factors, like multi-path effects, reflection effects, etc. This situation effects mostly positioning and location estimation applications that rely on RSSI for estimating the distance of a mobile user from a stationary point. For such systems, it is risky to rely purely on signal strength, as an indicator of distance that the signal has travelled. Concerning our system, the fact of not using precise positioning methods, like measuring the RSSI for distance estimation, makes multi-path and reflection effects less important. Our approximate positioning results cannot be highly affected by these factors, something proved by our testing results. Of course in a more cluttered with metal objects and crowded environment, like a supermarket, these effects might alter the signal at some point. Even so, the worst case scenario is for a base station not to detect a user, if he is near the boundaries of the stations' coverage area. There, the signal of the user might be too weak for the base station to detect it. In all other cases, this scenario is most unlikely to happen.

CONCLUSION AND FUTURE WORK

In this chapter we presented a Wireless Indoor User Positioning application for use in m-commerce. The purpose of this application is to locate users and inform them. The application uses a positioning method that is based on the triangulation method. The method's simplicity does not affect its efficiency, meaning that we don't use complex high precision positioning methods like measuring the signal strength of the Bluetooth connections, but a simpler method giving the amount of precision needed for m-commerce applications.

The positioning method provides the application with information about users' location, making it possible for the latter to send the appropriate messages to them. The application needs 40 to 50 secs to send the messages, meaning that almost every user will receive the messages on time, provided that they move in normal speed for shopping. The application requires no additional software or hardware from the users' devices.

Such an application could be upgraded in the future using cabled LAN like Ethernet connect-

ing the base stations. The Ethernet can make the stations-server connections quicker as it is faster than Bluetooth. The drawback of Ethernet is the cables, making the application less flexible for use outdoors. This is why we used Bluetooth for all our connections. Also, other wireless LAN technologies can be used for the connections we mentioned, like 802.11b.

By having the server sending the messages, a device being in the edge of the coverage area of the application might not receive them. This happens because the server has a range of only 10m (in fact he can send messages to devices at distances 12-13m. Figure 14). Increasing the range of the server will not solve the problem, since the users' devices will still be of 10m range.

An upgrade, which we have just developed and is under evaluation, is to let the stations and not the server send the messages to the users. The advantages of this scenario are: i) the mobile devices will be able to receive the messages anywhere in the coverage area of the system and ii) the messages will be transmitted in less time than before. This is because each station sends the messages corresponding only to those mobile devices that are positioned in its own coverage area. For the sub-areas that belong to two or more stations, we predefine which station will cover each one of them. In this way the stations send the messages simultaneously, achieving better timing than having the server sending all the messages sequentially.

A drawback of this upgrade is that it increases the number of messages in the system, since the server must forward the data to the stations be-

Figure 14. The server with range 10m can send messages to devices at distances 12-13m

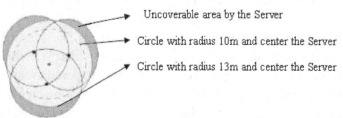

Uncoverable area by the Server

Circle with radius 10m and center the Server

Circle with radius 13m and center the Server

fore the stations send the messages to the mobile devices. This delay is noticeable only if there are few mobile devices in the system's coverage area. In this case, the message forwarding by the server to the stations and the simultaneously transmittance by them to the mobile devises is not really needed, as the server needs little time to send the messages sequentially. The forementioned are currently under validation.

REFERENCES

Aalto, L., Göthlin, N., Korhonen, J., & Ojala, T., (2004). Bluetooth and WAP Push Based Location-Aware Mobile Advertising System. *International Conference On Mobile Systems, Applications And Services,* Proceedings of the 2nd international conference on Mobile systems, applications, and services, Boston, MA, USA, 2004 (pp 49 - 58).

Anastasi, G., Bandelloni, R., Conti, M., Delmastro, F., Gregori, E. & Mainetto, G. (2003). Experimenting an Indoor Bluetooth-Based Positioning Service. *Distributed Computing Systems Workshops, 2003.* Proceedings. 23rd International Conference, May 2003 (pp 480- 483).

Anonymous. (2002). JavaTM APIs for Bluetooth-TM Wireless Technology (JSR-82). Specification Version 1.0a, JavaTM 2 Platform, Micro Edition (2002).

Anonymous. (2003). Specification of the Bluetooth System. Wireless connections made easy, specification Volume 0, Covered Core Package version: 1.2.

Anonymous. (2006a). Avetana OBEX-1.4. Retrieved March 2, 2006, from http://sourceforge. net/ projects/avetanaobex/

Anonymous. (2006b). Blue Cove. Retrieved March 2, 2006, from http://sourceforge.net/ projects/bluecove/

Anonymous. (2006c). The official Bluetooth Web site. Retrieved January 18, 2006, from http://www. bluetooth.com/bluetooth/

Anonymous. (2007). GPS Applications Exchange. *National Aeronautics and Space Administration.* Retrieved January 19, 2008, from http://gpshome. ssc.nasa.gov/

Bahl, P. & Padmanabhan, V. (2000). Radar: An in-building RF_based user location and tracking system. *INFOCOM 2000. Nineteenth Annual Joint Conference of the IEEE Computer and Communications Societies.* Proceedings. IEEE Volume 2, (pp 775-784).

Bandara, U., Hasegawa, M., Inoue, M., Morikawa, H., & Aoyama, T., (2004). Design and Implementation of a Bluetooth Signal Strength Based Location Sensing System. *Mobile Networking Group,* Nat. Inst. of Inf. & Commun. Technol., Yokosuka, Japan; Radio and Wireless Conference, 2004 IEEE 2004 (pp 319- 322).

Burger, K. A., (2007). M-Commerce Hot Spots, Part 2: Scaling Walled Gardens. E-Commerce Times. Retrieved May 9, 2008, from http://www. ecommercetimes.com/story/57161.html

Coursey, D., (2002), "Bluetooth vs. WiFi: Why it's NOT a death match". Retrieved February 10, 2006, from http://reviews-zdnet.com.com/4520-6033_16-4207317.html

Hallberg, J., Nilsson, M. & Synnes, K. (2003). Positioning with Bluetooth. *Telecommunications, 2003. ICT 2003. 10th International Conference. March 2003,* Volume 2, (pp 954- 958).

Hightower, J., Vakili, C., Borriello, C. & Want, R. (2001). Design and Calibration of the SpotON AD-Hoc Location Sensing System. University of Washington, Department of Computer Science and Engineering, Seattle. Retrieved January 19, 2008, from http://www.cs.washington. edu/ homes/jeffro/pubs/hightower2001design/hightower2001design.pdf

Kotanen, A., Hännikäinen, M., Leppäkoski, H. & Hämäläinen T. (2003). Experiments on Local Positioning with Bluetooth. *Information Technology: Coding and Computing [Computers and Communications], 2003. Proceedings. ITCC 2003. International Conference.*

Mahmoud, Q., (2003), Wireless Application Programming with J2ME and Bluetooth. Retrieved February 11, 2006, from http://developers.sun.com/techtopics/mobility/midp/articles/ bluetooth1/

Ni, L. M., Liu, Y., Lau, C. Y. & Patil, A. (2003). LANDMARC: Indoor Location Sensing Using Active RFID. *percom, p. 407, First IEEE International Conference on Pervasive Computing and Communications (PerCom'03).*

Nilsson, M. & Hallberg, J., (2002). Positioning with Bluetooth, IrDA and RFID. Master thesis Lulea University of Technology, Department of Computer Science and Electrical Engineering.

Paciga, M., & Lutfiyya, H., (2005). Herecast: An Open Infrastructure for Location-Based Services Using WiFi. *Wireless And Mobile Computing, Networking And Communications, 2005.* (WiMobapos 2005), IEEE International Conference, Volume 4, Aug. 2005 (pp 21 – 28).

Priyantha, B., N., Chakraborty, A., & Balakrishnan, H., (2000). The Cricket location-support system. *Proc. of the Sixth Annual ACM International Conference on Mobile Computing and Networking* (MOBICOM), August 2000.

Proc, J. (2006a). Decca Navigator System. Retrieved February 4, 2008, from http://www.jproc.ca/ hyperbolic/decca.html

Proc, J. (2006b). LORAN. Retrieved February 4, 2008, from http://www.jproc.ca/hyperbolic/loran_a.html

Proc, J. (2006c). Omega Navigation System. Retrieved February 6, 2008, from http://www.jproc.ca/ hyperbolic/omega.html

Singh, R., Gmdetto, M., Guainazzo, M., Angiati, D., & Ragazzoni, S., C., (2004). A novel positioning system for static location estimation employing WLAN in indoor environment. *Personal, Indoor and Mobile Radio Communications, PIMRC 2004.* 15th IEEE International Symposium Volume 3 (pp 1762 - 1766).

Varshney, U. (2001). Location Management Support for Mobile Commerce Applications. *International Workshop on Mobile Commerce, 2001.* Proceedings of the 1st international workshop on Mobile commerce, New York, NY, USA, ACM, 2001. (pp 1-6).

Wang, Y., Jia, X., & Lee, K., H., (2003). *An indoors wireless positioning system based on wireless local area network infrastructure.* Paper presented at SatNav 2003, The 6th International Symposium on Satellite Navigation Technology Including Mobile Positioning & Location Services Melbourne, Australia 22–25 July 2003.

Xiaojun, D., Junichi, I. & Sho, H., (2004). Unique Features of Mobile Commerce. *Journal of Business Research.*

KEY TERMS

Indoor User Positioning: Methodology used to detect the position of a user indoors.

Bluetooth: A well known Wireless Technology.

M-Commerce: Mobile Commerce.

Triangulation Method: Positioning method.

JABWT: Java API for Bluetooth Wireless Technology (JSR82).

RSSI: Received Signal Strength Indicator.

OPP: Object Push Profile.

Obex: Object Exchange Protocol.

Chapter III
RFID for Identification of Stolen/Lost Items

John Ayoade
American University of Nigeria, Nigeria

Judith Symonds
Auckland University of Technology, New Zealand

ABSTRACT

Standards organisations such as EPC Global work to provide global compatibility between RFID readers and tags (EPCGlobal, 2007). This is essential to ensure that product identification numbers can be accessed along a supply chain by a range of producers, manufacturers and retailers. If all that is stored on the RFID tag is a universal product code, then public access is appropriate. However, where the tag might store more information than just the product identification details, and this data might be private, there is a need to protect such information. The objective of this chapter is to test a security framework designed to authenticate RFID readers before allowing them to access private data stored on RFID tags.

INTRODUCTION

RFID is an area of automatic identification that is gaining momentum and is considered by some to emerge as one of the most pervasive computing technologies in history (Robert, 2006). Today RFID is a generic term for technologies that use radio waves to automatically identify people or objects (RFID Journal). There are several methods of identification, the most common of which is to associate the RFID tag unique identifier with an object or person. A typical RFID system will consist of a tag, a reader, an antenna and a host system (Berthon, 2004). In most commonly touted applications of RFID, the microchip contains Electronic Product Code (EPC) with sufficient capacity to provide unique identifiers for all items produced worldwide. When an RFID reader emits a radio signal, tags in the vicinity respond by transmitting their stored data to the reader (Position, 2003).

The principal advantages of RFID system are the non-contact, non-line-of-sight characteristics of the technology. Tags can be read through a variety of visually and environmentally challenging conditions such as snow, ice, fog, paint, grime, inside containers and vehicles and while in storage (Robert, 2006).

AUTHENTICATION

Authentication is one of the best methods to deter the growing concerns of unauthorized readers from accessing the RFID tag information which could result into the violations of information stored in the tag (Ayoade, 2005). Ayoade et al developed (Ayoade, 2005) a framework that makes it compulsory for the readers to authenticate themselves with the APF (Authentication Processing Framework) database prior to having access to registered tags information.

In this chapter our objective is to develop a system that will demonstrate the RFID Authentication framework in action. The system will be used to identify stolen high cost items recovered by the police. This is an interesting application on which to test the RFID Authentication Framework because, in the hands of the wrong people, the private information stored on the RFID tags could work against the authorities. Our system will read RFID tags attached to expensive items like laptops, PDAs, mobile computer systems, cars, and other expensive equipments and to identify such items by a specific (authentic) reader. For security purposes, the system will make sure that only authentic readers authorized to access specific tags embedded in the items can have access to those tags.

The business benefits expected from this system are:

i. It will be a means of protecting items in various departments in the universities, or industries.
ii. It will enhance police effort in locating and recovering stolen items.
iii. It will help police to determine the rightful owner of the recovered item.

Most times it is very difficult for the police to identify recovered stolen items. However, with the help of this system, once the stolen item is within the range of the RFID reader in the hand of the police officers, it will be possible for the police to identify the item embedded with the RFID tag quickly and accurately. This technology would be a great benefit to police officers as the process of identifying and returning recovered equipment to its owners is a very difficult and painstaking process that uses up precious time and resources. In a nutshell, this research work will be of great benefit to the community which deploys it.

RELATED WORK/LITERATURE REVIEW

Automatic identification technologies like RFID have valuable uses, especially in connection with tracking things for purposes such as inventory management (Wikipedia, n.d.). RFID is particularly useful where it can be embedded within an object, such as a shipping container. RFID tags communicate information by radio wave through antennae on small computer chips attached to objects so that such objects may be identified, located, and tracked. The fundamental architecture of RFID technology involves a tag, a reader, and a database. A reader scans the tag (or multiple tags simultaneously) and transmits the information on the tag(s) to a database, which stores the information (DHS, 2006).

RFID READ RANGE

Table 1 shows the classifications of RFID tags and their read range. The tags are classified according to the frequency range. Table 1 also briefly describes the specific merits and demerits of the tags according to their read range and typical applications. Some information were extracted from (NJE, 2006) about the frequency ranges for RFID in North America, along with their characteristics.

As can be seen from Table 1, RFID tags come in many different shapes and sizes. Passive tags can be very small and easily to conceal. So small

Table 1. RFID tags characteristics

RFID TAGS CHARACTERISTICS					
Frequency	**125kH & 140-148.5kHz** **Low frequency**	**13.56 MHz** **High Frequency**	**433 MHz** **Ultra High Frequency**	**868-928MHz** **Ultra High Frequency**	**2.45 GHz** **Microwave**
Active or Passive Tags	Passive	Passive	Active	Passive/ Active	Active and Passive
License Requirement Issues	Can be used without a license	Can be used without a license	Can not be used globally as there is no single global standard.	Can not be used globally as there is no single global standard with the exception of 902-928MHz in the U.S.A and 918-926MHz as well in Australia and New Zealand but restrictions exist for transmission power.	Can be used without a license
Merit	Liquid does not affect it.	Allows larger data volume and speed rate than LF.	Active RFID stands in a class of its own due to long read-range.	It has the highest read-range for passive tags.	It is highly directional, and it is more accurate.
Demerit	Tags are costly than HF and UHF and it has low anti-collision capability. It has low data speed and capability.	It is affected by metal and other materials.	Tags are expensive.	It is highly affected by metals and liquids and subject to reflection.	It is most affected by metals and liquids.
Tag Sizes	Up to 1-foot disks.	Very thin. Postage stamp to credit-card size and larger.	Approximately 3.5 to 1.2 inches, Credit card sized.	3.5 to 1.2 inch, Credit card sized.	
Read Range	Up to 1 m.	Up to 1.5 m.	3 to 100m and even more	Up to about 4 m.	Up to 1 m.
Common Uses	For animal tracking. industrial process tracking. access control.	Item tracking. document/library, smart cards.	Asset tracking.	Logistics pallet tracking and baggage handling.	For highway toll collection.

in fact that consumer groups are concerned that RFID tags could be embedded into products at the time of manufacture and sold to the consumer without their knowledge (Want, 1999). In effect, the RFID tags can be invisible to the consumer and therefore could be invisible to the criminal (Stanford, 2003). (Want, 1999) report that the flexibility to RFID tags allowed them to attach tags to highly curved shapes and objects that would not normally be able to identified with a barcode. (Juels, 2004) reports that small inexpensive RFID tags exist that permit both reading and writing to the contents of its memory exist and can be used to perform functions.

RESEARCH APPROACH

The authors of the chapter adopt a design science research approach in order to test the authentication framework. In this research we have drawn upon the guidelines presented by Hevner et al. (Hevner, 2004). The authors of the chapter discuss the design and development of a software program that operationalize the authentication framework

(our artifact) and then we evaluate the software using a descriptive technique (Hevner, 2004). The descriptive technique involves constructing detailed scenarios around the artifact to illustrate its utility.

THE FRAMEWORK FOR THE RFID SYSTEM FOR THE RECOVERY OF EXPENSIVE ITEMS

The Objective of the Proposed System

- To enhance protection and recovery of missed or stolen items
- To enhance the performance level of the police in recovering expensive stolen items
- To identify the rightful owner of an object

The system will have three components:

i.   RFID tag writer
ii. RFID tag reader
iii. RFID database

Figure 1. System overview of the RFID recovery system

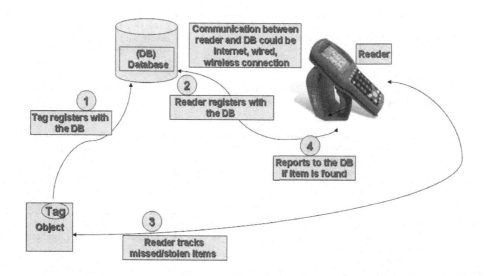

The purpose of the tag writer is for writing useful information about the item into the tag and the purpose of the tag reader is for reading information written about the item into the tag. The purpose of the database is to store information about the item read from the tag and link the information about the tag and the reader with the specific information about the items. The database system also will consider some security applications regarding the content of the information stored in the tag and the database. An administrator of this system will be controlling the tag reader, the tag writer and the database.

In a nutshell, in case the item embedded with a tag in the system is missed or stolen then, it will be possible to locate and recover the stolen item within the range of the RFID reader of this system.

- **Readers and tags:** RFID readers and RFID tags are used to identify recovered objects and the information about the object. As the reader moves around in the range of the tag embedded in the object, the reader detects the presence of the object in that particular environment.

  RFID covers a range of RF frequencies with specific uses based on the frequency and packaging. We have used the RFID tags that operate at 13.56 MHz in the High frequency category. The reason for using this RFID is because is the only one readily available for the development of the prototype system. The 433MHz frequency reader will be more appropriate because of its longer read range. The tag will be embedded in the expensive item and will store both the tags ID and some information about the expensive item for identification purpose.

- **RFID database:** In this research the database is working on two levels. Firstly, because we are not using active technology with this initial research, we are not able to store details about the object on the

tag. Therefore, the database will store the information about the RFID tag, that is, the tags' IDs and the information about the expensive item. Secondly, the database server registers the readers in the system for identification of recovered unidentified objects. The reader communicates with the server through either a wired or wireless connection to confirm the objects found. The reader will be able to have access and locate tags that were registered with this database system if it is within the range of the authentic readers. We now provide an example to illustrate this concept.

Imagine a laptop was embedded with an RFID tag. In the future, the tag might be embedded at the time of manufacture and would be invisible to both the consumer and the would be criminal. The registered authentic RFID reader in this system will be able to identify the laptop, provided the laptop embedded with that tag is in the range of that reader. Now, consider if that laptop is stolen and subsequently recovered by the police. The police will be able to identify the laptop if it is within the range of the authentic reader. One important point in this model is that only authenticated readers will be able to identify the item embedded with the RFID tag. Remember that generally RFID readers should be able to access any tag in the range of the reader. We have developed a prototype system that will authenticate registered reader before allowing access to data on RFID tags in the range of the reader. In essence only authentic readers will be able to access authentic tag (Ayoade, 2006). In this chapter any reader that was not registered with this RFID system that we are proposing will not be able to have access to the tag that was embedded in the expensive item

To achieve this, the system that manages the RFID readers and tags operates a registration system. For the readers, it allows registration of a Reader ID. For the tags, the system can register tag IDs and a key to decode the content written

Figure 2. Tag identification system

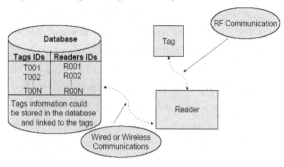

into the tag. In essence, it will be difficult for an unauthorized reader to access the unauthorized tags.

Figure 2 illustrates the database that stores the tags IDs and readers IDs. The purpose for this is to authenticate all the readers and tags in this application system for security purposes. Information about expensive items will ideally be stored in the tags. However, in our initial prototype system, the information is stored in the database and this information is linked to the respective tags within the application system. Also, it should be understood that communication between the readers and database could be wired or wireless. In the deployment of this application system, a wireless communication is preferred since the reader will be used as a portable reader and the database will be stored on a lightweight laptop or a PDA. In a situation where a stolen object is recovered, provided it is embedded with an RFID tag, it is possible to identify the rightful owner of that object immediately and accurately.

THE DEVELOPMENT OF THE PROTOTYPE SYSTEM

The authors were able to develop a prototype system as discussed previously. The U1000 RFID reader that contains 3.7V 600Ah Li-on battery was used. The frequency range of this RFID reader is 13.56MHz. Unfortunately, this RFID reader has some disadvantages compared to the one proposed

for this application. For example, it uses passive tags and its read range is up to 15cm. However, portable RFID readers with active tag read/write capacity were not readily available at the time of development of this research.

However, the author was able to write information into the tag regarding the expensive items and other information and the reader was able to identify the expensive item which in this case was a computer laptop and a PDA. Since, the reader was a handheld reader it was convenient to move it around with ease. Also, the reader could identify and recover the laptop and the PDA that were attached with the registered tags in the recovery application system. The author needs to note that the reader could locate and recover only items within the read range of the reader. In the laboratory, the reader's read range was approximately 10cm. We believe that the proposed (433MHz) reader has a better read range and future work will utilise this technology.

THE PROTOTYPE SYSTEM: SMARTDEVICE

In this section we describe the prototype system (our artefact) to demonstrate its utility. We have called the prototype system 'SmartDevice'. Throughout this discussion, we also provide

Figure 3. The prototype system

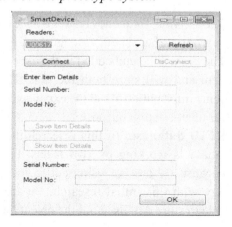

scenarios which describe the security features and we use this to evaluate our design.

Figure 3 shows the prototype application system developed to show how the data stored in the tags embedded in objects could be protected from unauthenticated readers. The data stored in the tag is encrypted in this prototype system. Due to the limited tag memory only the serial number of the object (for example PDA, laptop) is encrypted and this is linked with some other information about object in the database. In case an unauthorized reader wants to read the serial number of the information stored in the tag it will make no meaning to the reader because it will only be able to read encrypted data and it will be meaningless to the unauthenticated reader.

The symmetric encryption was used because of the limited tag memory of the tag. Advanced Encryption Standard (AES) algorithm was used to encrypt the data stored in the tag embedded in the item. AES uses 3 different key lengths 128, 192 or 256bits.

The authors used 256bits key length which provides roughly 10^{77} possible keys which makes the information stored in the tag secured.

Since, AES is a symmetric encryption algorithm, this means that the same key and the same algorithm are used both to encrypt and decrypt a message. One important thing to remember is that the key used for encryption and for decryption in this algorithm has to be kept secret for the message to be secured (Sawicki, 2006).

THERE ARE TWO SECURITY MEASURES DEPLOYED

The two levels/stages of security measures were deployed in order to make sure that the system is highly secured

1. The application ensures that only authentic/registered user (system administrator) or RFID reader is connected to the application and can read the data stored in the tag.
2. The data stored in the tag is encrypted so that in case an unauthorized RFID reader managed to access the system and read the information stored in the tag. The information will be meaningless to the reader.

Figure 4 is the screen shot of the SmartDevice prototype system. The prototype was developed with the security and privacy concerns of the users in mind. Figure 4 demonstrates that before anybody can have access to the prototype system the person must enter the username and password, these measures serve as security deterrence to unauthorized user of the system and it makes the prototype system secured.

Figure 4. Main form

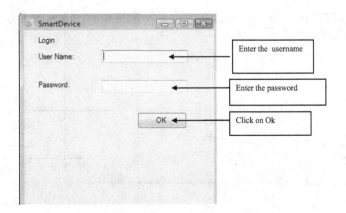

Figure 5. Administrator's log in

Figure 5 demonstrates how the authorized administrator logs in to the SmartDevice prototype system.

Step 1:

Scenario i:

Login to the application.

If user's credentials i.e. password and username are correct then the login will be successful and will allow the user access to the SmartDevice application.

Figure 6 demonstrates that unauthorized user will be denied access to the SmartDevice prototype system.

Figure 6. Administrator's log in failure

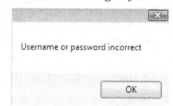

Figure 7. Smart device prototype

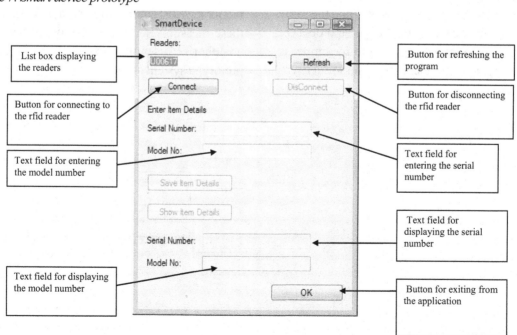

Scenario ii:

Login to the application.

If the user's credentials i.e. password and username are incorrect then the user will be denied access to the SmartDevice application.

There will be a dialog box informing the user that the user credentials entered are incorrect.

Figure 7 shows the steps to be taken before the authentic readers could have access to the SmartDevice prototype system.

Step 2:

Scenario i:

Connect to the RFID Reader.

The application will only allow authenticated readers access as shown in Figure 7. Once the reader is an authentic reader the user or the administrator will be able to use other part of the application such as entering the serial number, model number of the expensive items or objects.

Once the readers are connected either by wired or wireless (Bluetooth) interface the readers identification number will be displayed as shown in Figure 8 and the user or administrator will click connect button. If it is an authentic reader it will be connected and if otherwise it will be disconnected. The prototype system knows the authentic reader from unauthorized because only registered readers in the SmartDevice application database are allowed access to the application.

Figure 8. Reader's log in failure

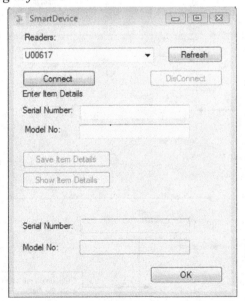

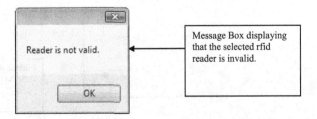

Figure 9. Tag data

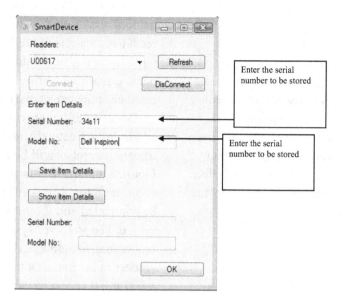

Figure 10. Update the item's data in the database

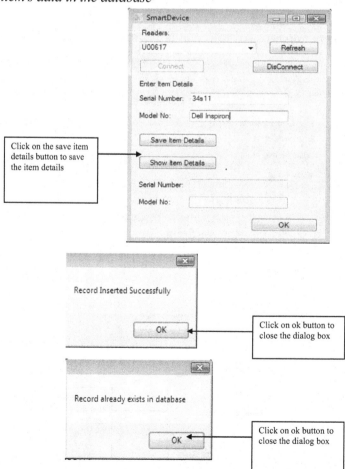

Scenario ii:

Figure 8 shows that the RFID reader is not authentic therefore the application does not allow the reader to connect to the application and the application displays a dialog box informing that the reader is "invalid".

Figure 9 demonstrates that once the authentic reader has been granted access to the SmartDevice application, the user or the administrator of the application can enter the serial number and the model number of the expensive items, and can also check the items that are already in the database.

Step 3:

Entering the Data for Authenticating Reader

The user or the administrator will enter the serial number and the model number of the item and save the item details in the application database.

Figure 10 shows that the tag could be embedded in the item/object and in case this item is lost or stolen it will be easier to identify the rightful owner of the object when the object is found. On the other hand, if the item/object is within the read range of the authenticating reader deployed for this application the object will be easily detected and recovered.

Figure 10 also demonstrates that once item information has been stored in the SmartDevice database it will confirm this by displaying a confirmation box that the item's information is recorded successfully.

Figure 10 also demonstrate that if item information has been stored in the SmartDevice database and the user/administrator is making mistake of overwriting it, the database will detect and confirm that the item information is already existed in the database.

This section shows a situation in which an item/object is recovered the smart device application could easily check from the database whether or not the item/object was registered before. If it was registered with the smart device it will be in the database and if otherwise, the item/object will be returned to the rightful owner. Figure 11 shows the serial number in this case, it is "34s11" and this is encrypted and it would only be decrypted and be made readable to the authenticating reader else it will be almost impossible for any attacker

Figure 11. Item details

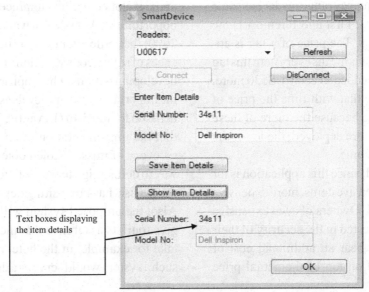

to have access to this information because it is encrypted with 256 bit encryption key length which makes the information very secure. This prototype system demonstrate that expensive objects could be easily identified when recovered in case it was lost and or stolen and also that it will enhance the police performance to determine the rightful owner of the recovered item.

THE LIMITATIONS OF THIS RESEARCH

In this research we used 13.56mhz technology. The main disadvantage of using this technology is that the read range is limited to a maximum of about 10cm. From Table 1, the best option for the implementation of this research work is the reader in the 433MHz frequency range. This reader has a long read range of 3 to 100m or more. The tag for this reader frequency range is active and is not affected by the metal or liquid unlike other tags in different frequency ranges. This characteristic makes it stand out among other readers and tags. Also, this reader has the highest read range which makes it perfect for identification of expensive items in an environment where it is difficult to identify what is legally possessed by an individual and what might be stolen.

The 433MHz frequency range reader has some disadvantages as well. First and foremost is the high price of the tags. The price of a tag is approximately US$20.This means every item this tag is attached to or embedded in costs US$20 more. However, we believe that with time the price of this tag will decrease because the more of these types of applications are deployed, the lower the price of tags will become.

On the other hand, since this application is for the protection of expensive items, more expensive tags may be justified. Owners of such expensive items would be interested in the security of their items and happy to bear an additional cost of for example, US$20 on top of the actual price of the expensive item. The reason being that the deployment of this application that can identify tagged items in the vicinity of the reader should convince the owner of such expensive items is that the items can be identified accurately and quickly once recovered.

In a situation where the expensive item is not within the read range of the RFID reader, it might be difficult to recover such an item. This is the reason why the author of this chapter proposed that the 433MHz RFID reader will be the best RFID reader to use for this kind of application. This application system will be useful to detect and recover expensive items within the read range of the RFID reader used. However, if the expensive item is within the read range of the RFID reader, the rightful owner of this item will be easily identified.

However, for the purposes of evaluating the RFID authentication framework, there is no difference between a 10cm, 3m or 100m read range.

DISCUSSION

Crime Effect on Tourism

It is a fact that the international tourism industry is booming and this has given many developing and developed nations unprecedented economic opportunities. However, it was noted in (Levantis, 2000) that little attention has been given to influences of safety considerations for tourists visiting developing nations. The empirical results confirm the importance of crime levels as a hindrance to the demand for tourism (Levantis, 2000). We believe that the implementation of an RFID system for recovery of missed/stolen objects will go a long way to defuse high tension of security anxiety that the tourists have in visiting developing countries. Also, the proposed system will go a long way to give tourists assurance that their goods are safe, take for example, in the hotel rooms. Moreover, such a system would serve as a deterrent to thieves so that they will not want to steal objects once they know that eventually such objects could be located and which could lead into their apprehension and punishment. In a nutshell, this chapter argues that the system can serve as a deterrent to theft and also it can serve as a way to recover lost objects and be able to determine who the rightful owner of the recovered object is when found.

WHO CONTROLS THE RFID APPLICATION SYSTEM?

The system could be owned by the owner of the expensive items. In this case, the owner could have many expensive items that will be embedded with the tags and just one reader could be reading the tags embedded in the items. In case any of these items is missing or stolen then the owner of the items could use this system as part of the technique to recover the item.

On the other hand, Police could use this technology to enhance their search of lost or stolen expensive items that the RFID tags of the recovery system had been embedded with. Note that alone it will assist the Police to identify the rightful owner of the expensive items. The setback of Police controlling this kind of systems is that the Police could misuse the information stored in the database and that could be linked to the tags embedded in the expensive items. Usually this is not the case but in order to ally the fears that the owners of expensive items have there could be a legal law that will prosecute the Police that invades and violates the privacy of the owners of expensive items.

One possible limitation of this system is that criminals may gain access to and use RFID tag blockers which will effectively disable the embedded RFID tag and remove all data stored on the tag. Blocker tag technology is cheap and easily developed (Juels, 2003). Blocker tags can find and destroy embedded tags even before the user knows they are present and have been devel-

oped to help consumers concerned that retailers might embed tags in products and use the RFID information to gain access private details about the consumer after the purchase is complete and the product is removed from the store. However, since the system will be predominantly used for the identification of lost equipment once it is recovered from the thieves, it is unlikely that the criminals will take the effort to find and remove tags and there may even little motivation to block or kill the tags as whilst the equipment is in the possession of the thieves there is very little danger of identification.

PROSPECTS FOR CRIMINALS TO SCREEN THESE DEVICES

It is almost impossible for a criminal to screen the RFID recovery of items application because the all tags and readers in this application will be authenticated by the database before it can be admitted in the system. In essence, no unauthorized reader can have access to the database and invariably would not be able to have access to the tags in the application. Interested readers could have access to the way in which this is done in (Ayoade, 2005) that is how to have mutual authentication of tags and readers in a particular application.

DATA-ON-TAG

Now, more than ever, since the industry is beginning to experiment with data-on-tag RFID storage (Diekmann, 2007), it is important to be able to vouch for the security of data stored on RFID tags. Our contribution to the research community is to provide a framework for authentication of RFID readers and tags. Once more researches are developed that store data on tags, it will become essential that only authenticated readers can access and read the information stored on the RFID tag.

As RFID tags converge with sensors and other microprocessors and devices, there is a potential for a much wider application for the authentication framework to take on any data stored locally at the source of collection where access to that data is available wirelessly.

CONCLUSION

In this chapter we have designed, built and evaluated a software artefact to demonstrate a security authentication framework for use with RFID. In systems where passive tags are used to store only an EPC which is used to link with data stored in a database, there is little justification for such a system. However, as the industry moves toward applications that utilise active tags (Diekmann, 2007), there is more potential for security breaches of information by unauthorised reading of the data. In our example of a security system of identification of expensive objects for ease of identification on recovery if stolen, the potential for breach of the system is high. We predict that as RFID technology becomes more readily available (RFID readers are planned for mobile phones for example), the need for such an authentication framework will be essential and in a similar way that EPCGlobal is an international framework, the authentication framework will also need to be global. Therefore, future work should concentrate both on exploring other aspects of the authentication framework and making the framework scalable enough to be able to apply it to other similar wireless microcomputer environments.

REFERENCES

Ayoade, J., Takizawa, O.,& Nakao, K. (2005). A Prototype System of the RFID Authentication Processing Framework. Keynote Speaker at IW-WST 2005 3rd International Workshop in Wireless Security Technologies, London, UK.

Ayoade, J. (2006, May). Security implications in the RFID and Authentication Processing Framework. *Journal of Computers and Security.*

Berthon, A. (2000, July). Security in RFID. Retrieved from http://www.nepc.sanc.org.sg/html/techReport/NN327.doc.

DHS (2006). The use of RFID for Human Identification: A draft Report from DHS Emerging Applications and Technology Subcommittee to the Full Data Privacy and Integrity Advisory Committee, version 1.0

Diekmann, T., Melski, A. Schumann, M. (2007). Data-on-Network vs. Data-on-Tag: Mananging Data in Complex RFID Environments. *Proceedings of the 40th Hawaii International Conference on System Sciences.* IEEE

EPCGlobal (2007). *EPC Standards Overview.* Retrieved November 23, 2007, from http://www.epcglobalinc.org/standards.

Hevner, A.R., Salvatore, T.M. Park, J. & Ram, S. (2004). Design Science in Information Systems Research. *MIS Quarterly 28*(1), 75-105.

Juels A., Rivest R.L. & Szydlo M. (2003). *The Blocker Tag: Selective Blocking of RFID Tags for Consumer Privacy.* CCS'03, Washington, DC, USA, October 27-31]

Juels A. (2004) *Minimalist Cryptograhy for Low-Cost RFID tags.* The Fourth International Conference on Security, Colombia.rsa.com

Levantis, T. & Gani, A. *Tourism Demand and the Nuisance of Crime.* Retrieved from http://www.emeraldinsight.com/Insight/ViewContentServlet?Filename=/published/emeraldfulltextarticle/pdf/0060270718.pdf#search=%22crime%20deterrent%20in%20the%20south%20pacific%20region%22

NJE Consulting (2006). *RFID Technical Information.* Retrieved from http://www.nje.ca/Index_RFIDTechnical.htm

"Position Statement on the use of RFID on consumer products" (2003, November). Retrieved from http://www.spychips.org/jointrfid_position_paper.html

RFID Journal (n.d.). *RFID Journal frequency asked questions.* Retrieved from http://www.rfidjournal.com

Roberts, C. (2006). Radio Frequency Identification (RFID). *Journal of Computers and Security.*

Sawicki, E. & Wells, N. (2006). *Advanced Guide to Linux Networking and Security.*

Stanford, V. (2003). Pervasive Computing Goes the Last Hundred Feet with RFID Systems. *Pervasive Computing, 2*(2), 9-14.

Want, R.., Fishkin, K.P., Gujar, A. & Harrison, B.L. (1999). *Bridging Physical and Virtual Worlds with Electronic Tags.* CHI 99 Pittsburgh P.A., USA, 15-20 May

Wikipedia (n.d.). Retrieved from http://en.wikipedia.org/wiki/Automated_identification_and_data_capture

KEY TERMS

AES: Is block cipher adopted as an encryption standard by the U.S. government.

APF: Stands for Authentication Processing Framework. A protocol developed to circumvent unauthorized reader from accessing the information stored in the tag.

Authentication: Is the act of establishing or confirming something as authentic, that is, that claims made by or about the thing are true.

Encryption: Is the process of transforming information using an algorithm to make it unreadable to anyone except those processing special knowledge, usually referred to as a key.

RFID: Is an automatic identification method, relying on storing and remotely retrieving data using devices called RFID tags or transponders.

RFID Tag: Is an object that can be applied to or incorporated into a product, animal, or person for the purpose of identification using radio waves. Some tags can be read from several meters away and beyond the line of sight of the reader.

RFID Reader: Is a device that is used to interrogate an RFID tag. The reader has an antenna that emits radio waves, the tag responds by sending back its data.

Chapter IV
RFID Technology for Agri–Food Traceability Management

Filippo Gandino
Politecnico di Torino, Italy

Erwing Ricardo Sanchez
Politecnico di Torino, Italy

Bartolomeo Montrucchio
Politecnico di Torino, Italy

Maurizio Rebaudengo
Politecnico di Torino, Italy

ABSTRACT

This chapter deals with the use of RFID technology for improving management and security of agri-food products. In order to protect health and to make transparent the production flow of alimentary commodities, traceability is becoming mandatory for food products in an increasing number of countries. Everywhere, innovative solutions are investigated by agri-food companies in order to improve their traceability management systems. The RFID technology seems to be able to solve in a very efficient way the requirements for traceability systems, however some technological problems, such as the lack of consolidated systems, and the costs are the main obstacles to the wide adoption of RFID-based traceability systems. In this chapter the peculiarities of agri-food traceability and the most relevant results reached by the state-of-the-art research studies are detailed.

INTRODUCTION

Traceability is considered today a crucial factor for the agri-food sector. An effective traceability system brings many benefits, such as increasing the security of customers, and so their confidence, and controlling the effects of commodity withdrawal. Furthermore, in many countries traceability is a mandatory requirement for the agri-food sector. In EU, The European Parliament And The Council (2002) establishes that "1. The traceability of food, feed, ... shall be established at all stages of production, processing and distribution. 2. Food and feed business operators shall be able to identify any person from whom they have been supplied with a food, ... To this end, such operators shall have in place systems and procedures which allow for this information to be made available to the competent authorities on demand. 3. Food and feed business operators shall have in place systems and procedures to identify the other businesses to which their products have been supplied. This information shall be made available to the competent authorities on demand. 4. Food or feed which is placed on the market or is likely to be placed on the market in the Community shall be adequately labeled or identified to facilitate its traceability, through relevant documentation or information in accordance with the relevant requirements of more specific provisions."

The Traceability in the agri-food sector is often managed by systems that employ labels or barcodes for the commodity identification. However, the new requirements of accuracy and efficiency have promoted the research of more efficient and effective solutions for traceability management. One of the most promising alternatives to traditional solutions is represented by the Radio Frequency Identification (RFID) technology. RFID systems, constituted by passive low cost transponders, are currently being used in a variety of applications and environments as detailed in this book. Many research projects have been developed to evaluate if RFID technology can be properly exploited for agri-food traceability activities.

The ISO 9001:2000 (ISO, 2000) standard defines traceability as the "ability to trace the history, application or location of that which is under consideration". The activities involved by Traceability Management (TM) are also strongly linked to Supply Chain Management (SCM).

For The Council of Supply Chain Management Professionals "SCM encompasses the planning and management of all activities involved in sourcing and procurement, conversion, and all Logistics Management activities. Importantly, it also includes coordination and collaboration with channel partners, which can be suppliers, intermediaries, third-party service providers, and customers. In essence, SCM integrates supply and demand management within and across companies" (Gibson, Mentzer, & Cook, 2005). On the one hand, TM aims at detecting and recording the path and the history of items; on the other hand, SCM aims at improving the production chain, so SCM can manage the traceability of products, but it is only an optional intermediate step to reach business improvements. Furthermore there are issues that characterize agri-food sector, and that affect both TM and SCM: (a) the management of perishable products requires special solutions like controlled storages in refrigerating rooms; (b) The Out-of-Shelves problem (Corsten & Gruen, 2004) is a threat for all kinds of brands and in particular for perishable products (Kranendonk & Rackebrandt, 2002), producing direct losses to retailers and manufacturers, such as lost sale, brand switch, and store switch. Therefore many research projects provide data about SCM and Automatic Identification and Data Capture (AIDC) that concern activities comprised by TM.

New traceability systems based on RFID technology are starting to be effectively employed, but small and medium companies, which represent a large part of the agri-food enterprises, are wayward to invest in technologies that are not conventional. Hence, it is evident the importance of studies that present the knowledge about features and properties of the RFID technology application. The aim of this chapter is to provide readers with a complete overview of studies about agri-food traceability characteristics and about how RFID technology can be applied to traceability activities. Conceptual and simulation papers and field studies, concerning topics related to RFID-based traceability, will be discussed and analysed. The results obtained by state-of-the-art research projects will be compared in order to identify benefits and drawbacks of the exploitation of RFID technology for agri-food traceability.

The remaining of the chapter is organized as follows. The second section will introduce the properties of RFID technology, and its peculiarities in the applications for traceability management. Details about traceability management in agri-food sector will be provided to the reader. The features of traceability and its relations with SCM will be detailed, then the characteristics of traceability systems employed in agri-food sector will be shown. The third section will present to the reader a state-of-the-art overview for RFID traceability applications. Results from studies about different topics, which pertain to RFID applications and which can bring important information about RFID benefits and drawbacks for traceability applications, will be shown. The fourth section will present a set of benefits and drawbacks for the employment of RFID technology for traceability management in agri-food sector. Finally, the fifth section will present reached targets and open issues for the near future.

RFID FOR TRACEABILITY

As described in this book, RFID technology is used for different kinds of applications. This section aims at providing the reader with the background necessary to analyse RFID-based agri-food traceability systems. In the following the characteristics of RFID technology that specifically affect its application to agri-food traceability management are described, a short background about agri-food sector is presented, and the characteristics of agri-food traceability systems are detailed.

RFID Architecture

RFID architectures are improving constantly and technology global standardisation is arriving to a stable point. As reported in a previous chapter, specific RFID standards, e.g., the EPCGlobal (2005) Class 1 Generation 2 UHF standard, have been created to address traceability management concerns. Due to the particular requirements, RFID standards addressing traceability management share common characteristics that shape an RFID architecture. New opportunities come from the Near-Field Communication (NFC) standard, which provides devices that can communicate with peer devices and with RFID tags compatible with LF standards (Want, 2006). NFC could widen the spread of RFID by allowing people to interact with RFID tags and many wireless devices by using their NFC mobile phone (Ortiz, 2006). Good opportunities for NFC application to agri-food sector come from near-field UHF RFID systems (Nikitin, Rao, & Lazar, 2007), which can operate also in close proximity to metals and liquid.

In general, RFID tags used for traceability management are passive ones, so they have no battery and acquire their power from the external RF communication; this characteristic allows reducing tag costs as much as possible in order to make it almost disposable. Another common architectural choice in RFIDs is related to its memory; it should be large enough to hold the tag identification number. A typical EPC identification number has 96 bits, however a tag may have up to several kilobits of capacity. Indeed, some applications may require a large user memory in order to record relevant information about the good, or to add redundancy to the system by backing up database information included into the tag.

Agri-Food Sector

The typical production chain in the agri-food sector is composed by the following entities:

Figure 1. The agri-food chain

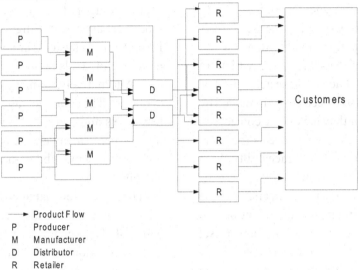

```
→   Product Flow
P   Producer
M   Manufacturer
D   Distributor
R   Retailer
```

1. **Producer:** An entity that produces the agri-food raw materials, and sells them to a manufacturing enterprise, e.g., a farm that cultivates grain or a cattleman that breeds beefs.

2. **Manufacturer:** An enterprise that treats and transforms the agri-food raw materials; the most elaborated products require the use of several agri-food raw products and a complex manufacturing, e.g., a company that produces biscuits needs many ingredients, such as sugar, flour, and butter, from different suppliers, and adopts many processes from cooking and leavening to packaging; also the products that are sold to customer apparently without manufacturing need several treatments, e.g., fruits need to be cleaned, divided by caliber, stored in refrigerating rooms, and packed.

3. **Distributor:** An enterprise that moves alimentary commodities; some large enterprises have their own distribution centers; mainly distributors get commodities from manufacturing enterprises and they give the commodities to retailers; normally, in a distribution center commodities are not treated, but they are only stored under determined conditions and then shipped to their destination.

4. **Retailer:** An enterprise that sells alimentary commodities directly to customers; this category includes many kinds of enterprises, from little alimentary shops to large hypermarkets, that sell all kind of commodities.

Figure 1 shows the agri-food production chain and the interactions among its members.

Traceability Management

Today, the businesses in the agri-food sector have to manage carefully the traceability of their commodities, in order to satisfy the expectations of customers and the law requirements. However, some years ago the demand of security and transparency was limited, and several companies in the agri-food sector have not still completely adjusted their processes. The gap between requirements and actual situation has motivated the research of innovative solutions for TM. In the meat sector DNA-based traceability can be used to check presence of genetic modification, and to overcome security problems of label-based systems (Loftus, 2005). However, the management of traceability inside the production flow requires the use of labels for an immediate identification of products.

TM can be divided in four activities, which are described in Table 1. Each of these activities has its peculiarities, and so it needs to be managed by a specific system, but they have to be considered all together, since each activity affects the other ones. In Figure 2, an example of traceability chain in the agri-food sector is shown.

Internal Traceability. The ITr in an agri-food enterprise may require: (a) the identification and the registration of food entering in the enterprise; (b) the registration of the food that is produced; (c) the tracking of the food movements; (d) the registration of the treatments that are executed on the food; (e) the registration of the interactions among alimentary commodities; and (f) the registration of the exit from the enterprise of the food.

The kind and the number of information about every operation, treatment and alimentary commodity, change according to the accuracy of the ITr system. ITr systems are typically based on the matching of labels to objects that must be identified. Alternatively, some systems tag containers of objects. The container tagging method requires less labels and work, but it is less accurate than the former. However, with both methods the obtained data must be gathered and recorded in a database.

The ITr is often managed by systems based on *paper labels* or *barcodes*. Systems that employ paper labels are characterized by low automation and low costs for the infrastructures involved. Normally, these systems are slow, so they can treat only a limited number of information. Systems based on barcodes are characterized by more automation than paper label-based systems, but the number of information stored on a bar code is still limited. However some barcode-based systems employ

Figure 2. The traceability chain

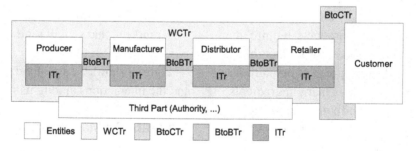

Table 1. The traceability activities

Activity	Description
Internal Traceability (ITr)	correct matching of input and output food information inside a company; the internal traceability system has to follow the path of a specific unit within the company
Business to Business Traceability (BtoBTr)	management of the information exchange from a business to the next one, throughout the production chain
Business to Customer Traceability (BtoCTr)	management of the transfer of information from the retailer to the final customer
Whole Chain Traceability (WCTr)	management of the information on the whole path of a commodity, from the producer to the final customer

the barcode like a link to a record in a central database, where all the information are stored. In a ITr system based on RFID technology, the tags can be used to replace paper labels and barcodes. Every tag could be matched to a commodity, or to a bin of commodities; the tag could directly hold the information about the commodities, or it could simply store a code that is used as a record in a database. The tag could be detected by portal readers, when it is moved through a portal or with hand-held RFID readers.

Business to Business Traceability. The main scope of BtoBTr is to preserve the information about the path of an alimentary commodity between two enterprises. The BtoBTr for agri-food enterprises may require: (a) the registration of the food exit from the enterprise of provenance; (b) the tracking of the food movements; and (c) the registration of the food entrance in the destination enterprise.

The data collected for the BtoBTr should be stored by both the enterprises, or in a common database. Typically, the BtoBTr systems identifying the single alimentary commodities, match a barcode to the commodity. The number of recorded information and precision of the identification, from item level to pallet level, change according to the accuracy of the BtoBTr system.

RFID could be used for BtoBTr by matching an RFID tag to all the commodities that are moved between the two businesses. The tag could hold the information about the commodity, or the identification code of the tag could be used to store a record in a common database, so a portal reader could identify the incoming commodity.

Business to Customer Traceability. The BtoCTr is the connection between the traceability systems and the customer, transferring the obtained information to the customer.

Normally, the BtoCTr is based on labels and texts written on the package of alimentary commodities, but this method allows the transfer of limited information.

Currently the employment of RFID tags is applicable only for expensive commodities. The tag could hold the information about the commodity, or the identification of the tag could be used to access, eventually through Internet, to information stored in a database. In order to access to data in the tag memory, customers could use RFID readers available in the shops.

Whole Chain Traceability. WCTr provides the information on the whole path of the commodity; it should link all the stored data. The WCTr can be used by businesses in the chain, in order to manage also the BtoBTr, furthermore it can be used by a third part, like the food security competent authority, in order to check the path of commodities for food disease prevention.

Typically, the WCTr is managed by searching the information in the database of the single companies of the production chain, step by step, looking in each database for the enterprises that had supplied the alimentary commodity. Alternatively, all the information are stored by the operators of the production chain in a common database, in order to allow a fast access to the required data.

The RFID technology could be used for WCTr in different ways. These information could be recorded on the tag memory, or the identification of the tag could allow the access to the information stored in a distributed database composed by the databases of all the operators of the production chain. This is a very important activity for agri-food traceability, because its aim is to make accessible all the useful information about food immediately, and the fast availability of traceability information can be crucial in case of food security emergency.

STATE-OF-THE-ART ANALYSIS

In this section an overview of the state-of-the-art research studies on RFID for agri-food traceability is presented. In addition, some remarkable research projects about RFID, supply chain, and food traceability are reported in order to provide a deep comprehension of the treated topics. All the studies are analysed and compared with the model described in the second section.

This section is divided in the following parts: theoretical model, where some critical features useful for the design of a model of traceability systems are described; business impact analysis, where the influence of RFID adoption on business processes is evaluated; system proposals, where characteristics and performances of RFID-based traceability systems are described; simulation analysis, where the effects of a real RFID application are simulated; and field studies, where the experimental results on the field are reported.

Theoretical Model

Traceability in the US Food Supply: Dead End or Superhighway (Golan et al., 2003). This paper, which is focused on traceability systems in US food supply and on the comparison of mandatory and voluntary systems, presents some interesting elements of food traceability systems that can be useful to be considered when analysing an RFID traceability system.

The identified motivations of food suppliers to adopt traceability systems are: (a) to improve supply-side management; (b) to differentiate and introduce added value on food with subtle or undetectable quality attributes; and (c) to facilitate traceback for food safety and quality.

The identified characteristics are: (a) breadth, the quantity of recorded information; the number of data about food is huge, so enterprises have to select the ones with the highest value; (b) depth, the number of recorded members, back and forward in the traceability chain; many enterprises record only direct suppliers and customers; and (c) precision, the degree of tracking assurance, that is composed by the acceptable error rate, which is the number of faulty elements, and the unit

of analysis, which is the dimension of tracking groups of elements.

Business Impact Analysis

The studies presented in this section are focused on the processes executed in the supply chain to manage the traceability. The adopted research methodology is based on interviews and field analysis. The main result of these studies is the identification of changes in the processes due to RFID adoption.

White Paper. Auto-ID Use Case: Food Manufacturing Company Distribution (Prince, Morán, & McFarlane, 2004). This use case is focused on a generic auto-ID implementation in the food manufacturing company distribution, and especially on the operation of placing the products onto trailers for transportation. The use case does not analyse the technological characteristics, but only the impact of the auto-ID on a business.

The use case describes the Auto-ID procedures and the gained benefits, it analyses the present situation, and it searches business benefits in order to justify the proposed solution.

The barcode is identified as the only current technology available for identification but it is considered slow and expensive. Instead RFID technology can solve some typical problems, e.g., portal readers can avoid incoherence due to possible errors in the list of shipped pallets. A benefit of the auto-ID is the reduction of human labor applied to repetitive tasks. A problem for the implementation of an auto-ID system is the resistance by the workforce to change the work processes. Pre-requirements to be guaranteed are

Figure 3. Use case traceability activities

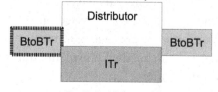

the 100% of scanning accuracy and the scanning rate, since the system have to scan pallets with different rates, and maybe also simultaneously passing. Different possible implementations with different costs were identified; the low cost implementation involves fixed portal readers, pallet level tagging and a basic integration with the information system (IS); instead the medium cost implementation involves also mobile readers and more integration with the IS; the high cost implementation involves also case level tagging, a higher number of readers, and a tight integration with the IS.

Authors conclude that basic implementations require only few changes to the IS and the introduction of auto-ID infrastructure, and that this kind of implementation brings benefits for organizations. High cost implementations can bring all described benefits of auto-ID, and they could be adopted by passing through basic implementations.

Figure 3 shows the traceability activities managed in the use case. The main activity managed by the system is the ITr of the distributor, which is leaded at different levels according to the implemented version of the system. The BtoBTr is managed by using the tags, but the system considers the option in which suppliers had not tagged the pallets, and so they are tagged at their entrance in the distributor building.

RFID as an Enabler of B-to-B e-Commerce and its Impact on Business Processes: A Pilot Study on a Supply Chain in the Retail Industry (Lefebvre et al., 2006). This paper presents empirical data collected by analysing four firms that are part of three layers of the same supply chain. The analysis is focused on the potential of RFID in a supply chain in the retail industry, and especially on open-loop supply chain applications, which involve multiple members of the chain together. The main research site is a distribution center; the other analysed firms are the two first-tier suppliers of the distribution center and one retailer. The paper does not treat directly agri-food traceability,

Figure 4. Case use traceability activities

but it explores general aspects of BtoBTr that are valid also for the agri-food sector.

The research was devised in different steps, grouped in three macro phases: Opportunity Seeking; Scenario Building; and Scenario Validation. The data collection was based on: (a) a focus group with 9 functional managers and IT experts; (b) on-site observations; and (c) semi-structured interviews conducted in the four research sites. The identified motivations for RFID adoption are: to reach an agile supply chain, the reduction of cost for traceability activities, the reduction of incoherences between the inventory and the reality, and the reduction of lead times. The author identified the list of processes executed in the distribution center. The four firms employ barcode-based systems, however the distributor employs some automatic information management systems.

The scenario obtained integrating RFID was validated with the focus group. The results are that: (a) the RFID technology facilitates the emergence of a model named cross-docking, where products move through the distribution center without being stored, or with short stop, since the automation in traceability activities makes less relevant the putting-away and the picking; this model allows faster delivery of commodities, which is very relevant for short life products, which are a large part of agri-food products; (b) many processes become automatic or disappear; (c) the time consuming is reduced, the quantity and the integrity of information are larger; (d) RFID-based system can bring additional value, and it includes intelligent processes managed by automatic decisions; (e) the integration among supply chain members is increased, and each member can continuously get updated information about products in the chain.

Authors conclude that the application of RFID in supply chain requires: (a) radical changes of the business processes, with significant reduction of human work for traceability; (b) systems that can manage a large quantity of data; (c) the authorization to share, between chain members, information that were previously considered proprietary. The changing to the cross-docking model is considered the major changing. A problem for RFID large adoption is considered the lack of standards.

Figure 4 shows the traceability activities analysed in the use case. The paper is focused on the impact on business processes in BtoBTr, which is managed by using the RFID tags.

System Proposals

In this section different kinds of studies are reported. All of them are characterized by the presentation of a traceability system and by its evaluation.

Agri-food traceability management using a RFID system with privacy protection (Bernardi, et al., 2007). In this paper an agri-food traceability system is presented. The aim of the system is to provide the traceability information to authorities. In order to avoid privacy problems, two privacy protection algorithms based on public key cryptography are proposed.

In order to trace back an alimentary commodity the authority in charge of controlling the agri-food safety has to inspect the company database, step by step along the traceability chain. In the proposed system every alimentary commodity is labeled by an RFID tag, so authorities can read all the traceability information directly from the tag memory. The tag memory is divided in logic areas, and each operator of the production chain has to record, in a specific area, its data and the data about the treatments executed on the food. All the data are stored in the RFID tags, and in a company database.

Authors present two cryptographic algorithms, which allow only competent authorities to read the data, in order to avoid privacy problems. One method reaches a higher security, the other one proofs the authenticity of the information. Experimental results show that the encryption algorithm is the part of the tool that requires the longest time.

Authors conclude that the time required by the algorithms allows the use of PDA only with short keys. The presented system protects only from some privacy threats, e.g., the monitoring of personal belongings, but it can be used with other privacy protection methods.

Figure 5 shows the traceability activities managed in the described paper. The system manages only the WCTr in order to provide information to authority. The WCTr is managed by using the tags, and the recorded information are fully detailed. The tagging level is the single commodity.

Analysis of an RFID-based Information System for Tracking and Tracing in an Agri-Food Chain (Gandino, Montrucchio, Rebaudengo, & Sanchez, 2007). The paper is focused on ITr. Authors present and evaluate a traceability system that was designed and tested in a fruit warehouse.

Figure 5. Traceability management system activities

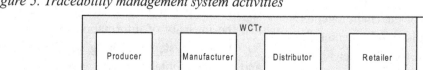

The fruit warehouse is a manufacturing company that treats the fruit. The fruit comes in the warehouse from different farmers. The main operations that can be executed on the fruit are: (a) storing in refrigerating room; (b) calibration; and (c) fruit packing.

In the presented system every fruit bin is tagged with an RFID tag; every tag is theoretically matched to a bin for their whole life. The data about fruit and treatments are recorded both directly on tag memories and in a central database. The operators working in the warehouse use PDA RFID readers to read and write the tag. The data recorded on the tag are also stored in the PDA memory and periodically copied in the central database.

The targets of the system are mainly: to facilitate the global traceability, to join traceability management to other activities, to reach a structure easy to upgrade, and to satisfy the fruit warehouse needs gathered from on-site observations and interviews with fruit operators. The main identified needs are an easy integration with an actual production process, the low costs, the reliability, a granularity precision, the time saving, the usability and the brand prestige. The system was tested in a laboratory and in a working fruit warehouse. Data presented on the paper show that all the operations, except the initialization of the system, requires at most 1 second.

Authors conclude that the time performances of the presented RFID-based traceability system are suitable for fruit warehouse, so also low

Figure 6. Fruit traceability system activities

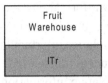

cost RFID-based systems can be adopted in the agri-food sector, but they should be considered an intermediate step toward a fully automatic RFID system.

Figure 6 shows the traceability activities managed by the system presented in the paper. The paper treats only the ITr, which is managed by using the tags in parallel to a central database; the paper provides the details about both stored information and technological characteristics of the system. The focus of the paper is the evaluation of an actual implementation of the system.

Radio Frequency Identification in Food Supervision (Zhen-hua, Jin-tao, & Bo, 2007). This paper presents a food security supervision system that manages the food chain traceability. The paper is focused on the producer and the retailer, since these members of the chain are considered the most critical for food security threats.

The supervision system is based on a Food and Drug Administrator (FDA), which supervises the chain, and which includes a food security database. UHF RFID-based systems of the members of the food chain interact with RFID tags; an RFID middleware elaborates the data and communicates with the FDA. The system architecture is based

Figure 7. Food supervisor traceability activities

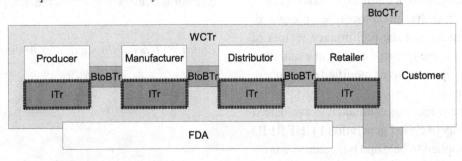

on the following steps: (a) the producer stores on the tag memory information concerning the food and the producer himself; (b) FDA checks the food and writes the relative information on the tag; (c) when the product is transported to a member of the chain the relative information are sent to the FDA; (d) each member of the chain records its own information; (e) the customer can check the food in the public database of the FDA; (f) when problems occur the FDA sends a warning to all members of the chain.

Authors found several issues that obstruct adoption of the RFID-based traceability systems: (a) the recognition rate of liquid food is very low; (b) the cost of tags is too high; (c) the read rate must reach 100%; (d) the enterprises want to adopt technology characterized by clear and sure standards. Therefore the authors indicate that the development of an RFID simulator can allow to reach wider range of data about RFID systems.

Figure 7 shows the traceability activities managed by the presented system. The main activity managed by the system is the WCTr, which is managed by communicating the information about the food and its movements to the FDA. The system manages also the BtoCTr, by using the information recorded in the tag memory and the Internet access to the database of the FDA. The BtoBTr is managed by writing the information about the commodities directly in the tag memories and by querying the database of the FDA. It is assured that the ITr is managed by the RFID-based traceability system.

Electronic Tracking and Tracing in Food and Feed Traceability (Ayalew et al., 2006). In this paper printed graphic identifiers, RFIDs and electronic data interchange protocols are presented. The description and the preliminary results of an experiment are reported aiming at evaluating UHF RFID application of modified atmosphere packaged meat.

The experiment was conducted to evaluate if the readability of class 1 generation 1 UHF RFID system as applied to beef and pork samples is af-

fected by material properties inside and around the meat. The results of the experiment are that the linearly polarized type antennas yielded better reading rates over larger distances, but no significant differences between linearly and circularly polarized antennas are detected up to a distance of 0.5 m. Preliminary results show a better readability over longer distances with the presence of bone in meat samples; authors suggest that the bone causes less loss than meat. The paper presents some graphical examples of the preliminary results of the described test. The graphics show clearly that the system works effectively only with short distances, up to 0.7 m, or with high power, next to 2 W.

Authors conclude that the adoption of RFID system for beef and pork items requires to improve performance in detection. The problems to operate in a wide high-attenuation environment and the high cost of the technology are considered an open issue for the large adoption of RFID.

Simulation Analysis

Exploring the impact of RFID on supply chain dynamics (Lee, Cheng, & Leung, 2004). In this paper a quantitative analysis of impact of RFID technology on supply chain performance is presented. The analysis is based on a simulation model developed by the authors in order to quantify the indirect benefits of RFID. The model considers: (a) the inventory accuracy, that is affected by problems like stock loss, transaction error, and incorrect product identification; (b) the shelf replenishment policy, that thanks to RFID technology can be based on a real time inventory;

Figure 8. Traceability activities in the simulation

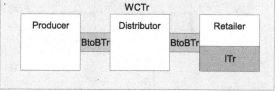

and (c) the visibility of the inventory throughout the entire supply chain.

The model consists of a three layer supply chain that is composed by a manufacturer, a distribution center and a retail store. The RFID readers are placed at the receiving and shipping points, at the end of the production line, and in the backroom and at the shelves of the retail store. Tags are applied at the item level. The model is characterized by some parameters, and the most important ones are the reorder point, which is the number of products that requires a replacement, and the target inventory, which is the number of products to reach by the replacement; these parameters are used for the replacement of both shelves and backroom. The physical inventory is performed every 3 months. The simulations use metrics such as lost sales, surpluses and costs.

Some simulations with different parameters are analysed in order to find the impact of RFID application. The simulations show some benefits due to RFID application: (a) a reduction of 99% for the back order quantity, in cases with the same parameters; (b) it is possible to reach a smaller inventory with a lower reduction; (c) there is a reduction of 99% of the lost sales also with restricting parameters; (d) the reached reduction of lost sales is of 84% with a lower backroom inventory target; (e) both assuming that by means of RFID the manufacturer knows the inventory of the distribution center, and assuming that it knows also the inventory of the retailer, the back orders of the distribution center are deleted and the average quantity of products in the inventory is lower.

Authors conclude that RFID technology can provide benefits to supply chain, but analysed scenarios are too simple and not completely realistic, so the results can not be directly used.

Figure 8 shows the traceability activities managed in the model. The main activities managed by the system is the BtoBTr, which is managed by writing the information about the commodities directly in the tag memories, and the WCTr. The producer and the distributor seemingly use the RFID traceability system only for BtoBTr and WCTr, instead, the retailer uses the system also for the ITr, indeed inside the shop the RFID system is used to detect the movement through and from the backroom and to detect the commodities in the shelves. The tagging level is the single commodity. The technological and practical aspects of the traceability system are not considered in deep by the model, which is focused on the business impact of AIDC, possibly RFID-based, so implementation problems and error rate are not evaluated.

Field Studies

Increasing efficiency in the supply chain for short shelf life goods using RFID tagging (Karkkainen, 2003). Karkkainen, in order to discuss the application of RFID technology in the supply chain of short shelf life products, analyses a trial conducted at Sainsbury's, which is a chain of supermarkets in the UK that sells a large volume of different short shelf-life goods. The author discusses the impact of RFID for retailers and also for other supply chain participants.

Shelf life is the period when the defined quality of the goods remains acceptable. Short shelf-life goods are a large part of agri-food commodities, they are characterized by a high number of product

Figure 9. The Sainsbury's trial traceability activities

variants, need of temperature control and all the traceability requirements of agri-food commodities. Therefore short shelf-life food needs a strictly rotation monitoring.

At Sainsbury's short shelf-life commodities are packed on recyclable plastic transportation crates that are tagged by barcodes. The path of the crates starts from a producer, then they are moved to a distribution depot and finally to a store. The focus of the trial is the retail store, since it was considered the operator with the major difficulties due to the effort required for barcode-based traceability management.

The trial, which started with one ready-meal supplier, one depot and one store, was designed as follows. RFID tags are applied to recyclable plastic crates; the information stored in the tag memories are: (a) the description and quantity of products in the crate, (b) the use-by date of products, and (c) the ID number that identifies the crate. An RFID reader, which writes on the tag the information related to the products in the crate, is located at the end of the production line. A gate reader at the depot detects the incoming of the products. At the store, another gate reader, between the chilled storage and the store areas, detects the incoming into the chilled storage of the products from the depot and the moving out through the store areas. After the first phase, the trial was scaled up. During the second trial phase, all the products for the store that come from any supplier are tagged, but the information about the product from the suppliers out the trial are written by a gate reader that is located at the depot. The scaled-up phase took three months.

The labor standards, which are work study timings for key activities in store processes, are used by Sainsbury's to calculate the benefits of different store activities. Recalculating the standards for the RFID trial, the total benefits for Sainsbury's, without the supplier participation, were estimated to be £8.5 million a year; the largest origins of the savings are the stock loss reduction, stock check saving, and replenish-

ment productivity improvement. The requested investment to adopt the system was calculated to be between £18 million and £24 million. The payback period was estimated to be between two and three years. With the participation of suppliers the benefits are estimated to be notably larger, despite the higher investment costs.

The analysis of the trial focused on retailers concludes that a traceability system based on RFID applied to recyclable transports offers possibilities with a large return of investment. The system is evaluated useful also for suppliers, mainly for the reduction of out-of-stock rate, since short life products are highly subject to brand switching for stock-outs and the difficulties in their management bring to a high stock-out rate. During the trial it was evaluated that the used RFID tag memories can store additional information to get added value.

Figure 9 shows the traceability activities managed in the presented system. The main activity managed by the system is the BtoBTr, that is managed by writing the information about the commodities directly in the tag memories. The producer and the distributor seemingly use the RFID traceability system only for the BtoBTr, instead the retailer uses the system also for the ITr, indeed inside the shop the RFID system is used to detect the movement through and from the chilled storage.

Does RFID Reduce Out of Stocks? A Preliminary Analysis (Hardgrave, Waller, & Miller, 2005). This paper presents the preliminary results of a trial conducted between February 14 to September 12 2005 in 24 stores at Wal-Mart, which is the world's largest public corporation by revenue and which runs a chain of large, discount department store. The aim of the study is to assess the impact of RFID technology on out of stocks, which generate a huge economic lost, especially for agri-food firms (Kranendonk and Rackebrandt, 2002).

In the implemented system the commodity cases were labeled by RFID tags; a set of RFID readers detect the tags that pass in their field and record their data. In the distribution center there are: receiving door readers, conveyor readers and shipping door readers; these three reader points allow to detect the entrance, the sorting phase, and the exit of each case, however when cases are in a pallet it is not possible to read all the tags, so the reading can be completed only after the case are put out of the pallet. In the retailers there are: receiving door readers, backroom shelf readers, sales floor door readers, and box crusher readers; these three reader points allow to detect the entrance in the backroom storage area, the movement into the sale area, and the crashing of cases.

A method used at Wal-Mart for replenishing stock on the shelves is based on a picklist; employers put a new element to be replenished in the list, maybe by using a hand-held barcode scanner, when they see a shelf near to out of stock. This method is laborious and the replenishment is slow. By using point of sale RFID readers is possible to generate an automatic picklist, based on the number of cases moved in the sale area, and on the number of sold commodities.

The trial was executed in 12 "test" stores; other 12 stores with similar characteristics were chosen to compare the results. Along the 29 weeks of the trial, the test and the control stores were scanned daily at the same time along the same path, in order to detect Out-Of-Stock, empty shelf spaces, in the majority of the sections of the stores. The trial in the test stores evolved through three phases: (a) no RFID, (b) partial RFID on some selected products, and (c) full RFID.

The results of the trial are: (a) a reduction of 13% of Out-Of-Stock from no RFID phase to partial RFID phase and a reduction of 26% of Out-Of-Stock from no RFID phase to full RFID phase; (b) also in control stores there was a reduction of Out-Of-Stock, which was probably due to the other Wal Mart supply chain improvement initiatives and to influence of evaluation on employers, however in the test stores the reduction is 63% higher than in control stores; (c) a comparison among Out-Of-Stock of tagged products and non tagged products in the same stores, shows that the reduction of Out-Of-Stock for non tagged ones is lower; (d) the adoption of automatic picklist in parallel to traditional picklist, shows that a variable amount of Out-Of-Stock was found by the automatic picklist.

Authors conclude that the adoption of RFID technology can reduce consistently the Out-Of-Stock without large changes of the work processes. However a better isolation of RFID effect is considered essential to determinate its contribution.

Figure 10 shows the traceability activities managed in the Wal-Mart trial. The main activity of the trial is the ITr in retailers, this activity allows to manage the Out-Of-Stocks problem, by utilizing the information about the number of products in the retailer, and their approximative collocation. The tagging is at case level, however the authors think that a tagging at item level can bring better improvements. The only variable stored on a tag is the EPC code, the other information are recorded in a database. The system manages also the BtoBTr and the ITr in the distribution centers, but the analysis in focused on the ITr in the retailers.

RFID Technology and Applications in the Retail Supply Chain: The Early Metro Group

Figure 10. The Wal-Mart traceability activities

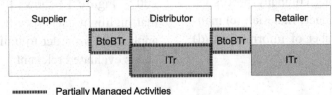

Figure 11. The Future Store traceability activities

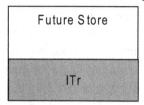

Pilot (Loebbecke, 2005). This paper provides the results of the trial conducted at Metro Group's Future Store. The Metro Group is one of the most globalised retail and wholesale corporations. The trial is conducted in the Future Store that was build in one of the Metro Group's supermarkets in Germany.

In the trial the tagging is exploited at item level, on three products, among which a cream cheese; the tags are prepared by suppliers and then attached in the Future Store. The shelves of these products were equipped with RFID readers, that can detect the tags of the commodities on the shelves. In addition to the standard traceability system activities, a specific application is tested on each product: anti-theft protection, marketing improvement, and, on the cream cheese, the management of expiration dates.

The trial underlined benefits and drawbacks of RFID application for traceability systems. The main advantages are: (a) better inventory monitoring, and consequent improvement of replenishment management; (b) reduction of out-of stock due to the better monitoring of shelves; (c) better knowledge of the demand that improves production planning; (d) better knowledge of the conditions under which goods are sold; (e) reduction of storage space; (f) reduction of labor time due to automation. On the other hand the trial underlined also some challenges: (a) need of standardisation among company processes; (b) problems due to products material; (c) management of a huge number of information; (d) privacy issues.

Authors conclude that RFID technology can bring many benefits but its adoption in supply chain management and traceability requires a stronger roll-out for achieving necessary economies of scale and quantitative insights.

Figure 11 shows the traceability activities managed in the Metro Group's Future Shop trial. The trial is focused on the ITr in a retailer, this activity allows to manage problems such as Out-Of-Stocks and expiration date, thanks to the tagging at item level. The system potentially manages also the BtoBTr but the study treats only the ITr.

DISCUSSION

By analyzing the described studies it is possible to highlight the main opportunities and drawbacks of RFID technology application to agri-food traceability.

Several studies identify obstacles to the RFID large adoption such as: (a) the lack of universal technology standards (Lefebvre et al., 2006; Karkkainen, 2003; Zhen-hua et al., 2007; Lefebvre et al., 2006); (b) the need of changes in process standard (Loebbecke, 2005; Lefebvre et al., 2006); (c) the low detection rate due to problems such as interferences with product and package materials (Loebbecke, 2005; Ayalew et al., 2006; Zhen-hua et al., 2007); (d) the need to deal with a huge number of data (Loebbecke, 2005; Lefebvre et al., 2006); (e) the need of cooperation, cost division, and sharing of information between the chain members (Karkkainen, 2003; Lefebvre et al., 2006; Ayalew et al., 2006); (f) the lack of final system suppliers (Karkkainen, 2003); (g) the privacy problems (Loebbecke, 2005; Bernardi et al., 2007); (g) the high costs (Ayalew et al., 2006; Zhen-hua et al., 2007; Gandino et al., 2007). Figure 12 shows the quantity of papers that highlight each specific drawback of RFID application, in order to indicate how much each one is evaluated relevant.

Figure 12. RFID traceability drawbacks

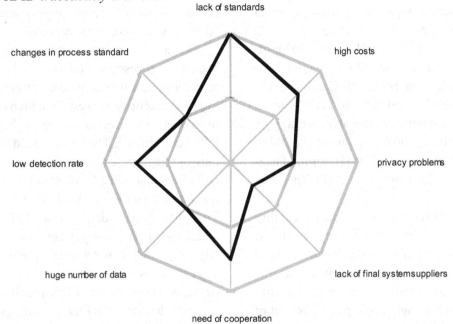

Some studies (Prince et al., 2004; Gandino et al., 2007) underline the opportunity for an enterprise to implement low cost systems, in order to evaluate their effectiveness, and then eventually to adopt a more advanced system.

The described studies identify some key benefits of RFID-based traceability system adoption: (a) improvement of the production planning along the whole chain (Lee et. al., 2004; Loebbecke, 2005); (b) reduction of storage space (Lee et. al.,

Figure 13. RFID traceability benefits

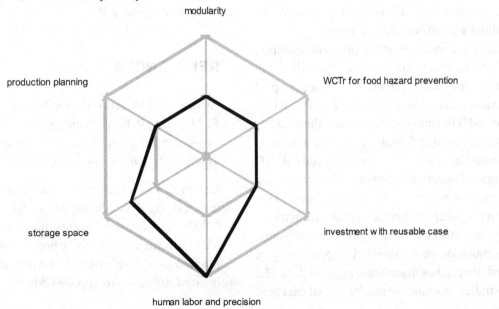

2004; Loebbecke, 2005; Lefebvre et al., 2006); (c) improvement of replenishment management and reduction of out-of-stock (Hardgrave et al., 2005; Lee et. al., 2004; Karkkainen, 2003,); (d) reduction of human labor and relative precision improvement (Loebbecke, 2005; Gandino et al., 2007; Prince et al., 2004; Lefebvre et al., 2006); (e) reduced investment with reusable case tagging level (Karkkainen, 2003; Gandino et al., 2007); (f) efficient management of WCTr, for food hazard prevention (Bernardi et al. 2007; Zhen-hua et al., 2007).

Therefore RFID can improve the traceability management in terms of efficiency, accuracy, human labor, and used area; however these improvements require cooperation among the chain companies. Figure 13 shows the quantity of studies that highlight each specific benefit of RFID application, in order to indicate how much each one is evaluated relevant.

CONCLUSIONS AND FUTURE TRENDS

In this chapter the characteristics of agri-food traceability were detailed, and the most relevant results reached by the international research about the employment of RFID for agri-food traceability and about similar topics were shown.

The described research projects examine RFID-based traceability systems from different points of view. The studies in the business impact analysis section are focused on the effects of RFID and auto-ID business processes, and their results are mainly based on field analysis and discussions. These studies conclude that an advanced auto-ID system implementation requires radical changes in the company processes. The studies described in system proposals section present different traceability systems and evaluate practical problems. The simulation paper shows the opportunity of analysis that comes from the use of simulators. The field studies describe the results of trial executed in real-life conditions; these studies demonstrate the economic and technological feasibility of RFID-based traceability systems.

The agri-food traceability management is becoming necessary, and system based RFID technology can efficiently manage it and guarantee high food security, however the high cost of this technology requires to utilize all benefits that RFID can provide. Thereby the food traceability must be integrated with supply chain management, and all other possible RFID applications, such as expiration time management, must be evaluated. Though many trials demonstrate the feasibility of RFID-based traceability system wide adoption, it requires to tackle many open issues. In order to solve these issues wider trials and very accurate simulation systems are still required.

The adoption of RFID technology for agri-food traccability will be mainly affected by two elements: (a) the growing requirements of food security, commodity quality, and food origin certification, which characterize the agri-food market; (b) the economic benefits that RFID technology brings, especially to the perishable food sector, where an efficient supply chain management can avoid consistent waste, and to the high cost food sector, where the price of a single product allows the use of RFID tags for reaching value added after the point-of-sell.

REFERENCES

Ayalew, G., McCarthy, U., McDonnell, K., Butler, F., McNulty, P. B., & Ward, S. M. (2006). Electronic Tracking and Tracing in Food and Feed Traceability. *LogForum, 2*(2), 1-17.

Bernardi, P., Demartini, C., Gandino, F., Montrucchio, B., Rebaudengo, M., & Sanchez, E.R. (2007). Agri-food traceability management using a RFID system with privacy protection. *The 21st International Conference on Advanced Networking and Applications* (pp. 68-75).

Corsten, D. & Gruen, T.W. (2004). Stock-Outs Cause Walkouts. *Harvard Business Review*, 26-28

EPCglobal (2005). EPCTM Radio-Frequency Identity protocols Class-1 Generation-2 UHF RFID Protocol for Communications at 860 MHz - 960 MHz. Version 1.0.9.

The European Parliament and The Council (2002). Article 18. Regulation (EC) No 178/2002 Of The European Parliament And Of The Council of 28 January 2002. *UE: Official Journal of the European Communities.*

Gandino, F., Montrucchio, B., Rebaudengo, M., & Sanchez, E.R. (2007). Analysis of an RFID-based Information System for Tracking and Tracing in an Agri-Food Chain. *The 1st Annual RFID Eurasia Conference.*

Gibson, B. J., Mentzer, J. T., & Cook, R. L. (2005). Supply chain management: the pursuit of a consensus definition. *Journal of Business Logistics, 26*(2), 17-25.

Golan, E., Krissoff, B., Kuchler, F., Nelson, K., Price, G. & Calvin, L. (2003). Traceability in the US Food Supply: Dead End or Superhighway? *Choices, 18*(2), 17-20.

Hardgrave, B.C., Waller, M., Miller, R. (2005). *Does RFID Reduce Out of Stocks? A Preliminary Analysis.* Tech. report, Information Technology Research Center, University of Arkansas.

ISO 9001:2000 Standard.

Kärkkäinen, M. (2003). Increasing efficiency in the supply chain for short shelf life goods using RFID tagging. *International Journal of Retail & Distribution Management, 10*(31), 529-536.

Kranendonk, A. & Rackebrandt, S. (2002). *Optimising availability - getting products on the shelf!* Official ECR Europe Conference, Barcelona.

Lee, Y.M., Cheng, F., & Leung, Y.T. (2004). Exploring the impact of RFID on supply chain dynamics. *Proceedings of the 2004 Winter Simulation Conference.*

Lefebvre, L.A., Lefebvre, E., Bendavid, Y., Wamba, S.F., & Boeck, H. (2006). RFID as an Enabler of B-to-B e-Commerce and its Impact on Business Processes: A Pilot Study on a Supply Chain in the Retail Industry. *The 39th Annual Hawaii International Conference on System Sciences.* 6, 104a-104a.

Loebbecke, C., (2005). RFID Technology and Applications in the Retail Supply Chain: The Early Metro Group Pilot. *The 18ᵗʰ Bled eConference eIntegration in Action.*

Loftus, R., (2005). Traceability of biotech-derived animals: application of DNA technology. *Scientific and Technical Review The Office International des Epizooties, 2005, 24*(1), 231-242.

Nikitin, P.V., Rao, K.V.S., and Lazar, S., (2007). An Overview of Near Field UHF RFID. *IEEE International Conference on RFID 2007.*

Ortiz, S., Jr., (2006). Is Near-Field Communication Close to Success? *Computer, 39*(3), 18-20.

Prince, K., Morán, H., & McFarlane, D. (2004). *Auto-ID Use Case: Food Manufacturing Company Distribution.* Cambridge University, UK.

Want, R., (2006). An introduction to RFID technology. *IEEE Pervasive Computing, 5*(1), 25-33.

Zhen-hua, D., Jin-tao, L., & Bo, F. (2007). Radio Frequency Identification in Food Supervision. *The 9th International Conference on Advanced Communication Technology.* 542-545.

KEY TERMS

Agri-Food: Concerning production, processing, and inspection of food products made from agricultural commodities.

AIDC: Automatic Identification and Data Capture.

BtoBTr: Business to Business Traceability.

BtoCTr: Business to Customer Traceability.

ITr: Internal Traceability.

Traceability: ability to trace the history, application or location of that which is under consideration.

WCTr: Whole Chain Traceability.

Section III
Smart Health

Chapter V
Interpreting Health and Wellness Information

Lena Mamykina
GVU Center, Georgia Institute of Technology, USA

Elizabeth D. Mynatt
GVU Center, Georgia Institute of Technology, USA

ABSTRACT

In the last decade, novel sensing technologies enabled development of applications that help individuals with chronic diseases monitor their health and activities. These applications can generate large volumes of data that need to be processed and analyzed. At the same time, many of these applications are designed for non-professional use by individuals of advanced age and low educational level. These users may find the data collected by the applications challenging and overwhelming, rather than helpful, and may require additional assistance in interpreting it. In this chapter, we discuss two different approaches to designing computing applications that not only collect the relevant health and wellness data but also find creative ways to engage individuals in the analysis and assist with interpretation of the data. These approaches include visualization of data using simple real world imagery and metaphors, and social scaffolding mechanisms that help novices learn by observing and imitating experts. We present example applications that utilize both of these approaches and discuss their relative strengths and limitations.

INTRODUCTION

Rapid developments in the sensing technologies lead to the introduction of sensors and object auto-identification in new areas of human life and activities. One such area that became a topic of extensive research is healthcare. In the healthcare domain, auto-identification takes a form of health and wellness monitoring and applies not only to objects, but also, and even more commonly, to activities, and to bio-indicators of individuals' health. For example, new sensing techniques attempt to determine individuals' diets by audio recording chewing sounds (Amft et al, 2006); individuals' interactions with RFID-tagged objects is used to infer the activities they engage in (Intille, 2003), and various sensors are designed to monitor new and traditional vital signs, such as heart rate, blood glucose, or gate.

Oftentimes, introduction of these new sensing techniques can lead to an exponential growth of the volumes of data available for interpreting. At the same time, many of the monitoring applications that utilize such sensors are designed in context of chronic disease management and are meant to be used by lay individuals and their non-clinical caregivers. As a result, the attention of researchers is starting to shift from sensing technologies to ways to incorporate these data into individuals' sensemaking and decision-making regarding their health and disease. After all, the richness of the captured data is of little value unless it can inform decisions and empower choices.

In this chapter we discuss two distinct approaches to enhancing the utility of auto-identification data for lay individuals, discuss recent research projects that utilize these approaches and compare and contrast their advantages and disadvantages. The two approaches we focus on are: 1) introduction of novel data presentation techniques that facilitate comprehension and analysis of the captured data and 2) incorporation of social scaffolding that helps individuals acquire skills necessary for data analysis by learning from experts.

We will begin our discussion by introducing three applications that utilize novel visualization techniques to represent health-related information captured by sensors. These applications include Digital Family Portrait (later referred to as DFP, Mynatt et at, 2000) designed by the Graphics, Visualization and Usability Center of the Georgia Institute of Technology, Fish 'n' Steps (Lin et at, 2006) designed by Siemens Corporate Research, Inc. and UbiFit Garden (Consolvo et

at, 2007) designed by Intel Research, Inc. All of these applications use sensors to collect health or wellness data and rely on a particular approach to visualizing the resulting data set, namely they use metaphors of real world events or objects to assist in comprehension.

An alternative approach to facilitating analysis of health data captured by ubiquitous computing applications is by providing social scaffolding mechanisms. One example of such applications is Mobile Access to Health Information (MAHI, Mamykina et al, 2006) designed and developed by the Georgia Institute of Technology and Siemens Corporate Research, Inc. In contrast to DFP, Fish'n'Steps, or UbiFit Garden, MAHI uses relatively simple data presentation techniques. However, it includes a number of features that allow diabetes educators help individuals with diabetes acquire and develop skills necessary for reflective analysis of the captured data.

Evaluation studies of the applications we describe here showed that all of them were successful in reaching their respective design goals and led to positive changes in behaviors or attitudes of their users. While these studies did not specifically focus on data comprehension, such comprehension was the necessary first step in achieving these positive results. In addition, our own experiments comparing different types of visualizations showed that not all of them are equally effective. However, we believe that novel visualizations and social scaffolding have their unique advantages and disadvantages that need to be considered when making a choice as to which strategy to follow. In the rest of this chapter we describe the applications mentioned above in greater detail and talk about the results of their deployment studies. We then describe our attempts to evaluate the effectiveness of different types of data visualization. We conclude with the analysis of comparative advantages and limitations of the two approaches.

VISUALIZING HEALTH INFORMATION

As the world's elderly population increases in numbers, chronic diseases common to older adults stretch the capacity of traditional healthcare. As a result, aging adults and other individuals affected by chronic diseases must take an increasingly proactive stance towards personal healthcare, adopting roles and responsibilities previously fulfilled by professionals. One such responsibility is the monitoring of longitudinal medical records for patterns that may indicate important changes in conditions or that may signal an impending crisis.

Shifting medical monitoring activities to lay individuals is not without consequence. According to a recent report of the Committee on Health Literacy (Nielsen-Bohlman et al, editors, 2004), "nearly half of all American adults — 90 million people — have difficulty understanding and acting upon health information." Often at issue are the methods with which this health information is visually represented. Traditional techniques represent data using graphs, charts, or tables, all of which can pose impassable barriers to individuals of advanced age or lower socio-economic status and education. However, these individuals have the highest risk of developing chronic diseases, and thus the greatest need to be meaningfully engaged in self-care.

The problem of assisting individuals in comprehending complex and extensive datasets is at the heart of the field of Information Visualization. Building upon a set of principles first developed in the late eighteenth century, modern day visualizations range from common graphs and bar charts to space-time narratives and data maps (Tafte, 1999). Common to these methods is the notion of abstractly representing data so that large quantities of information can be depicted and compared in a condensed space. However, whereas these visualizations may be suitable for educated users, some researchers question their appropriateness for individuals of advanced age and lower education and seek alternative visualization techniques.

People rely on a number of methods when faced with the need to understand complex phenomena. One such method is the use of metaphors, whereby a complex concept is related to a simpler situation exhibiting similar properties. Metaphors permeate modern languages and deeply impact human cognition, lay as well as scientific (Lakoff and Johnson, 1981). Within the world of computer interfaces, metaphors can be found at the core of graphic user interfaces; the ubiquitous "desktop" metaphor is familiar to millions of computer users. Lately, metaphors served as an inspiration to a number of applications that visualize health related information for lay individuals that we discuss below.

Metaphor-Based Visualizations

Throughout history, analogies with real world objects and situations have served as powerful inspiration for visual communication. For example, maps have been grounded in real-world geographic analogies for over a thousand years, making them one of the most persistent and ubiquitous forms of analogical, pictorial communication in the Western world.

In the eighteenth century, Lambert and Playfair, among others, popularized new forms of graphical representation: statistical charts used for communicating economical and political data (Tafte, 1981). The techniques they pioneered later developed into plots, which utilize Cartesian coordinates, time-series, or relational graphics. Whereas previous data visualizations relied heavily on real-world analogies, these new charts required one to learn mappings between particular visual properties (such as position, color, shape or size), and the information represented by these encodings.

Computing technologies naturally lend themselves to relational visualizations because they make it easy to decouple data from representation. In fact, much of the power of computer-based visualizations lies in their ability to produce abstract, high density, relational visualizations efficiently for a wide range of data sets. However, these techniques require a certain level of abstract thinking and appreciation of basic mathematical concepts (Tversky et al, 1991).

While relational visualizations permeate computer-based Information Visualization, there exist alternatives, more commonly explored within the fields of ambient or peripheral displays. For example, InfoCanvas (Stasko et al., 2004) visualizations utilize real world imagery to map information but allow users to create arbitrary mappings. Further departing from the relational tradition, visualizations such as People Garden (Xiong and Donath, 1999), or the Presence Display (Huang and Mynatt, 2003) relay information, such as the flow of conversations or individuals' presence in the office, by using metaphors that compare the information with familiar real world situations.

Metaphors allow individuals to understand one set of experiences in terms of another through a relation of the form "A is B," where B is said to be the source of the metaphor and A is the target. Common examples of metaphors include "time is money," or "life is a journey." According to Lakoff and Johnson (Lakoff and Johnson, 1981), human thought processes are largely, although implicitly, metaphorical. Through the use of metaphors, complex or abstract concepts, such as emotions or thought processes, become more accessible through their relation to concrete objects and situations. Visual metaphors are means to visually represent a linguistic metaphor. One of the most familiar examples of visual metaphors, or metaphor-based data visualizations, is a genealogical tree, which represents a history of a family as a tree with each branch depicting a particular "branch" of the family. The roots of this visualization can be traced to "life is a tree" metaphor common in many languages (Lakoff and Johnson, 1981)

Although there exist examples of symbolic or metaphorical visualizations in User Interfaces, they are rarely seen as superior to relational alternatives in facilitating analysis and comprehension. Instead, they are often valued for aesthetic properties or their ability to blend into the surrounding environment. At the same time, the historical importance of metaphors suggests they may possess particular strengths for audiences or situations which are lacking skills necessary for interpreting relational graphics.

Recently, however, there emerged a number of applications that utilize real-world imagery to convey health and wellness related information to lay individuals. These applications came from different research organizations and were designed by different research teams, perhaps without explicitly targeting usage of metaphors as an inspiration for the design. However, the conceptual similarity in the approaches adopted by these applications is intriguing, and positive results of the deployment studies described by the researchers recommend metaphor-based visualizations as a promising approach for health monitoring applications. We discuss several such applications: Digital Family Portrait by the Georgia Institute of Technology (Mynatt et al, 2001), Fish 'n' Steps by Siemens Corporate Research (Lin et al., 2006) and UbiFit Garden by Intel Research (Consolvo et al., 2008). These applications represent only a limited selection, however we believe together they form a relatively representative sample of this new class of software designed for health and wellness monitoring.

Digital Family Portrait

Digital Family Portrait (DFP, Mynatt et al., 2000) is a pioneering application designed by researchers at the Graphics, Visualization and Usability center of the Georgia Institute of Technology that helps adult children remain connected with their aging parents living remotely. DFP is inspired by the observation that many decisions to transition to assisted care facilities are initiated by adult children who want to ensure wellbeing of their parents. In modern times, when children and parents rarely live together and are often separated by hundreds of miles, they lack the usual lightweight indicators of each other's daily activities. For example seeing that mom picked up the newspaper in the morning or the light in the kitchen window around dinner time might be sufficient to conclude that things are in order if you live in a house next door. DFP uses modern sensing technology to recreate the feeling of collocation without undue intrusion on the privacy of the aging parents. A number of motion detection sensors placed around the parent's house capture a rough picture of daily activities. The design of the display further supports the notion of lightweight unobtrusive awareness: a digital frame of a parent's picture is enhanced with icons indicating the general amount of activity in the parent's house. The choice of icons includes butterflies, trees, or other simple and aestheti-

Figure 1. Digital Family Portrait. The picture of the aging parent is surrounded by a digital frame with icons indicating the amount of activity in the parent's house in the last 14 days. Each butterfly represents a day of activity (the current day is indicated with a lighter background color); the size of the butterflies shows the amount of activity captured with motion detection sensors

cally pleasing images; each icon represents one day, and its size represents the amount of activity (Figure 1). Thus, while each icon taken by itself is not sufficiently informative, together they form a pattern and allow the users to notice changes in the amount of activity overtime.

DFP was deployed with one family for an extended period of over a year. It is easy to imagine that the volume of sensory data collected during this time could be quite overwhelming and difficult to interpret. However, the simple, yet articulate visualization made it easy for both users to cope with the data volume and extract useful aggregated information. During the time of the study, both the parent, Helen, and the child, Will, participating in the study learned to rely on the display for awareness. Helen volunteered that because of the display she felt less lonely, knowing that Will is looking over her. Will found several creative ways for using the display, such as anticipating Helen's return from travel, or inferring when she was out doing errands. While the more detailed and more typical visualization of Helen's movements around the house could provide more detailed information, simple butterflies contributed to the desired piece of mind and sense of awareness.

Fish 'n' Steps

Fish'n'Steps designed by Siemens Corporate Research, Inc. (Lin et al., 2006), is an application that combines ubiquity and simplicity of pedometers, wearable devices that measure one's step counts, with the engagement of social computing games. Individuals enrolled in the game use pedometers to measure their daily step count. Fish'n'Steps then links the number of steps taken each day to the growth and emotional state of a virtual pet "belonging" to each individual: a fish in a fishtank. Additional incentives incorporate social dynamics, such as competition between teams of players.

"Fish'n'Steps" was built as a distributed software application that included several functioning components as well as some "Wizard of Oz" components. Simple commercially available pedometers, Sportline 330, were used to measure the step count of individual participants. To collect data from pedometers, individuals placed their pedometer on a platform at a public kiosk, and took a picture of their pedometer screen, including the unique pedometer ID. The picture was captured and sent to a member of the research team who entered the appropriate data into a database.

The fourteen-week deployment study with nineteen participants showed that the game served as a catalyst for promoting exercise and for improving game players' attitudes towards physical activity. Furthermore, although most player's enthusiasm in the game decreased after the game's first two weeks, analyzing the results using Prochaska's Transtheoretical Model of Behavioral Change (Grimley et al, 1994), suggested that individuals had, by that time, established new routines that led to healthier patterns of physical activity in their daily lives. Once again, as with DFP, the simple visualization allowed to condense large volumes of data captured with pedometers and present a coherent aggregated picture of

users' overall activity levels. Such compelling visual presentation had an additional benefit of creating a resemblance of emotional attachment and motivated a number of users to increase their activity.

UbiFit Garden

Another application that utilizes a similar idea was designed by researchers at Intel Research (Consolvo et al., 2008). UbiFit Garden is a mobile application designed to monitor and encourage physical activity by its users. On-the-body sensing component monitors individuals' physical activity and can reliably differentiate between various types of exercise. The display, designed for a mobile phone, represents levels of activity through flowers in a garden: the number of flowers and types of flowers in the garden indicate amount and variety of different types of exercise. Butterflies above flowers signify achievement of activity goals.

As with the previous two applications, Ubi-Garden uses simple, familiar imagery to convey specific information in a way consistent with using

Figure 2. Fish'n'Steps. One participant's display after approximately two weeks into the trial in the Fish'n'Steps team-condition, also the public kiosk and pedometer platform, which rotated through each of the team fish-tanks. The components of the personal display include: 1) Fish Tank - The fish tank contains the virtual pets belonging to the participant and his/her team members, 2) Virtual Pet – The participant's own fish in a frontal view on the right side next to the fish tank, 3) Calculations and feedback - improvement, burned calories, progress bar, personal and team ranking, etc., 4) Chat window for communicating with team members

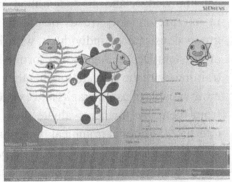 

Figure 3. UbiFit Garden's Glanceable Display. a) at the beginning of the week; b) after one cardio workout; c) a full garden with variety; and d) a full garden on the background screen of a mobile phone. Butterflies indicate met goals

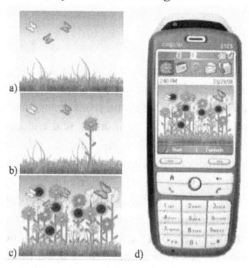

linguistic metaphors. While the initial deployment studies of UbiFit Garden focused primarily on the activity sensing side of the application, the display received a positive reaction from the users. Once again, large volumes of data were condensed to a simple coherent picture that was informative, aesthetically pleasing, and had an additional capability of inspiring emotional reaction and consequently motivating users.

Evaluating Metaphor-Based Interfaces

The deployment studies of the three applications described above have demonstrated their overall utility for the users. However, they did not specifically focus on the effectiveness of their chosen approach to visualizing the data through the use of metaphors. More generally, while there exist many examples of studies examining relative benefits of different visualizations, to the best of our knowledge none of them focuses specifically on visualizations that use metaphors. To address this

limitation we conducted two small pilot studies that examined these questions. In these studies we specifically focused on data comprehension with different visualization types measured by an individuals' ability to answer pointed questions regarding the depicted data using the classic criteria of comprehension such as error rate and time required to answer the questions.

In the first of the studies we designed two visualizations to present diabetes-related data usually targeted by diabetes monitoring applications, such as records of blood sugar values and records of daily activities. The first visualization used a more traditional, relational approach (Figure 4, top image); the second visualization used a number of metaphors to represent temporal aspect of the records, and for the design of the icons (Figure 4, bottom image). In a controlled experimental setting the participants were exposed to both visualizations for a limited amount of time and asked to answer a series of questions regarding the data.

Thirty-five participants were paid $125 to participate in a two-hour experimental session. Participants with diabetes were recruited from two age groups, younger adults (17 participants, mean age 36.24 years, range 25-40) and older adults (eighteen participants, mean age 69.18 years, range 60-75). Each participant had been living with diabetes for at least 2 years. Within age groups, our goal was to have individuals who differed in their ability to interpret graphs and data trends. Accordingly, one group consisted of high school graduates with little formal statistical knowledge, and no specialized experience in interpreting data trends or graphs. Another group consisted of individuals with Bachelors or Masters Degree, and some formal statistical training, with the expectation that they would be more capable of using graphs and extracting data from them. To further evaluate their ability to interpret traditional graphical presentations and validate our sampling methods, each participant was given a test taken from the graph understat-

Figure 4. Comparing Relational and Metaphorical Visualizations. Both visualizations (top and bottom) show a day worth of activity records and health indicators (emotional state, blood glucose values, etc.) The visualization on top utilizes more traditional, relational techniques, such using coordinate systems. The visualization below uses a metaphor of a clock to show temporality of the data and uses icons to signify different activities

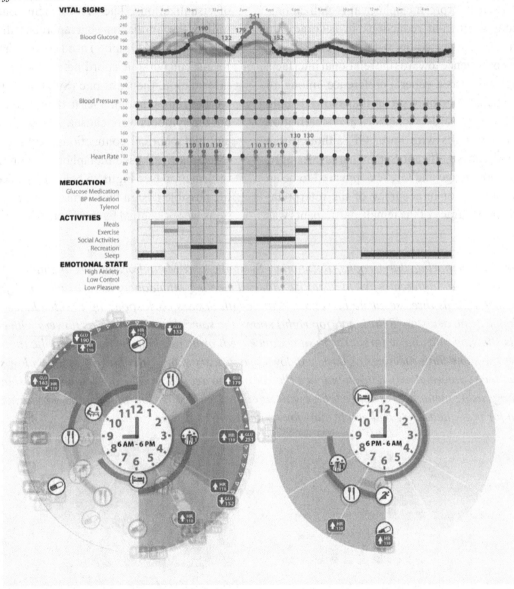

ing portion of the Graduate Record Examination (GRE) (ETS, 2004). Participants were split into high (2-4 correct answers) and low (0-2 correct answers) Graphical Facility (GF). This produced an approximate median split, with 16 low and 19 high GF participants. Sex was not a variable of interest, but each group was approximately gender-balanced. We expected that age and Graphical Facility would influence the subjects' success with different visualizations, with subjects of younger age and higher GF performing better with relational graphics and subjects of older age and lower GF performing better with metaphorical graphics.

As expected, younger adults with higher GF required less time to interpret relational visualizations, whereas older adults with lower GF required less time to interpret metaphorical visualizations, without significant reductions in accuracy. In addition, younger adults with high GF showed strong preference towards the relational interface, though this was a general preference among all participants. The only group that showed slight preference towards metaphorical visualization was older adults with lower GF, although that trend was not significant. Somewhat surprisingly, in addition to age and GF, sex appeared to be an important factor in accuracy of the interpretations; the accuracy of the female participants was

significantly higher on the metaphorical visualization. Further research is required to account for this finding.

In the second study, we expanded the scope of our investigations to include four different types of visualizations. The first of them (Bar Chart) utilized the familiar bar chart approach; the second one (Relational Graphic) used colors, shapes and forms but without coordinate systems to code information, the third one (Symbolic) used real world symbols and images to depict information, but the symbols were chosen arbitrarily, without any metaphorical connections, and the last one (Metaphorical) used metaphors to communicate information (see Figure 5 below). To account for the possible design bias some of these visualizations were designed by members of our team and

Figure 5. Comparing Bar Graphs, Relational, Symbolic and Metaphorical Visualizations. The four images represent different ways to visualize planned meeting attendance. Bar Graph (top left) shows three meetings as three separate bar charts with length of bars corresponding to attendance, non-attendance or no decision. Relational (top right) shows the same three meetings as flowers with colors of petals showing attendance (green), non-attendance (red) or no decision (white). Symbolic (bottom left) shows the same three meetings as three windows in a grocery shop with objects in the window showing attendance (watermelons), non-attendance (flowers) or no decision (apples). Metaphorical shows three meetings using metaphors of coffee tables with cups filled with coffee for attendance, cups turned upside down for non-attendance and empty cups for no decisions

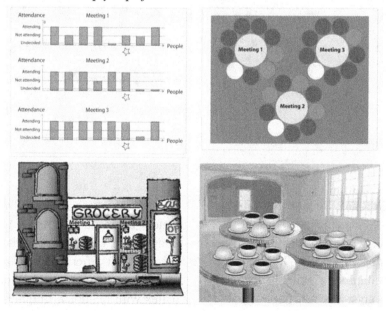

some borrowed from the works of others (Huang and Mynatt 2003, Stasko et al, 2004). Based on our previous findings we specifically focused on individuals of advanced age (above 65) with various levels of education. As in the previous study, we expected that individuals with higher levels of education will perform better with more traditional graphics (Bar Chart and Relational), whereas individuals with lower levels of education will perform better with metaphorical visualizations.

Nine participants were recruited from senior centers to participate in the study. Participants' age ranged from 65 to 85 (mean age 70.8), with the majority of the participants being female (7 out of 9). Six participants completed high school and had some college experience, whereas three did not complete high school. The testing took place at the senior centers, and the participants were compensated $50 for participating in the 1½ hour session.

During the session, participants were presented with visualizations one at a time, with an explanation accompanying each visualization on the screen. After reviewing explanations, the participants answered four multiple choice questions about each visualization. The questions required participants to interpret the visualization (e.g., "How many people are planning on attending meeting 1?"); identify overall trends in the data ("There is an overall high attendance of the meetings"); or form an inference ("Meeting 2 seems the most interesting based on the planned attendance"). Participants' accuracy and time per question were recorded. A subjective rating for ease of questions, ease of visualization, and comparative quality of visualizations was captured via a paper questionnaire after each visualization was presented. Time required for answering each question and the accuracy of the answers were captured by the researchers.

For Accuracy, the results showed a significant main effect of the visualization type across education levels [$F(3, 18) = 13.68$, $p < 0.001$].

Pair-wise comparison showed that metaphorical and symbolic visualizations were comparable with bar-charts, while relational graphics led to significantly less accurate answers [$F(1, 6) = 22.65$, $p < 0.01$]. Further analyses revealed a significant interaction between Visualization Type and Education [$F(3, 18) = 5.36$, $p < 0.01$; the means are presented in Table 1]. For individuals with higher education, metaphorical visualizations led to slightly inferior performance as compared to bar graphs. This trend reversed for those with lower education: These participants performed best with metaphorical visualizations; however, the differences in performance within this group were not significant.

There were no significant effects on response time, perhaps owing to large individual differences between participants.

These findings demonstrate considerable differences for older adults in their comprehension of information visualized in different ways. Although the small sample size of this study prohibits strong claims and conclusions, the trends identified in the experiment deserve further investigation. Across educational levels, relational graphics proved to be the most challenging for the older adults. In addition, education proved to play an important role in helping individuals benefit from traditional forms of presentation, such as bar graphs and relational graphics.

With these two small pilot studies we only scratched the surface of this issue, and uncovered new research questions. For example, in our ex-

Table 1. Results presented in the form of mean accuracy for responses and standard deviations

	Higher Education		Lower Education	
	Mean	St.D	Mean	St.D
Bar Graph	0.63	0.49	0.56	0.50
Relational	0.28	0.45	0.38	0.49
Symbolic	0.63	0.49	0.40	0.49
Metaphorical	0.56	0.50	0.67	0.48

periments the participants received a limited exposure to each of the visualizations. Consequently, there remains a question of whether metaphorical visualizations will have similar benefits even after users gained substantial experience with them or their advantages are short-lived. However, even these preliminary results show that at least for individuals of advanced age and lower education metaphorical visualizations are a promising approach to depicting information.

SOCIAL SCAFFOLDING FOR DATA ANALYSIS

The applications we describe above successfully helped their users cope with large volumes of data captured by sensors. However, due to the significant level of data aggregation, these applications may have limited utility in facilitating detailed data analysis. Below we describe a complimentary approach for the design of health monitoring application that focuses not on a particular type of data presentation, but on helping users acquire and develop data analysis skills by observing and imitating experts.

There are a variety of ways people learn and acquire new skills. Some researchers argue that the acquisition of new skills in personal and even professional worlds is different in nature from formal schooling. Observations of a number of professional (butchers, tailors) and non-professional (Alcoholics Anonymous) communities of practice by Lave and Wenger (Lave and Wenger, 1991) led them to conclude that learning in these communities occurs through observation and imitation in a style known as apprenticeship. They argue that knowledge in these communities is preserved by core members or masters, who mastered the necessary skills in the course of their careers. New members join these communities at the periphery, and engage in observation and imitation of the masters, while often performing small and well-defined tasks. With time and

acquisition of new skills, novices move from the periphery closer to the center of the community until they in turn become masters and keepers of community's practices.

In our work, we adopted the view of learning as a social activity that happens through observation and imitation. We incorporate features that facilitate these activities into the diabetes-monitoring application, MAHI (Mobile Access to Health Information). MAHI was developed in collaboration between the Graphics, Visualization and Usability Center of the Georgia Institute of Technology and Siemens Corporate Research, Inc.

MAHI is a distributed mobile application that includes a conventional blood glucose meter, such as LifeScan's OneTouch Ultra, a Java-enabled cell phone, such as Nokia N80 and a Bluetooth adapter, such as a modified and custom-programmed Brainboxes BL-819 RS232 Bluetooth Converter to support communication between the glucose meter and the phone (see Figure 6). Individuals with diabetes can use MAHI in two modes, as a diary and as an experience sampling tool. As a diary, MAHI allows individuals to capture their diabetes-related experiences, such as records of activities or questions and concerns they may have through voice notes and photographs (using a cell phone camera) taken with a straightforward and easy-to-use user interface. As an experience sampling tool, MAHI initiates recording sessions when individuals use their blood glucose meter. At that time, MAHI establishes a Bluetooth connection between the meter and the phone, allowing the phone to query the meter for the recently captured readings and prompt individuals to record the reasons for using the glucose meter, and the context of usage by capturing voice notes and photographs. The captured records are packaged by MAHI and transferred to a MySQL database hosted on a dedicated web-server.

The last component of MAHI is a web-based application built using PHP that offers access to dynamic, password-protected websites where individuals and their educators can review cap-

Figure 6. Components of MAHI: MAHI website (screenshot of the actual site usage). The columns include: 1) record number, 2) date and time of capture, 3) blood glucose value, 4) picture(s), 5) audio, 6) participant's comments posted directly to the website, 7) educator's comments posted directly to the website; MAHI phone; Glucose meter with Bluetooth adapter

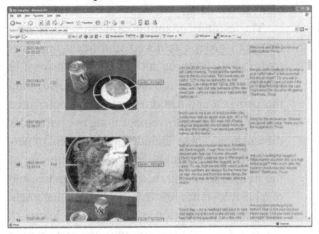  

tured records, and engage in a dialog by providing comments, feedback and additional questions in a message board style.

Deployment Study

The deployment study was conducted in collaboration with the St. Clare's Hospital Diabetes Education Center in Dover, NJ. The education program includes a number of personalized sessions with certified nurses and certified diabetes educators and registered dieticians to establish personal care goals, and weekly diabetes education classes, in which the students are familiarized with the physiological nature of the disease and different aspects of care. The two recruitment criteria included age (below 65) and experience owning and using a cell phone (over 1 year) to minimize confounds due to cell phone usability.

The research team invited all the newly enrolled students of the center to participate in the study as part of their educational program; 49 new students volunteered to participate. The study used a between-subjects design. Half of the participants (25) were assigned to the experimental group, provided with mobile phones,

glucose meters and Bluetooth adapters and were asked to use MAHI during the four weeks of the program. Another half (24) were assigned to a control group and received all of the benefits of the diabetes education but did not use MAHI. General demographics questionnaires conducted prior to the study showed no significant differences between the experimental and the control groups in regards to age, gender, marital status, educational level, or the severity of their general medical condition and their diabetes.

Once the classes started, the individuals in the experimental group were expected to use MAHI independently, with no additional meetings with the research team beyond their attendance of the classes. During the class time, their glucose meters with Bluetooth attachment were collected for battery exchange. At the same time, the individuals were given an opportunity to ask questions, and discuss their experience with the researchers. The researchers attended and audio recorded all the classes that had recruited participants. Once the classes were completed, the individuals were invited for another qualitative interview and reimbursed $30.

Results

As with other applications mentioned earlier in this chapter, the deployment study of MAHI focused on the general utility of the application for individuals with diabetes and its ability to assist them in the management of their disease. We evaluated the impact of MAHI along three different dimensions: individuals' analytical state, or changes in their understanding of their disease, emotional state, or changes in their attitudes towards the disease and changes in their actual behavior. These three factors can help to recreate a comprehensive picture of one's diabetes management. The actual measures for each of these factors were selected together with the personnel of the Diabetes Education Center and included the following:

- **Analytical state:** A multiple choice questionnaire testing basic diabetes understanding developed by the Diabetes Education Center
- **Emotional state:** The two measures used included the standard Health Locus of Control (Wallston et al 1976) and Diabetes Quality of Life (Burrough et al, 2004) questionnaires
- **Behavior:** As part of the educational program, the personnel of the center helped new students to establish their individual management goals, specifically diet goals based on their established habits and desired results. The achievement of these goals was evaluated by the registered dietician during the post-study interview

In addition, we used the Grounded approach Theory (Strauss and Corbin, 1990) to analyze qualitative data, which included qualitative interviews with the participants and online conversations between participants and educators captured in MAHI. The complete findings of this study are described elsewhere (Mamykina et al,

2008). In this chapter we briefly summarize the results that demonstrate the overall effectiveness of MAHI and specifically focus on ways individuals engaged with the application and learned to analyze the data.

The results of quantitative measures indicated that both groups achieved significant improvements along all three anticipated dimensions. In regards to the specific benefits of MAHI, we found that using the application significantly contributed to individuals' improvement along two particular dimensions. These included achievement of personal diet goals, established at the beginning of the study, and acceptance of a more proactive and responsible stance towards diabetes management indicated by adoption of the Internal Locus of Control. Both of these findings are encouraging since they demonstrate that MAHI not only helped individuals meet their diabetes management goals but also helped them change their attitude towards the disease, a good indicator that the behavioral changes achieved during the study will endure overtime (Wooldridge et al, 1990).

These positive results can serve as an indicator that individuals were in fact able to comprehend the data collected by MAHI and draw meaningful conclusions from it. The analysis of online conversations and interviews with the participants gave us some cues as to what influenced individuals' comprehension. As we expected, the educators played a decisive role in helping individuals engage with the applications and learn the necessary analytical skills.

Many online conversations followed a similar pattern. They started with the identification of a specific problem, most commonly a surprisingly high blood glucose value noticed either by the participant or by the educator. After articulating the problem, the educator engaged in the analysis of the possible causes of the problem in individual's behavior by reviewing records captured by MAHI and filling gaps in the data through extensive question and answer exchanges captured on MAHI website. These exchanges played a critical role in illustrating to the participants the expert way of engaging with the data, formulating relevant questions and hypotheses and testing initial conclusions. For many participants these exchanges became the most valuable experiences of the study:

Half the time I didn't even answer her questions. But I knew that those were questions for me; this is how I should be thinking. Now I can look at these records and I know what to look for and how to look for it.

Thus empowered by the expert example, the participants could incorporate the newly learned strategies into their own data analysis techniques and experiment with the new approaches. During this time, the educators observed participants' progress and provided feedback and recommendations until there was sufficient evidence that the participants adopted the new skills and no longer required any scaffolding. This three-step approach including demonstration of the new skills by the expert, internalization of the skills by the student with coaching from the expert and subsequent removal of the scaffolding have striking resemblance with the teaching style that Collins, Brown and Newman named "cognitive apprenticeship" (Collins, Brown and Newman, 1989). Through observing the experts and imitating their techniques the participants were able to master the volumes of data collected by MAHI and learn to draw meaningful conclusions from it.

DISCUSSION

In the last decade novel sensing technologies enabled the development of applications that help individuals with chronic diseases monitor their health and activities. These applications can generate large volumes of data that need to be processed and analyzed. At the same time, many of these applications are designed for non-professional use by individuals of advanced age and/or lower educational levels. These users may find the data collected by the applications challenging and overwhelming, rather than helpful and may require additional assistance in interpreting it.

We discussed two different approaches to designing computing applications that not only collect the relevant health and wellness data but also find creative ways to engage individuals in the analysis and assist with interpretation of the data. These approaches include the visualization of data using simple real world imagery and metaphors, and social scaffolding mechanisms that help novices learn by observing and imitating experts. Both of these approaches have a number of advantages and limitations that we discuss below.

Presentation of data, in particular data captured by health and wellness monitoring applications that use various sensors, has a number of clear benefits, as is demonstrated by the applications we described above. Their interfaces were able to condense large volumes of data inevitable with any monitoring application to a clear and comprehensible picture that was easy to understand by lay individuals, specifically by individuals of advanced age and lower educational level, who may otherwise have difficulties adopting novel technologies. These interfaces are aesthetically pleasing and consequently more appropriate for non-professional environments, such as homes, or for personal mobile devices. In addition, such visualizations as the ones utilized by Fish 'n' Steps and UbiFit Garden can inspire emotional response and further reinforce the behavior change they are designed to inspire. Finally, they tend to be intuitive enough to be used without any training and often require only a simple explanation.

With these advantages, however, come a number of limitations. The study of Fish 'n' Steps demonstrated that the emotional attachment can have a negative side: some participants limited their participation in the game because they found crying fish too upsetting. The researchers noted that adopting only positive reinforcements and avoiding negative ones might be a safer strategy. In addition, mapping with visual as well as linguistic metaphors is not precise and could be misinterpreted. Finding an appropriate visual metaphor for all and any data might be a serious challenge: all three applications described here focus on wellness and activity data, which might have more direct mappings to metaphors than more abstract clinical data, for example. Finally, because these visualizations help to condense large volumes of data they inevitably lead to data loss and thus may not be appropriate if the goal of the application is detailed data analysis.

Similarly, MAHI demonstrated that social scaffolding mechanisms can be successful in helping individuals engage with the data and learn to independently interpret it. This approach does not lead to any reduction in the data, consequently it can be used with relatively complex data displays that facilitate detailed analysis. It also avoids the necessity to search for metaphors, which may be challenging in cases of abstract data.

At the same time, the clear limitation of this approach is that it requires a significant commitment and time investment from the expert and depends on the personality of the expert. In MAHI studies, the expert providing advice was a member of the research team and was highly motivated to engage the participants, which may not always be the case. However, if further analysis of conversational patterns between experts and participants reveals a certain level of consistency in experts' approaches, there is hope that the expert's role can be fully or at least partially substituted by automated agents. Conversational agents in healthcare is already a vibrant and active research area and future research will show whether these agents can play a role in autoidentifaction applications as well.

REFERENCES

Amft, O., Stager, M., Lukowicz, P., & Troster, G., (2006) Analysis of Chewing Sounds for Dietary Monitoring. *Pervasive 2006* (pp. 56-72). Springer-Verlag Berlin Heidelberg

Burrough, T.E., Desikan, R., Waterman, B.M., Gilin D, & McGill, J. Development and validation of the diabetes quality of Life brief clinical inventory. Diabetes Spectrum. 2004;17(1):41-49.

Consolvo, S., Froehlich, J., Harrison, B., Klasnaja, P., LaMarca, A., Landay, J., Legrand, L., Libby, R., McDonald, D., Smith, I., & Toscos, T. (2008). Activity Sensing in the Wild: A Field Trial of UbiFit Garden. *Proc. Of CHI 2008*. Florence, Italy

Collins, A., Brown, J. S., & Newman, S. E. (1989). Cognitive apprenticeship: Teaching the crafts of reading, writing, and mathematics. In L. B. Resnick (Ed.), *Knowing, learning, and instruction: Essays in honor of Robert Glaser* (pp. 453-494). Hillsdale, NJ: Lawrence Erlbaum Associates.

Cooper, A. (1995).The Myth of Metaphor. *Visual Basic Programmer's Journal.*

Grimley, D., Prochaska, J.O., Velicer, W.F., Vlais, L.M., & DiClemente, C.C., (1994). The transtheoretical model of change. In T.M. Brinthaupt & R.P. Lipka, *Changing the self: Philosophies, techniques, and experiences. SUNY series, studying the self* (p. 201 – 227). Albany, NY: State University of New York Press

Huang, E. M. and Mynatt, E. D. (2003). Semi-public displays for small, co-located groups. In *Proceedings of the ACM Conference on Human Factors in Computing Systems, CHI 2003* (pp. 49-56).

Intille, S. S. (2003). Ubiquitous Computing Technology for Just-in-Time Motivation of Behavior Change (Position Paper). In *Proceedings of the UbiHealth Workshop' 2003.*

Lakoff, G., Johnson, M. (1981). *Metaphors We Live By*. Chicago: The University of Chicago Press.

Lave, J. & Wenger, E. (1991). *Situated Learning: Legitimate Peripheral Participation*. New York: Cambridge University Press

Lin, J., Mamykina, L., Delajoux, G., Lindtner, S., & Strub, H. (2006). Fish'n'Steps: Encouraging Physical Activity with an Interactive Computer Game, UbiComp'06, Springer-Verlag Berlin Heidelberg

Mamykina, L., Mynatt, E.D., Davidson, P.R., & Greenblatt D. (2008). MAHI: Investigation of Social Scaffolding for Reflective Thinking in Diabetes Management. In *Proceedings of ACM SIGCHI Conference on Human Factors in Computing, CHI 2008.*

Mamykina, L., Mynatt E.D., & Kaufman, D. (2006) Investigating Health Management Practices of Individuals with Diabetes. In Nielsen-Bohlman et al (Eds.), *Proceedings of the ACM SIGCHI conference on Human factors in computing systems, CHI'06*, Montreal, Canada/

Mynatt, E. D., Rowan, J., Craighill, S., & Jacobs, A. (2001). Digital family portraits: supporting peace of mind for extended family members. In *Proceedings of the SIGCHI Conference on Human Factors in Computing Systems* (pp. 333-340). Seattle, Washington, United States.

Nielsen-Bohlman, L., Panzer, A.M., & Hindig, D.A. (Eds.) (2004). *Health Literacy: A Prescription to End Confusion*. Washington, D.C.: The National Academic Press.

Stasko, J., Miller, T., Pousman, Z., Plaue, C., & Ullah, O. (2004). Personalized Peripheral Information Awareness through Information Art, In *Proceedings of UbiComp '04* (pp. 18-35). Nottingham, U.K

Tafte, E.R. (2001). *The Visual Display of Quantitative Information*. Cheshire, Connecticut: Graphics Press.

Tversky, B., Kugelmass, S., & Winter, A. (1991). Cross-Cultural and Developmental Trends in Graphic Production. *Cognitive Psychology, 23,* 515-557.

Wallston, BS, Wallston, KA, Kaplan, GD, & Maides, SA. (1976). Development and validation of the health locus of control (HLC) scale. *J Consult Clin Psychol 44*(4), 580-585.

Wooldridge, K, Graber, A, Brown, A, & Davidson, P. (1992). The relationship between health beliefs, adherence, and metabolic control of diabetes. *Diabetes Educator, 18*(6), 495-450

Xiong, R. & Donath, J. (1999). PeopleGarden: creating data portraits for users. In *Proceedings of the 12th Annual ACM Symposium on User interface Software and Technology* (Asheville, NC, United States, November 07 - 10, 1999). UIST '99, pp. 37-44.

KEY TERMS

Chronic Disease Management: A set of practices that allow individuals with chronic diseases to control the development of their disease and avoid or delay development of complications. For example, for individuals affected with diabetes, disease management usually involves close monitoring of blood sugar levels, adjusting diet and maintaining an exercise routine.

Health Monitoring: A collection of techniques that allow collection of data pertaining to individuals' health. This collection could be performed manually or with the use of computing technologies. For example, in case of diabetes, health monitoring may include capture of blood sugar levels, records of individuals' diets and exercise routines.

Information Visualization: A set of techniques for visually presenting certain data or concepts. Common examples of information visualization include graphs, plots, various maps or illustrations. Recently this term became associated with a branch of computer science that focuses on computer-based techniques for generating such presentations. These computer-generated visualizations could be static or interactive and are usually meant to assist in analyzing and comprehending large volumes of data.

Metaphor-Based (or Metaphorical) Visualizations: Presentations of complex data that use common linguistic metaphors and real-world imagery as a their basis. One of the most familiar examples of metaphorical visualizations are genealogical trees that use a "life is a tree" metaphor implicit to many languages to depict a history of a family, using branches of the tree to represent "branches" of a family.

Relational Graphics: Visualizations of data that rely on abstract mapping between the data and particular visual properties, such as position in space, color, shape or size. Examples of relational graphics include different types of graphs, such as line, bar or pie, and most charts.

Social Scaffolding: A set of techniques and methods that allows teachers or experts to support novices or students in their learning process. Common examples of socials scaffolding include coaching, when a coach is observing a student's performance and provides feedback or learning by example, when an exert demonstrates certain techniques to students.

Chapter VI
RFID in Hospitals and Factors Restricting Adoption

Bryan Houliston
Auckland University of Technology, New Zealand

ABSTRACT

Hospitals are traditionally slow to adopt new information systems (IS). However, health care funders and regulators are demanding greater use of IS as part of the solution to chronic problems with patient safety and access to medical records. One technology offering benefits in these areas is Radio Frequency Identification (RFID). Pilot systems have demonstrated the feasibility of a wide range of hospital applications, but few have been fully implemented. This chapter investigates the factors that have restricted the adoption of RFID technology in hospitals. It draws on related work on the adoption of IS generally, published case studies of RFID pilots, and interviews with clinicians, IS staff and RFID vendors operating in New Zealand (NZ) hospitals. The chapter concludes with an analysis of the key differences between RFID and other IS, and which RFID applications have the greatest chance of successful implementation in hospitals.

INTRODUCTION

In 1989 management guru Peter Drucker described hospitals as prototypical knowledge-based organisations (Drucker, 1989). Considering the variety and volume of information that hospitals, and other health care organisations, deal with, it is easy to see why they might be expected to be early adopters of IS. Kim and Michelman (1990) identify the components of a typical integrated Hospital Information System (HIS): General accounting and budgeting; Staff payroll; Patient demographic information and medical records; Nursing care plans; Treatment orders; Test results;

Surgery and resource schedules; and Databases of clinical information relating to Radiology, Pharmacology, Pathology, and other specialist departments.

Yet research suggests that in comparison to other industries, the health care sector invests relatively little in IS. Twelve years on from Drucker's statement, a British survey of annual IS spending per employee found that the health care sector spent approximately one-third that of the manufacturing sector, one-fifth that of the distribution sector, and one-ninth that of the financial sector (Wallace, 2004). This low level of investment has led various stakeholders to demand greater use of IS in the health care sector. Two key areas in which significant potential benefits have been identified are improving patient safety, and sharing electronic medical records amongst all the health care organisations that may treat a patient.

Patient safety is, of course, paramount in health care. 'First, Do No Harm' is the fundamental principle of the medical profession. Yet each year medical mistakes take a heavy toll in both human life and health care resources. For example, errors in administering drugs, known as Adverse Drug Events (ADEs), are believed to result in tens of thousands of deaths, many more serious injuries, and to cost the health care sector tens of billions of dollars (Classen, Pestotnik, Evans, Lloyd, & Burke, 1997; Davis et al., 2003; Johnson & Bootman, 1995; Wilson et al., 1995). The US Institute of Medicine (IOM) strongly advocate the use of IS to reduce the incidence of ADEs (Institute of Medicine, 2001). Regulatory agencies, such as the Food and Drug Administration (FDA) and Joint Commission on Accreditation on Healthcare Organisations (JCAHO), have mandated the use of barcode technology in US hospitals to improve identification of medications and patients (Merry & Webster, 2004). The NZ Ministry of Health has recently announced plans to spend NZ$115 million to implement systems such as Computerised Physician Order Entry (CPOE) and Barcoded Medication Administration (BCMA) (Johnston, 2007).

The leading cause of ADEs is the prescription of unsuitable drugs (Bates, Cullen, & Laird, 1995; Leape, Bates, & Cullen, 1995). Unsuitable prescriptions result primarily from clinicians lacking ready access to patients' medical records, and thus being unaware of drug allergies, existing conditions, and current prescriptions. Storing medical records in electronic form, in a centralised database, enables timely access to such information for all clinicians who may treat a patient. In the UK, the government is planning to spend around £6 billion on an Electronic Patient Records (EPR) system for the National Health Service (NHS) as part of the 'Connecting for Health' initiative (Wallace, 2004). In NZ, the WAVE (Working to Add Value through E-information) Advisory Board to the Director-General of Health recommended a similar system (WAVE Advisory Board, 2001), which has been included in the country's Health Information Strategy (Health Information Strategy Steering Committee, 2005). In Australia a non-profit company created by federal and state governments, the National e-Health Transition Authority (NEHTA), invests in IS that supports sharing of EPRs. The same approach has been taken in Canada, with the Health Infoway corporation. In the US, major insurers, such as Medicare, require hospitals to provide details of treatment in electronic form (Jonietz, 2004).

One technology that has been gaining attention in the health care sector for its potential to address these issues is RFID. It offers very similar functionality to barcode technology, but with a number of advantages (Schuerenberg, 2007). Most notably, RFID allows multiple labels to be scanned simultaneously without requiring a line-of-sight between the scanner and the label. A range of RFID applications, from real-time stocktaking, to tracking patients, staff and equipment to storing patient data, have been successfully trialled by hospitals around the world (Wasserman, 2007). Based on published case studies, relatively few hospitals have fully implemented such systems. At the time of writing, NZ hospitals are just beginning to RFID pilots.

This chapter seeks to investigate the factors that have restricted the adoption of RFID technology in hospitals. The next section, RFID and Hospital IS, describes the various RFID applications piloted in hospitals. It then reviews research on the adoption of IS generally by hospitals, identifying a number of key organisational and technological factors. To gain greater insight of these factors in the NZ context, a series of interviews were conducted with clinicians, IS staff and RFID vendors operating within the NZ hospital environment. The section Interviews and Findings briefly describes the interview process and presents the results. The Discussion section considers some implications of this research for RFID pilots in NZ hospitals, and some possible areas for further research.

RFID AND HOSPITAL IS

This section describes the various RFID applications piloted in hospitals. It then reviews research on the adoption of IS generally by hospitals, and concludes with the aims of the current research.

RFID Applications for Hospitals

Hospitals all around the world have successfully trialled RFID applications. These applications can be broadly organised into four types. Identification applications involve a single reader interrogating a single tag. Data storage applications are those where a single reader reads and writes to a single tag. Location-based applications involve a single reader reading multiple tags. Tracking applications involve multiple readers reading single or multiple tags. Examples of each application are given below.

Identification Applications

Identification of people, objects and locations is an obvious application of RFID technology. Security systems that use RFID proximity cards to control access to restricted areas are perhaps the most common RFID application in use today. Even in developing countries, such as Bangladesh, hospitals are using RFID-enabled staff ID cards (Bacheldor, 2008). Other hospitals have extended the use of staff ID cards to control access to computers and applications (Bacheldor, 2007d).

Patient identification appears to be the next most common application, after access control. A survey of US health care organisations found that 29% expected to be using RFID wristbands for patient identification by the end of 2007 (Malkary, 2005). One example is the US Navy, whose medics in Iraq have trialled RFID dog-tags and wristbands in the field, attaching them to injured servicemen, refugees and prisoners of war. The tags can be read even in harsh desert and battlefield conditions (Greengard, 2004).

Drug identification is an application attracting growing interest, as it is the basis for both medication administration and e-pedigrees. Intended to combat the counterfeiting, dilution and diversion of drugs, e-pedigrees are mandated in the US under the Prescription Drug Marketing Act. The FDA, which will administer the law, advocates RFID as their preferred technology for keeping e-pedigrees. Drug manufacturers such as Pfizer, GlaxoSmithKline, and Johnson & Johnson have trialled RFID 'e-pedigrees' for their products (Herper, 2004)

At the Georgia Veteran's Medical Centre RFID has been used for location identification (Ross & Blasch, 2002). Patients with visual impairments can navigate around the hospital by reading these location tags with using a cane containing an RFID reader.

Location-Based Applications

Once patients, staff, and drugs and other medical consumables are identified by RFID tags, it becomes possible to automate a number of manual processes that happen at specific locations. One example is prevention of retained surgical items.

Sometimes known as the NoThing Left Behind (NTLB) policy, this involves checking that surgical implements and supplies used during an operation have been removed from the patient before they leave theatre. More than 30 hospitals around the US already employ a system that allows surgeons to use an RFID wand to detect tagged surgical sponges left inside patients (Japsen, 2008).

Medication administration is another example. At the University of Amsterdam Medical Centre, patients awaiting blood transfusion are issued RFID wristbands. The blood products are also tagged. By reading the two RFID tags prior to starting the transfusion, the risk of a patient receiving incorrect blood is reduced (Wessel, 2007b). Similar systems apply the same principle to patients receiving general, anaesthetic, and chemotherapy drugs.

'Smart' cabinets, are already in use in a number of hospitals (Collins, 2004). Drugs and other consumables are tagged, allowing RFID readers inside the cabinets to read them. Inventory levels can then be monitored in real time, and warnings given about expired items or items low stock levels. The cabinets may also read the RFID badges of staff, allowing only authorised people to access restricted drugs. Smart cabinets are relatively expensive, and tagging large numbers of items can be costly and time-consuming. As a result, some companies have started to provide and monitor cabinets as a managed service, with monthly fees rather than a large up-front cost (Bacheldor, 2007a, 2007f).

RFID makes it safer to take inventory of sterilised items, hazardous chemicals, and other objects with which people should have minimal contact. Sokol and Shah (2004) describe how a US surgical supplies company have embedded RFID tags in over 1 million re-usable surgical gowns and drapes. These are cleaned, assembled into surgical packs, and sterilised. As a final step in the process an RFID reader scans the contents of the pack, verifying that it is complete without compromising the sterilisation.

National University Hospital and Alexandra Hospital in Hong Kong used a location-based application for quarantine management during the SARS epidemic of 2002/03 (Roberti, 2003). Two areas were set aside for patients with SARS-like symptoms. All patients, staff and visitors entering these areas were issued with RFID-enabled cards and their movements recorded. Had any patients within these areas been diagnosed with SARS, it would have been possible to identify all the people they had been in contact with during the incubation period.

Tracking Applications

RFID technology is being used to track thousands of wheelchairs, beds, IV pumps and other pieces of expensive medical equipment at several hospitals, including Bielefeld City Clinic in Germany (Wessel, 2007a), Lagos de Moreno General Hospital in Mexico (Bacheldor, 2007c), and the Walter Reed Army Medical Centre in the US (Broder, 2004). Each item is tagged and can be located in real time via a network of RFID readers throughout the hospital. Some such systems, often referred to as Real Time Location Systems (RTLSs), also keep track of whether the equipment is available, in use, awaiting cleaning, or undergoing maintenance.

If patients and staff are tagged for identification, then patient tracking and staff tracking are also possible. Systems are already available commercially for tracking babies. Osborne Park Hospital in Australia places RFID bands on the legs of newborn babies (Deare, 2004), following a kidnapping from its maternity ward. Readers around the ward allow the location of each baby to be tracked. Readers at the exits set off an alarm if they detect a baby being removed from the ward without the presence of an authorised staff member. Alerts are also raised if the ankleband is cut, or if it remains stationary for some time. This may indicate that the band has been removed, or that there is something wrong with the baby.

By collecting tracking data over time, hospitals can also use workflow analysis to gain insights into, and identify possible improvements to, their procedures. Huntsville Hospital (Bacheldor, 2007e) is using a system to analyse patients and staff movements up to and following surgery. Ospdedale Traviglio-Caravaggio in Italy has been using RFID to analyse the progress of patients from first arrival in the Emergency Department (ED) (Swedberg, 2008).

The cost of tracking systems can be significant, depending on the area to be covered, the number of items to be tracked, and the accuracy required. This cost can be reduced by employing existing wireless networks. For example, Lagos de Moreno General Hospital's system operates over its Wi-Fi (802.11) network, using the access points as RFID readers and simplified network cards as tags. Walter Reed Army Medical Centre's RTLS works over a Zigbee (802.15) network. RTLS systems are also available as a managed service, with monthly fees rather than a large up-front cost (Bacheldor, 2007b).

Data Storage Applications

The applications described above typically read only the RFID tag's identifier, and retrieve or update data across a network. But more advanced tags also permit data to be stored on the tag itself. Georgetown University Hospital has trialled a system where the patient's RFID wristband stores their blood type, allergies and medications (Schuerenberg, 2007). This allows the data to be viewed quickly even when network access is not available.

IS Adoption in Hospitals

The case studies above contain individual hospitals' experiences with RFID technology. But there is little research on the overall uptake of RFID in the health care sector. In comparison, there is a more significant body of research on adoption of IS generally.

The research suggests that hospitals, and the health care sector as a whole, spend relatively little on IS. A recent survey of US hospitals shows that almost 50% spend between 1% and 2.5% of their budget on IS, with 20% spending less and 30% spending more (Morrissey, 2004). According to the IOM, the health care sector ranks 38th out of 53 industries in IS spending per employee, at about 1/25th the level of securities brokers (Institute of Medicine, 2001). A more recent survey in the UK showed a similar pattern, with IS spending per employee in the health care sector approximately one-ninth of that in the financial industry (Wallace, 2004).

There are a number of reasons why measuring IS investment per employee may give low figures for the health care sector. One reason is the nature of work in a hospital. Hospitals generally operate 24/7. Medical staff spend a large part of their day on rounds or in theatre, rather than at a desk (Reddy & Dourish, 2002). So while a personal computer (PC) in an office may be used by one person for eight hours a day, a hospital PC is likely to be used by three shifts a day and multiple people during each shift. A second reason is that in comparison to a financial institution, hospitals employ a lot of support staff. Cleaners, caterers, orderlies and the like typically have less need for IS than, for instance, securities brokers.

IS has also frequently proven to be a bad investment for hospitals in the past. Rosenal et al (Rosenal, Paterson, Wakefield, Zuege, & Lloyd-Smith, 1995) state that "the set of all successful HIS implementations is only slightly larger than the null set". Littlejohns et al (Littlejohns, Wyatt, & Garvican, 2003) suggest that around 75% of hospital IS projects fail. Heeks et al (Heeks, Mundy, & Salazar, 1999) offer a brighter picture, giving a failure rate of only 50%.

The work of Heeks et al is one of the few pieces of research to analyse a number of HIS projects and attempt to generalise some theory as to why they fail. They conclude that the probability of failure is proportional to the size of 'Concept-

Reality' gaps. The larger the gap between the HIS designers' concept of a system and the end users' reality, the more likely the system is to fail. While this conclusion is hardly novel, and is not specific to hospitals, the authors do identify seven dimensions on which gaps may occur: Information, Technology, Processes, Objectives, Skills, Management and Resources.

A more common approach taken by researchers of HIS success and failure has been to contextualise a general model. For example, England et al (England, Stewart, & Walker, 2000) apply some of Rogers' seminal work on the diffusion of innovation within organisations (Rogers, 1995) to the diffusion of IS within hospitals. Rogers identified eight organisational factors, shown in Table 1, and five technological factors, shown in Table 2. Evaluating the organisational factors from an analysis of Australian hospitals, England et al conclude that IS innovations would be expected to diffuse slowly. Based on the technological factors, they further conclude that administrative IS, such as accounts and payroll, would diffuse more quickly than more strategic or clinical IS.

Although England et al have attempted to base their arguments on previously published research, they note that there is a dearth of suitable mate-

Table 2. Technological factors affecting the diffusion of IS (adapted from Rogers, 1995)

New technology will diffuse faster to the extent that it...
Provides relative advantage over existing technology
Is compatible with existing technologies
Has low complexity
Has been observed to be successful for other users
Can be trialled with minimal disruption to normal activities

rial. Thus a number of their arguments seem to be based on their personal experience, which is not documented in any detail. In addition, their framework is relatively simple. Pettigrew et al (Pettigrew, Ferlie, & McKee, 1992) and Greco and Eisenberg (1993), for instance, have developed models of innovation in hospitals that also include their general environment. An earlier model developed by Stocking (1985) also includes the characteristics of individuals. Rogers' own work highlighted the importance of this factor. He classified individuals into five types, based on how early they adopt innovation: Innovators, Early adopters, Early majority, Late majority, and Laggards.

The work of England et al does have the advantage of being the most recent of the models considered. In addition, it relates to the Australian hospitals, which are commonly used as comparisons in NZ health research (Jackson & Rea, 2007).

Organisational Factors

The findings of Rogers and England et al on organisational factors are summarised in the following sections. Related information on the NZ health care sector is also presented, based on the general environmental factors identified by Pettigrew et al and Greco and Eisenberg.

Table 1. Organisational factors affecting the diffusion of IS (adapted from England et al., 2000)

Factors that lead to faster diffusion	Present in Australian hospital environment?
Executive sponsorship	Unclear
Decentralised IS control	No
Complex work and educated staff	Yes
Lack of formal procedures	No
Highly interconnected departments	No
Readily available resources	No
Large size	Yes
Openness to outside ideas	No

Executive Sponsorship

Rogers finds that if an organisation's leaders have a positive attitude towards change, then innovations will diffuse more quickly. England et al find that there is not enough published research on the attitude of hospital executives towards IS to evaluate this factor.

In the NZ health care sector there are a number of executive layers that may impact on hospital operations. As figure 1 illustrates the Minister of Health, the Health Ministry, and the relevant District Health Board (DHB) have direct input. The Accident Compensation Corporation (ACC), an agency of the Department of Labour, also has some indirect input.

Figure 1. Stakeholders in the NZ health care sector (Ministry of Health, 2008b)

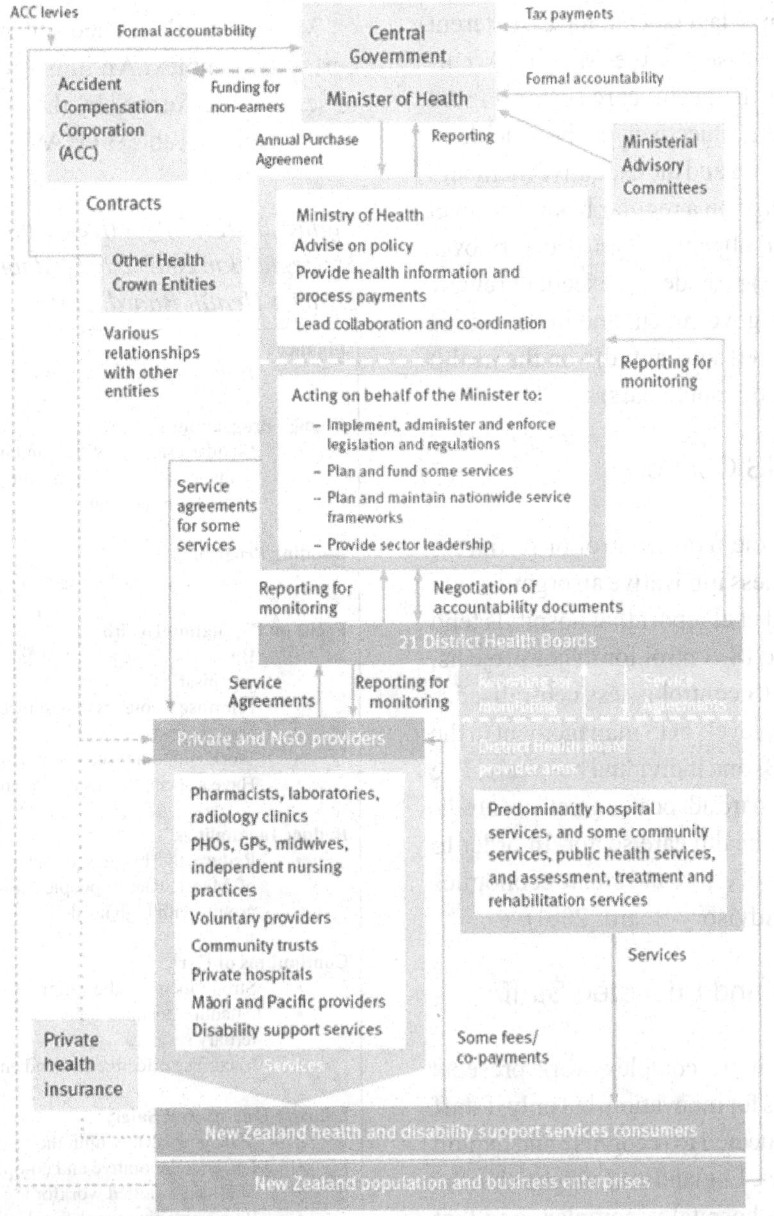

NGO = Non-Government Organisation
PHO = Primary Health Organisation

Figure 2. Ministry of Health's Health Strategy objectives (Ministry of Health, 2003b)

- Acknowledge the special relationship between Maori and the Crown under the Treaty of Waitangi.
- Good health and wellbeing for all New Zealanders throughout their lives.
- An improvement in health status of those currently disadvantaged.
- Collaborative health promotion and disease and injury prevention by all sectors.
- Timely and equitable access for all New Zealanders to a comprehensive range of health and disability services, regardless of ability to pay.
- A high-performing system in which people have confidence.
- Active involvement of consumers and communities at all levels.

These executive layers can have different objectives. Figure 2 shows the Ministry's current objectives for the health care sector. Figure 3 shows the current objectives of the Auckland DHB. As the Minister and the executive members of each DHB change on a regular basis, the level of sponsorship and objectives can also vary over time. Easton (2002) provides an excellent review of how changes in government and in the role of DHBs have impacted substantially on the health sector over the last twenty years.

Decentralised IS Control

Rogers finds that the more control of resources is centralised, the less innovative an organisation becomes. England et al report that hospitals tend to have centralised IS control for major projects, while day-to-day IS control is less centralised.

In NZ, there are levels of IS management in the Ministry, the DHBs and individual hospitals. The WAVE Advisory Board advocates greater centralisation of IS in the health care sector, in order to reduce duplication of effort and create economies of scale (WAVE Advisory Board, 2001).

Complex Work and Educated Staff

Rogers finds that more complex work presents more opportunities for innovation, but only if staff are sufficiently educated to recognise and exploit those opportunities. England et al suggest that the medical work in a hospital is complex, and that the staff who carry it out are highly educated.

Medical work carried out in NZ hospitals is certainly complex. An illustration of the variety of services performed by the NZ health care sector is given in Table 3 (WAVE Advisory Board,

Figure 3. Key objectives from Auckland DHB Strategic Plan 2002-2007 (adapted from Auckland District Health Board, 2002)

Finances
- Reduce the current level of deficit

Change Programme
- Standardise, consolidate and integrate services
- Collaborate across all health services to streamline care and to secure more cost-effective health gain

Building Programme
- Finish the building programme

Focus on Population Health
- Build the research and analytical base of the organisation
- Prioritise resources to best meet health and disability service needs
- Work with other sectors and agencies
- Have a special focus on the prevention of diabetes

Reduce Inequalities
- Reduce the barriers to service to meet the needs of Maori, Pacific people, new migrants and other groups with high needs

Continuums of Care
- Strong focus on the patient
- Attention to links between primary, secondary and tertiary services
- Maximise effectiveness and encourage integration

Improve Quality and Safety
- Manage growth within the resources available
- Foster collaborative and co-operative relationships
- Maintain a skilled workforce
- Reduce waiting times for elective surgery

2001). It is less clear whether the administrative work is any more complex than that carried out in other organisations.

Medical staff in NZ must be well educated. However, as Chassin points out, medical training conditions doctors to be self-reliant, and to reject support systems (Chassin, 1998). This is supported by a recent survey of administrative staff, nurses and general practitioners (GPs) in NZ (Engelbrecht, Hunter, & Whiddet, 2007).

Lack of Formal Procedures

Rogers finds that an organisation with formal procedures is less likely to innovate. England et al suggest that hospitals do officially have many formal procedures, but in everyday work are somewhat more flexible. An example of this is provided by Heeks et al, who describe a scenario where nurses followed a procedure that was morally and clinically sound, but officially prohibited.

Highly Interconnected Departments

Rogers finds that highly interconnected departments lead to a faster rate of diffusion, because innovations can flow more easily between them. England et al point out that hospital departments are not generally highly interconnected. They particularly note the different perspectives of medical staff and managers, and the professional sub-cultures or 'tribes' that are formed by medical staff with the same specialities.

Readily Available Resources

Rogers finds that innovation is more likely to happen if time and resources are available to do it. England et al suggest that public hospitals are unlikely to have such resources due to "constant funding pressure".

The NZ government funds around 77% of total health care funding. The remaining 23% is paid by individuals or private insurers for treatment

Table 3. Health care events in an average day in New Zealand (adapted from 1 Ministry of Health, 2008a; 2 Ministry of Health, 2006)

160 people are born[1]
78 people die[1]
83,000 prescriptions are filled[1]
66,000 laboratory tests are analysed[2]
6,000 outpatients visit hospitals for treatment[1]
275 people have elective surgery[1]
29 people are diagnosed with diabetes[2]
1,450 people visit an Accident and Emergency department[2]
1,350 people are admitted to hospital[1]
94,000 people take an anti-depressant medication[2]
235,000 people take a cholesterol lowering drug[2]
25 people have a heart attack[1]
127 children are immunised[2]
2,124 children and teenagers visit the dentist[2]
47 asthmatics are admitted to hospital[2]
ACC receives 4,100 new claims[2]
55,000 people visit their GP[1]

in private hospital. Public and private spending on health care have both risen by an average of 5% per year over the past 10 years. According to Organisation for Economic Co-operation and Development (OECD) figures, NZ's health care spending per capita and as a proportion of GDP are both just below the median for developed countries. Health care spending per capita is approximately 81% of that in the UK health care sector, 66% of that in Australia, and 34% of that in the US (Ministry of Health, 2007).

Public hospitals in NZ are extremely limited in their ability to borrow from private sector financial institutions (Ministry of Health, 2003a).

The government runs the Crown Funding Agency (CFA) to provide loans and credit to public sector bodies, including DHBs.

Large Size

Rogers finds that innovation happens more quickly in larger organisations, as they have more people to identify opportunities and more resources available to exploit those opportunities. England et al have classified hospitals as large, but don't state what metric they have based this on.

Hospitals are certainly large organisations in the NZ context, where 96% of businesses employ fewer than 20 people (Ministry of Economic Development, 2007). But in comparison to hospitals in other countries, NZ's are relatively small by most measures. Considering budget, the figures given above illustrate that NZ's is substantially less than the UK, Australia and the US. Considering infrastructure, as approximated by the number of public hospital beds per capita, NZ has half the level of Australia and 60% that of the UK (Jackson & Rea, 2007). Considering the number of staff, NZ pales in comparison to the UK's NHS, which is the third largest employer in the world (Wallace, 2004).

Table 4. Levels of evidence in EBM (adapted from Canadian Task Force on Preventive Health Care, 1997)

I	Evidence from at least one well-designed randomized controlled trial
II – 1	Evidence from well-designed controlled trials without randomization
II – 2	Evidence from well-designed cohort or case–control analytic studies, preferably from more than one centre or research group
II – 3	Evidence from comparisons between times and places with or without the intervention; dramatic results from uncontrolled studies (e.g., results of treatment with penicillin in 1940s)
III	Opinions of respected authorities, based on clinical experience; descriptive studies or reports of expert committees

Openness to New Ideas

Rogers finds that organisations that are open to new ideas are able to learn about innovations and evaluate them more easily. England et al state that medical staff tend to be open to new ideas only from within their professional sub-culture.

In terms of Rogers' classification of individuals' adoption of IS, Mathie (1997) finds that doctors generally view Innovators as "misfits", but respect Early adopters as "opinion leaders". Mathie suggests that the adoption of clinical IS is slowed by the principle of Evidence-Based Medicine (EBM). EBM requires that a new medical practice should not be used until there is sufficient evidence that it is safe and effective. Table 4 shows a typical scale for levels of evidence (Canadian Task Force on Preventive Health Care, 1997). In reviewing literature for this chapter, no IS evaluations were found that might be considered 'well-designed randomized controlled trials'.

Even when an IS is adopted by some clinicians, there is no assurance of widespread diffusion. For example, Morrissey (2003) reports that Computerised Physician Order Entry (CPOE) has recently been approved as an evidence-based standard by an, albeit privately managed, medical standards organisation in the US. Yet only 24% of hospitals are planning to implement it. Of those that aren't, 54% state that it is because doctors are resistant to using it.

Technological Factors

The findings of Rogers and England et al on technological factors are summarised in the following sections.

Relative Advantage

Rogers finds that innovations that offer many advantages over the status quo tend to diffuse more quickly than those that offer few or no advantages. England et al seem to suggest that IS managers in hospitals believe that IS produces relative advantage, but don't know how to prove it.

The literature clearly indicates that hospitals have problems evaluating IS. As Littlejohns et al (2003) point out, "the overall benefits and costs of hospital IS have rarely been assessed". Ammenwerth et al (2004) discuss some of the common barriers to performing and publicizing evaluations. These reflect a number of the organisational factors above, including a lack of formal procedures, a lack of resources, and insular departments. The authors summarise previous attempts at HIS evaluation frameworks, and conclude by drafting the Declaration of Innsbruck. Although it contains 12 valid recommendations, they are quite generic and relate to the evaluation process rather than to the evaluation details. For example, one recommendation is that an evaluation should be sufficiently funded.

Compatibility

Rogers finds that innovations that are highly compatible with the status quo tend to diffuse more quickly than ones that aren't. England et al suggest that, in the hospital context, administrative applications have the most compatibility because most people know how to use them. Larger, strategic applications have less compatibility because they generally require accompanying organisational changes. Clinical applications can also have frequent compatibility problems because of the difficulty of translating paper-based medical forms to electronic format.

Complexity

Rogers finds that innovations that are less complex tend to diffuse more quickly than those that are more complex. England et al don't appear to explicitly address complexity in their analysis.

Observability

Rogers finds that innovations that can be observed working successfully elsewhere will diffuse more quickly than those that can't. England et al suggest that successful HIS projects are so rare that observability is problematic.

At the time of writing, the only RFID application that is observable in NZ hospitals is access control. There are a small number of vendors developing or importing RFID systems for hospitals, that are observable in other countries (Hedquist, 2007). Outside of the health care sector, a number of RFID systems have been trialled or fully implemented in NZ: Livestock identification and tracking (Stringleman, 2003); Tracking carcasses on a meat processing line (Anonymous, 2004b); Identification of dogs and other pets (Department of Internal Affairs, 2005; New Zealand Veterinary Association, 2002); Timing runners competing in road races (Timing New Zealand, 2004); Identifying and tracking books in libraries (Anonymous, 2004a); and Identifying farm and forestry equipment to support a fuel delivery service (Anonymous, 2007). There have also been trials conducted by a small number of major retailers and manufacturers, and by customs officials for tracking cargo containers and identifying passports (Bell, 2004).

Trialability

A trial is defined by Rogers as testing an innovation in part before committing to it fully. He finds that innovations that can be easily trialled diffuse more quickly than those that can't. England et al suggest that small, stand-alone operational systems are more easily trialled than strategic or clinical systems.

Research Aims

At the time of writing, NZ hospitals are just beginning trials of RFID. Two pilot projects are in the early planning stages. The first will employ RFID for patient identification and patient tracking in an ED. The second will use RFID to replace or complement barcodes in an existing BCMA system used during anaesthesia (Houliston, 2005). The researcher has been an observer of the former project, and an active participant in the latter. This research has been conducted partly to inform the further development of these two projects, and others that may follow.

The analysis of England et al lead them to conclude that the organisational characteristics of Australian hospitals partly explain why they have been slow to adopt IS generally, and that they would be expected to adopt small, stand-alone, operational IS more quickly than strategic or clinical IS. The first aim of the current research was to investigate whether these conclusions are equally valid for NZ hospitals.

The second aim of the research was to consider RFID applications for hospitals in light of these conclusions. As NZ hospitals begin to pilot RFID applications, what implications do the hospitals' organisational characteristics, the applications' technology factors, and the strengths and weaknesses of RFID, as discussed in previous chapters, have for the likelihood of success?

INTERVIEWS AND FINDINGS

This section briefly describes the interview process and presents the findings.

Interviews

A number of research methods were considered for this research project. Surveys were ruled out primarily because other recent surveys on IT in NZ hospitals had shown a very low response rate (Lau, 2003). Observation was considered to be especially appropriate for gauging 'fuzzy' factors

Table 5. Backgrounds of interviewees

Interviewee	Background
M	M is a practicing doctor. He has recently been successful in getting a BCMA system implemented for anaesthesia in his DHB. He is the main sponsor for the anaesthetic RFID pilot. Interviews with M took place in person and by e-mail.
G	G is also a practicing doctor, and a colleague of M. Interviews with G took place in person.
C	C is doctoral researcher, primarily interested in systems that support patient safety. He has been researching alongside M. Interviews with C took place in person and by e-mail.
S	S is an experienced nurse in an Intensive Care Unit (ICU). She is an early adopter of IS, and is currently researching in the area of medical data mining. Interviews with S took place in person and by e-mail.
E	E is a nursing manager, with previous experience as a practicing nurse. Her current role includes some responsibility for the design, implementation and support of nursing IS. Interviews with E took place in person.
R	R is currently a management consultant in the private sector, but was previously the Chief Information Officer (CIO) of a DHB, and a project manager within the Ministry of Health. Interviews with R took place by e-mail.
D	D is a vendor who markets an RFID application for tracking staff and equipment to hospitals (so far with no sales in NZ) and companies in the transport industry. Interviews with D took place in person.
P	P is a vendor who does bespoke IS development for various organisations including hospitals. He is leading the vendor consortium involved in the ED RFID pilot. Interviews with P took place by telephone.
B	B is a technician for electronic medical equipment. Interviews with B took place by telephone.

such as 'Executive sponsorship', 'Complex work' and 'Interconnected departments'. However, this was judged to be a high-risk approach, given the researcher's inexperience with observational methods and the hospital environment. Interviews offered the best balance. They could be performed in less time than observation, but go into more detail than surveys. Given the lack of experience with RFID, interviews also provided an opportunity to introduce the technology to interviewees.

A total of nine people were interviewed. All were known to the researcher or his supervisor, or were referred by another interviewee. It had been the researcher's intention to interview more people, but availability was an issue. This may in itself be an indication of the time pressures resulting from organisational factors such as 'Complex work' and 'Readily available resources'. A brief background on each interviewee is shown in Table 5.

The interviews with M, G and C were done primarily in the context of designing a prototype for the anaesthetic RFID pilot. Therefore the technology factors were discussed more than the organisational factors. Organisational factors were mostly discussed in relation to their experiences in getting the existing BCMA system implemented.

The interviews with S, E and R were more structured. All followed a similar, two-part pattern. In the first part, interviewees were asked to describe at least one IS they had been involved with. For each IS, they were then asked whether it had been a success or failure, and what factors they perceived as being most significant in that outcome. The researcher explicitly mentioned Rogers' organisational factors only once, when E appeared to struggle with identifying factors. In the second part, the researcher briefly described RFID technology and the four types of application identified in the previous section. If the interviewee had not already done so, they were asked to indicate which application they thought

would be most useful to them. They were then asked to point out obvious problems that they could foresee with any of the applications.

The interviews with D and P were also structured. They were asked questions about making initial contact with a hospital, the management level of hospital staff they dealt with, how well-informed the staff were about RFID and its applications, requirements for reference sites and trials, and the most common reasons for IS implementations being delayed or abandoned.

The interview with B covered only RFID technology, particularly compatibility with existing hospital equipment and applications.

Findings

This section presents the findings from the interviews. The findings are grouped under the eight organisational and five technology factors identified in the previous section.

Organisational Factors

The organisational factors considered were: Executive sponsorship; Decentralised IS control; Complex work and Educated staff; Lack of formal procedures; Highly interconnected departments; Readily available resources; Large size; and Openness to new ideas.

Executive Sponsorship

England et al suggested that hospital executives could not be considered to have a consistently positive or consistently negative attitude towards IS. The interviews supported this.

S described a barcode-based costing system that she had implemented several years previously. Although the system was a success in her eyes, she eventually stopped using it because it had no executive sponsorship. As she puts it:

Management just didn't want to know that we spent $250,000 on this burns patient.

A lack of executive sponsorship does not necessarily mean the demise of an IS. M successfully implemented an anaesthetic BCMA system apparently without executive sponsorship. However, it should be noted that M is a senior staff member in his department, and getting his system implemented was:

... a long, and not altogether happy, tale.

An example of positive executive sponsorship was provided by E:

There's a pattern when you implement a new system. For the first two weeks users moan and complain because it's different. Then they're quiet for about a month. At six weeks there's another peak of grumbling. Then they realise that management are committed to the system, and they just accept it...

R noted that even when an IS had executive sponsorship, it did not necessarily make the IS a success:

We had systems on our books that should have been scrapped but weren't, because they were a manager's pet project. Officially they still exist, but no-one, except maybe the manager, uses them...

P stated that he had never had a DHB or hospital manager present at one of his product presentations. D also stated that he rarely has contact with managers, although the ED RFID pilot is an exception. The DHB's Chief Information Officer (CIO) been involved with the project since its inception.

E expressed a belief that executive sponsorship can be diluted by the large number of executives around hospitals. D gave an example from the ED RFID pilot. While the project has sponsorship from the DHB's CIO, IS management in the Ministry are ambivalent. They have expressed concern that it may conflict with Ministry plans for barcode-based systems.

Decentralised IS Control

England et al suggested that hospitals tend to have centralised IS control of major projects, but not necessarily of day-to-day operations. The interviews seem to support this.

As far as R was aware, the ministry and each DHB had a central IS group. However, he agreed that these IS groups exercise control mostly at the level of IS strategy and significant new projects. A large measure of this control is to satisfy the requirements of government. He noted that this is criticised in the WAVE report (WAVE Advisory Board, 2001): "There is a strong focus on spending [IS] money on governance and compliance, rather than on systems aligned to health goals".

R suggested that in day-to-day dealings with end-users, each hospital's IS group focused on support, not on control. This is supported by S, E and G, who were not aware of any policies enforced by the IS group at their hospital. E went so far as to suggest that the IS group wouldn't have sufficient influence with management and clinicians to enforce any major policies. She recalled an incident:

IS sent out a memo saying they were no longer going to support systems developed by the departments, without IS knowledge. They were very quickly asked, or instructed rather, by management to drop that particular policy.

P generally has IS staff attending his product presentations, but only from the individual hospital, never from the DHB or Ministry.

Complex Work and Educated Staff

England et al suggest that the medical work in a hospital is complex, and that the staff who carry it out are highly educated. The interviews support both these points.

All interviewees agreed with both points. R noted that:

I believe that all the medical staff I encountered, regardless of their paper qualifications, had the equivalent of a Masters' education.

Rogers found that educated staff are more likely to recognise and exploit opportunities for innovation. However, this is not always the case in hospitals. E pointed out that even highly educated and experienced staff are not necessarily natural innovators:

We get lots of complaints when new systems go in. But hardly any suggestions on how to make things better. Normally they just ask to go back to the way the previous system did things.

R suggested that senior doctors who work only part-time for the hospital might be more inclined to apply innovations in their private practice than in the hospital.

Lack of Formal Procedures

England et al suggested that hospitals had formal procedures, although they were not always followed. The interviews support this point.

R noted that, in his experience as a CIO:

Clinicians will typically not be comfortable with being limited to a single method of operation for any given system. This can be at variance with the desire of the IS professional to develop integrated and efficient systems.

This is illustrated well by M and C's anaesthetic BCMA system. It is a highly procedural system, carefully designed to reduce the likelihood of drug administration errors during surgery. Yet during simulated operation trials, half of the participants neglected the simple step of scanning the barcode before administering the drug (Merry, Webster, Weller, Henderson, & Robinson, 2002).

Another example was given by both S and E. Patients in their hospital were given barcoded wristbands, but neither knew which staff or procedures actually made use of the barcodes.

Highly Interconnected Departments

England et al suggest that hospital departments are not generally highly interconnected. The interviews support this.

R expressed his outsiders view:

The [healthcare] sector is highly tribal: There are at least 12 different practitioner groups. Within the doctors' ambit alone there are around 15 specialist colleges. There is traditionally a high level of distrust between practitioner groups. Even within one group of practitioners, there can be a high level of mistrust [sic]. All of this was exacerbated in NZ by the endless reforms and re-structures.

S expressed this 'mistrust' indirectly:

Whenever we (the ICU) get a new patient, we always go through the admission form again. The people in admissions never do it properly. It's not surprising – they're very busy.

Readily Available Resources

England et al suggest that public hospitals are unlikely to have readily available resources. The interviews support this point.

R believed that NZ hospitals do have readily available resources. He pointed to repeated increases in government funding and recent statistics on DHB deficits. The 21 DHBs had a combined deficit of NZ$58 million as at June 2004, although that was a significant decrease from the NZ$170 million deficit the previous year (Pink, 2004). But those resources were not readily available to IS:

Another factor that is, I think, unique to healthcare is that there is never enough money. Every dollar that is not directly spent on the delivery of care is questioned.

E agreed that investment in IS is very closely scrutinised, due to its unfortunate track record. Quoting from one of her Ministry of Health directives: "Following concern regarding the quality of health [IT] investment, the Minister of Health has directed that a stepped approval be required for information systems and communication technology" (Ministry of Health, 2003a). Any IS investment over $500,000 must be approved by the Director-General of Health. Any investment over $3 million must be approved by the Minister.

P believed that the time and effort required for hospital operational staff to get IS funding was the major cause for projects being delayed, cancelled or reduced in scope. He gave an example:

One hospital wanted [his product] to track their wheelchairs. I gave them a quote for a full system to cover the entire complex. They went with someone else who just put readers at the exits. They wanted something quickly and couldn't wait for approval.

S still had the barcode scanners from her abandoned costing system in a box under her desk. This raises the interesting question of what other unused IS resources from failed projects are in a similar position.

Large Size

England et al have classified hospitals as large. The issue of size was not raised in any of the interviews.

Rogers finds that innovation happens more quickly in larger organisations, as they have more staff to identify opportunities and more resources to exploit those opportunities. Given that 'Readily available resources' and 'Openness to new ideas'

already appear as separate factors, it may be that size is redundant in the case of hospitals.

Openness to New Ideas

England et al suggested that medical staff were generally not open to new ideas. The interviews support this point.

R suggested that being closed to new ideas was the result of medical training:

Healthcare workers take a very long term view. It takes ten years for a doctor to become fully qualified, so there is an inherent conservatism.

M and C provide an illustration of the challenges posed by the requirements of evidence-based medicine. They carried out two sets of simulated operation trials of their barcode-based ID (Merry et al., 2002; Webster, Merry, Gander, & Mann, 2004). The trials were level II-1 on the evidence-based medicine scale shown in table 4. The results were positive, yet there are still only a limited number of doctors using the system.

P and D both agreed that initial interest in RFID nearly always came from operational staff, and never from the medical staff. As P put it:

My first contact always comes from the guy who looks after, say, the wheelchairs. He finds that a lot are going missing. He searches the 'net and finds us.

P believes that operational staff are generally open to new ideas. Part of his standard product presentation is discussing how the staff could employ RFID beyond their initial problem.

Technological Factors

The technological factors considered were: Relative advantage over existing technology; Compatibility with existing technology; Low complexity; Trialability; and Observability.

Relative Advantage

M, G, C, S, E and R were asked which of the RFID applications described in the previous section would be the most useful to them. The responses illustrate that relative advantage is in the eye of the beholder.

M and G selected drugs identification. In particular, M was interested in using RFID to replace barcodes in their anaesthetic BCMA system, leading to the initiation of the anaesthetic RFID pilot. This would remove the need for anaesthetists to scan barcodes, which has proven to be a major usability issue for the BCMA system.

C was most interested in RFID 'smart' cabinets. He expressed particular interest in having alerts when drugs were about to reach their expiry date, and when quantities reached minimum levels.

S nominated data storage. If every person had an RFID chip containing their medical history embedded under their skin, this would mitigate the problem of having inaccurate or incomplete details on patient admission forms. She went so far as to suggest a 'Top 10' list of data to store.

E believed that nurses would be interested in anything that made their medication rounds easier. She thought that a medication administration would be most useful.

R suggested RTLS. He noted a problem that many hospitals have with theft of laptop computers, personal digital assistants (PDAs) and similar items. The ability to raise an alert when a piece of equipment leaves a particular area, and to track it, may help to prevent stolen items from leaving the building.

The issue of evaluating IS was raised with E and R, as the only two interviewees with any official responsibility for evaluation. R had a formal evaluation process, albeit inherited from a previous role in the private sector. E had no formal evaluation process, and tended to rely heavily on user feedback. She gave the example of an IS being selected by the doctors in one particular department:

They've been looking for nearly four years, and they're finally about to make a choice. Basically, we're so desperate to get something in place, we'll go along with whatever they decide.

D and P were asked how often the systems were replacing existing systems, and what benefits their clients expected. The ED RFID pilot, in which D was involved, was not replacing any existing system. P stated that his RTLS is often intended as a replacement for some form of manual 'equipment booking' system that hospital staff are too busy to use. The advantage is having a system automatically detect where a piece of equipment is, rather than staff having to write that on a board or enter it into a PC.

Compatibility

The interviewees raised a number of compatibility issues that they believed might impact on the adoption of particular RFID applications. They are discussed here grouped under the dimensions identified by Heeks et al.

Information: Two major issues regarding compatibility of information were raised by S. First, the medical data stored in embedded RFIDs must be compatible with the needs of end users. As noted above, the major reason for the failure of S's costing IS was that management did not want the information it produced. She also cited the National Health Index system (NHI) (NZ Health Information Service, 2004). Although an estimated 95% of the population are recorded in the system, the information kept is too basic to be of use. Second, the data must be consistent with that held in paper-based records.

Technology: B confirmed that there were potential compatibility issues with RFID technology and existing electronic medical devices, such as pacemakers. However, he suggested that a more likely problem would be other devices interfering with communication between RFID readers and tags. Surgical and medical diathermy machines are two examples of devices that emit much stronger electromagnetic fields than RFID. They are widely recognised as major sources of interference (Bassen, 2002).

D highlighted the importance of technology compatibility in his RFID pilot:

We had a few hospitals express an interest in running the trial. We chose [the pilot DHB] *because they have the wireless network infrastructure that makes it easiest for us.*

The other interviewees didn't mention any issues related to technology compatibility. Although RFID is novel in the hospital environment, all interviewees were familiar with related technologies such as barcodes and proximity cards.

Processes: All interviewees made the point that adopting RFID for a particular process should not prevent the process from being carried out as it is now. For example, M, G and C required that, if RFID labels were to replace barcode labels in their drug identification application, then the barcode must be printed on them. Then, if the RFID application failed, the existing barcode application could be reverted to.

E and S both suggested that staff would be reluctant to wear RFID tags. Both accepted that there were valid reasons for wearing them, such as authenticating access to smart cabinets. However, they expressed concern that the data gathered might be used for other purposes, such as covert tracking. As E put it:

There are managers who would love to know exactly how much time doctors and nurses spend on their feet.

E, S and R all believed that management would have to make the adoption of any RFID applications that involve tagging staff as transparent as possible.

Skills: D and P both reported that the hospital staff they interacted with knew little or nothing about RFID technology when they first gave product presentations. But all interviewees seemed to agree that medical staff already had the skills to deal with the RFID applications discussed. When it was found that few of the staff in S and E's departments used barcode scanners, the researcher pointed out that patient and drug identification applications would probably require the use of handheld devices, such as PDAs or tablet PCs. Even though the staff had little or no experience with these either, S and E believed they would have no difficulty learning to use them.

Some RFID applications may also require new skills to be learned by patients. S noted that if medical data were to be stored on embedded RFID chips, then the general public may have to be educated in protecting that data.

Resources: M, G and C are the only interviewees with whom the costs of RFID were discussed in any detail. The tag and reader prices mentioned did not appear to be a major concern. The researcher suggested that with the interest shown in RFID by pharmaceutical manufacturers, and the possible influence of DHBs and PHARMAC over pharmaceutical suppliers, the cost involved in tagging drugs may largely be met at those levels of the supply chain. M considered this unlikely at the current time.

Complexity

Two interviewees also raised complexity issues that they believed might impact on the adoption of particular RFID applications.

E suggested that getting all parties involved in the health care sector to agree on what medical data should be stored on an embedded RFID chip would be:

...next to impossible. That's why data in the NHI is so basic. It's mostly stuff that's available publicly from other sources.

B believed that designing networks of RFID readers to support an asset tracking application would be complex. While some IS groups have experience with RF engineering through the implementation of wireless networks, such networks consist largely of homogeneous components. In contrast, RFID tags are more heterogeneous. Patient identification applications, for example, are likely to use short-range, passive tags while RTLSs are likely to use longer-range, active tags. He also expected that keeping up to date with the RFID standards would be a challenge.

Trialability

The importance of trialability varied between the interviewees. It was vital for M, G and C. They regard the principles of evidence-based medicine as very important, particularly for the clinical systems that they use in theatre. This is illustrated by the simulated operation trials they performed on their own IS. D and P both stated that they always recommend trials of their systems before full implementation.

E provided a contrasting view. When asked specifically about trialability, her reply indicates that it isn't essential:

We don't normally have time for trials. We just put systems in. If they don't work we stop using them.

Observability

Observability appeared to be important for most of the interviewees. It was one of R's evaluation criteria, and he noted that it regularly appeared in proposals for major new IS projects. For instance, a recent proposal for a clinical HIS by one DHB is based largely on the success of the same system at a neighbouring DHB (Wright, 2003).

Both D and P stated that their clients always asked for reference sites. D recalled a meeting he attended where a few DHB CIOs were hosting a visiting Canadian CIO:

He asked what their innovation strategy was. [A NZ CIO] replied 'We look at what other hospitals have been doing for at least three years.

A further example of the importance of observability was provided at a demonstration of the prototype anaesthetic RFID system. In previous demonstrations the application had been standalone, simply displaying the RFID tag numbers of the items it was reading. In the last demonstration it was integrated with the existing BCMA system, providing the same functionality as using barcodes. As G commented:

It's one thing to see the tag numbers come and go on the screen. It's something quite different to see the drug names come up in [the existing IS].

DISCUSSION

This section proposes some refinements to the conclusions of England et al in light of the interview findings, and considers the implications for RFID applications. Some possible research areas for further grounded theory iterations are also highlighted.

Diffusion of IS in NZ Hospitals

The interview findings seem to suggest that there are three organisational factors where England et al's evaluation of Australian hospitals may differ for NZ hospitals. These are: Decentralised IS control, Lack of formal procedures, and Large size. Assigning *No* to 'Decentralised IS control' conceals the fact that day-to-day IS control is largely decentralised. Likewise, assigning *No* to 'Lack of formal procedures' conceals the fact that such procedures exist primarily at high levels. It is therefore suggested that these factors be assigned a value of *Unclear.*

Table 6. Organisational factors affecting the diffusion of IS in NZ hospitals (adapted from England et al., 2000)

Factors that lead to faster diffusion	Present in Australian hospital environment ?	Present in NZ hospital environment ?
Executive sponsorship	Unclear	Unclear
Decentralised IS control	No	*Unclear*
Complex work and educated staff	Yes	Yes
Lack of formal procedures	No	*Unclear*
Highly interconnected departments	No	No
Readily available resources	No	No
Large size	Yes	*Unclear*
Openness to outside ideas	No	No

It is suggested that the 'Large size' factor also be assigned a value of *Unclear*. The basis on which England et al classified Australian hospitals as large is not clear. However, on measures such as number of employees, spending per capita, and public hospital beds per capita, NZ hospitals are significantly smaller. Finally, the factor 'Large size' may be redundant, given the presence of the 'Readily available resources' factor.

Table 6 shows a comparison of the values suggested by England et al and the values suggested by this research, with differences highlighted. If each of these organisational factors had equal weighting in determining the rate of diffusion, then removing two *No*s and one *Yes* should result in a higher rate. Thus it might be expected to observe NZ hospitals diffusing IS, including RFID, more quickly than Australian hospitals. Yet that does not appear to be the case. This anomaly may be explained in a number of ways.

One possibility is that the organisational factors do not have equal weightings in determining the rate of diffusion, perhaps specifically in hospitals. The factors 'Highly interconnected departments', 'Readily available resources', and 'Openness to new ideas' appear to outweigh the factors 'Decentralised IS control', 'Complex work and educated staff', 'Lack of formal procedures', and 'Large size'. Based simply on the number of times that these factors were mentioned in the interviews, this seems plausible. However, that is based on the researcher's interpretations of interviewee responses. A more explicit, quantitative research method, such as a questionnaire with all the factors listed, should be used to confirm this.

Another possibility is that there are additional organisational factors, perhaps specific to hospitals, that are not included in Rogers' work and have not been considered by England et al. In analysing the interviews for this research, statements were associated with the established factors. Analysing the interviews without these *a priori* classifications may highlight new factors.

A third possibility is that RFID technology is sufficiently different from the generic innovation considered by Rogers and the general IS considered by England et al, that some of the organisational factors have a different effect on its diffusion. Specifically, the factor 'Large size' may have an exaggerated effect on the diffusion of RFID, or the factors 'Decentralised IS control' and 'Lack of formal procedures' may have a minimal or even negative effect.

Decentralised IS control may in fact decrease the diffusion rate of RFID. RFID is an infrastructure technology, similar to other networking technologies such as mobile phones or wireless networks. The pattern seen with other infrastructure technologies is that diffusion is slow until a critical mass of end users is reached, at which point diffusion increases sharply (Rogers, 1995). Reaching the critical mass of end users is likely to be easier for an organisation with centralised IS control than for an organisation with decentralised IS control. Centralised IS control should ensure that all end users have compatible technology. With decentralised IS control, end users may independently choose incompatible technologies. This is likely to result in a longer wait for one technology to reach a critical mass of end users. Even when this does occur, there may be resistance from end users of other technologies to adopt a new one. This resistance may be exacerbated in the health care sector by the presence of non-interconnected departments.

A lack of formal procedures may also decrease the diffusion rate of RFID. A formal, documented procedure lends itself to automation more easily than an informal, unwritten procedure. This is illustrated by the fact that physical security, a domain with many formal procedures, is currently the most widespread application for RFID technology. Walker et al suggest that the greatest value of RFID will come from using it for "the real work of organising data to help trigger transactions and business rules" (Walker, Spivey Overby, Mendelsohn, & Wilson, 2003).

It is less obvious how large size might directly affect the diffusion of RFID. Large size implies more staff who may identify opportunities to apply RFID technology. But it has already been established that clinicians tend not to be open to outside ideas. Large size suggests more resources to exploit opportunities. But in the health care sector, resources are not readily available for investment in IS. Large size in terms of physical area or services provided may increase diffusion, as it offers improved trialability. RFID applications are frequently trialled in distinct areas of the hospital, such as the ED, or for specific services, such as blood transfusion. But diffusing an RFID application over a large physical area would be impeded by the lack of readily available resources to create a reader network. Diffusing across a range of services would be complicated by non-interconnected departments and a lack of openness to outside ideas.

Diffusion of RFID Applications

The interviews seem to suggest that all of Rogers' technological factors will impact on the diffusion of particular RFID applications, but not to the same extent. For instance, all interviewees raised issues about compatibility, but complexity issues were noted by only two. The interviews also seem to support England et al's conclusion that small, administrative or operational IS should diffuse more quickly than large, strategic or clinical IS. The three largest, most strategic applications discussed were data storage - RFID chips holding a person's medical data embedded under their skin - and hospital-wide staff tracking, and RTLS. More concerns were raised about the first two of these applications than any others.

Four classes of RFID application were identified in the section on RFID and Hospital IS. A discussion of the factors impacting on each class is presented in the following sections.

Identification Applications

Patient identification supports the major health care concern of easily sharing medical information. Drug identification directly supports the major concern of patient safety. In addition, drug identification was nominated by two interviewees as the applications that would be of the most benefit to them. Overall this suggests a high level of relative advantage. Thus it is no surprise to see that patient and drug identification are the major components of the first two RFID pilots in NZ hospitals.

As the first experience with RFID technology, there are likely to be issues around technology standards, integration with existing IS, training and other aspects of compatibility and complexity. But there are many patient identification systems already deployed overseas, so it should be more observable than other types of application. Trialability is possible by limiting the application to a single area of the hospital, as is being done in the NZ anaesthetic drug and ED patient RFID trials.

The cost of handheld RFID readers suitable for identification applications is relatively small. The cost of RFID wristbands for patient identification is minimal, since they can be re-used. However, the cost of tagging individual drug doses is likely to be the major impediment to the adoption of drug identification applications. The Ministry of Health gives cost as the primary reason for recommending the use of barcodes in its proposed BCMA system. Cost may become less of an issue if more pharmaceutical manufacturers and distributors choose, or are required by law, to adopt RFID for drug e-pedigrees.

Location-Based Applications

A number of location-based applications directly support the major health care concern of patient safety. Medication administration, prevention of retained surgical items, and quarantine management are clear examples. Smart cabinets offer indirect support by ensuring that sufficient quantities of drugs and supplies are in stock, and that they are not expired. Medication administration and smart cabinets were each nominated by one interviewee as the application that would be of the most benefit to them. Overall this suggests a reasonably high level of relative advantage.

These systems are typically automating standard operational practices, so should not be complex. But the interviewees did raise some compatibility issues, notably that staff may feel they are being monitored. Trialability of smart cabinets, for example, may be difficult if staff are able to avoid using them by obtaining drugs or supplies from other storage areas. The number of such systems implemented around the world is relatively low, which may make observability an issue.

As noted above, the cost of tagging individual drug doses and surgical items will be significant. Smart cabinets themselves are also expensive.

There are currently no companies in NZ providing them as a managed service, as there are in other countries.

Tracking Applications

Patient tracking applications directly support the major health care concern of patient safety. Staff tracking and RTLSs offer indirect support by ensuring that staff and equipment can be found quickly if required for an emergency. RTLS was nominated by one interviewee as the application that would be of the most benefit to them. Both vendors interviewed also deal mainly in patient tracking and RTLS, although not with any sales in NZ. Overall this suggests a medium level of relative advantage.

Tracking applications are the most complex of the four types discussed here. Some idea of the complexity is given by Sokol and Shah's detailed cost-benefit analysis for an RTLS (Sokol & Shah, 2004). Designing an effective RFID reader network requires expertise in RF engineering. Making use of existing wireless networks is one way to reduce complexity, but that creates potential compatibility issues with existing IS and requires more expensive tags. Tracking applications also have the most potential compatibility issues identified by interviewees. Most significant are the privacy of staff, and potential electromagnetic interference between RFID readers and common medical electronic devices. Despite these issues there have been a relatively high number of RTLSs piloted overseas, so observability should not be difficult. Trialability can be made easier by limiting the tracking to a specific area, such as a single ward.

The cost profile of tracking applications differs from the other four types discussed. They require more RFID readers, but significantly fewer tags than, for example, drug identification. The cost can be controlled by varying the degree to which existing wireless networks are used, the area to be covered, the number of people or items to be tracked, and the accuracy required. There are currently no companies in NZ providing RTLSs as a managed service, as there are in other countries.

Data Storage Applications

Data storage applications offer one solution to the major concern of easily sharing medical records. Storing patient medical data in an RFID tag was nominated by one interviewee as the application that would be of the most use to them. Overall this suggests a reasonably low level of relative advantage.

Compatibility of information is the most significant issue identified by interviewees. There must be agreement among potential users on what information is stored. Assuming that the information is encoded for security, and to compress it into the small storage space available on an RFID tag, there must also be agreement on encoding standards.

Writable RFID tags are currently more expensive than the read-only versions, but the cost difference is likely to decrease over time.

Future Research

This research would benefit from further interviews with a more representative range of people. The current group of interviewees is dominated by clinicians, who could be considered to be 'Innovators' or 'Early Adopters' under Rogers' classification, and whose experience is in public hospitals in the same DHB. Further interviews should include staff from other DHBs, and health care organisations other than public hospitals, more managers, more 'Late Adopters', and possibly some patients.

There is a danger in interviews that people give 'correct' responses rather than truthful responses. While the researcher didn't sense such behaviour during interviews conducted in person, it is more difficult to discern in an e-mail or telephone interview. As already noted, observation may have been a more suitable methodology for judging the true state of factors such as 'Executive sponsorship', 'Complex work and educated staff' and 'Highly interconnected departments'.

Privacy has emerged as a clear concern for RFID applications that involve staff tracking and smart cabinets. Further investigation seems warranted. What exactly are the privacy concerns of staff? What measures, if any, could be taken to reduce these concerns?

Security of RFID tags has been identified as a key issue for data storage applications. A number of approaches have been suggested in the research (Juels, Rivest, & Szydlo, 2003) but these mostly relate to the retail scenario. Are they suitable for securing tags containing medical information? Chao, Hsu and Miaou (2002) propose a scheme intended specifically for keeping medical data on an RFID chip confidential. There remain a number of aspects still to be investigated. For instance, how will the source of data written to a tag be authenticated? If it is done by a medical data certification authority, how might that function?

It is clear that most RFID trials and implementations are taking place in US hospitals. This may simply reflect the fact that the recent development of RFID technology has taken place largely in the US. It might also indicate that some aspect of US hospitals increases the diffusion of RFID. The major feature distinguishing US hospitals from those of other countries is the level of competition. Might operating in a competitive market affect the diffusion of RFID? Is the 'Need to compete' reflected in Rogers' organisational factors?

Executive sponsorship is widely regarded as a critical success factor for most types of IS. Further research on the attitude of hospital executives to IS, and RFID in particular, would be valuable.

CONCLUSION

This chapter has investigated the factors that have restricted the adoption of IS by hospitals, and specifically of RFID technology in NZ hospitals. The health care sector has historically invested relatively little in IS, in comparison to the manufacturing sector, the financial sector and most others. But this is to be expected. Hospitals and other health care organisations exhibit characteristics associated by Rogers with slow diffusion of innovation: No clear executive sponsorship; Centralised IS control; Formal procedures; Shortage of readily available resources; Little or no connection between departments; and Lack of openness to new ideas. When hospitals have implemented IS, there has been a high rate of failure.

In recent years governments, regulators, insurers, and consumers have been calling for the greater use IS to, among other things, make it easier to improve patient safety and more easily share patient medical records. The NZ government has played its part, supporting a National Health Index and Health Information Strategy, and planning to invest in CPOE and BCMA systems.

Innovative hospitals overseas, notably in the US, have been applying RFID technology to these problems. A range of applications, from simple patient identification to medication administration to real-time tracking of patients, staff and equipment have been successfully piloted. Despite this, and successful applications of RFID in other industries in NZ, local hospitals are just beginning RFID pilots.

Interviews conducted with practicing clinicians, a nurse manager, a CIO, an RF technician, and RFID vendors suggest that NZ hospitals may operate day-to-day with less centralised IS control and fewer formal procedures than hospitals in Australia, and perhaps other countries. While this might be expected to hasten the adoption of IS generally, it may explain why an infrastructural technology such as RFID has been slower to diffuse.

The two RFID pilots that are about to begin – anaesthetic drug identification and patient tracking in ED - will be closely observed by other NZ hospitals. The pilots have technological profiles that give them a good chance of success. They don't raise issues of privacy, security, or any of the other major concerns highlighted in the interviews. However both will be expensive to implement beyond the trial, and will have to demonstrate real benefits to the inherently cautious health care sector.

REFERENCES

Ammenwerth, E., Brender, J., Nykanen, P., Prokosch, H. U., Rigby, M., & Talmon, J. (2004). Visions and strategies to improve evaluation of health information systems: Reflections and lessons based on the HS-EVAL workshop in Innsbruck. *International Journal of Medical Informatics, 73*, 479-491.

Anonymous. (2004a). *Radio Frequency ID*. Retrieved November 1, 2004, from wiki.lianza. org.nz

Anonymous. (2004b). *RFID - Tracking every step you take*. Retrieved February 12, 2008, from www.istart.co.nz

Anonymous. (2007). *Tracient Technologies helps Mini Tankers NZ deliver to its customers*. Retrieved February 12, 2008, from www.istart. co.nz

Auckland District Health Board. (2002). *Proposed Strategic Plan for the Auckland District Health Board 2002-07*. Auckland.

Bacheldor, B. (2007a). *ASD Healthcare Deploys RFID Refrigerated Drug Cabinets*. Retrieved December 20, 2007, from www.rfidjournal.com

Bacheldor, B. (2007b). *AT&T Debuts Managed RTLS for Health Care Organisations*. Retrieved December 20, 2007, from www.rfidjournal.com

Bacheldor, B. (2007c). *Local Hospital Spearheads Mexico's Digital-Hospital Initiative*. Retrieved February 12, 2008, from www.rfidjournal.com

Bacheldor, B. (2007d). *N.J. Medical Center Uses LF Tags to Protect Patient Records*. Retrieved February 12, 2008, from www.rfidjournal.com

Bacheldor, B. (2007e). *RFID Documents Surgery at Huntsville Hospital*. Retrieved February 12, 2008, from www.rfidjournal.com

Bacheldor, B. (2007f). *UMass Med Centre Finds Big Savings Through Tagging*. Retrieved December 20, 2007, from www.rfidjournal.com

Bacheldor, B. (2008). *RFID Take Root in Bangladesh*. Retrieved February 12, 2008, from www.rfidjournal.com

Bassen, H. (2002). Electromagnetic Interference of Medical Devices and Implications for Patient Safety. *International Journal of Bioelectromagnetism, 4*(2), 169-172.

Bates, D. W., Cullen, D. J., & Laird, N. (1995). Incidence of Adverse Drug Events and Potential Adverse Drug Events. *Journal of the American Medical Association, 1995*(274), 29-34.

Bell, S. (2004). *Kiwi firms radio in RFID progress*. Retrieved April 12, 2004, from www.computerworld.co.nz

Broder, C. (2004). *Hospitals Wade into Asset-Tracking Technology*. Retrieved October 30, 2004, from www.ihealthbeat.com

Canadian Task Force on Preventive Health Care. (1997). *Levels of Evidence - Research Design Rating*. Retrieved October 1, 2004, from www.ctfphc.org

Chao, H. M., Hsu, C. M., & Miaou, S. G. (2002). A Data-Hiding Technique With Authentication, Integration, and Confidentiality for Electronic Patient Records. *IEEE Transactions on Information Technology in Biomedicine, 6*(1), 46-53.

Chassin, M. R. (1998). Is healthcare ready for sigma six quality. *Milbank Quarterly, 76*(4).

Classen, D. C., Pestotnik, S. L., Evans, R. S., Lloyd, J. F., & Burke, J. P. (1997). Adverse Drug Events in Hospitalized Patients: Excess Length of Stay, Extra Costs, and Attributable Mortality. *Journal of the American Medical Association, 277*, 301-306.

Collins, J. (2004). *Healthy RFID Rivalry for Hospitals*. Retrieved September 9, 2004, from www.rfidjournal.com

Davis, P., Lay-Yee, R., Briant, R., Ali, W., Scott, A., & Schug, S. (2003). Adverse events in New Zealand public hospitals II: preventability and clinical context. *New Zealand Medical Journal, 116*(1183).

Deare, S. (2004). *Hospitals Ga-Ga Over RFID*. Retrieved October 30, 2004, from www.pcworld.idg.com.au

Department of Internal Affairs, Dog Control (Microchip Transponder) Regulations 2005, (2005).

Drucker, P. (1989). *The New Realities*. New York: Harper & Row.

Easton, B. (2002). The New Zealand health reforms of the 1990s in context. *Applied Health Economics and Health Policy, 1*(2), 107-112.

Engelbrecht, J., Hunter, I., & Whiddet, R. (2007). Further Evidence of How Technology Availability Doesn't Guarantee Usage. *Health Care and Informatics Review*.

England, I., Stewart, D., & Walker, S. (2000). Information technology adoption in health care: when organisations and technology collide. *Australian Health Review, 23*(3), 176-185.

Greco, P. J., & Eisenberg, J. M. (1993). Changing physicians practices. *New England Journal of Medicine, 329*, 1271-1274.

Greengard, S. (2004). *A Healthy Dose of RFID*. Retrieved September 8, 2004, from www.rfid-journal.com

Health Information Strategy Steering Committee. (2005). *Health Information Strategy for New Zealand 2005*. Wellington: Ministry of Health.

Hedquist, U. (2007). *Orion Health teams with Oracle and Intel in Spain*. Retrieved February 12, 2008, from www.computerworld.co.nz

Heeks, R., Mundy, D., & Salazar, A. (1999). Why Health Care Information Systems Succeed or Fail. In A. Armoni (Ed.), *Health Care Information Systems: Challenges of the Next Millenium*: Idea Group Publishing.

Herper, M. (2004). *Tiny Chips Could Combat Counterfeit Pills*. Retrieved August 1, 2004, from www.forbes.com

Houliston, B. (2005). *Integrating RFID Technology into a Drug Administration System*. Paper presented at the Health Informatics NZ Conference, Auckland, New Zealand.

Institute of Medicine. (2001). *Crossing the Quality Chasm: A New Health System for the 21st Century*. Washington DC: National Academies Press.

Jackson, G., & Rea, H. (2007). Future hospital trends in New Zealand. *The New Zealand Medical Journal, 120*(1264).

Japsen, B. (2008, 2 January 2008). *Technology cuts risk of surgical sponges*. Retrieved February 12, 2008, from www.chicagotribune.com

Johnson, J. A., & Bootman, J. L. (1995). Drug-related Morbidity and Mortality: A Cost of Illness Model. *Archives of Internal Medicine, 155*, 1949-1956.

Johnston, M. (2007). Wired for saving lives. *Weekend Herald, August 25*, p. B4.

Jonietz, E. (2004). *Making Medicine Modern*. Retrieved August 1, 2004, from www.technologyreview.com

Juels, A., Rivest, R. L., & Szydlo, M. (2003). *The Blocker Tag: Selective Blocking of RFID Tags for Consumer Privacy*. Paper presented at the Tenth International Conference on Computer and Communication Security, Washington, DC.

Kim, K. K., & Michelman, J. E. (1990). An Examination of Factors for the Strategic Use of Information Systems in the Healthcare Industry. *MIS Quarterly, 14*(2), 201-215.

Lau, L. (2003). *Pen Based Computers in Health Care*. Unitec New Zealand, Auckland.

Leape, T., Bates, D. W., & Cullen, D. J. (1995). Systems Analysis of Adverse Drug Events. *Journal of the American Medical Association, 274*, 35-43.

Littlejohns, P., Wyatt, J. C., & Garvican, L. (2003). Evaluating computerised health information systems: hard lessons still to be learnt. *British Medical Journal, 326*, 860-863.

Malkary, G. (2005). *Healthcare without Bounds: Trends in RFID*. Menlo Park, CA: Spyglass Consulting Group.

Mathie, A. Z. (1997). Doctors and change. *Journal of Management in Medicine, 11*(6), 342-356.

Merry, A., & Webster, C. (2004). Bar Codes and the Reduction of Drug Administration Error in Anesthesia. *Seminars in Anesthesia, Perioperative Medicine and Pain, 23*, 260-270.

Merry, A., Webster, C., Weller, J., Henderson, S., & Robinson, B. (2002). Evaluation in an anaesthetic simulator of a prototype of a new drug administration system designed to reduce error. *Anaesthesia, 57*, 256-263.

Ministry of Economic Development. (2007). *SMEs in New Zealand: Structure and Dynamics*. Wellington: Ministry of Economic Development.

Ministry of Health. (2003a). *Guidelines for Capital Investment*. Wellington: Ministry of Health.

Ministry of Health. (2003b). *New Zealand Health and Disability Sector Overview.* Wellington: Ministry of Health.

Ministry of Health. (2006). A Day in the Life statistics. In DayInTheLife.xls (Ed.). Wellington, New Zealand.

Ministry of Health. (2007). *Health Expenditure Trends in New Zealand 1994-2004.* Wellington: Ministry of Health.

Ministry of Health (2008a). Every Day in New Zealand: DVD. Wellington: Ministry of Health.

Ministry of Health. (2008b). *Statement of Intent 2008-11.* Retrieved September 26, 2008, from www.moh.govt.nz

Morrissey, J. (2003). An info-tech disconnect. *Modern Healthcare, 33,* 6.

Morrissey, J. (2004). Capital crunch eats away at IT. *Modern Healthcare, 34,* 32.

New Zealand Veterinary Association. (2002). *Annual Report.* Retrieved November 1, 2004, from www.vets.org.nz

NZ Health Information Service. (2004). *National Health Index FAQ.* Retrieved August 31, 2004, from www.nzhis.govt.nz

Pettigrew, A., Ferlie, E., & McKee, L. (1992). *Shaping Strategic Change.* London: Sage.

Pink, B. (2004). *District Health Board Deficit Decreases.* Retrieved November 1, 2004, from www.stats.govt.nz

Reddy, M., & Dourish, P. (2002). *A Finger on the Pulse: Temporal Rhythms and Information Seeking in Medical Work.* Paper presented at the ACM Conference on Computer-Supported Co-operative Work, New Orleans, Louisiana.

Roberti, M. (2003). *Singapore Fights SARS with RFID.* Retrieved August 1, 2004, from www. rfidjournal.com

Rogers, E. M. (1995). *Diffusion of Innovations.* New York: The Free Press.

Rosenal, T., Paterson, R., Wakefield, S., Zuege, D., & Lloyd-Smith, G. (1995). *Physician involvement in hospital information system selection: a success story.* Paper presented at the Eighth World Conference on Medical Informatics, Vancouver, Canada.

Ross, D. A., & Blasch, B. B. (2002). Development of a Wearable Computer Orientation System. *ACM Personal and Ubiquitous Computing, 6*(1), 49-63.

Schuerenberg, B. K. (2007). *Bar Codes vs RFID: A Battle Just Beginning.* Retrieved October 2, 2007, from www.healthdatamanagement.com

Sokol, B., & Shah, S. (2004). *RFID in Health-care.* Retrieved October 30, 2004, from www. rfidjournal.com

Stocking, B. (1985). *Initiative and Inertia.* London: Nuffield Provincial Hospital Trust.

Stringleman, H. (2003). *Electronic identification comes a step closer.* Retrieved November 1, 2004, from www.country-wide.co.nz

Swedberg, C. (2008). *Italian Hospital Uses RFID to Document Patient Location, Treatment.* Retrieved February 12, 2008, from www. rfidjournal.com

Timing New Zealand. (2004). *Winning Time Timing System.* Retrieved November 1, 2004, from www.poprun.co.nz

Walker, J., Spivey Overby, C., Mendelsohn, T., & Wilson, C. P. (2003). *What You Need to Know About RFID in 2004.* Retrieved February 9, 2004, from www.forrester.com

Wallace, P. (2004). The Health of Nations. *The Economist, 372,* 1-18.

Wasserman, E. (2007). *A Healthy ROI.* Retrieved October 12, 2007, from www.rfidjournal.com

WAVE Advisory Board. (2001). *From Strategy to Reality: The WAVE Project.*

Webster, C., Merry, A., Gander, P. H., & Mann, N. K. (2004). A prospective, randomised clinical evaluation of a new safety-orientated injectable drug administration system in comparison with conventional methods. *Anaesthesia, 59,* 80-87.

Wessel, R. (2007a). *German Hospital Expands Bed-Tagging Project.* Retrieved February 12, 2008, from www.rfidjournal.com

Wessel, R. (2007b). *RFID Synergy at a Netherlands Hospital.* Retrieved October 31, 2007, from www.rfidjournal.com

Wilson, R. M., Runciman, W. B., Gibberd, R. W., Harrison, B. T., Newby, L., & Hamilton, J. (1995). The quality in Australian health care study. *Medical Journal of Australia, 163,* 458-471.

Wright, D. (2003). *Business Case for Clinical Information System - Phase 1.* Auckland: Waitemata District Health Board.

KEY TERMS

Clinical HIS: IS that supports day-to-day clinical activity in radiology, pathology, pharmacy, and other specialist areas.

Diffusion of Innovation: The process by which adoption of an innovation spreads through an organisation. Diffusion may be informally, through social peer networks, and/or formally, through organisational hierarchies.

Electronic Patient Record (EPR): Also known as Electronic Health Record (EHR) or Electronic Medical Record (EMR).

An electronic longitudinal collection of personal health information relating to an individual, entered or accepted by health care providers, and organised primarily to support ongoing, efficient and effective health care.

Evidence Based Medicine (EBM): The use of current best evidence in making decisions about the care of patients. Evidence comes from both the individual physician's clinical expertise, to accurately diagnose a patient, and external research, to identify the safest and most effective treatment for a given diagnosis.

Operational Hospital Information System (HIS): IS that supports day-to-day non-clinical activity, such as accounting, payroll, inventory, and patient (customer) management.

Patient Safety: The minimisation of unintended injury to a patient as a result of health care practices (as opposed to injury resulting from the patient's underlying disease). Injury includes death, permanent and temporary disability, prolonged hospital stay, and/or financial loss to the patient.

Strategic HIS: IS that supports analysis of day-to-day activity in order to identify potential improvements, such as traffic patterns in ED, equipment utilisation, and workflow.

Chapter VII
RFID and Assisted Living for the Elderly

David Parry
AUT University, New Zealand

Judith Symonds
AUT University, New Zealand

ABSTRACT

Radio-frequency Identification (RFID) offers a potentially flexible and low cost method of locating objects and tracking people within buildings. RFID systems generally require less infrastructure to be installed than other solutions but have their own limitations. As part of an assisted living system, RFID tools may be useful to locate lost objects, support blind and partially sighted people with daily living activities, and assist in the rehabilitation of adults with acquired brain injury. This chapter outlines the requirements and the role of RFID in assisting people in these three areas. The development of a prototype RFID home support tool is described and some of the issues and challenges raised are discussed. The system is designed to support assisted living for elderly and infirm people in a simple, usable and extensible way in particular for supporting the finding and identification of commonly used and lost objects such as spectacles. This approach can also be used to extend the tagged domain to commonly visited areas, and provide support for the analysis of common activities, and rehabilitation.

1 INTRODUCTION

Assistive technology has been recognised as a vital component of care for the increasing numbers of elderly and chronically sick people in western countries who will require help to stay in their homes and carry out the activities of daily living(ADL) (UK Audit Commission, 2004). Therefore, there is a need for homes and the objects within them to become intelligent- that is to be able to actively assist their inhabitants. A further development has been the concept of ubiquitous nursing (u-nursing) (Honey et al., 2007). In this vision for 2020 the nurse is able to care for his or her patients assisted by an invisible ubiquitous web of sensors and information flows. Throughout the world there has been an increase in the occurrence of long term conditions (LTC), such as stroke, cancer, diabetes and heart disease, and hence an increase the importance of delivering effective care efficiently to sufferers. Both for quality of life issues and economic ones, care at home is becoming more important and is being studied intensively(Pare, Jaana, & Sicotte, 2007). The demographic shift of the population, from a generally young population, to that of one where the number of workers supporting each elderly person is much smaller, is becoming more visible, and many LTC's are associated with increasing age. Data from Statistics New Zealand (Statistics New Zealand, 2005) based on the "medium" assumption of changes until 2051, estimates that by 2051 the percentage of the population aged 65 years and over will double from 12% to 26% .A similar scenario is happening in the UK where the number of people over the age of 65 has doubled since 1935 and today one fifth of the population is over 65 (Curry, Trejo Rinoco, & Wardle, 2002) Further, one in every five adults is reported to have some form of disability (Statistics New Zealand, 2006) with motor and cognitive disability being the most frequent. At the same time, the information flow between healthcare providers, patients and other stakeholders is being investigated as part of the Health Information Strategy action committee process, and being found to be wanting at present, and in need of improvement as part of an action area (Health Information Strategy Action Committee, 2007).

Thus, a pattern emerges whereby there is a convergence of requirements between the need to assist people to continue to live at home, an increasing need to treat chronic diseases and manage the information required for such processes, and to do so in the context of a holistic healthcare system. The vast majority of people needing such services are elderly although it should be emphasised that this need is not universal, and does not begin at any specific age.

There are a wide range of technologies used to support people who need assistance in the tasks of daily living. These technologies range from modifications to houses, alarm and fall detection systems, mechanical devices to assist with particular functions (e.g. shoe horns), as well as self and telemonitoring devices such as glucose blood testing kits or blood pressure monitors. Of course, living at home implies less contact with the routine measurement of health status, as may occur in high level care. This may in turn lead to undiagnosed exacerbations or decline in function, which could possibly have been avoided if more information was available to the health professionals with responsibility for the person. In terms of information flow, telemonitoring devices seem an attractive prospect to improve home management of chronic conditions. A recent review (Pare et al., 2007) has demonstrated that in the case of hypertension and diabetes, clinical improvement has been shown, but this is not the case for pulmonary and cardiac disease. The review also reported the fact that many published studies were not suitably designed to prove clinical benefit and that quality of life and economic issues (although vital) were not usually addressed reliably. A more general study of the reasons for adoption or non-adoption of telemedicine services(May et al., 2003) emphasises the institutional requirements for implementation, adoption, translation and stabilization of telemedicine so that it becomes normal to use it.

Some nations are investing heavily in telecare – for example the United Kingdom has produced a white paper on community health (UK Department of Health, 2005), and the telecare knowledge network(Telecare Knowledge Network, 2007) has some examples of projects in development and practice.

This chapter describes a combination of telemonitoring and assistive technology; the chapter is based around a Radio Frequency Identification (RFID)-based system for object location in the home currently being developed. The background to the system is described followed by a description of the system and its use, including the potential information flows. Issues that may arise from such a system in terms of privacy and ethical problems are then described. A short discussion and some conclusions end the chapter.

2 BACKGROUND

The concept of the "intelligent home" is not particularly new, (Stauffer, 1991) describes a "Smart House", including a network for home automation. More recently work has been done on the use of instrumented houses as technology test beds (Helal et al., 2005), and there has been increasing recognition that networking and computer control of electronic devices in the home is only one element of a solution for a supportive environment. A recent paper (Stefanov, Bien, & Bang, 2004), gives an overview of some of these requirements. Appropriate interface design, context-awareness, standards for interoperability and, most importantly, usefulness are necessary for success. This work focuses on a number of features of an intelligent home that may be particularly useful for assisted living; Object location and identification, activity measurement and assistance to mitigate the effects of short-term memory loss.

2.1 Object Location

Finding objects in the home is a task that everyone performs. Given the size of houses, location to around +/- 1 metre or even higher resolution is required. Houses also have structures – such as walls and furniture – that are a barrier to humans, but not radio waves. Lost objects or landmarks may not be in line of sight to the users. Memory failure is a common problem in the elderly with 25-50% of people reporting it (Jonker, Geerlings,

& Schmand, 2000). A system to assist with finding objects in the home may therefore be useful for supporting elderly people in tasks of daily living.

Essentially the object location problem either requires a direct triangulation of the object, by the object having some sort of beacon attached, or the recording of the object's location in relation to some sort of map, which can be stored in a computer. An example of the first sort of system is the object finder (Holbrook; Paul Robert), or the common sound-activated key rings. In this approach, the device emits a sound when the search function is activated. The user then follows the sound. Obvious disadvantages to such a system include the fact that many elderly people are deaf, and that precise object location by sound is difficult. In addition, the active beacons require batteries, and the beacons can themselves be quite large and interfere with the use of the object.

2.2 A Review of the Technology of Object Identification and Location

GPS systems are difficult to use within buildings, because of reflection and attenuation with walls and other factors. Although this problem has been addressed (Ni, Liu, Lau, & Patil, 2003), the solution involves triangulation of several different types of data. Any such system also requires that the plan of the building and furniture be translated into appropriate coordinates, so that the location of an object with respect to walls etc. is known. Triangulation techniques using either WiFi or mobile phone networks require available availability of wireless network infrastructure and are generally imprecise on the scale necessary, although there are techniques to reduce this error.

RFID has been proposed for object detection by several studies and the limitations of such development are well documented. Some systems, such as the one developed by Intel (Smith et al., 2005) , use short range technology and can trace when objects are used in the environment by recording when the glove or bracelet is in close proximity to a tagged object in the environment. It should be pointed out that the main aim of this project is in activity tracking rather than object detection. Another such system by GaTech called the memory mirror (Quan T. Tran, 2005) tracks removal and return of items from a specific storage area. The limitation of these systems is that they can only detect the location of objects when they are within range of the bracelet/glove/sandal and due to technical limitations the range is very short. This problem has led to augmentation with other types of data such as video analysis (Mihailidis, Carmichael, & Boger, 2004), motion detection sensors (Smith et al., 2005) and sonic data (Adam, Hari, Michel, & Nissanka, 2004). A recent summary from the University of Essex ((Prashant Solanki & Huosheng Hu, 2005) has covered a number of projects that use object recognition by visual means – for example, mobile phone based work on object recognition in museums, active tagging or triangulation. Object recognition has the disadvantage that the system is computationally expensive and relies on the user pointing the device in the right direction. The use of additional hardware and sensors also adds to the cost of the overall system. However, the main disadvantage of such systems is that they are really only useful for self location or object identification. Lost objects will not be findable with this approach.

Long range RFID hardware uses either high frequency with high power supplies or ultra high frequency technology. The read range achieved starts from around 30cm and extends out to 10 metres. The exact location of an object is derived by triangulating the time difference in communication between the tag and reader to calculate an exact location. An example of this is the Paric system (Paric Limited, 2006)This system is extremely precise but requires a network of active tags which may be expensive.

This difference in user requirements can be illustrated by the type and differences in the kind of information provided by topographical and topological maps (Monkhouse & Wilkinson 1978).

Topographic maps show a scaled representation of the area in question and significant objects within it. A topological map does not attempt to accurately represent distances between objects or landmarks, but rather distorts the layout so that routes between significant locations can be clearly seen, although the actual distance and absolute bearings are not correct. In an environment where the exact route taken between landmarks is not important, or routes are constrained for some reason, topological maps can be a great deal clearer than topographic ones. Topological maps are easily represented as a series of points and do not show exact coordinates.

Figure 1. The London transport topological map (Source: Transport for London)

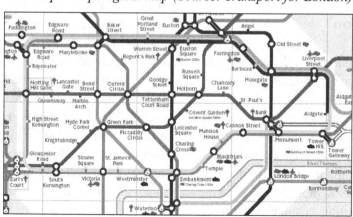

Figure 2. Topographic map of the Zone 1 area of London

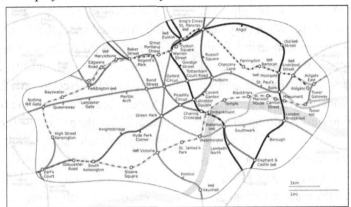

A famous example of a topological map is the London underground map produced by Harry Beck in 1932(Figure 1) Compared to the topographic map in Figure 2, the map is inaccurate in terms of location of stations, but it is extremely useful for route planning and progress monitoring.

In a system of object location using RFID, the Paric system referred to in the previous section would be very useful in preparing a topographic map of a room where the landmarks of the room were represented accurately to scale. However, such a system would be expensive overkill for preparing a topological map of the room in terms of providing the user with useful information.

2.3 Object Identification and Characterization

In the object identification scenario, characteristics of the object being examined are important. This becomes important when there is some mismatch between the user's ability to perceive the attribute, and the requirement to know it in order to undertake certain tasks. Examples include identifying use-by dates, correct washing or cooking methods, instructions relating to the taking of prescribed drugs, the presence of gas or water leaks and interaction with mechanical and electronic devices.

Traditionally these requirements are met using visual indicators, whether symbolic or textual, in the form of instructions. Other sensory clues are also given – such as smell or sound. Even when the object incorporates specific affordances such as a handle or knob, vision assists in orientation. People with very poor eyesight may not be able to identify the colours of clothes, which can restrict their ability to dress themselves effectively.

Issues therefore arise for those with loss of vision, people who have difficulty reading, or those who are not speakers of the language in use. Loss or restriction of other senses can often raise problems when sound or smell is used as for attention focusing (such as a doorbell) or as a warning as in the odorant mixed with natural gas. In addition, the complexity of instructions and the number of possible interactions can give rise to difficulties if concentration or memory is impaired.

2.4 Activity Measurement and Person Tracking

One of the major concerns facing elderly people living alone is suffering a fall or other incapacitating event and being unable to summon help. Falls remain a common cause of morbidity and are difficult to prevent (Gillespie, 2006). Changes in levels of activity can indicate exacerbations of chronic disease – e.g. Chronic Obstructive Airways Disease (COAD). Some people with dementia may require warnings when they venture outside the home or begin wandering. Brain injured patients and others with some types of memory loss may have difficulty completing tasks that need to be undertaken in a sequence, and will require reminders and training to allow them to finish them.

Gross activity measurement has been performed by many groups. A recent paper (Suzuki et al., 2006) has used information fusion from a number of sensors to monitor activity, and wrist-based sensors have also been used for this purpose. Fall alarm systems have become popular and more sophisticated (Doughty, Lewis, & McIntosh, 2000). However, such systems do have their drawbacks. In particular the activity-monitoring systems tend to measure gross activity, rather than whether the activity is directed and purposeful. Systems to notify carers of people straying are effective, but are single-use and tend to only perform this task (Altus, Mathews, Xaverius, Engelman, & Nolan, 2000).

Algorithms to convert RFID log files into activity reports are an area where more development is needed. A simple mapping from tag to location is unlikely as tags can fail to be detected within the expected range, because of interference from other radio-frequency sources, manufacturing differences and even humidity. Conversely tags can sometimes be detected via reflection paths- and the shape of the detection zone from an aerial can be modified by the presence of conducting materials. As noted previously systems have been developed to monitor activity via RFID, and (Smith et al., 2005), used a Bayesian belief network to infer likely current behaviour.

3 PROPOSED SYSTEM

This section deals with some of the requirements for a solution, and some of the results we have obtained during the development of a prototype.

3.1 Object Location System

The system being developed has been described elsewhere (Symonds, Parry D., & Briggs J., 2007). Briefly the system uses a number of RFID tags located around the user's home (landmarks), and

Figure 3. Landmark Locations for potential landmark locations

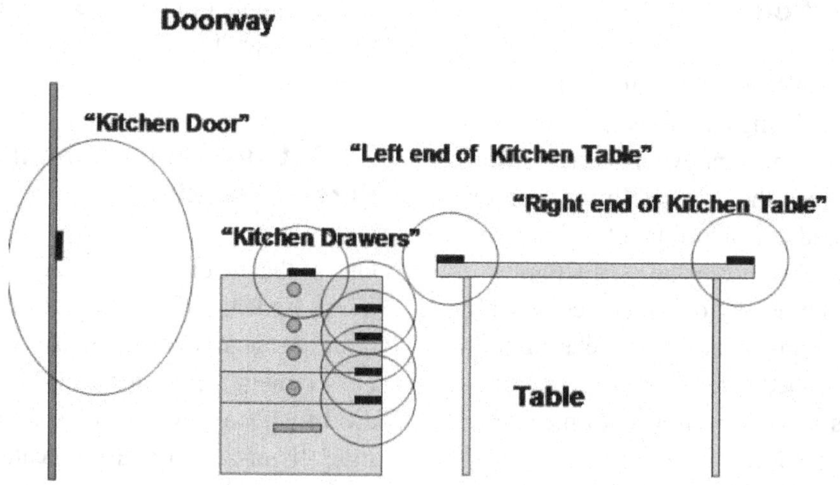

attached to objects that may be lost. The user is equipped with a tag reading device that allows interaction via screen or voice. The tag reading device operates continuously, recording the detection of landmarks and objects within the range of the detector, also known as the user's "aura". When the user deposits an object, then it is no longer visible to the system and its location is recorded in reference to the landmarks visited before and after. See

The system differs from other RFID approaches such as LANDMARC (Lionel, Yunhao, Yiu Cho, & Abhishek, 2004), in that the reader is carried by the user and the tags remain in the same place, rather than the other way round. This approach was taken in order to reduce costs, limit the effect on others sharing the space (e.g. spouses) and also to allow the system to be installed in less frequently used areas, or even public spaces. The use of landmark tags, which could have different effective read ranges, allows the spatial resolution of the system to be adjusted as required, so that there can be areas where a difference of 10cm is important (e.g. in the drawer area), whereas in a corridor, 5 metres may be the resolution needed. The user in effect builds up a topological rather than a topographic map, so that the relative arrangement of items is more important than some absolute coordinate. The result "Your glasses are between the toaster and the fridge is more useful to a human than "your glasses are on a bearing of 90 degrees and 7.5 meters away". The latter approach is valuable for a featureless environment such as for avalanche rescue, but not in a complex, obstacle strewn space like the average home.

Essentially, each time an object or landmark RFID tag comes into range of the RFID interrogator (and therefore the user); a database system is updated with a record. This record forms a comprehensive log of where the user has been and what objects they have been in contact with. There is a continuous stream of data coming from the RFID interrogator. However, we sample this data to facilitate the manageability of the database

while still providing enough information to be able to use the system. We also delete some of the history on the basis of age and whether new information about that object or landmark has been stored for storage capacity reasons. There is a tremendous opportunity to analyse this data to provide useful information and triggers for care or to help users to learn from the data that is stored in the device. However, simply uploading all of the data collected or making it available to a remote health professional for example, would be counter productive. Therefore, there is a need with all systems that provide information flows for some sort of intelligence or data management to enable the provision of useful information. Such intelligence would need to relate to the individual case scenario as every patient is unique.

3.2 General Characteristics of a Solution

According to our previous work investigation (Basrur and Parry 2006), a system designed for the location of lost objects, within the home as an assistive technology would have the following characteristics:

1. It should be relatively cheap
2. Objects should not have to be modified greatly
3. It should support multiple ways of searching
4. The interface and interaction should be intuitive
5. It must survive a reasonable degree of home rearrangement
6. It should not interfere with other occupants' lifestyle
7. A single system, rather than data fusion, is preferable for simplicity's sake.

Fortunately, adding activity tracking and object identification is relatively straightforward. Object characterisation can be achieved by including more data – either embedded in the object or as data retrieved from a database using an object identifier such as a barcode. Activity tracking can occur as a by-product of object location – as the objects are picked up and landmarks passed, the path of the user and the objects they are interacting with can be recorded.

Initially, losable objects (LO) and landmarks are labelled with RFID tags. A database in the interrogator system allows association between the tag ID (TID) and the description. For each TID a description that can be spoken and understood by the user is recorded. In choosing locations for landmarks, the user should have a higher density of landmarks near likely locations of loss as well as a regular pattern identifying navigation landmarks such as doorways, stairs etc. See Figure 4 and Figure 5 for a potential scheme.

It may be useful to give such higher-level navigation tags high visibility colours so that they can be identified. Generally higher-level navigation landmarks will require longer range detection, so tags with larger aerials may be used. The approach is similar to that of (Satoh, 2005), where the "aura" component represents the final location of the object.

When the user is holding the losable object, the interrogator registers the presence of the object and records the high-level navigation tags that the user passes. The TID and timestamp are recorded in the database. Interrogation happens at around 10 millisecond intervals, depending on the number of tags within range. In order to reduce storage requirements, only the time of first detection and the time of last detection of a tag are stored for each tag detection episode. This avoids large amounts of data being stored when the user is stationary or holding an object. When the user drops the LO, then the system detects this by noting the absence of the LO's TID in the input stream. Any other navigation tags being detected at this point are noted.

When the user wishes to recover the LO, he or she names the object verbally and the speech

conversion system finds the nearest LO name. When the required LO is identified, the topological map is searched via the timestamps, radiating outwards from the time that the LO was last detected. The navigation locations that were detected at the closest point to the dropping of the LO are declared. Should this not be clear, a dialogue could continue, with other nearby navigation points being declared until the user is satisfied that he or she knows the location of the object.

When the user gets to the nearest navigation point they can begin a detailed search for the LO. Patterns such as those used in avalanche search may be useful (Michahelles, Matter, Schmidt, & Schiele, 2003). Another alternative is to retrace steps, where the system declares the sequence of navigation points around the time before and after the LO is dropped.

For object characterisation, the tags can either be used as the data storage medium, or as a pointer in a database stored in the interrogator or any central database. In some cases in the future many consumer items may have RFID tags already attached, which may provide some data or at least a unique identifier. Libraries may encode the name of the book although privacy issues may mitigate against this (David & David, 2004). It may be more attractive to use this system to store user-generated data – for example whether the item of clothing is for warm or cold weather, along with any data that may be placed there automatically by the manufacturer. Short-range tags are most suitable for this application as the user will wish to distinguish between items that are stored close together.

Activity monitoring could use a number of approaches. The simplest is to measure movement of the user in relation to landmarks or tagged items. If the movement is below a certain amount, an alarm could be sent to a monitoring system. Adding the next level of complexity and invasiveness would identify landmarks that are the gateway to "no-go" zones such as out of the front door. This would assume that the user is

Figure 4. Topographic plan of the landmarks

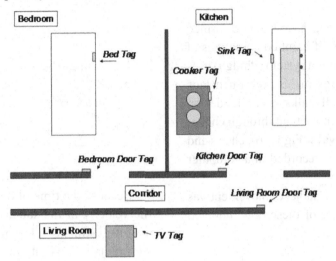

confused enough to wish to leave when they are at risk, but not determined enough to remove the interrogator device. A warning to the user that they were at risk from the device may be helpful. There is no reason why different zones may not be set up – for example within one's own room, within a building or on a campus – which may make this approach more acceptable. Certain users may wish to have the system remind them of objects that they should have with them when they go to certain areas – such as their front door keys or even a coat.

More precise and task-focussed tracking may be useful in the rehabilitation of brain-injured patients. These people often have difficulty remembering to complete tasks, and effectively have to begin again halfway through a task. The tracking system may be able to identify characteristic patterns of movement around the topographic map associated with certain tasks, and prompt the user to complete them when the sequence halts or the user indicates they have forgotten what they are doing. A similar approach would generate speech that indicates what the next task is in the sequence as each one is completed.

Figure 5. Topographic map of the landmarks

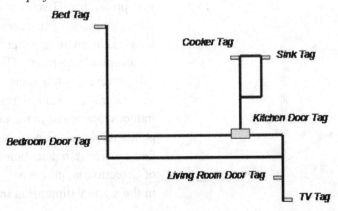

3.1 Implementation Results

A number of experiments have been performed with the system using different combinations of reader and tag. The Phidgit system (Phidgit) uses 125 KHz short range tags. In this experiment tags were mounted on small stalks, and a reader on the hip of the subject, movement through choke-points – such as doorways (Figure 6), chairs and sinks etc. The data was recorded in a computer in a backpack.

Information about the subject's movement was derived from a number of these tags mounted around the testing space.

Figure 6. Reader interacting with doorframe tag

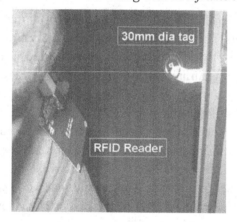

Figure 7. Path generated from recording of tag detection

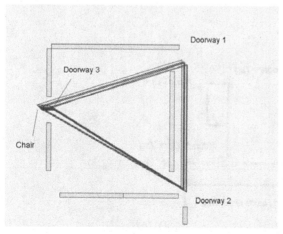

Figure 8. Results of doorway-passing detection

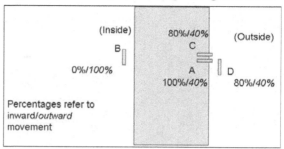

Because the time of detection was recorded, the velocity of the subject can be derived, and activity estimated. The main experimental issues remain reliability of tag detection and user acceptance.

A second set of experiments involved the use of an UHF reader (Tracient) located on a lanyard, with a coil aerial resting around the lower end of the sternum (Figure 9). The Tracient designs for readers are a comparable size to a 1st generation mobile phone, and allow Bluetooth communication, as well as USB. UHF tags (Alien) were placed as shown in Figure 8 Tag A was at the height of the aerial during normal walking. The UHF tags are around 4cm long and 1 cm wide. Best results were shown when tags were attached via a non-conducting medium as "flags" (A and C) and away from the metal doorframe (D and B). This was a very small study but it indicated that UHF tags were able to be detected by a reader worn on the body and that having tags on all sides of the doorway i.e. left and right and front and back was preferable. Given the relatively low cost of tags, redundancy in placement – that is many tags located closely together at key landmarks seems an acceptable approach. There is an upper limit to this however, as too many tags within range will cause signal collision. Normal walking movement induces movement in the tag reader – much as a pendant around the neck will swing, and this effect can assist in detection when the aerial angle of detection is quite small – around 30 degrees in the x and y dimension in this case.

Figure 9. Tracient reader on Lanyard

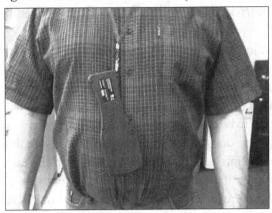

Smaller computing devices, such as the Sony Vaio UX which weighs only 600 grams but is effectively a full PC with USB port, are currently being investigated. A small demonstration of a "smart bag" application that reads out the name associated with a tagged object, and identifies missing objects by name has been developed using this device and a Tracient reader. Because this device supports standard office software, a simple ACCESS (Microsoft) database holds the lookup between tag ID and object name, and the expected contents list of a bag. When the bag tag is detected, the application reads out the names of the objects have not been detected but that are associated as part of a contents list of the bag. In this way a user could check that they have their keys etc. before leaving the house.

Other work has shown effective detection of loss of signal in order to detect objects being put down, and there has been some work on the usability of the system, with volunteers performing various detection tasks (McPherson, Parry, & Symonds, 2007).

4 DISCUSSION

In our discussion we will cover the main practical and conceptual design problems that we face in this project.

4.1 Practical design problems

In our study the main practical design problems are a function of our use of "Commercial off-the-shelf" (COTS) approach. This approach has some great advantages and has been used by others in a similar domain (Behringer et al., 2000). Mainly these problems relate to issues around adaptation of existing technology. However, it is useful to report these as they provide guidance for hardware developers and open avenues for application of RFID other than in the mainstream areas of tracking and traceability.

4.1.1 Size & Weight

One major issue is the size of the 'aura', which is dependent on the read range of the interrogator, and the size and alignment of the tag. We think that the ideal size of the aura is large enough to incorporate the personal interaction space of the user. In this context, personal interaction space means the area in which objects that are currently being interacted with or carried are located. This is likely to be around 70-150cm circumference. It would be attractive to be able to control this – for example by using tags with smaller antennae in areas such as within cupboards. Tag size is not a particular issue although flag-type deployment gives greater range on small objects. Some tag detection devices allow control of the power output and hence detection range. The use of metallic sliding covers over tags – as in the case of a door lock indicator has been proposed.

Generally longer range is associated with larger antennae on the detection device and higher power output. These may make the system unwieldy in some cases, and cause a reduction in battery life. Using Bluetooth for communication allows the readers to be independent of cables, but the issue still arises of communication between the user and the computing device if it is not being carried on the person.

4.1.2 Privacy Issues and Autonomy

There have been some privacy concerns, however all of the data is stored locally and is controlled exclusively by the user. Access to activity data derived from the system is limited to the user of the system unless they choose to share such information. Data coded onto object identification tags could be encrypted to prevent others reading them at a distance. One key element will be to emphasise that the system is a helper and not in charge of the user's life. Thus any reminders will have to be useful and appropriate. A model that treats this system as more like a guide dog than a human associate may be useful.

4.1.3 User acceptance

We are working on the assumption that many people are accepting of personal electronic devices (iPod, mobile phone, personal organiser for example). The public are also generally quite accepting of various types of tags on merchandise that they purchase – e.g. barcodes or tags on clothing. However, usability testing is a major feature of the final stages of our work and findings have not yet been collected.

4.1.4 Health

As all the devices used in our prototype are licensed for use without restriction there is thought to be no risk associated with the RF energy. Moulder et al. (1999) have conducted a comprehensive study of the risks associated with exposure to radio frequency (chiefly cell phone) and risk of developing cancer. They find no proof of a link, but also conclude that proof that there is a complete lack of health hazards from cell phone exposure is impossible because of the wide range of contexts and areas of investigation possible.

4.1.5 Multiple Users (Multiple Interrogators in the Same Environment)

Major work is needed on ways to deal with multiple users and occupants operating in the same environment. If multiple users are moving objects, their individual annotated maps will have to be collaboratively updated. Our proposed system does have some inbuilt robustness in that each time losable objects come within the aura of the user, they are recorded and so our system should recover from object misplacement rather quickly. An intriguing suggestion has been made to incorporate RFID identification with social networking and semantic web approaches (Matsuo et al., 2006), but this is not proposed in our environment.

4.1.6 Other Tags in the Environment

Our system has an initial set-up procedure to register tags in the system and the system 'ignores' tags that are not registered.

4.1.7 User Interface

The user interface is a critical success factor. Following design of current personal consumer devices such as mobile phones, iPods and PDAs, the keypad/screen interface is probably not the best communication approach. Voice recognition could be helpful, but some limitations in the technology might mean that a combination of voice and menu selection might be most practical at the moment. The concept of a large, fixed interface centre – e.g. a TV or PC with suitable input devices, linked by Bluetooth has been proposed.

4.1.8 Antenna Design

The current loop antenna is designed with manufacturing applications in mind. The antenna is rigid and is of an inconvenient shape. In our proof of concept experiments, we have used the antenna in a backpack configuration placed with the top edge just under the shoulder blades and on a 'shield' attached to the user's forearm. Ideally, it would be better to be able to design the antenna to be inserted into a cuff or watchstrap for the forearm. Other approaches we have used include the smaller pendant aerial worn on a lanyard.

4.2 Conceptual Design Problems

The chief conceptual design problem that we have encountered is that the aura concept has the potential for false readings in a multi-room environment. That is, because the tags can be read through some building materials that would be used in the home, there are possibilities for a landmark to be associated with the last known location of an object when the tag is on the other side of an internal wall from the landmark. There are a number of ways that this problem could be addressed:

- Hardware
- Tag placement
- Database stored information, and
- Software intelligence.

4.2.1 Hardware

One possible solution to the problem of false (or rather inappropriate) reads would be to shield the tag from being read through walls. We thought about using tin foil, which is a very good shield for RF signals, to shield the tag from being read through objects. In our tests we found that it was impossible to shield the tag from only one direction – that is, the foil stopped the signal from all directions even though applied only to the back of the tag. We also experimented with a thickness of card to separate the tag from the foil at the back, and while this did allow the tag to be read from one direction, the signal was severely weakened and this seemed like a poor solution

since an efficient read range for the tags is so important for our system.

4.2.2 Tag Placement

Another possible solution to the problem is tag placement. It is possible to generate a set of rules about tag placement that would limit the potential for false results. For example, there could be a rule that all tags must be placed at least 70cm from walls. However, this could become quite complex and require expert installation of the tags in the final system, and could restrict the performance of the object location system. Therefore, it does not seem to be a viable solution to the problem.

4.2.3 Database

It is also possible to add some fields to the database tables in the application to allow a room location to be stored. These locations could then be checked using a simple SQL query to ensure that the tags on the object and the landmark are in the same room. This solution will work quite effectively once the system is set-up, but does complicate the registration process and would limit the plug and play capability of the system. For example, it would be difficult to ship the application with a set of pre-set tags and objects if you had to also store the room location as these will differ from environment to environment. However, a practical implementation will involve at least one confirmatory tour around the landmarks at some stage and this problem is not insurmountable.

4.2.4 Intelligent Software

It is possible for the software to implement a type of topological logic inherent in topological mapping (see section 2). That is, not only does the system feedback and track landmarks that are within the user's aura, the system also applies a sensibility test using a known topological route to check that the items are not in a different room of the house from the user before storing the information. This seems the most sensible solution and is the one that we are trying to implement in our software after initial proof-of-concept experimentation.

5 CONCLUSION

Earlier in our chapter we put forward seven criteria for the success of the assisted living environment system design. In this section we address each in an attempt to evaluate our progress. There is also a small section on future work.

5.1 Relatively Cheap

Essentially, the topological approach to the system, with the reader on the user, makes our system relatively cheap when compared with systems that follow the topographical approach to object location

5.2 Low Modification of Objects

Placement of tags on the outside of losable objects means that they do not need to be modified greatly to be part of the system, and if the system came with pre-registered tags, this would limit the amount of setting up needed in the system before initial use.

5.3 Multiple Search Methods

We intend to allow the system to use a 'roam' search option as well as the historical object tracking system to allow the system to support multiple ways of searching. There are other possibilities – such as using a grid for searching – but this is outside the scope of this paper. The size of the aura, and the complexity of the environment may determine the exact search procedure, and it may be that this device should be linked to eg a photographic record of the location of objects

which may be possible with a lightweight camera mounted in the computing device.

5.4 Intuitive User Interface

Moving to the ultra portable PC has allowed a wider range of interfaces to be tested using touch and speech. A "menu" based around reading particular tags associated with starting a task may also be a useful approach. Given the small size of the screens used, placing the computing device in a cradle and linking it up to a large screen may be appropriate for relatively complex tasks such as setting up bag content lists.

5.5 Survive Home Rearrangement

The topological approach to finding lost objects copes quite well with the prospect of home rearrangement, especially if locations of objects are not stored in the database tables. After landmarks and objects have been moved and the first instance of their location has been stored in the database, effectively a new virtual topological map is created. The only limitation would be that the user would need to check that the placement of the tags was not affected, such as not being shielded by metal or water. However it is easy to see this as part of an installation process, and continuing technical support for these devices is probably essential in the short term.

5.6 Not Interfering with Other Occupants Lifestyle

The ultimate goal is to develop a system that will not interfere with other occupants' lifestyle. Presently, the size of the prototype is an obvious limiting factor. We also need to develop a sensible cuff/strap embedded antenna to allow usability trials to test for problems with it interfering with daily life. Certainly, something on the user's arm seems less restricting than a glove that would restrict washing up, food preparation and toileting.

5.7 Single System

For obvious reasons, a single, well-integrated system is preferable to the complications of combining disparate systems. By associating the system with the user- rather than the house, the paradigm of the mobile phone or PDA can be used, thus making it a personal system. This removes the need to interface multiple sensors, or make the user learn multiple interfaces. As a side effect of this, many homes or spaces, such as hotel rooms or public transport, could be fitted with the RFID tags even if the occupants do not currently need the system.

Overall, the concept of attaching the reader to the person and distributing tags around the assisted living space seems viable. Costs of readers and tags continue to fall, and these systems are becoming easier to implement. Future challenges will include integrating information from these and other devices into health information systems in the community and establishing appropriate rules for the use and transfer of this data. As with mobile phones, it is possible that such devices will induce some change in social behaviour, especially if uptake is large and public spaces become tagged. There is obviously an opportunity for other groups aside from those needing assistance in ADL to use location tags for other purposes. It is hoped that these approaches will increase autonomy, by removing barriers to activity, and allowing more people to continue to live a normal life.

5.8 Future Work

Developments in reader technology are very rapid. The current system requires a computing device e.g. a palmtop or PDA, to be carried on the user. Adding such a computing device to store and interpret the data increases weight and complexity including requiring cables. One solution may be to use on-board storage of data on the reader - currently information regarding tag ID and time of reading can include thousands of records on

the Tracient device with battery life for around 6000 reads. Interpretation could then take place by a fixed location machine that captures the data opportunistically via Bluetooth

6 REFERENCES

Adam, S., Hari, B., Michel, G., & Nissanka, P. (2004). *Tracking moving devices with the cricket location system.* Paper presented at the Proceedings of the 2nd international conference on Mobile systems, applications, and services, Boston, MA, USA.

Altus, D. E., Mathews, R. M., Xaverius, P. K., Engelman, K. K., & Nolan, B. A. D. (2000). Evaluating an electronic monitoring system for people who wander. *American Journal of Alzheimer's Disease and Other Dementias, 15*(2), 121-125.

Behringer, R., Behringer, R., Tam, C., McGee, J., Sundareswaran, S. A. S. S., & Vassiliou, M. A. V. M. (2000). *A wearable augmented reality testbed for navigation and control, built solely with commercial-off-the-shelf (COTS) hardware:*

A wearable augmented reality testbed for navigation and control, built solely with commercial-off-the-shelf (COTS) hardware. Paper presented at the Augmented Reality, 2000. (ISAR 2000). *Proceedings. IEEE and ACM International Symposium.*

Curry, R. G., Trejo Rinoco, M., & Wardle, D. (2002). *The Use of Information and Communication Technology (ICT) to Support Independent Living for Older and Disabled Peopl*e. 2008, from http://www.rehabtool.com/forum/discussions/ictuk02.pdf

David, M., & David, W. (2004). *Privacy and security in library RFID: issues, practices, and architectures.* Paper presented at the Proceedings of the 11th ACM conference on Computer and communications security, Washington DC, USA.

Doughty, K., Lewis, R., & McIntosh, A. (2000). The design of a practical and reliable fall detector for community and institutional telecare. *Journal of Telemedicine and Telecare, 6*(Supp. 1), S150-154.

Gillespie, L. G., Robertson, M. C., Lamb, S. E., Cumming, R. G., & Rowe, B. H. (2006). *Interventions for preventing falls in elderly people.* (Publication. Retrieved 31st January 2007, from Cochrane Database of Systematic Reviews.

Health Information Strategy Action Committee. (2007, 30th January 2007). *Action Zone 7 - Chronic Care and Disease Management: An Initial View.* Retrieved 1st July 2007, 2007, from http://www. moh.govt.nz/moh.nsf/pagescm/532

Helal, S., Mann, W. H., King, J., Kaddoura, Y., & Jansen, E. (2005). The Gator Tech Smart House: a programmable pervasive space. *Computer, 38*(3), 50-60.

Holbrook, P. R. L. D. R. G. B. S., Born, J. Hurtado, R. E., & Buczkiewicz, R. T. (2004). USA Patent No. 6,674,364.

Honey, M., Øyri, K., Newbold, S., Coenen, A., Park, H., Ensio, A., et al. (2007). *Effecting change by the use of emerging technologies in healthcare: A future vision for u-nursing in 2020.* Paper presented at the Health Informatics New Zealand (HINZ), 6th Annual Forum., Rotorua.

Jonker, C., Geerlings, M. I., & Schmand, B. (2000). Are memory complaints predictive for dementia? A review of clinical and population-based studies. *International Journal of Geriatric Psychiatry, 15*(11), 983-991.

Lionel, M. N., Yunhao, L., Yiu Cho, L., & Abhishek, P. P. (2004). LANDMARC: indoor location sensing using active RFID. *Wirel. Netw., 10*(6), 701-710.

Matsuo, Y., Hamasaki, M., Takeda, H., Mori, J., Bollegala, D., Nakamura, Y., et al. (2006). *Spinning Multiple Social Networks for Semantic*

Web. Paper presented at the Association for the Advancement of Artificial Intelligence, Boston.

May, C., Harrison, R., Finch, T., MacFarlane, A., Mair, F., Wallace, P., et al. (2003). Understanding the normalization of telemedicine services through qualitative evaluation. *Journal of the American Medical Informatics Association, 10*(6), 596-604.

McPherson, K., Parry, D., & Symonds, J. (2007, 4th December 2007). *Radio Frequency Identification (RFID) for Assisted Living: Testing the Aura Object Location (AOL) Model.* Paper presented at the 18th Australasian Conference on Information Systems, Toowoomba, Queensland, Australia.

Michahelles, F., Matter, P., Schmidt, A., & Schiele, B. (2003). Applying wearable sensors to avalanche rescue. *Computers and Graphics, 27*(6), 839-847(839).

Mihailidis, A., Carmichael, B., & Boger, J. (2004). The use of computer vision in an intelligent environment to support aging-in-place, safety, and independence in the home. *IEEE Transactions on Information Technology in Biomedicine, 8*(3), 238-247.

Ni, L. M., Liu, Y., Lau, Y. C., & Patil, A. P. (2003). *LANDMARC: indoor location sensing using active RFID.* Paper presented at the Pervasive Computing and Communications, 2003. (PerCom 2003). *Proceedings of the First IEEE International Conference.*

Pare, G., Jaana, M., & Sicotte, C. (2007). Systematic Review of Home Telemonitoring for Chronic Diseases: The Evidence Base. *J Am Med Inform Assoc, 14*(3), 269-277.

Paric Limited. (2006). Paric homepage. Retrieved 1st December 2006, 2006, from http://www.paric. co.nz/

Prashant, S., & Huosheng, H. (2005). *Techniques used for Location-based Services: A survey.* University of Essex.

Quan, T., & Tran, E. D. M. (2005). The Aware Home - Memory Mirror. Retrieved 1st December 2006, 2006, from http://www-static.cc.gatech. edu/fce/ahri/projects/Memory_Mirror.pdf

Satoh, I. (2005). *A location model for pervasive computing environments.*

Smith, J. R., Fishkin, K. P., Jiang, B., Mamishev, A., Philipose, M., Rea, A. D., et al. (2005). RFID-based techniques for human-activity detection. *Communications of the ACM, 48*(9), 39-44.

Statistics New Zealand. (2005). *National Population Projections 2004(base) – 2051.* Retrieved 28th November 2005, 2005, from http://www2. stats.govt.nz/domino/external/pasfull/pasfull. nsf/7cf46ae26dcb6800cc256a62000a2248/c2567e f00247c6acc256f6b00095c46?OpenDocument

Statistics New Zealand. (2006, October 2007). *The 2006 New Zealand Disability Survey.* Retrieved 1st May 2008, 2008, from http://www.stats.govt. nz/NR/rdonlyres/799A77CC-4DF6-445C-96DA-F5A266538A72/0/2006disabilitysurveyhotp.pdf

Stauffer, H. B. (1991). Smart enabling system for home automation. *IEEE Transactions on Consumer Electronics, 37*(2), xxix-xxxv.

Stefanov, D. H., Bien, Z., & Bang, W.-C. (2004). The smart house for older persons and persons with physical disabilities: structure, technology arrangements, and perspectives. *IEEE Transactions on Neural Systems and Rehabilitation Engineering, 12*(2), 228-250.

Suzuki, R., Ogawa, M., Otake, S., Izutsu, T., Tobimatsu, Y., Iwaya, T., et al. (2006). Rhythm of daily living and detection of atypical days for elderly people living alone as determined with a monitoring system. *Journal of Telemedicine and Telecare, 12*(4), 208-214.

Symonds, J., Parry D., & Briggs J. (2007, June 8-10 2007.). *An RFID-based system for assisted living: Challenges and Solutions.* Paper presented at the ICMCC 2007 Event: Empowering the Patient. , Amsterdam.

Telecare Knowledge Network. (2007, 1st June 2007). *Telecare Knowledge Network.* Retrieved 1st July 2007, 2007, from http://www.tkn.port. ac.uk/

UK Audit Commission. (2004, 12th Feburary 2004). *Assistive Technology Independence and Well-being 4.* Retrieved 1 November 2006, 2006, from http://www.audit-commission.gov. uk/reports/NATIONAL-REPORT.asp?Categor yID=&ProdID=BB070AC2-A23A-4478-BD69-4C19BE942722

UK Department of Health. (2005, 2nd March 2007). Our health, our care, our say. Retrieved 1st July 2007, 2007, from http://www.dh.gov.uk/ en/Publicationsandstatistics/Publications/Publi-cationsPolicyAndGuidance/DH_4127453

KEY TERMS

Assisted Living: Assisted living and assisted living technology are terms that deal with the use of devices to make the tasks of everyday living easier for people with some sort of disability. Often many different sorts of device are used, from the very simple such as handrails etc. to complex monitoring devices. Although the elderly may be seen as a major market for assisted living technology, groups with particular disabilities may well benefit from appropriate technology.

Bluetooth: Bluetooth and other wireless communication protocols such as WiFi and Zigby allow electronic communication between computing devices. Bluetooth is an especially popular standard because of its relatively low cost and the fact that suitable devices can discover each other automatically. Bluetooth works in an unlicensed part of the electromagnetic spectrum around 2.4GhZ and supports frequency hopping to minimize interference. One of the major application areas has been the development of wireless headsets and hands-free devices for mobile phones. Such development has reduced the cost, size and power requirements of chipsets to support Bluetooth connectivity.

Radio Frequency Identification: Usually abbreviated as RFID, this is a method of identifying objects using radio-frequency communication. The identifying tag contains some data storage and a logic circuit along with an aerial. A "reader" unit sends out a signal, which is picked up by the tag. This then sends back data such as a unique identifier and sometimes other data. There are a wide variety of types of tags and readers, identified by the frequency band used, whether the tag uses a battery or is passive and the data and security format used. RFID is being used in a wide variety of application areas, including supply-chain, security and healthcare.

Rehabilitation: Rehabilitation is the branch of healthcare that deals with attempts to restore functional abilities to people who have suffered some sort of disability. It is often used to describe the process that takes place after an accident or other loss of ability, that features interventions by clinical professionals including physiotherapists, occupational therapists and nurses.

Telecare: Telecare refers to the use of electronic communication networks to support the care of patients remotely. It is often associated with the term telemedicine, but generally has a wider meaning in that it includes non-medical interventions such as support for activities of daily living as well as purely medical interventions such as glucose monitoring etc. Telecare is generally seen as part of a care package that also includes face-to-face visits as well as assisted living technology.

Topographic: Topographic maps are those that attempt to accurately represent the actual physical layout of the mapped area. This contrasts with topological maps which represent the relationships between key items, often in the form of a network diagram.

Chapter VIII
RFID in Emergency Management

Ashir Ahmed
Monash University, Australia

Ly-Fie Sugianto
Monash University, Australia

ABSTRACT

This chapter introduces an activity-based framework for the adoption of radio frequency identification (RFID) in emergency management. The framework is based on a rather loose interpretation of the task-technology fit (TTF) theory. The chapter provides an overview of emergency management, a description of RFID characteristics and a scheme for classifying emergency management activities. It also reports literature survey on emergency management models, the use of RFID and RFID adoption models. Last but not least, it outlines the perceived benefits associated with the use of RFID in emergency management. It is hoped that the proposed framework can serve as a useful guidance for RFID adoption in emergency management.

INTRODUCTION

In this chapter, we extend the use of technologies from fulfilling secondary needs in society, such as to bring convenience, comfort and gratification, to primary needs for safe, rescue and survival. In ensuring the effective use of the new technologies, the adoption process must be planned carefully. In the past few decades, researchers have introduced various adoption models, such as technology acceptance model (TAM), diffusion of innovation and task-technology fit (TTF) model. These models provide theoretical guidelines for adoption process, and suitable for some specific domains. The aim of this study is to propose a framework for adopting RFID in emergency management based on TTF model.

Technology adoption is a non-trivial process that requires many questions to be answered. For example, what is the most suitable technology to adopt for a particular domain? Which activities can be better facilitated by the technology? How can the technology be utilized to leverage productivity? This chapter is structured into three sections. Section one highlights the nature of emergency situations, its impacts on the society, as well as literature review on emergency management models. Section two emphases on RFID and highlights the use of this technology in the context of emergency management. This section also provides an overview of other technologies which can potentially be used in emergency management. Section three discusses the adoption process. A guideline to adopt RFID in emergency management is also presented in this section.

Table 1. Major categories of emergencies

CATEGORY	TYPE	DESCRIPTION
Manmade	**Biological Threat**	A biological attack is the deliberate release of germs or other biological substances that can make someone sick, like the smallpox virus, can result in diseases one can catch from other people.
	Chemical Threat	A chemical attack is the deliberate release of a toxic gas, liquid or solid that can poison people and the environment.
	Nuclear Threat	A nuclear blast is an explosion with intense light and heat, a damaging pressure wave and widespread radioactive material that can contaminate the air, water and ground surfaces for miles around.
	Radiation threat	A radiation threat, commonly referred to as a "dirty bomb" or "radiological dispersion device (RDD)", is the use of common explosives to spread radioactive materials over a targeted area.
Natural	**Earthquakes**	An earthquake is a sudden movement of the earth, caused by the abrupt release of strain that has accumulated over a long time.
	Extreme heat	Heat kills by pushing the human body beyond its limits. In extreme heat and high humidity, evaporation is slowed and the body must work extra hard to maintain a normal temperature.
	Fires	Fire produces poisonous gases that make you disoriented and drowsy. Heat and smoke from fire can be more dangerous than the flames. Asphyxiation is the leading cause of fire deaths, exceeding burns by a three-to-one ratio.
	Floods	Floods are one of the most common natural hazards. Floods can occur due to excessive rain, broken rivers' bank or dam brakeage.
	Hurricane	A hurricane is a type of tropical cyclone, the generic term for a low pressure system that generally forms in the tropics. Hurricanes can cause catastrophic damage to coastlines and several hundred miles inland. Winds can exceed 155 miles per hour.
	Landslides and Debris Flow	In a landslide, masses of rock, earth, or debris move down a slope. Landslides may be small or large, slow or rapid. They are activated by storms, earthquakes, volcanic eruptions, fires, and human modification of land.
	Thunderstorms	All thunderstorms are dangerous. Every thunderstorm produces lightning. Although most lightning victims survive, people struck by lightning often report a variety of long-term, debilitating symptoms.
	Tornados	Tornadoes are nature's most violent storms. Spawned from powerful thunderstorms, tornadoes can cause fatalities and devastate a neighbourhood in seconds. A tornado appears as a rotating, funnel-shaped cloud that extends from a thunderstorm to the ground with whirling winds that can reach 300 miles per hour.
	Tsunamis	Tsunamis (pronounced soo-ná-mees), also known as seismic sea waves (mistakenly called "tidal waves"), are a series of enormous waves created by an underwater disturbance such as an earthquake, landslide, volcanic eruption, or meteorite.
	Volcanos	A volcano is a vent through which molten rock escapes to the earth's surface. When pressure from gases within the molten rock becomes too great, an eruption occurs. Eruptions can be quiet or explosive. There may be lava flows, flattened landscapes, poisonous gases, and flying rock and ash.
	Winter storm and extreme cold	Heavy snowfall and extreme cold can immobilize an entire region. Even areas that normally experience mild winters can be hit with a major snowstorm or extreme cold. Winter storms can result in flooding, storm surge, closed highways, blocked roads, downed power lines and hypothermia.

EMERGENCY: DEFINITION, MANAGEMENT AND IMPACT

Definition

In our study, we understand "emergency" as defined by the Church World Service (2006), namely:

An extraordinary situation where there are serious and immediate threats to human life as a result of disaster such as floods, earthquakes, tsunamis and hurricanes; imminent threat of a disaster, cumulative process of neglect, civil conflict, environmental degradation and socio-economic conditions. An emergency can encompass a situation in which there is a clear and marked deterioration in the coping abilities of a group or community.

As mentioned in the definition, emergency covers several situations such as floods, earthquakes, tsunamis and hurricanes, cumulative process of neglect, civil conflict, environmental degradation and socio economic conditions. This chapter does not cover the process of neglect, civil conflict and socio-economic aspects of emergencies, but only emphasizes on the serious and immediate threats to human life as a result of manmade and natural disasters. Emergency situations often lead towards big disasters. Incidents happened in last few years have changed the dimensions of this domain. Incidents like the terrorist attack on the US in September 2001, Indian Ocean Tsunami in 2004, and the earthquake in Pakistan in 2006 placed a disastrous impact on mankind.

Table 1 lists several major disasters with an explanation of possible dangers associated with each situation. Please refer to the Colorado ready website (www.readycolorado.com/disasters.php) for a more comprehensive description of other type of disasters. These disasters had implausible impact on mankind, may it be in monetary term or human casualties.

Figure 1(a) shows the death toll reported over the last five years in various types of natural disasters. During this five years period, the death toll reaches over to 482,000 as a result of such disasters.

Death toll reported in various disaster types over the last five years is shown in the Figure 1(b). Several earthquakes around the world proved to be the most deadly disasters which caused 406,866 deaths for last five years.

Emergency Management

The past decade has seen many attempts to develop strategies to cope with emergency situations. Emergency management is the collective term encompassing all aspects of planning for responding to emergency situations. Research in emergency management includes the adoption

Figure 1(a). Annual death toll caused by natural disasters since 2003 (Wikipedia, 2008)

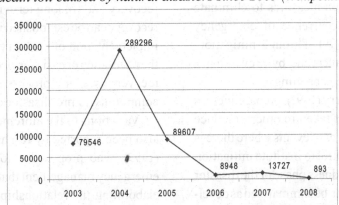

Figure 1(b). Major Disasters Since 2003 (Wikipedia, 2008)

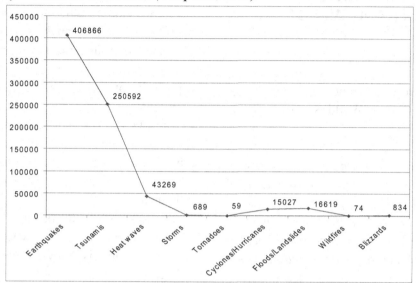

of technologies and utilization of computerised systems for sensor, communication, simulation, forecast and information management. Emergency management concerns with all aspects of emergency situations: risks, consequences, as well as pre and post emergency activities, such as prevention, mitigation, preparedness, response, recovery and rehabilitation. Research in emergency management discipline reported different models to conceptualise types of emergency management activities. A commonly used model consists of four phases such as mitigation, preparedness, response and recovery (Peterson & Perry, 1999)

Mitigation is a process of planning and taking long term risk-reduction measures to eliminate hazards before the occurrence of emergency (Peterson & Perry, 1999). Through mitigation, organizations try to intervene by preventing a destructive event from happening.

As described by Perry (1991), preparedness is "a collection of actions taken in order to reduce the vicious consequences of events where there is insufficient human control to institute mitigation measure". The preparedness phase of the disaster management process can be summarized as devel-

oping action plans in order to handle emergency scenarios. Such plans depend upon the analysis of hazard severity and vulnerability conducted in mitigation phase.

McEntire (1999) defined response as "actions taken in anticipation of, during, and immediately after a disaster to ensure that the effects are minimized and immediate attention is provided to victims".

The actions taken following the emergency phase are often defined as recovery phase. This phase includes both rehabilitation and reconstruction. The objective of this phase is to make the system normal, or near normal. Recovery can be decomposed into two main types (a) short-term recovery and (b) long term recovery. Short-term recovery can be established immediately with the implementation of recovery plan and it involves the restoration of basic services whereas long-term recovery is a long process aiming to return the community to pre-disaster condition.

Variations to the aforementioned model have also been reported by researchers such as Kelly (1999), who proposed a four phase model for emergency management that help in defining and elaborating the relationship inputs and impacts rather than simply classifying various stages in complete emergency management life cycle. Asian Development Preparedness Centre (2000) and Atmanand (2003) analysed the different phases of emergency management as a continues process rather than a sequential one. According to their model, all four phases of emergency management run parallel to each other with variation in the degree of emphasis. Furthermore, this model suggests that emergency management consists of various activities that occur simultaneously. Kimberly (2003) proposed an emergency management model that consists of four phases including mitigation, preparation, response and recovery. This model declares *response* as most important and visible phase as compared to other phases of emergency management. It places *mitigation* and *preparation* at the base, suggesting that they are both driving forces behind a successful response. As recovery takes more time and is most costly phase therefore it has been placed at the top. Tuscaloosa (2003) suggested emergency management as an open ended process that contain four phases as mitigation, preparedness, response and recovery. This model further argues that mitigation is a starting and ending point of this cyclic model.

Other emergency management models consist of different groupings. Turner (1976) introduced a model for emergency management life cycle that consists of six stages: (1) notionally normal starting points, (2) incubation period, (3) precipitating event, (4) onset, (5) rescue and salvage, (6) full cultural readjustment. Mayer (1993) proposed a disaster management process in four periods, namely normal operations, emergency response, interim process and restorations. Richardson (1994) proposed a disaster model which defines three stages for disasters: (1) before disaster, (2) during disaster and (3) after disaster. Prabhu et al. (2004) used the Turner's Six Stage model, and proposed a seven stage model for disaster management: (1) the incubation period, (2) the operation-socio-technical system, (3) the precipitating event, (4) the disaster itself, (5) rescue and salvage,

(6) inquiry and report, and (7) feedback. Lastly, Ibrahim-Razi et al. (2003) proposed a model that represents the technological disaster pre-condition stages. The model is composed of eight phases: (1) inception of error, (2) accumulation of errors, (3) warning, (4) failure of correction, (5) disaster impending stages, (6) triggering events, (7) emergency stage, and (8) disaster.

CLASSIFICATION OF EMERGENCY MANAGEMENT ACTIVITIES

From the foregoing, it is evident that there is a lack of uniformity to perceive emergency management activities. Rather than focusing on the different phases in emergency situations, this chapter introduce an activity based perspective. In the proposed model, common activities involved in emergency management are noted and categorised into four distinctive classes: authentication, automation, tagging and tracking, and information management (AATI). The identification of these four activities is based on thorough consideration and review of the existing emergency management models. Furthermore, the aim of identifying these activities is to facilitate the technological adoption process in emergency management.

Authentication

Authentication is any process by which a system verifies the identity of a user who wishes to access it. Reliable authentication is the basis for protecting financial data, valuable assets, and confidential information from theft, misuse, and fraud. If users are not properly identified, and if that identification is not verified through authentication, an organization has no assurance that access to resources and services is properly controlled; everything hinges on the true identity of the user", as cited in (Kelley, 2001).

Rigorous and flawless authentication system is highly desired in emergency management. It has the ability to prevent most of the disasters before their occurrence. Strong authentication assures that only valid users can interact with the system which will eventually minimizes the risks of various man-made disasters such as technological disasters and terrorist attacks. In the context of emergency management, authentication covers the following sub-activities:

- Define policies to implement authentication protocols
- Assigning privileges to access the system
- Verify all access requests
- Block the unauthorized access/use of system.

Authentication is not only important during "prevention" of manmade disasters, but it is equally important in natural disasters as well. Emergency management life cycle requires several types of information and objects to secure from illegal and unauthorized use.

Automation

Automation is a process of using control system, such as computers, to control machinery and processes, replacing human operators (Wikipedia, 2006). Replacement of humans with control systems has some advantages as well as disadvantages. Reduction in labor cost, working in harsh climatic conditions, and consistent working hours are few advantages of automation whereas human pattern recognition, language recognition, and language production ability is well beyond anything currently envisioned by automation engineers. Importance of automation in emergency management is quite significant. Emergency related experiences suggest that in most emergency cases, the real barriers are not lack of data or insufficient technological capabilities. The real bottleneck is the automatically handling of information. Consistency and efficiency in information processing is highly required in an emergency situation, and it can be achieved by automating the most critical information processing tasks (Zlatanova et al., 2004). Automation includes:

- Identification of tasks which can be done by control systems; replacing humans
- Automatic detecting of inputs using sensors
- Automatic decision making based on the received data; using artificial intelligence
- Using technology to assist in human decision making process.

Tagging and Tracking

Tracking is a process of capturing and maintaining the information of any moving object and it has been a real challenge for researchers and scientists. Various types of tracking techniques and technologies have been introduced. Global Positioning System (GPS) and Pattern Recognition are few examples of such techniques. The purpose of tagging and tracking is to identify the target object in a group of similar objects as well as to keep real time information about its position. People and object management are the main objective of tagging and tracking. Most of the emergency management experiences show that during an emergency situation, one of the most important and urgent problems at the scene is the overwhelming number of patients that must be monitored, tracked and managed by each first responders. The ability to automate these tasks could greatly relive the workload for each responder. Tagging/tracking can be further decomposed into following sub activities:

- Marking or tagging of humans and objects
- Use these tags to track humans and other objects
- Use these tags for human/object management before, during and after emergencies.

Information Management and Communication

Information management is the collection and management of information from one or more sources and distribution to one or more audiences who have a stake in that information or a right to that information. Initially it was largely limited to files, file maintenance, and life cycle management of paper and a small number of other media. With the proliferation of information technology starting in the 1970s, the job of information management took on a new light. No longer was information management a simple job that could be performed by almost anyone. An understanding of the technology and the theory behind it became necessary, as information was ever more stored via electronic means. By the late 1990s when information was regularly disseminated across computers and other electronic devices, information managers found themselves tasked with increasingly complex devices. With the latest tools available, information management has become a powerful resource for organizations (Wikipedia, 2006). In emergency management, information management and communication plays a vital role. Study of recent emergencies shows that at some level or another, information was available which could have prevented the emergency from happening. Information management in emergency management is a collection of several other activities which comes under the umbrella of information management. These sub-activities include:

- Trainings/drills/exercises
- Collect information from various resources
- Broadcast warnings/alerts
- Building and maintaining information pools
- Communication with other emergency management organizations.

OVERVIEW OF RFID TECHNOLOGY

History of RFID

According to Landt (2005), the thoughts of RFID occurred on the heels of the development of radar. Both technologies use radio waves as a medium of communication, in contrast to radar technology, RFID technology is relatively economical mean of communication for short-medium range of distance. Effective range for RFID is increasing as the new advancements takes place in this technology. We can observe tremendous developments since its invention in 1948. Landt (2005) summarized major RFID-related activities in last five decades.

Characteristics of RFID

RFID is a term coined to use short to medium range of radio technology used to communicate between two objects without any physical contact. Objects on two sides of RFID link can be either stationary or moveable. A typical RFID system consists of (a) tag (b) reader/interrogator and (c) an antenna. Tags are relatively simple devices and normally attached to the objects to be managed. Tags can be classified into active tags and passive tags. Active tags operate with a battery attached to them whereas passive tags are powered by the rectification of radio signals sent by the reader. Readers are comparatively complex device which is to send radio signals to the tags and locate them. These are connected with a host computer or a network. Antenna is connected with RFID tag and mainly responsible to absorb radio signals sent by the reader and pass them to RFID tag. The working principle of RFID technology is illustrated in Figure 2.

When reader sends out the electromagnetic signals to couple with tag antenna, the tag gets electromagnetic energy from waves to power its circuits in the microchip. The chip located

Figure 2. Working Principle of RFID Technology

inside the tag then sends back electromagnetic waves to the reader, and the reader receives and returned waves and coverts them into digital data. The data transmitted by the tag actually provide the data and information of the object, and the information can be processed in any information system or network connected to the reader. A typical RFID system is able to communicate in a range of radio frequencies including low frequency, high frequency, ultra high frequency and microwave.

SCOPE OF RFID IN EMERGENCY MANAGEMENT

In the previous section, we have outlined the importance of emergency management. It is not surprising that researchers have attempted to apply many technologies to facilitate emergency management procedures. Research by Gunes & Kovel (2000), Kerle (2002), Cutter et al. (2003) suggested mapping technologies into emergency management phases. Other researchers, such as Love, Mariam, & Vogel (1998), Kelly (1999), Manitoba-Health-Disaster-Management (2002), Cyganik (2003) and Tuscaloosa (2003) also reported the use of technologies for disaster management. These models represent various phases, processes and activities involved in emergency management. The following section provides a summary of technologies used in authentication,

automation, tagging and tracking, and information management.

Technologies for Authentication

Biometric Authentication: In biometrics-based personal authentication, biometric data that is to be used for reference in comparison (referred to as template data) is registered in advance in the same way as when passwords are used. In the authentication processing, another biometric data that was input from a sensor is compared with the pre-registered template data and a degree of similarity is calculated. This degree of similarity serves as the basis for deciding whether or not this person is the authorized person.

Smart Card: Smart cards serve as security tokens by securely storing users' personal data and service providers' private information. The cards interact within a system using special communication interfaces and dedicated protocols. Smart cards provide highly reliable mechanisms for storing, accessing, and using data in nonvolatile memory. Data access control and data management follow a security policy based on cryptographic services and defined for a specific application (Dhem & Feyt, 2001). Hence it can be used as a reliable mode of authentication.

Authentication by Password: In a computer network, if a user wants to log in to a remote server, he/she must submit his/her personal identity (ID) and password (PW) to the server. Once the ID and the PW match the corresponding pairs stored in the server's verification table, the user will be granted access to the server's facilities.

RFID: RFID can help in the authentication. The process of authentication by using RFID technology is as follows. When a product (any object) passes a RFID reader, the reader checks whether the necessary and authentic product and reference information is present on the tag. For this purpose it runs a protocol with the tag. If the necessary information is there and verified to be authentic, the product is declared to be genuine and otherwise not.

Technologies for Automation

Artificial Intelligence: It can also refer to intelligence as exhibited by an artificial (*man-made, non-natural, manufactured*) entity. Research in artificial intelligence is concerned with producing machines to automate tasks requiring intelligent behavior. Examples include control, planning and scheduling, the ability to answer diagnostic and consumer questions, handwriting, natural language, speech and facial recognition. As such, the study of AI has also become an engineering discipline, focused on providing solutions to real life problems, knowledge mining, software applications, strategy games like computer chess and other video games.

Robot: A robot is a mechanical or virtual, artificial agent. A robot is usually an electro-mechanical system, which, by its appearance or movement, conveys a sense that it has intent or agency of its own.

RFID: Strong power of RFID for authentication and tracking makes it suitable for automation process. Reliability and efficiency of a technology are the key things to qualify for automation. In automation process there is least involvement of humans and technology is by its own at most of the times. Therefore, its reliability should be well proven. RFID has proved itself for automation in various capacities. Supply chain management,

inventory control, transportation and manufacturing are few examples of RFID as an automation technology.

Technologies for Tagging and Tracking

Optical Gyroscopes: Gyroscopes are used to make angular velocity measurements. Optical gyroscopes operate on TOF principle. They use laser light (Fibre optics gyroscopes or FOG, Ring laser gyroscope or RLG) and time of propagation to extract angular velocity of a target. They are light, durable, and low in power consumption.

Spatial Scan: The principle of spatial scan trackers is based on either the analysis of 2D projections of image features or on the determination of sweep-beam angles to compute the position and the orientation of a target. The optical sensors are typically cameras (CCD), lateral-effect photodiodes, or 4-quadra detectors.

Video Metric: The video metric technique employs several cameras placed on a target (e.g. the head of a user). The reference has a pattern of features (e.g. the ceiling panels) whose locations in 3D space are known. The cameras acquire different views of this pattern. The 2D projections of the pattern on the sensor can be used to define a vector going from the sensor to a specific feature on the pattern. The position and orientation of the target is computed from at least three vectors constructed from the sensor(s) to the features.

Beam Scanning: This technique uses scanning optical beams on a reference. Sensors located on the target detect the time of sweep of the beams on their surface. The time variable is transformed into a variable (e.g. angle) for extracting the position and the orientation of the target.

Phase Difference: Phase-difference systems measure the relative phase of an incoming signal from a target and a comparison signal of the same frequency located on the reference. As in the TOF approach, the system is equipped with three emitters on the target and three receivers on the reference.

RFID: The basic premise behind RFID systems is that you mark items with tags. These tags contain transponders that emit messages readable by specialized RFID readers. Most RFID tags store some sort of identification number; for example a customer number or product SKU (stock-keeping unit) code. A reader retrieves information about the ID number from a database, and acts upon it accordingly. RFID tags can also contain write able memory, which can store information for transfer to various RFID readers in different locations. This information can track the movement of the tagged item, making that information available to each reader.

Technologies for Information Management

Mobile Devices: Mobile devices such as cellular phones, Personal Data Assistants (PDA), handheld PCs, laptops have given new direction to information management system. Real-time data gathering, concurrent data transformation and instant data transmission become possible with the use of such mobile devices. Developers are augmenting these handheld devices with ever-increasing functions that cross boundaries, such as GPS-enhanced PDAs and games or cameras on phones. Communication technologies such as Blue tooth, WiFi, and G3 will make it easier for these devices to communicate with other handheld, appliances, and computers.

Computers: Computers are considered to be the most common and popular device used for information management. It is used as data storage, data transformation and data transmission. Currently there would be hardly any field of life that is not using computers where information management is required. Recently it was introduced as an integrated disaster management communication and information System (Meissner et al., 2002)

Sensors: Sensors are playing an important role in information management. A sensor information management system is a component of a sensor network; it is the information management component. Sensor information management systems essentially extract information out of the sensor data and manage the information. Sensor data management systems manage the sensor databases. These databases may not be full-fledged secondary storage databases as in the case of relational databases being used, for example, for banking and airline reservation applications. These databases could be main memory databases. Essentially sensor information systems encompass both sensor information management systems and sensor data management systems (Thuraisingham, 2004).

RFID: RFID is a technology that can play an important role in information management. Its characteristics such as no-line-of-sight and read/write make it a top choice for data gathering and data transmission. Recent researches proposed the use of RFID for information management in various domains such as supply chain management, manufacturing, procurement and transportation (Raza et al., 1999).

Other reports on the use of RFID include the following. RFID is being used in some hospitals in order to track a patient's location, and to provide real-time tracking of location of doctors and nurses in the hospital. In addition, RFID can be used in hospitals to track the expensive and critical equipments, and even to control the access of drugs and other clinical instruments. In Taiwan the application of RFID in hospitals has accelerated since 2003 due to rapid spread of SARS. In 1997, Exxon Mobile introduced "*SPEEDPASS,*" an RFID based system that allowed customers to make credit gasoline purchases by waving a tiny transponder in front of the gas pump. *MASTER-CARD* introduced "a contact-free RFID payment chip called "*PAYPASS*" that will be available in credit cards and Nokia cell phones" (Garskof, 2004). In Rheinburg, Germany, Metro opened the "Store of Future", which has RFID technology installed for checkout and for replenishment of store shelves (Collins, 2004). Shoppers log into the system by scanning a customer id-card into the touch screen, according to "metro Opens," in 2003. The device lets them scan bar coded goods as they place them in grocery cart, which then sends the price to checkout through the wireless network. This eliminates scanning at checkouts.

LITERATURE REVIEW ON ADOPTION MODELS

The use of different technologies in various domains has been presented in the previous section. The application of those technologies is not without challenges and difficulties. Therefore, it is important that the adoption of a particular technology in a domain should be carefully studied. In our study, we submit that the use of RFID in emergency management activities can be most effective when the process is guided by the Task-Technology mapping. The background theory for our adoption model together with literature review on adoption models are presented as follows.

Sharma, Citurs, & Konsynski (2007) studies the adoption factors of RFID technology which is considered to be an inter-organizational tool. For this purpose, a research model is proposed based on integrating two innovation adoption theories namely the strategic choice theory, with an emphasis on improving efficiency and the organizational performance, and the institu-

tional theory, with an emphasis on conforming to external organizational pressures. Based on the integration of aforementioned theories, the model examines four types of adoption factors that are technological, inter-organizational pressure, organizational readiness, and external environmental factors. The model determines the influence of each factor in the adoption of RFID as well as post adoption integration decision by a firm. Tornatzky et al. (1990) proposed a model for technological adoption in e-business. This model identifies three aspects that influence a firms adoption and implementation processes. These factors are classified in three categories including technological, organizational and environmental factors. An exploratory adoption model proposed by Iacovou et al. (1995) regarded technological as perceived benefits, organizational as organizational readiness and environmental factors as external pressures. This model called these factors as adoption influencers.

Goodhue & Thompson (1995) shed a different light with their Task-Technology Fit (TTF) model. They define Task Technology Fit as "the degree to which a technology assists an individual in performing his or her portfolio of tasks. More specifically, TTF is the correspondence between task requirements, individual abilities, and the functionality of the technology." The concept of TTF is depicted in Figure 3.

Goodhue & Thompson (1995) reported that the characteristics of a technology or a tool are

Figure 3. Task-technology fit model

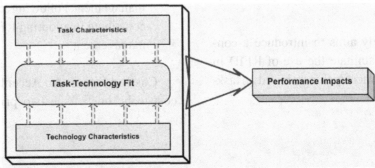

used in performing some tasks. Generally, the technologies/tools are computers, sensors, robots, data, artificial intelligence, and information technology and these technologies are often used for data manipulation, data gathering, intelligent decision making and transferring data from one data point to another.

Goodhue & Thompson (1995) also proposed a theoretical model (known as The Technology-to-performance chain (TPC) model) by integrating Task Technology Fit (TTF) model and Utilization Focus Model (UFM). The purpose of TPC is to better understand the linkage between information systems and individual performance. Furthermore, this model claims that, to have positive impact of information technology on individual performance it must be utilized; and must be a good *fit* to the tasks (jobs) it supports.

The aforementioned literature review highlights several adoption theories and strategies which can be used for proposing the use of RFID in emergency management. After careful analysis of these models, we decided to use task-technology fit model as a foundation for our conceptual model. Decision of using TTF is based on the following reasons:

- Emergency management is a group of various activities (tasks) namely authentication, automation, tagging and tracking, and information management
- RFID is used to carry out various tasks in this domains
- The tasks in the emergency management and the functionalities of RFID seem to fit well.

Hence, this study aims to introduce a conceptual model to facilitate the use of RFID in emergency management activities based on task-technology fit model.

PROPOSED FRAMEWORK

Little evidence is found in the current literature which explicitly deals with the adoption of a technology in emergency management. In the attempt to fill the research gap, we propose a conceptual framework to guide the adoption of RFID in emergency management based on TTF model. Task characteristics are the actions performed in turning inputs to outputs. To perform such actions, the support of any appropriate technology is highly desired. Task-Technology Fit is the degree to which a technology assists an individual in performing his/her tasks. Furthermore, TTF is the correspondence between risk requirements, individual abilities and the functionality of the technology. By using the basic concepts of TTF and CEMA, we propose an activity based framework that provides the foundation for using RFID in emergency management. Our proposed model is shown in Figure 4.

The proposed framework consists of three tiers (layers):

1. Emergency management activities Tier (EMAT) also known as AATI tier deals with the type of emergency, characteristics of emergency, emergency management model and the activities involved in that model. This tier highlights the activities in a particular emergency management model and segregates them into AATI.
2. Adoption Issues Tier (AIT), highlights the issues or factors which play important role in adoption process of RFID in emergency management. Following are the issues which contribute in adopting RFID in emergency management.

Costing Issues: An Accenture survey found cost to be one of the two primary barriers to

Figure 4. Activity based framework for use of RFID in emergency management

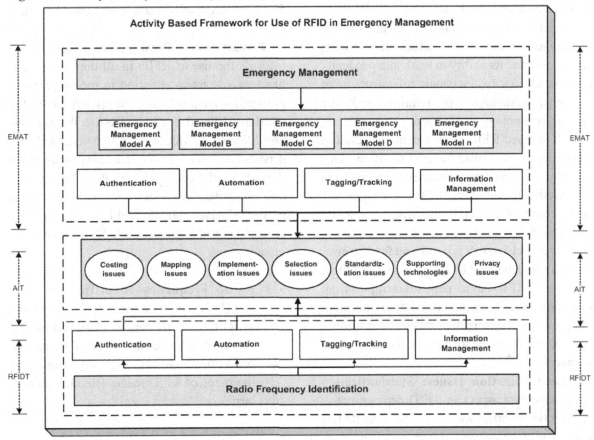

the implementation of RFID (McGinity, 2000). Reports on the current cost of RFID tags varies, however they all find common ground in noting that the current cost of tags is too high. Cost is an important factor that influences the decision whether or not to adopt the technology. Although in emergency management, cost of technology will be less important when compared to benefits achieved by the use of such technology. Nevertheless, this module identifies various cost-related issues that can be encountered during the deployment of RFID in emergency management.

Mapping Issues: Based on the concept of TTF, technology characteristics should be carefully mapped on the task characteristics so that technology adoption can yield maximum benefits. This module highlights the importance of proper

mapping of RFID for certain task in emergency management. It addresses the task-technology fit characteristics of RFID in emergency management.

Implementation Issues: Implementing a particular technology in emergencies is a complex process. The main problem in the implementation process is the unfavourable conditions during emergencies. It is highly desirable for emergency workers to be able to immediately deploy the new technology in the affected areas, including those with destroyed infrastructure, such as no electricity supply. Similarly, the technology should require less resources and support (including training, maintenance, troubleshooting and upgrade) during emergencies. RFID instruments have the ability to operate in uncontrollable climate, and often, extreme conditions like harsh weather and unsuitable working environment. It has promising potential to meet most of the challenges of emergency situations. Simple, easy to use and its ability to work independently (without electricity, telephonic infrastructure or any other technological pre-requisite) make it a suitable technology in emergency management. A well planned RFID deployment can result in robust performance in emergency situations. This module aims to address implementation concerns like physical installation of RFID devices, protection, security and overall maintenance of RFID infrastructure.

Selection issues: It is important for organisations to select the right RFID type devices. Often, selection of RFID device depends on inputs from other aforementioned modules. Hence, this module provides a systematic procedure to select a suitable RFID device for a particular emergency scenario.

Standardization Issues: Standardization is an important aspect in RFID deployment. It ensures the seamless working of different RFIDs regardless of their types and frequency bands. According to Michael & McCathie (2005) there is an apparent lack of standards hindering the technology adoption and its global use. Currently EPC Global network (a member based organization) is working RFID standardization, but its standard is yet to be backed by International Standard Organization (ISO). Authors further argued that there is no standard supported by all stakeholders that meets the need of all users. Therefore, the aim of this module is to investigate and resolve the standardization issues involved in the use of RFID in a particular disaster scenario.

Supporting Technologies: In order to achieve optimise the outcome of the RFID deployment in emergency management, supports of other existing technologies such as information technology, computer technology and bio-technology might be desired. This module draws the coordination

of supports from other technologies for successful deployment of RFID in emergency management.

Privacy Issues: Privacy poses a huge barrier towards the use of RFID in all domains and it has received much attention in recent years as journalists, technologists, and privacy advocates who have debated the ethics of its use. Want (2006) and Michael & McCathie (2005) claimed that privacy issues loom as one of the biggest threats to the unbridled success of RFID. Privacy concerns have the potential to "stop a technology dead in its tracks". This module highlights the privacy issues involved in the use of RFID in emergency management.

3. Radio Frequency Identification Tier (RFIDT) encompasses different types of RFIDs. RFID can be classified on the Tag type (active or passive tag), frequency band (low, high, very high, ultra high) and the range of RFID reader (small, medium, large).

POTENTIAL BENEFITS

It is anticipated that successful deployment of RFID in emergency management will bring benefits. As activities in emergency management have different characteristics and requirements, RFID may reveal different degree of task-technology fit to match with each activity. In our study, we propose to measure the task-technology fit using five factors, namely response time, efficient tagging and tracking, enhanced compatibility, reduced labour cost and robustness. These factors along with their significance in emergency management perspective are shown in Figure 5.

The following is a brief description of potential benefits from using RFID in emergency management.

Figure 5. Potential benefits of use of RFID in emergency management

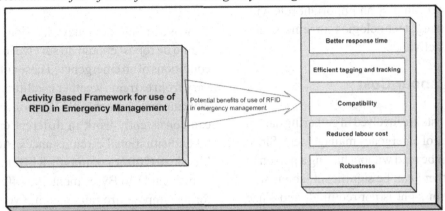

Better Response Time

Response time is a crucial factor during and after an emergency situation. Emergency managers are very concerned with the time required to respond to any emergency, and the time taken during an emergency situation. RFID has the ability to minimize the time required to respond any emergency situation and also shrinks the procedural delays in all phases in the emergency management life cycle. Fry & Lenert (2005) proposed an integrated hardware-software system (MAS-CAL) based on RFID technology that enhance management of resources at a hospital during a mass causality situation. It includes interfaces for a hospital command centre, local area managers (emergency room, operating suites, radiology, etc.) and registration personnel.

Efficient Tagging and Tracking

Efficiency is generally described as useful work per quantity of energy. As compared to the other technologies used for tracking such as GIS, RFID needs less setup in order to put it in action. Furthermore, the characteristics of RFID such as contact-less and no-line-of-sight put this technology on top priority where efficient and reliable tracking is required. During and after an emergency situation, tracking humans (people management) and other objects (management) are very important. RFID can help in managing people and other objects before, during and after an emergency situation. Example of using RFID during an emergency situation is the placement of radio frequency identification device (RFID) microchips inside victim bodies that provided a practical solution to problems of body tagging and attribution in the DVI setting encountered by the Austrian DVI team in Thailand in early 2005 (Meyera et al., 2005).

Compatibility

In emergencies, working conditions are not normal. To deal with such unfavourable conditions, several technologies have deployed in emergencies. All requirements of emergency management are hard to carry out by the use of only one technology. Emergency management really needs "teamwork" of technologies. In such scenario, a technology which offers better compatibility with other technologies is highly desired. RFID has ability to work along with various other technologies. Compatibility of RFID with other technologies such as telecommunication, information technology, and robotics has already been proven (Fry & Lenert, 2005; Kleiner et al., 2006;

Zhu et al., 2005). Hence, to deal with emergency situation, RFID can play an important role with other supporting technologies in emergency management activities.

Reduced Labour Cost

High labour costs are involved in gathering data in various phases of emergency management. Since RFID tags can be read without having a person to gather data, there can be significant labour savings. As line of sight is not required, and since multiple tags can be read simultaneously instead of one at a time, the efficiency savings could be huge. Reduction in labour cost with RFID deployment in many sectors is already proven. For example, in distribution systems, it was reported that the labour cost reduction can be as high as 30% (Pisello, 2004); while retail stores can see a labour reduction of 17% estimates by Kurt Salmon Associates (1993). Kearney (2004) estimated the labour cost savings in manufacturing industry to be 9% and at retailer stores and warehouses to be 7.5%. Accenture estimated, as reported in Lacy (2005), that the savings in receipt is 6.5%, while 100% of the labour in physical inventory count could be eliminated. Gavin et al. (2003) also report labour savings in receipt as 5% to 40%, stocking as 22% to 30%, cycle counting as 95%, and checkout as 5% to 45%. Quarterly (2003) estimates are 0.5% to 1.6% in distribution, and 0.9% to 3.4% in the stores. SAP (2003) estimated an more aggressive reduction. At retailer warehouses, they estimated a reduction of 20% to 30% in receiving cost, and 40% to 50% in picking cost. At stores, they estimate a reduction of 65% in receiving, 25% in stocking, and 25% in cycle counting. Finally, Booth-Thomas (2003) reported that Marks and Spencer achieved labour savings equivalent to 1% of its revenue in their RFID project. Similarly, the labour saving due to RFID use in various emergency management activities could be significant and it could be an important potential benefit of adopting RFID in emergency management.

Robustness

To work in an emergency situation, technology should be robust enough to survive in the varying conditions of an emergency. These conditions can vary from extreme weather conditions to adverse working environments. RFID is a technology that can consistently work in different environmental and situational circumstances. According to Massload (2007), commonly RFID tag specifications include 16 Bytes memory, $-40°C$ to $185°C$ for its temperature range, with 3 years standard life cycle at 1 data pulse every 2 seconds. This specification makes RFID tag an attractive option to be used in many emergency management activities because of its technological robustness that can survive even in unfavourable environmental conditions.

CONCLUSION

This chapter has presented some of our initial work in developing a framework for adopting the use of RFID in emergency management. It includes literature reviews on current emergency management models, use of RFID and adoption models. The proposed framework is based on task-technology mapping, following the Task-Technology Fit model. Common tasks in emergency management life cycle have been categorised into four core activities, namely authentication, automation, tagging and tracking, and information management. Likewise, core capabilities of the technology have been identified. Interaction among emergency management activities (task characteristics) and RFID characteristics (technology characteristics) is represented in the proposed framework. To validate the proposed framework, case study method is used. Five emergency management organizations are selected worldwide. An interview protocol including open and close ended questions is prepared to collect the empirical evidence from case organizations. Work in progress includes analysis of empirical evidence by using pattern matching technique. Results generated from the analysis of collected data will validate the actual potential of RFID in emergency management.

REFERENCES

ADPC. (2000). Community Based Disaster Management (CBDM): Trainers Guide Module 4: Disaster Management. *Asian Disaster Preparedness Center (ADPC) Bangkok, Thailand.*

Associates, K. S. (1993). *Efficient Consumer Response: Enhancing Consumer Value in the Grocery Industry.* Washington DC.

Atmanand. (2003). Insurance and Disaster Management: The Indian Context. *Disaster Prevention and Management, 12*(4), 286-304.

Booth-Thomas, C. (2003). *The See-It-All Chip.*

Collins, J. (2004). Self-checkout gets RFID upgrade. *RFID Journal*, August 25, 2004 from http:/www.rfidjournal.com/ article/view/1082.

Church World Service (2006). Church World Service Emergency Response Program. Retrieved 17 November, 2006 from http://www.cwserp.org

Cutter, S. L. (2003). GI Science, Disaster, and Emergency Management. *Transactions in GIS, 7*(4), 439-445.

Cyganik., K. (2003). Disaster preparedness in Virginia Hospital Center-Arlington after Sept 11, 2001. *Disaster Management and Response, 1*(3), 80-86.

Dhem, J. F., & Feyt, N. (2001). Hardware and Software Symbiosis Helps Smart Card Evolution. *IEEE Micro, 21*(6), 14-25.

Fry, E. A., & Lenert, L. A. (2005). MASCAL: RFID Tracking of Patients, Staff and Equipment to Enhance Hospital Response to Mass Casualty Events.

Garskof, J. (2004). The Many Faces Of RFID Tech: Luggage, cellphones, casino chips. The "smart tag" is starting to live up to its potential.(Headlines/ Trends; radio frequency identification). . *Popular science.*

Gavin, C., David, D., Greg, G., Lyle, G., Jeff, S., & Joseph, T. (2003). *Auto-ID in the Box: The Value of Auto-ID Technology in Retail Stores.* Cambridge, USA: Massachusetts Institute of Technology.

Goodhue, D. L., & Thompson, R. L. (1995). Task-Technology Fit and Individual Performance. *MIS Quarterly,, 19*(2), 213-236.

Gunes, A. E., & Kovel, J. B. (2000). Using GIS in Emergency Management Operations. *Urban Plng. and Devel, 126*(3), 136-149

Iacovou, I. C., Benbasat, I., & Dexter, A. S. (1995). Electronic Data Interchange and Small Organizations. *MISQ, 19*(4).

Kearney, A. (2004). RFID/EPC: Managing the Transition (2004-2007).

Kelley, D. (2001). Authentication as the Foundation for eBusiness *Security Focus.*

Kelly, C. (1999). Simplifying disasters: developing a model for complex non-linear events *Australian Journal of Emergency Management, 14*(1), 25-27.

Kleiner, A., Prediger, J., & Nebel, B. (2006). RFID Technology-based Exploration and SLAM for Search and Rescue.

Lacy, S. (2005). RFID: Plenty of Mixed Signals. *BusinessWeek Online, January 31, 2005.*

Landt, J. (2005). The History of RFID. *Potentials, IEEE, 24*(4), 8- 11.

Love, J., Mariam, & Vogel, C. (1998). White Paper on Disaster Management. *Journal.* Retrieved from http://www.local.gov.za/DCD/policydocs/wpdm/ wpdm_app.html

Manitoba-Health-Disaster-Management. (2002). Disaster Management Model for the Health Sector: Guideline for Program Development.

Massload. (2007). RFID-Brochure. Retrieved March 30, 2007, from http://www.massload.com/Brochure-RFID.pdf

Mayer, K. N. (1993). Total Contingency Planning for Disasters: Managing Risk, Minimizing Loss, Ensuring Business Continuity.

McEntire (1999). Issues in Disaster Relief. Journal of Computer Science and Information Management, 8(5), 351-361.

McGinity, M. (2000). RFID: Not Your Father's Bar Code. *IEEE Distributed Systems Online.*

Meissner, A., Luckenbach, T., Risse, T., Kirste, T., & Kirchner, H. (2002). Design Challenges for an Integrated Disaster Management Communication and Information System. *The First IEEE Workshop on Disaster Recovery Networks (DIREN 2002).*

Meyera, H. J., Chansueb, N., & Monticellia, F. (2005). Implantation of Radio Frequency Identification Device (RFID) Microchip in Disaster Victim Identification (DVI). *Forensic Science International, 157*(2-3).

Michael, K., & McCathie, L. (2005). The Pros and Cons of RFID in Supply Chain Management. *Mobile Business, 2005. ICMB 2005. International Conference.*

Mustapha, I. M. S. F.-r. A. S. a. (2003). Technological disaster's criteria and models. *Disaster Prevention and Management, 12*(4), 305-311.

Perry, R. W. (1991). Managing Disaster Response Operations. *Emergency Management International City/Country Management Association, Washington, DC 201-223 Drabek.*

Peterson, D. M., & Perry, R. W. (1999). The Impact of Disaster Exercises on Participants. *Disaster Prevention and Management, 8*(4), 241-254.

Pisello, T. (2004). The Three Rs of RFID: Rewards, Risk, and ROI from http://www.ism.co.at/analyses/RFID/Three_Risks.html

Prabhu, B. S., Su, X., Ramamurthy, H., Chu, C., & Gadh, R. (2004). WinRFID: A Middleware for the Enablement of Radio Frequency Identification (RFID) Based Applications.

Quarterly, M. K. (2003). *Why Retail Wants Radio Tags.*

Raza, N., Bradshaw, V., & Hague, M. (1999). Applications of RFID technology. *RFID Technology (Ref. No. 1999/123), IEE Colloquium.*

Richardson, B. (1994). Socio-Technical Disasters: Profile and Prevalence. *Disaster Prevention and Management, 3*(4), 41-69.

SAP. (2003). *SAP Auto-ID Infrastructure.*

Sharma, A., Citurs, A., & Konsynski, B. (2007). *Strategic and Institutional Perspectives in the Adoption and Early Integration of Radio Frequency Identification (RFID).* Paper presented at the Proceedings of the 40th Hawaii International Conference on System Sciences - 2007, Hawaii

Thuraisingham, B. (2004). Secure Sensor Information Management and Mining. *Signal Processing Magazine, IEEE 21*(3), 14-19.

Tornatzky, L., Eveland, J. D., Boylan, M. G., & Hetzner, W. A. (1990). The Process of Technological Innovation. *Lexington, MA.*

Turner, B. A. (1976). The Organizational and Interorganizational Development of Disasters. *Administrative Science Quarterly, 21*(3), 378-397.

Tuscaloosa. (2003). Tuscaloosa County Emergency Management Cycle. Retrieved June 4, 2007, from http://www.tuscoema.org/cycle.html

Want, R. (2006). An Introduction to RFID Technology. *IEEE CS and IEEE ComSoc.*

Wikipedia (2006). Wikipedia. *Journal.* Retrieved from http://en.wikipedia.org/wiki/List_of_wars_and_disasters_by_death_toll

Wikipedia. (2008). List of Disasters. Retrieved February 1, 2008, from http://en.wikipedia.org/wiki/List_of_natural_disasters_by_death_toll

Zhu, W., Wang, D., & Sheng, H. (2005). Mobile RFID technology for improving M-Commerce. *e-Business Engineering, 2005. ICEBE 2005. IEEE International Conference.*

Zlatanova, S., Oosterom, P., & Verbree, E. (2004). *3D Technology for Improving Disaster Management: Geo-DBMS and Positioning.* Paper presented at the XXth ISPRS congress.

KEY TERMS

Activity Based Framework: A research framework that combines the existing emergency management models based on their common activities such as authentication, automation, response and recovery.

Adoption Benefits: Adoption benefits refer to the advantages achieved by the use of RFID in emergency management. These benefits include better response time, efficient tagging and tracking, compatibility, reduced labor cost and robustness.

Adoption Issues: Adoption issues cover the influencing factors and the challenges involved in the adoption of RFID in emergency management. The role and significance of such issues are also part of adoption issues.

Emergency Management Life Cycle: Emergency management life cycle encompasses the major phases of emergency management cycle. Generally, emergency management life cycle comprises of four phases including mitigation, preparedness, response and recovery.

Emergency Management Model: Emergency management model illustrates the overall phases of emergency management life cycle. Several emergency management models represent these phases in different ways such as some models uses three phases, four phases, five phases, six phases, seven phases to represent the overall emergency management life cycle.

Technology Adoption: Technology adoption is a process of deploying and using a technology in a specific domain. This process further involves the evaluation of technology according to the requirements of the field and deals with the challenges involved in the technology adoption process.

Technology Characteristics: Technology characteristics refer to the strengths and weakness of a technology. It also considers the aspect of external environmental conditions which influence the performance of a technology.

Section IV
Smart Data & Convergence

Chapter IX
Subsequence–Wise Approach for Online Tracking

Bin Shen
Tsinghua University, Beijing, China

Yu-Jin Zhang
Tsinghua University, Beijing, China

ABSTRACT

This chapter is concerned with online object tracking, which aims to locate a given object in each of the consecutive frames. Many algorithms have been proposed to deal with this problem. Most make a decision in each frame, failing to consider the inner relationship among these decisions. However, the relation among these decisions is important if they can be fused together. Intuitively, human beings do not make a decision in a single frame and always explore the temporal information contained in neighboring frames, and then make decisions for all these neighboring frames. This chapter proposes a novel framework, which views the tracking as a sequence of decisions, with each subsequence of decisions corresponding to a subsequence of the video. Such an approach is described as a subsequence-wise approach. This framework considers the relation among the states in different frames, and it is ready to be incorporated into many related tracking techniques.

1. INTRODUCTION

With the development of computer vision, online object tracking is becoming a more and more active research area. It plays an important role in a lot of applications, such as area surveillance, navigation, video compression, and human computer interfaces. Besides, tracking paves the way for further process of videos, such as object classification or recognition.

1.1 Existing Approaches

Lots of algorithms have been proposed to deal with this task, from the simple feature point matching method to non-rigid object tracking.

The general idea inside these approaches can be simply described as two steps: (1) make use of the information available to model the target object or both the target and background; (2) decide where the target is in the current frame. For example, particle filter based tracking algorithm (Arulampalam, 2002, Isard, 1998) adopts the information available in the past frames to get the priori probability of the target's state for the current frame, and then the measurements are used to get the posterior probability distribution function via Bayesian Theorem. Based on the posterior the state in the current frame of the target is estimated. Mean shift based tracking algorithm (Cheng, 1995, Comaniciu, 2000) treats tracking as a mode seeking process. The model of the target for tracking is constructed based on the passed frames, and then it deploys the mean shift method to search the optimal mode the current frame. These algorithms make a decision based on the feature extracted from the current frame, while they fail to take into account the constraint among the decisions in consecutive frames, which we call a subsequence. Some other algorithms (Grabner, 2006, Nguyen, 2006) are aimed to explore not only the spatial context of the object but also the temporal spatial context. However, they still make one decision at a time, which is for the current frame, and do not consider the innate relation among the decisions in neighboring frames.

Now, to express our idea clearly, we introduce the term *tracking unit*. Here, we call a repeated component of a video sequence a tracking unit, if and only if the tracking algorithm treats each such component equivalently. For example, these algorithms listed previously treat every frame equivalently, and make a decision in an individual frame, no matter whether they make use of the temporal context. Therefore, the tracking unit for them is a single frame. While experiences tell us that when we humans track a target using our eyes, we do not make decisions about the states in several continuous frames separately. Or

rather, we will explore some inner relation among these decisions and fuse them before releasing the decision result. For instance, we are able to estimate the occluded target states if we know how the target enters occlusion and how it gets out. Therefore, it is intuitive that the constraint among decisions in consecutive frames will be helpful for our final better decisions if we can make use of it. From this example, we can further see that choosing a frame as the tracking unit may be not a good choice, for it probably fails to estimate the target's state when it is occluded. Before seeking a better choice for tracking unit, we denote these aforementioned algorithms as frame-wise approach, since they take a single frame as the tracking unit.

1.2 Proposed Approach

As discussed previously, we shall select a new tracking unit rather than a single frame in order to reasonably take into account the relation among decisions in consecutive frames. Naturally, we divide a video sequence into several subsequences, and a subsequence is adopted as the tracking unit in our framework. We denote our tracking framework as subsequence-wise approach. In this framework, we will not only be able to explore both spatial and temporal context in video, but also refine the decisions in the subsequence, and then output a reasonable sequence of decisions for all the frames in a subsequence. This approach can ensure that the set of decisions for a video subsequence is optimal according to some criteria, while the frame-wise approach can only ensure that each of the decisions is optimal to some criteria. Note that, the quality of a tracking algorithm on a video sequence should be measured based on the set of decisions in all frames, neither in a single frame nor in a subsequence, because when tracking a given object, our goal is to find the optimal path through the entire sequence. Apparently, subsequence-wise optimum is a better approximation of global optimum for a sequence than frame-wise optimum. This is our key observation. This will also be shown in the following theoretical analysis and experimental results.

If we treat the entire input video sequence as a subsequence, the result our framework gets will be a global optimal path according to some certain criteria, though in this case, the complexity may be too high. If let every single frame make up a subsequence, our framework will degenerate to the frame-wise approach.

The rest part of this chapter is organized as follows. The general framework of our subsequence-wise approach is given in section 2. In section 3, we give a simple implementation of our framework, which adopt dynamic programming as the path selection method in a subsequence. Then, a variety of experiment results on real data shows that our approach outperforms the traditional frame-wise approach. In last section, we conclude this chapter and discuss the future research.

2. SUBSEQUENCE-WISE APPROACH

A general framework is presented first, followed by the theoretical analysis.

2.1 General Framework

Subsequence-wise approach includes the following steps: 1) divide the input video sequence into several subsequences; 2) track in every subsequence; 3) fuse the results in different subsequences if the neighboring subsequence overlaps so as to get the final output.

The overview of this framework can be seen in Figure 1.

As summarized in Figure 1, we firstly divide the input video sequence into several subsequences, each of which is made up of several continuous frames. Use S_i to denote the i-th sub-

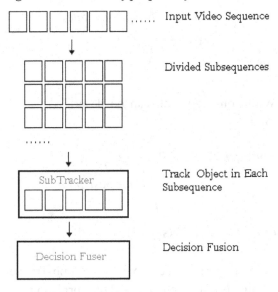

Figure 1. Overview of proposed framework

Input Video Sequence

Divided Subsequences

Track Object in Each Subsequence

Decision Fusion

sequence, f_j to denote the j-th frame, and assume the subsequence S_i contains k_i frames. There are N frames in the input video, and we divide the video into M subsequences. So,

$$S_i = \{f_{j_i}, f_{j_i+1}, \ldots\ldots, f_{j_i+k_i-1}\} \tag{1}$$

$$\forall m, n \qquad S_m \subseteq S_n \Leftrightarrow m = n \tag{2}$$

The equation (1) means that a subsequence has several frames, and different subsequences may have different lengths. We introduce the aforementioned constraint (2) to keep the division reasonable, which means not every subsequence is a subset of any other subsequence.

The traditional frame-wise approach makes a decision in a single frame without considering the constraint among the decisions around it—the decisions in previous or following frames. It can be described as follows.

Let $P_j = \{P_{ij}\}$, $i = 1, 2, \ldots, N$ denote the N possible states (e.g. position) in the j-th frame.

The frame-wise tracking algorithm is a function as follows.

For each $P_{ij} \in P_j$

$$T(P_{ij}) = \begin{cases} 1, & \text{if } P_{ij} \text{ is the optimal state} \\ -1, & \text{else} \end{cases} \quad (3)$$

$$Output = \arg_{P_{ij}} (T(P_{ij}) = 1)$$

While our approach can be described as follows.

For each $\mathbf{s}_j \in P_j \times P_{j+1} \times ... \times P_{j+k-1}$,

$$T_{sub}(\mathbf{s}_j) = \begin{cases} 1, & \text{if } \mathbf{s}_j \text{ is the best path}. \\ -1, & \text{else} \end{cases} \quad (4)$$

$$Output = \arg_{\mathbf{s}_j} (T_{sub}(\mathbf{s}_j) = 1)$$

In Figure 1, the input of the sub-Tracker module is a subsequence, and the corresponding output is the object locations in every frame in the subsequence.

Decision fusion is then required because neighboring subsequences may overlap and it is necessary to refine the output result.

2.2 Theoretical Analysis

We view tracking algorithm as an optimization process, in which we are search the optimal path throughout the entire video sequence for the given object. Frame-wise tracking can be viewed as making a decision in every frame to get the local maximum. It will have low computational complexity but may be not a good approximation of global optimum. While if we use the whole sequence as a tracking unit, we will get the global optimum as the result, but it will certainly have high computational complexity. Subsequence-wise tracking can be viewed as a tradeoff between the computational complexity and the result optimality.

Now, we show that this tradeoff does not sacrifice too much optimality. If we take all the N frames available, we will estimate the object state given the measurements in all the frames, which

are denoted as $y_0, y_1, y_2, ..., y_{N-1}$. Based on the information gained from $y_0, y_1, y_2, ..., y_{N-1}$, we obtain the estimation of the target's state in N frames x_0, $x_1, x_2, ..., x_{N-1}$. According to data processing inequality in information theory, the measurements near x_i will provide more information than the measurements far from it to estimate x_i. Therefore, $E(x_i \mid y_0, y_1, y_2, ..., y_{N-1}) \approx E(x_i \mid y_{i-\Delta'}, y_{i-\Delta'+1}, ..., y_{i+\Delta})$. This approximation can also be explained by the assuming the process as a Markov process.

Through this, we get a window, which we also call a subsequence. So, if we want to estimate the states x_i, we need only consider the $y_{i-\Delta'}, y_{i-\Delta'+1}, ..., y_{i+\Delta}$, rather than $y_0, y_1, y_2, ..., y_{N-1}$, because the measurements $y_{i-\Delta'}, y_{i-\Delta'+1}, ..., y_{i+\Delta}$ in the neighboring frames have enough information to help us estimate x_i. Therefore, each frame corresponds to a certain window with a width of $2\Delta + 1$. This window is the subsequence considered in our framework. To make the algorithm computationally feasible, we forbid several continuous frames correspond to the same window, which is the subsequence they belong to. As is analyzed previously, the frames in this subsequence maintain most information of the total video sequence to estimate the given object's state in the subsequence.

Our framework has at least two merits compared with general frame-wise framework.

1.   More information is employed for a decision-making than a frame-wise approach that does not consider spatial-temporal context.

For a frame-wise approach, we use the state before and the current measurement to estimate the current state, while in our approach we infer the current state based on the state ahead of the subsequence which current frame belongs to and all the measurements in this subsequence.

Here, $A \rightarrow B$ means that we use A to estimate B, x_i means the target's state in the i-th frame, and y_i means the measurement for the target's state in the i-th frame. Frame-wise approach can be described as follows:

$$(x_0, y_1) \rightarrow \hat{x}_1$$
$$(\hat{x}_1, y_2) \rightarrow \hat{x}_2$$
$$\cdots \tag{5}$$
$$(\hat{x}_{k-2}, y_{k-1}) \rightarrow \hat{x}_{k-1}$$

If we denote $\hat{x}_0 = x_0$, which is the initial state of the target, for any i, $(x_{i-1}, y_i) \rightarrow \hat{x}_i$, while $\hat{x}_{i-1}$ is determined by the state x_0 and all the past measurements, as $(x_0, y_1, y_2 ... y_{i-1}) \rightarrow \hat{x}_{i-1}$, so we get

$$(x_0, y_1, y_2 ... y_{i-1}, y_i) \rightarrow (\hat{x}_{i-1}, y_i) \rightarrow \hat{x}_i. \tag{6}$$

A subsequence-wise approach can be described as follows:

$$(x_0, y_1, y_2 ..., y_{k-1}) \rightarrow (\hat{x}_1, \hat{x}_2 ..., \hat{x}_{k-1}) \tag{7}$$

For any i, we estimate x_i base on $(x_0, y_1, y_2 ..., y_{k-1})$, in which k is the length of subsequence, $k - 1 \geq i$, which means

$$(x_0, y_1, y_2 ..., y_{k-1}) \rightarrow \hat{x}_i. \tag{8}$$

The mutual information $I(x_0, y_1, y_2 ..., y_{k-1}; \hat{x}_i)$ is the information we can use to estimate the x_i based on $(x_0, y_1, y_2 ..., y_{k-1})$.

Likewise, the mutual information $I(\hat{x}_{i-1}, y_i; \hat{x}_i)$ is the information we can use to estimate x_i based on $(\hat{x}_{i-1}, y_i)$.

As k is the length of subsequence and $k - 1 \geq i$, it can be seen that

$$I(x_0, y_1, y_2 ..., y_{k-1}; \hat{x}_i) \geq I(x_0, y_1, y_2 ..., y_{i-1}; \hat{x}_i) \tag{9}$$

So according to (6) and the data process inequality in information theory, we get

$$I(x_0, y_1, y_2 ..., y_{i-1}; \hat{x}_i) \geq I(\hat{x}_{i-1}, y_i; \hat{x}_i) \tag{10}$$

From (9) and (10), we can easily get

$$I(x_0, y_1, y_2 ..., y_{k-1}; \hat{x}_i) \geq I(\hat{x}_{i-1}, y_i; \hat{x}_i) \tag{11}$$

It means that more information we can rely on when we deploy subsequence-wise approach to estimate x_i than when we use frame-wise approach.

2. In our framework, it is reasonable to consider the constraint among decisions for the neighboring frames in the same subsequence, which will contribute to refining the results. However, this is directly related to the implementation of this framework, or rather, the optimization method adopted for the sub-Tracker module. The details of our example can be seen in the implementation in section 3.

3. IMPLEMENTATION OF PROPOSED FRAMEWORK

In this section, we give the details of our simple implementation of this proposed subsequence-wise framework.

3.1 The Division of Input Sequence

As mentioned before, we divide a sequence into several subsequences. The division has two parameters, one of which is the length of the i-th subsequence *sublength(i)*, the other is the length of the overlapping frames between the i-th subsequence and the (i+1)-th subsequence, which is denoted as *overlength(i)*.

As to the division of the video, here are two special cases: (1) Taking the entire input video sequence as a tracking unit to find the global optimal decisions. It is a special case of subsequence-wise approach when the length of the subsequence is equal to the input video, or rather, we take the entire input sequence as the only one subsequence. (2) frame-wise approach is also a special case of our framework. It is the same as our subsequence-wise approach when each subsequence contains only one frame, and neighboring subsequences do not overlap, which means *sublength(i)* =1, *overlength(i)* = 0.

3.2 Candidates Selection

In order to gain the optimal sequence of decisions about the states in the subsequence, we have to first determine $P_j \times P_{j+1} \times...\times P_{j+k-1}$. A simple histogram model combined with integral histogram (Porikli, 2005) is employed to search N_{cand} most likely candidates in every frame in the subsequence.

We use a 48-bin color histogram to model the object. Each of *R, G, B* corresponds to 16 bins. According to the correlation of the model and patches in every frame, we construct a confidence map for every frame, and then select N_{cand} biggest local maxima, set the corresponding position as the possible positions of object. Figure 2 shows one input frame and the constructed confidence map.

As a component of this proposed tracking framework, this module can be replaced by any other detector. For the merit of this framework, we pay adequate attention to the constraint among the decisions for the frames in a same subsequence, so the detector may be not very reliable. We'll explain why it works in section 3.3.

In each of the frames, we find the N_{cand} biggest local maxima, which make up P_j *or* $P_{j+1},...$. Accordingly, we get the candidate pool $P_j \times P_{j+1} \times...\times P_{j+k-1}$. Since there is overlapping between two neighboring subsequences, it is not necessary to detect all the frames in the subsequence. Even more simply, we can sample several frames in the subsequence, and detect only in them (Wei, 2007).

3.3 Subsequence Description

Consider the subsequence $S_i = \{f_j, f_{j+1},....., f_{j+k-1}\}$. There are *k* frames in the subsequence, and every frame contains N_{cand} candidates, which are possible states for the object.

All the candidates and x_{j-1}, the known object position in the frame ahead of this subsequence, can be modeled as a graph. What we want to gain is an optimal path connects x_{j-1} and all the frames in this subsequence. This optimal path is made up by x_{j-1} and *sublength(i)* candidates, each of which is in an individual frame.

Now we compute the cost of the path that connects two states in neighboring stages. Take three principals into account:

1. The appearance likelihood between the candidate and the model. In the framework, we maintain a 16×3-bin color histogram as a model for the object. The Bhattacharyya distance (Bhattacharyya, 1943) between the

Figure 2. Example of confidence map

model and candidate is computed to get the appearance likelihood. The model is online updated based on the previous subsequence. We use the average color histogram of the tracked object in all frames of the previous subsequence as the model in this subsequence. This model-updating scheme is able to decrease the impact of the local wrong decision in a frame, so this would be a more robust one than a one-frame based model-updating scheme, which is another advantage this subsequence-wise approach has over the frame-wise approach.

2. The consistency of the object appearance, which is measured by the likelihood between two states that the path connects. Again, we adopt the Bhattacharyya distance between the two states as the consistency.

3. Assume there is no abrupt motion. Therefore, if the one state is too far from the other, we add a penalty to the weight of the path connecting them. This means the velocity of the object will not change too quickly, which is unacceptable in most real scenarios. Note that this assumption reflects the relation among the decisions in the same subsequence. After gaining the cost map, dynamic programming is adopted to find out the optimal path through the subsequence. Therefore, the best path $\mathbf{s} \in P_j \times P_{j+1} \times P_{j+2} \times P_{j+3}$ is gained.

Obviously, many other description methods can be employed to model the candidates in a subsequence. If we take finding the true path as a pattern classification problem, any other methods, such as AdaBoost, or SVM can be adopted to deal with this problem.

When there is overlap between two subsequences, we use the decisions made in the next subsequence to obtain the final decision for the object in overlapped frames.

3.4 Track Refinement

In 3.3, we consider the constraint that there is no abrupt motion between two frames. We have added a penalty to the path that connects two states that are far from each other. We set the penalty serious enough so that a path with penalty will be selected only if all the other paths in the same stage are penalized, which means there is no reasonable detection result in this frame (stage). Therefore, when a penalized path is selected, we know that the corresponding state shall not be the true result. Instead, we estimate the result in the frame using linear interpolation based on the other reasonable results in the frames in the same subsequence.

4. EXPERIMENTAL RESULTS

We implemented the proposed framework with details described in Section 3 in C++, and tested it on a variety of challenging sequences with similar background, quick motion, and occlusion. We compare this approach with traditional frame-wise approach for the first two video sequences, the gained result show this approach outperforms the traditional one.

4.1 Quick Motion with Similar Background

We first test the algorithm with sequence moving mouse. The mouse is moving quickly and the background has the similar color with the mouse. We use simple color histogram as the only measurement. The result has been shown in Figure 3.

We set 5 as the length of subsequence, and 3 as the length of overlapping. Therefore, the algorithm makes 5 decisions in a subsequence at a time, and the first 2 of them are considered

Figure 3. Tracking Moving Mouse: Frame 1, 19, 44, 99, 164. The top row shows the result of our approach, the red rectangle means the final tracking result, and the green rectangles denote the detected candidate positions; the middle row shows the result of mean shift based method, the red circle denote the tracking result; the bottom row shows the result of particle filter based method, the red rectangle denotes the result

the final decisions. The top row shows the result of our algorithm, the green rectangles show the candidates in every frame, and the red one shows the final decision in that frame. The second row shows the result by a typical frame-wise approach: mean shift based tracker, which is implemented by (Intel OpenCV library). The third row shows the result by another typical frame-wise approach: particle filter based methods (Isard, 1998). From the results, we can easily find that in this video sequence, only our approach works well.

4.2 Occlusion

We then test our algorithm on the sequence bike man in Figure 4. The tracked person is occluded by the pole and tree branches. The first row shows the result of our approach. The second row shows the result of mean shift tracker. The third row shows the result of the particle filter tracker. On this video sequence, particle filter and our ap-

proach outperform the mean shift tracker, while our approach can efficiently avoid local error, thus more efficient than particle filter tracker, as is seen in frame 89 where occlusion occurs. A variety of other experiments has been conducted, which can be seen in Figure 5.

5. DISCUSSION AND CONCLUSIONS

Some discussion and concluding remarks are given as follows.

5.1 Discussion

It is well known that Radio frequency identification (RFID) has generated vast amounts of interest in the supply chain, logistics, and the manufacturing area. RFID can be used to significantly improve the efficiency of business processes by providing automatic data identification and capture. Object tracking, as a basic technique in computer vision, helps to capture a pre-defined object in video frames. Their combination would provide a novel object discovery framework at a high level of traceability.

Either for RFID or for object tracking, both accuracy and efficiency are mandatory. In fact, the accuracy and efficiency of video analysis are both important for information convergence. The approach presented in this chapter provide a balanced trade-off for accuracy and efficiency in object tracking, This would contribute to the fusion of object tracking and RFID in data processing and supply the potential to impact information systems in businesses as well as in our lives.

5.2 Conclusion and Future Work

In this chapter, we propose a novel framework, which we call a subsequence-wise approach. This approach takes a subsequence as a tracking unit, rather than a single frame as before. As it takes into account the constraint among the decisions about the states in the same subsequence, it is innately able to handle short-time occlusion, and can robustly avoid local error to better approximate global optimal tracking than traditional frame-wise tracking. Actually, it is a tradeoff of complexity and accuracy, a tradeoff between global optimal offline tracking (Agarwala, 2004, Buchanan, 2006, Wei, 2007) and frame-wise tracking. In addition, we can view it as a unified framework for all these algorithms as its parameters vary. Experimental results show that even if we adopt the simplest measurement, the performance is gratifying.

This framework is ready to incorporate other related tracking techniques, such as time reversibility (Wu, 2007), classification technique (Avidan, 2005, Tang, 2007) or other related techniques. Therefore, in future, we will conduct research on how to efficiently incorporate other modules into this framework to improve the performance.

ACKNOWLEDGMENT

This work has been supported by Grants NNSF-60872084 and SRFDP-20060003102.

REFERENCES

Agarwala, A., Hertzmann, A., Salesin, D., & Seitz, S. (2004). Keyframe-based tracking for rotoscoping and animation. *Proceedings of the SIGGRAPH Conference*, (pp. 584-591).

Arulampalam, M. S., Maskell, S., Gordon, N., & Clapp, T. (2002). A tutorial on particle filters for online nonlinear/non-Gaussian bayesian tracking. *IEEE Transation on Signal Processing, 50*(2), 174-188.

Avidan, S. (2005). Ensemble tracking. *Proceedings of the IEEE Conference on Computer Vision and Pattern Recognition, 2*, 494 – 501.

Bhattacharyya, A. (1943). On a measure of divergence between two statistical populations defined by probability distributions. *Bulletin of the Calcutta Mathematical Society, 35*, 99–109.

Buchanan, A., & Fitzgibbon, A. (2006). Interactive feature tracking using K-D trees and dynamic programming. *Proceedings of the IEEE Conference on Computer Vision and Pattern Recognition, 1*, 626 – 633.

Cheng, Y. (1995). Mean Shift, Mode Seeking, and Clustering. Mean Shift, Mode Seeking, and Clustering. *IEEE Transaction on Pattern Analysis and Machine Intelligence, 17*(8), 790-799.

Comaniciu, D., Ramesh, V., & Meer, P. (2000). Real-time tracking of non-rigid objects using mean shift. *Proceedings of the IEEE Conference on Computer Vision and Pattern Recognition, 2*, 142-149.

Grabner, H., & Bischof, H. (2006). On-line boosting and vision. *Proceedings of the IEEE*

Conference on Computer Vision and Pattern Recognition, 1, 260 - 267.

Intel OpenCV library. http://www.sourceforge. net/projects/ opencvlibrary.

Isard, M., & Blake, A. (1998). CONDENSATION--conditional density propagation for visual tracking. *International Journal of Computer Vision, 28*(1):5-28.

Nguyen, H. T., Ji, Q., & Smeulders, A. W. M. (2006). Robust multi-target tracking using spatio-temporal context. *Proceedings of the IEEE Conference on Computer Vision and Pattern Recognition, 1,* 578 - 585.

Porikli, F. (2005). Integral histogram: a fast way to extract histograms in Cartesian spaces. *Proceedings of the IEEE Conference on Computer Vision and Pattern Recognition, 1,* 829 - 836.

Tang, F., Brennan, S., Zhao, Q., & Tao, H. (2007). Co-tracking using semi-supervised support vector machines. *In IEEE International Conference on Computer Vision.*

Wei, Y., Sun, J., Tang, X., & Shum, H. (2007). Interactive offline tracking for color objects. *In IEEE International Conference on Computer Vision.*

Wu, H., Chellappa, R., Sankaranarayanan, A. C., & Zhou, S. K. (2007). Robust visual tracking using time-reversibility constraint. *In IEEE International Conference on Computer Vision.*

KEY TERMS

Classification Technique: The classifying methods in pattern recognition, which classify an object into its belonging category. For example, Support Vector Machine, AdaBoost, Neural Network, etc.

Color Histogram: Histogram of color image. Each of its bins counts the number of pixels whose values are in the corresponding range. It represents the distribution of colors in the image.

Computer Vision: A discipline in which people build computer systems to gain information, such as the identity of a face picture, from images or videos to represent, describe, and to understand the scene.

Object Classification: The process to classify an object into the corresponding category.

Object Tracking: The process to locate the given object(s) in a video sequence. Typically, it is based on the position of the object detected in the first frame, then it needs to locate the object in the following frames.

Offline Tracking: Given all the frames of the video and some initial positions in certain frames, then locate the object in all the other frames.

Time Reversibility: One property that the object's motion follows according to the physical laws of classical mechanics. In such a case, the object's motion is time-symmetric.

Chapter X
From Fixed to Mobile Convergence

John Ayoade
American University of Nigeria, Nigeria

ABSTRACT

The aim of Fixed-Mobile Convergence (FMC) is to provide both fixed-line and mobile telephony services to users through the same handset which could switch between networks and support both wide-area mobile network access and local-area connection to fixed-line technology, typically through a local wireless connection. An important feature of FMC is to allow users to access a consistent set of services from any fixed or mobile terminal via any compatible access point, independent of access network it is attached to. The chapter discusses the benefits and challenges of the FMC. It also analyse the efforts that have been put into realising the potentials that FMC promised in the nearest future.

INTRODUCTION

The introduction of wireless communication devices into the market, such as cell phones and PDA's, has significantly increased worker productivity, but has also increased costs, as cellular network usage has increased significantly.

Voice communication is one of the most costly pieces of an ICT service, and the costs are only growing as more employees become part of the mobile workforce. Fixed-Mobile Convergence (FMC) allows wireless users to utilise the enterprise's fixed line network to greatly reduce the number of billable cellular minutes while adding additional functionality to their mobile devices. An effective fixed-mobile strategy provides increased workforce productivity and a more reliable communication platform, while reducing overall costs. With the obvious benefits of fixed mobile converged services, the question now is how to implement an effective fixed-mobile strategy [FMCC 2007].

This chapter focuses on the FMC strategies issue. It presents an overview of fixed-mobile convergence and outlines an FMC architecture that displays the technical structure of the FMC framework.

A second section of the report is dedicated to the technological challenges, the specific requirements of FMC and the differences and barriers that may hinder the progress of the technology.

The research also highlights the benefits of fixed-mobile convergence technology. A number of organisation and companies have already taken the initiative in terms of convergence development; details of which are presented later in the chapter.

FMC warrants full industry support which is fundamental for successful development and implementation of this breakthrough technology. Several key players such as network equipment vendors, handset vendors and applications developers are required to collaborate as they all play a significant role in the FMC niche. This will also be discussed in the convergence recommendations section.

This chapter concludes with a view of the future of fixed mobile convergence and details of the enhancements in FMC technology through different stages are discussed.

About two decades ago, the mobile industry got its start on the strength of early adoption of mobile phones by business users. Despite the size and heft of those early cellular phones, business users latched on to the benefits of mobility and gave the wireless industry the boost it needed to get up on its feet and drive continued success through eventual penetration into the mass consumer space. Fast forward to today and the telecom industry is on the verge of yet another major inflection point: Fixed-Mobile Convergence [Baw 2006]

FMC is a breakthrough technology in pervasive communications with the convergence of the wired and the wireless technologies into a single solution. It is an innovative approach towards implementing a ubiquitous network infrastructure.

The technology will allow network and service operators to make more efficient use of existing access technologies (GSM, DSL, Wi-Fi) as well as taking advantage of the new access technologies such as 2.5/3G, DSL, WLAN, Bluetooth, etc by launching new voice and multimedia service. The most challenging aspect of FMC is to combine 3G cellular and Wi-Fi wireless networking into a single mobile handset and to combine the two services into a single wireless plan.

Convergence almost always results in cost savings and efficiencies because converging the traditional voice network with the cellular voice network reduces the number of devices, maintenance, and the ongoing costs of delivering voice services. In addition, the ability to deliver data over the converged voice handset allows for tremendous efficiency gains for the mobile workforce [Harrell 2007].

The technology warrants a review of the current infrastructure along with the participation and full cooperation of the various stakeholders in the industry. For example, there has to be a wide development support and manufacturing commitment from handset vendors such as Motorola, Nokia, Samsung for a dual-mode handset that would meet the FMC criteria.

Telecommunication Issues: Problem Statement

There are currently a number of physical barriers that exist between wired and wireless networks that prevent telecom service providers from reaching all of their potential customers with a full range of services.

This is particularly due to infrastructure restrictions and an insufficient support for convergence from the various players in the market. Although a few companies have already taken the initiative in terms of prototype development and implementation, industry wide collaboration is important in order to achieve the core objectives of FMC.

With FMC, wired service providers may no longer be restricted to landline networks while wireless network operators will be able to use the most robust network resources available to meet the growing demand from mobile subscribers.

FMC will eliminate such obstacles and will bring fundamental changes to the structure of telecommunications markets.

Fixed-Mobile Convergence: An Overview

People tend to access many different devices. For example, in a corporate organisation, staff, have desk phones in the office, mobile phones in their pockets, and IP phone services such as Skype on their laptops. In addition, they use voicemail, emails, instant messaging and so on in their PDAs, laptops, desktops and at public internet terminals.

The impracticality in accessing necessary and urgent information/messages becomes extremely inconvenient particularly for mobile workers and others who spend most of their time away from the office. Convergence is an ideal solution which will make workers more productive by giving them easier communications and cutting costs by putting services on the same bill. It can also give the flexibility of allowing people to work wherever they are, either on the way to or from work or from home. Figure 1 (IDC, 2005) illustrates the FMC layout.

Figure 1 represents a single mobile phone that has multiple access over GSM and Bluetooth technologies. The advantage of the multi-access mobile phone over a contemporary single access mobile phone is that the phone will decide which network is cheaper to communicate through. The next priority will be accessing the network that offers greater availability.

FMC: Understanding the Landscape

Fixed to Mobile Convergence is the mode of connection from the mobile phone to the fixed line infrastructure. It allows wireless users to transfer calls and call features from a cellular network to a wireless LAN (WLAN). With the convergence between the mobile and fixed line networks, telecommunications operators can provide services to users irrespective of their location, access technology and handset.

Figure 1. Single Phone for multi-access mobility over GSM and Bluetooth/Wi-Fi (source: IDC, 2005)

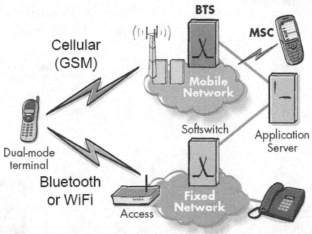

By using dual-mode handsets, devices that can connect to both cellular networks and voice-over-wireless LANs (VoWLAN), users will be able to roam between networks with a single device.

The idea behind such a technology is to allow users to access a consistent set of services by seamlessly switching networks.

FMC Scenario

NTE: Network Terminating Equipment, PSTN: Public Switch Telecommunication Network, VoIP: Voice over IP, ADSL: Asymmetric Digital Subscribe Line

Figure 2 depicts the FMC architecture. The convergent handset contains a number that supports both fixed line and cellular network. It shows that the convergent handset could actually converges all the calls from different networks and protocols for example, PSTN, VoIP, NTE, VoIP, ADSL,gateway and so on. The good thing about the FMC is that calls can be routed through various networks. The routing mechanism looks for the best route to take in terms of cost effectiveness, network and lines availability.

For example, calls could be routed to and from the fixed network through the Bluetooth or Wi-Fi access points provided the calls are within the range of coverage. However, out of range calls to the Bluetooth or Wi-Fi would definitely be routed through the cellular network.

FMC: A Pervasive Network Solution to Convergence

Figure 3 illustrates a pervasive network scenario whereby using a dual mode handset users will be able to seamlessly switch between networks in order to access both voice and data networks [Nortel 2006].

Using a single phone solution for multi-access mobility, shown in Figure 3, FMC will offer providers a converged service that will in turn allow the users to roam freely between the fixed network and the mobile network using one phone with one phone number.

FMC's seamless network switching feature is an ideal platform for ubiquitous infrastructure whereby a single handset allows users to make and receive fixed and mobile calls, eliminating multiple contact numbers, multiple voice mail and address books. This converged service, which automatically roams between a connection to the fixed network via Bluetooth or Wi-Fi and the mobile network, will surely save the user time and money.

Figure 2. Fixed-mobile convergence

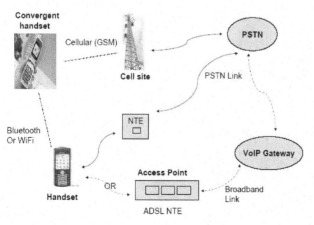

Figure 3. Pervasive solution to convergence (source: Nortel, 2006)

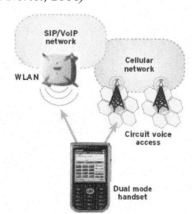

The pervasive communications scenario created by the FMC architecture will allow users freedom of movement in terms of mobile communications. Since the handheld devices are not restricted to a single channel such as GSM or GPRS the users will be allowed to exercise flexibility in terms of network switching.

Seamless switching between networks is what makes this technology fascinating and an ideal pervasive communication solution for mobility.

THE FMC ARCHITECTURE

Figure 4 illustrate the FMC architecture, which consists of an overlaid wireless LAN network that connects to an existing cellular network.

Wireless LAN access points are implemented in consumer and enterprise environments and connected to the FMC application server via domestic broadband connections or enterprise PSTN gateways. The access points use either Wi-Fi or Bluetooth to facilitate LAN connectivity to dual-mode handsets.

When a handset shifts between the coverage of the local and wide-area network environments, it seamlessly transfers between the respective networks. The wireless hotspots within the vicinity of the FMC network facilitate calls to and from the dual-mode handsets [Stoutenburg, 2005].

The FMC service is typically realised through an application server, or the FMC server. When a user on the PSTN network calls the FMC subscriber, the call is routed to the FMC server

Figure 4. FMC Wi-Fi architecture

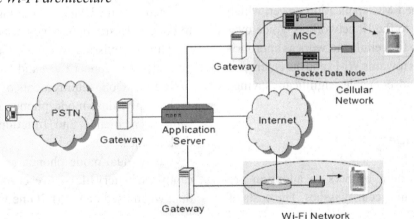

Figure 5. FMC Wi-Fi Architecture (source: Stoutenburg, 2005)

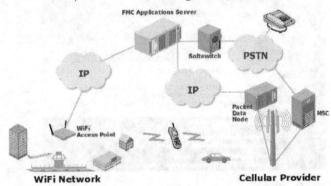

where it is anchored. Anchoring is achieved by having the FMC server act as a back-to-back user agent, which re-initiates the call toward the FMC subscriber. The FMC server can route the call into the cellular network or to the Wi-Fi network on the dual-mode device [Rosenberg 2006].

Figure 5 also illustrates the FMC architecture within a Wi-Fi network and cellular network.

Client software on the handset monitors the signal strength of both Wi-Fi and cellular networks and signals the application server which network is most suitable for a call. When each network offers a strong connection, the application has a bias towards Wi-Fi [Schwartz 2005].

The client software also serves as a fully functional IP phone that can take advantage of most business features hosted in the application server. Users can roam seamlessly between the enterprise's fixed Wireless LAN (WLAN) and the cellular network; the handset communicates directly with the FMC application server, which passes calls on to the IP network as Voice over Wi-Fi calls or to the cellular network as appropriate. With its bias towards Wi-Fi and the enterprise WLAN, the handset enables significant savings in calling costs.

FMC Challenges

The most important barriers to adoption are related to costs and security issues. The costs of time online and those involved in the upgrading of current business applications are both significantly important issues. The management and support of devices used on a converged network is also seen as a concern.

Figure 6 illustrates the various layers that form the foundation of the FMC Ecosystem. In addition to cost and security collaboration within the layers also presents a significantly challenging scenario [Gibson 2005].

FMC Requirements

Industry and researchers must overcome the following challenges to maintain a successful convergence platform:

Firstly, the service providers and cellular/VoIP/WLAN equipment manufacturers are to develop the equipment standards and build the infrastructure required to facilitate.

Secondly, the FMC's technology are required to be seamlessly transition between networks.

Thirdly, existing WLANs may need to be upgraded to support the bandwith and Quality of Service (QoS) requirements of VoIP.

Fourthly, dual-mode phones must have the same convenience and functionality as PBX desk phones.

Lastly, dual-mode phones will have significantly less battery life when used on Wi-Fi network than when used on GSM/3G networks.

Figure 6. The FMC ecosystem

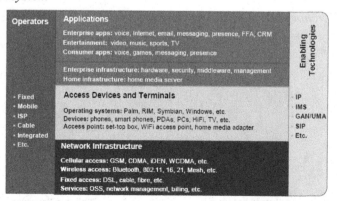

Source: IDC, 2005

Differences and Barriers

Some of the barriers linked to FMC are as follows:

- Infrastructure policies and regulations.
- Immature technologies.
- Barriers from the existing fixed and mobile networks.
- Availability of spectrum and the regime of licensing.
- Unbundling of the spectrum and wired access in the last mile.
- Pace of change, rapid obsolescence of technology and the need for fast return on investment.
- High risks in an era of competing technologies, business models, and market fragmentation.
- Security/authentication and legal framework.

Other FMC Issues

Users see mobile voice/data convergence and fixed/mobile convergence as ways to cut costs in the long term, but there are short-term imple-

mentation costs in terms of new devices and new applications. Also, there are also practical issues in keeping software updated on a set of mobile devices and in supporting users.

Furthermore, there are security and management issues: mobile convergence means complex devices are on the move in staff pockets. They may be carrying data that is at risk.

Benefits of Fixed-Mobile Convergence

As illustrated by Figure 7, there are a number of benefits associated with the FMC technology for businesses as well as consumers.

FMC Players: The Benefits

It is expected that all the players in the value chain of the telecommunications industry will benefit from the convergence of fixed and mobile technologies, leading to economies of scale.

Some of the players and their benefits are:

- **Service providers:** Service providers will be able to provide value added services to

Figure 7. Balancing service quality, convergence and bandwidth efficiencies (Source: IDC, 2005)

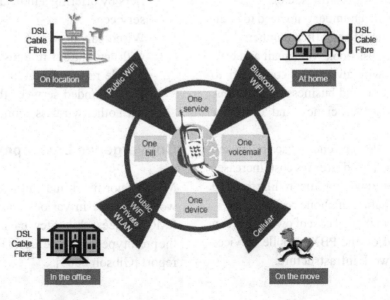

users on multiple access technologies, and retain and increase their customer base.

- **End users:** end users will be able to access their services from their home service provider anywhere, independent of the access technology and terminal they use.
- **Vendors:** vendors will develop the switching and services related products once and sell them in both the fixed and mobile markets, leading to reduced development costs.

Other Benefits

According to [Gibson 2005], fixed-mobile convergence aims to present mobile users with a uniform communications experience. FMC will combine the convenience, freedom of movement and personalised services of the wireless world with the high quality and speed of fixed communications.

The benefit would be one of convenience and simplicity, enabling new services at the same time. These benefits could include:

- Reduced cost through use of the optimum network for incoming and outgoing calls.
- Enhanced voice quality by providing fixed voice quality over a mobile phone, important where GSM coverage is spotty (inside buildings, in rural settings, etc).
- A single contact number – no need to manage fixed, mobile and office numbers.
- A single address book, voicemail and bill.
- Employees will always be connected to telephony, mail and business applications. This increases efficiency and customer satisfaction.
- Use of one device, one subscription and one number. This decreases cost, increases manageability and simplifies billing through the reconciliation of phone records.
- Improvement in total cost of ownership can be achieved on the PBX, mobile services and the network infrastructure.

- New business communication services such as presence, instant messaging, instant conferencing and other multimedia services will become available.
- Balancing service quality, coverage and bandwidth efficiencies.
- Managed FMC services improve user mobility and productivity, providing each user with one phone, one number, one voicemail, one directory, and one bill, as well as full, consistent features across multi-site enterprises and between both wired and wireless networks.
- Managed FMC services significantly reduce capital expenses per user and total cost of ownership.
- Outsourcing telephone services makes it easier to predict expenses, reduces the number of networks the enterprise needs to manage, helps control costs via least-cost routing over IP, and supports tele-workers and travelling employees by giving them access to enterprise telephony features no matter where they are.
- FMC gives enterprises an easy migration path to full voice over IP and even PBX replacement.
- FMC services will help wired carriers reverse the loss of business to cellular carriers by offering a more attractive wireless service.
- Wired carriers can create a stronger bond with new and existing customers by offering a wide range of highly differentiated and FMC branded services that are extensible with other wireless applications.

Convergence Development

Many major fixed-line and integrated operators worldwide are in various stages of developing FMC services while a few have already launched the prototypes as per the recent FMC development report [Gibson 2005].

Swisscom's Mobile Unlimited Service allows business users to roam seamlessly between different types of mobile network, UMTS, Wi-Fi, GPRS and EDGE, using a PC card. France Telecom's Business Everywhere allows mobile employees to access their network using a laptop or PDA using a single password to any access network (ADSL, 3G, Wi-Fi, GPRS or PSTN) they are closest to at the time [Gibson 2005].

According to Gibson, three operators, one in Korea, one in Japan and one in the UK, have moved further and begun to offer services where convergence is at both the device layer and the network layer:

- **Korea Telecom (KT):** KT launched One phone for consumer users. It uses Cordless Telephony Profile (CTP) technology, and consists of a dual-mode Bluetooth/CDMA handset and a Bluetooth-enabled access point. KT automatically switches calls from KT's mobile network to its local network whenever the subscriber comes within range of his or her landline's access device without the user's knowledge.
- **NTT DoCoMo's:** NTT DoCoMo's PAS-SAGE DUPLE was launched for enterprise customers. Mobile employees use a single converged handset as a 3G mobile phone outside of the office and as an IP cordless phone inside the office. Calls made within the office wireless environment are free of charge. Standard phone functions, such as call hold and call transfer, are possible in the wireless LAN mode. Through browser functionality on the phone employees can access their calendar, Web mail and other office applications in real time both in and out of the office. Presence-based services, such as IM, are also possible in wireless LAN mode.
- **BT Fusion:** BT Fusion was launched in June 2005 and is aimed at consumers and small businesses. Outside the home or office,

calls travel over BT Mobile's GSM network. Because BT does not have its own mobile network, it has entered a partnership with Vodafone to use its network. Once the user gets within range of a BT Hub, the call automatically switches over to BT's wireless broadband network. The BT Hub is a box that links the handset to a BT wireless broadband connection using Bluetooth technology. The BT Hub is also Wi-Fi enabled and can support future Wi-Fi-enabled BT Fusion handsets and be used as a Wi-Fi router as well. If the user already has a Wi-Fi network, the customer will receive a Bluetooth access point to plug into their existing Wi-Fi modem. The BT Hub has built-in quality of service to prioritise voice calls.

Many other operators in Europe, Asia and the Americas are currently holding trials of different types of FMC services across a range of technologies, and more FMC offerings will appear in the future.

The various players in the FMC ecosystem have begun working more closely on the technology and standardisation necessary for developing FMC services that address customer needs and expectations [Gibson 2005].

Convergence Recommendations

Full industry support is fundamental to the successful outcome of new initiatives in telecommunications. In the initial development of WLAN, 802.11b acted as a foundation, making it possible to progress WLAN technology to other more advanced versions. The result today is higher capacity, longer reach and a more user focused experience.

The success of FMC technology requires wider industry collaboration. The FMC network is comprised of several essential components and each component plays an integral role in the entire FMC ecosystem [Gibson 2005]. The essential players include:

- **Standard development and certification organisations (such as IEEE):** The significant role of standard development and certification organisations include setting the agenda for technology roadmaps. These organisations enable uniform approaches that are backed by the industry, which is essential sure there is a common foundation on which the industry can build its products and services.
- **Network equipment vendors:** The foundation for FMC is in the network. The infrastructure vendors have set the stage for the development of convergence. For FMC to work at network level, network equipment vendors have to work on technologies based on standards and protocols which will allow network traffic to be transported seamlessly between different types of networks.
- **Handset vendors:** For customers to access FMC services, they require handsets that are intelligent, with large storage capacity, long battery life and the capability to run complex software. The handsets should be equipped with Bluetooth and cellular technology.
- **Application developers:** Although voice is still the critical application for FMC, application developers are an integral part of an operator's ability to offer wider FMC services. FMC will initially provide seamless voice and data across Wi-Fi and cellular infrastructure. For sustained success, however, it must quickly evolve to include a number of more advanced converged applications. To enable the development of these converged applications, FMC infrastructure will present developers with the required components to achieve this, including authentication, presence and location. These will all span across networks.

The FMC Future

A future FMC service could look something like this:

Jane Smith subscribes to an FMC service. She likes the simplicity and convenience of a single phone. In the morning while she is getting ready to work, she receives a call from one of her friends. The intelligent network routes the call via her broadband connection and her home Wi-Fi network to her dual-mode Wi-Fi/cellular phone. Jane is eager to get to work and is already locking the door and getting in her car to drive to work. The FMC service routes the call seamlessly to the cellular access network and Jane continues her conversation without noticing the handover. On her way to work, Jane needs to stop at a petrol station. While paying for the petrol she calls her colleague in the office to tell him that she will be a little bit late. As it turns out there is Wi-Fi coverage available at the station. The FMC service has already routed the call over the Wi-Fi network. The FMC service is also aware of Jane's preferences in music and makes a balanced decision that the hotspot location and network speed are adequate for downloading the latest release of her favourite band on to her mobile. When Jane gets home tonight, the song will be automatically stored on her home media server. [Hills 2005]

Figure 8 illustrates the future of FMC [Cisco 2007]. The early stages include mobilising fixed applications using single-mode phone e.g. mobile email extensions, mobile access to private branch exchange (PBX) features and so on. As the infrastructure in access networks such as Wi-Fi, mesh networks, public hotspots, etc. becomes prevalent the industry will begin to move toward FMC 1.0 solutions. Finally, in FMC 2.0 users will want their services to be customised based on their own personal preferences.

Figure 8. The FMC Trend (source: Cisco Systems, 2007)

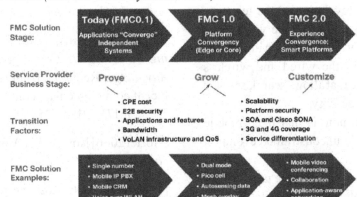

A single device will be capable of accessing services regardless of the underlying network technology and topology and a single service will be available across many devices, regardless of the underlying system architecture.

For the consumer, this means the ability to communicate anywhere, anytime with lifestyle-defining devices that offer convenience and simplicity at an acceptable price point. Consumers will have a choice in terms of what services to connect to - either automatically or through turning connectivity options on or off at will.

For the enterprise, this means that employees will always be connected to applications such as telephony, email, voice messaging, unified communications, conferencing, collaboration, contact centres and instant messaging. This unified network will decrease costs, increase control, increase employee efficiency and increase customer satisfaction [Gibson 2005].

Citywide wireless broadband networks will be implemented based on mesh and WiMax technologies. Consumers and business alike will be able to connect with these networks for voice, data or other new applications that will emerge as a result of this.

The move towards longer battery life, more storage, more memory, faster processing and smaller chipsets will continue. Future devices will be able to hold much more functionality at an increased battery time. Users and devices will be connected all the time and roam automatically to the best network for the application at the least possible cost.

Enterprises will be able to use thin mobile devices, deriving much of the applications and services over the network, and as a consequence would increase manageability and security and decrease costs [Gibson 2005].

According to [Gibson 2005], the world will enter into the invisible computing area, where the number of user and device touch points to the network will multiply exponentially. There will be an "embedded boom". Technologies and architectural components that are for a large part still separate silos today (networks, applications, services, systems, devices, etc.) will blend into a layered environment' [Gibson 2005].

CONCLUSION

This chapter evaluates the benefits of fixed-mobile telecommunications convergence and presents the challenges it faces. From the discussion it is clear that the benefits of fixed mobile convergence outweigh its challenges.

Fixed mobile convergence will open new revenue sources and realise cost savings in the long run although, until the full implementation of the technology, many challenges lay ahead.

Fixed-mobile convergence is an emerging technology that will revolutionise the telecommunications industry and will take voice communications to the new heights. It is an innovative ubiquitous solution to the wired and wireless networks convergence that allows seamless voice and multimedia connectivity.

Also important to note is that fixed mobile convergence will bring unconstrained evolution in the near future.

As discussed in this chapter, the user experience of FMC will revolutionise daily life. The key factor being that end-users will have freedom of choice in communication and ease of use because they won't need technical skills or knowledge of how to switch from one technology to the other since this will be done invisibly.

As presented in this chapter, many industries have single-handedly come up with innovative ideas regarding the implementation of fixed mobile convergence. However, for the rapid and smooth realisation of the technology, it requires joint collaboration across industry, researcher and the support of the governments and regulators.

REFERENCES

[Baw 2006] Baw, A,. *Delivering fixed-mobile convergence (FMC) services to the enterprise.* Technology Marketing Corporation, One Technology Plaza, Norwalk.

[Cisco 2007] Cisco Systems. *Generating new revenue with fixed mobile convergence.* Viewed 24 September, 2007

[FMCC 2007] *Fixed Mobile Convergence Conference (FMCC)*, 2007

[Gibson 2005] Gibson, J. F., Bilderbeek, P. & Vestergaard L. *Fixed-Mobile Convergence: Unifying the communications experience*, An IDC Whitepaper, pp. 1-43.

[Harrell 2007] Harrell R. *Fixed Mobile Convergence: Understanding the Landscape*, 2007

[Hills 2005] Hills, D. & Mercouroff, N. *Using Fixed/Mobile Convergence to Competitive Advantage.* Retrieved from http://www1.alcatel-lucent.com/com/en/appcontent/apl/T0512-FMC-EN_tcm172-521331635.pdf

[Nortel 2006] Nortel. *Why Nortel for fixed-mobile convergence?* Viewed 03 October, 2007

[Rosenberg 2006] Rosenberg J D. *SIP and fixed mobile convergence: Realizing the component architecture.*

[Schwartz 2005] Schwartz D. *InFocus: Why wireline carriers will be the early adopters of fixed mobile convergence.*

[Stoutenburg 2007] Stoutenburg, A. *Overview of FMC architecture & challenges.* Viewed 12 October 2007

KEY TERMS

3G: The third generation of mobile phone standards and technology, superseding 2G, and preceding 4G.

Bluetooth: Is a wireless protocol utilizing short-range communications technology facilitating data transmission over short distances from fixed and/or mobile devices.

CDMA: Is a channel access method utilized by various radio communication technologies. It should not be confused with the mobile phone standards called cdmaOne and CDMA2000 (which are often referred to as simply "CDMA"), that use CDMA as their underlying channel access methods.

GSM: Is Global System for Mobile communications. It is the most popular standard for mobile phones in the world.

PBX: Is a private branch exchange. It is a telephone exchange that serves a particular business or office, as opposed to one that a common carrier or telephone company operates for many businesses or for the general public.

PDA (Personal Digital Assistance): Hand held computers, also known as small or palmtop computers.

Wi-Fi: Is a wireless technology used in home networks, mobile phones, video games and more. In particular, it covers the various IEEE 802.11 technologies (including 802.11n, 802.11b, 802.11g, and 802.11a).

Chapter XI
Handling RFID Data Using a Data–on–Tag Approach

Sarita Pais
Whitireia Polytechnic, New Zealand

Judith Symonds
Auckland University of Technology, New Zealand

ABSTRACT

RFID tags can store more data and can update this data through local processing. This is in contrast to the EPC global standard of data-on-network. In order to illustrate this concept of data-on-tag a single case study of a smart laundry bin is undertaken. The laundry bin is able to process the count of soiled linen tagged with RFID at the time of Pickup. Thus the processing is taking place at the time of data capture and does not depend on the central database with expensive middleware. Further, data modelling for data stored at different objects like linen, laundry bin and pickup PDA is undertaken. Issues and solutions for this are discussed at the end.

1. INTRODUCTION

Mark Weiser (Weiser, 1993) envisioned a ubiquitous computing environment for the future where technology is omnipresent in the environment and 'invisible' to the user. This is also referred to as pervasive computing. The computing devices are small and well integrated into the environment to provide useful information where required at any time. Radio Frequency Identification (RFID) is one such promising technology in the field of pervasive computing. It is more advantageous than barcode technology having no line of sight for reading tags, can read several tags simultaneously, store more data on the tag and data on the tag can be manipulated (Haas & Miller, 1997; Hardgrave, Armstrong, & Riemenschneider, 2007). The cost of implementing RFID is also reducing, making realisation of Return of Investment (ROI) in commercial deployment more achievable.

Most commercial applications currently use passive tags and centralised data storage models

(Diekmann, Melski, & Schumann, 2007). With hardware costs falling, it is possible to think of accepting RFID tags with storage and processing capabilities. With data storage and manipulation capabilities in RFID tag, representing physical objects becomes a means of decentralised data storage (Melski, Thoroe, Caus, & Schumann, 2007). This was earlier envisioned (Gray, 2004) where smart objects are embedded with smart dust and local processing can take place at this level. Thus for some specific applications data intelligence is moving towards the periphery of a network and not relying on a central database. Hence it is important to understand how much data can be stored in an RFID tag and how it can be processed. Further, the data needs to be structured and modelled to be read and processed across the enterprise.

In order to illustrate the concept of storing more data on RFID tag and processing it, a case study of a smart laundry bin for a hospital laundry is considered. The bin should be smart enough to count the soiled linen in the bin. RFID tags are attached to linen and contain details of that linen. The bin is only not just smart enough to recognise the linen and count them but also able to write some updated data into the linen tag. Thus all data pertaining to the linen is stored in its tag close to the physical object. It does not depend on a central database or middleware software for any meaningful information from this tag data. Thus local processing can take place close to the vicinity of the objects.

In order to understand the required technology and infrastructure for the smart laundry bin, a review of the academic literature is undertaken. The main purpose is to understand the background of different RFID tags, the available standard architecture to integrate RFID data into the enterprise and whether there are any available data modelling schema and manipulation tools available.

Thus, the research focuses on finding the solution for the following question:

How can data from RFID tags be better managed in a data-on-tag approach?

First the literature will be considered. Then, the knowledge gained will be applied to a practical single case study situation. Finally, some discussion and findings will be presented to analyse the research question.

2. LITERATURE REVIEW

2.1 Background

Although barcode technology has been widely used for applications such as Supply Chain Management (SCM) to identify and track products, RFID has many advantages. First of all, a barcode has a unique identity for all items of a particular type. For example all books of the same title and author have the same barcode. However, RFID identifies each item using a unique identity. Thus each book copy has a unique product number stored on a RFID tag. Such unique identification further helps in tracing a particular book in the SCM or in an asset tracking system such as for a public library.

Secondly, barcodes need a line of sight between the label and the scanner device. The result is that using barcode technology, each book for example, needs to be handled individually and in close proximity to the scanner in order to be able to read each barcode. This process of individual handling involves expensive labour processes in the supply chain. RFID tags on the other hand are automatically scanned by interrogators from a wider range (depending on the generation of tag and reader) and multiple tags can be read in very quick succession.

In this paper we consider a case study where laundry inventory control management works on a system of five sets of linen for each bed serviced. No counting of linen is undertaken. However, stock control problems occur when linen is lost in the system and there are not enough sets of linen to service each bed in the system. Counting the linen at the point of collection is not an option due to the labour overhead and health hazards involved with handling soiled garments. Thus counting of linen at the point of collection needs to be automated and RFID technology is very efficient at automated counting. However RFID has many configurations, not all of which are suited to the laundry application.

RFID tags come with an antenna which picks the signal from a RFID reader (interrogator) and returns the signal back. There are five classifications of RFID falling into either passive or active tags (Chawanthe, Krishnamurthy, Ramachandra, & Sarma, 2004). Passive tags are mostly *read only* and some others have limited *write* capabilities. Passive tags have no power source themselves and are read by the reader by transferring energy in the form of radio frequency. Active tags have an inbuilt battery with a 3 to 5 year span(Ni, Liu, & al, 2004). Passive tags are normally cheaper than active tags. However, they have limited capabilities like some are read only, have a limited read range and a reader can read a few hundred tags at a time. On the other hand, active tags are programmable and read many tags from a bigger range more accurately. Moreover passive tags have been used in the same concept as a barcode technology by storing only limited data of the product on the tag. This could be the product id and more data needs to be fetched from the database and any manipulation on this data is done centrally in the database. This is why, it is widely used in applications like supply chain management, inventory management and asset tracking systems to identify physical objects. However, active tags could store all required data of the product in the physical object and do any data processing at the reader level which has the capability of a micro processor.

After understanding RFID tags it is also important to understand how RFID tag data is fed into the enterprise system for further processing. Literature about the architecture is researched and highlighted in the next section.

2.2 Data-on-Network versus Data-on-Tag

Initially, RFID technology developed without an appropriate tag standard. Hence Auto-ID Centre in MIT came up with the Electronic Product Code (EPC) to uniquely identify each RFID tag (Harrison, 2003). EPC specifies the minimum information on the tag, i.e. a unique identification, indexed to *look up* more details from a database via the enterprise network. Savant[1] enterprise software developed by Auto-ID centre runs on a distributed network, collecting the RFID data read by the readers. As RFID data are voluminous, there could be duplicate readings, error readings which need to be cleansed by the middleware before extracting meaningful information from the data. In most applications like Supply Chain Management, asset tracking system in libraries uses a data-on-network approach as seen in Figure 1. Data-on-Network systems also strive for data independence so that the object is never invisible to the network (Joseph, 2003). This process is often referred to as data centric routing and ensures that each data node is always available to the system. The need for all objects to be visible on the network is a disadvantage of the data-on-network system.

Recently, (Diekmann, Melski, & Schumann, 2007) highlighted a neglected aspect of 'Data-on-tag' in the literature. Here, complete data of the object is saved on the tag. It could be useful for local processing and does not depend on the backend data warehouse. This helps to reduce bottlenecks at the backend process. The data-on-network approach is a similar approach to traditional barcode systems. With the additional capabilities of RFID tags over barcode, this can open the way for new applications and approaches. This could be realised with the rapid reduction in the cost of passive tags equipped with read/write ability.

The concept of data-on-tag is not new. It has been used in production control and maintenance

Figure 1. Integrated data management architecture (Adopted from Diekmann, Melski, & Schumann, 2007)

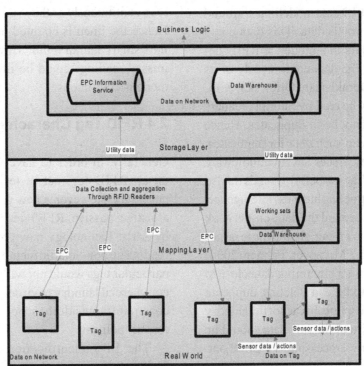

documentation in manufacturing, tracking patients and medical equipment in healthcare. In one example, additional information for garments was stored in the tag (Melski, Thoroe, Caus, & Schumann, 2007). This additional information was used to convey garment details along different stages of the supply chain. As these products travel long distances, accessing network details at different distribution centres is not possible as there is no central network connection at all times. In order to avoid bottlenecks at the central database, Ford manufacturing company stores the customised details of the production process in active tags. This does not disrupt production even if there is a network failure. Another advantage is keeping an update of maintenance documentation in Frankfurt airport's fire shutters scattered at different locations. The maintenance person reads the maintenance instructions from the tag and updates with the current date and time. In this

way, complete maintenance records can be kept and quality assurance targets can be met.

Although examples of the data-on-tag concept exist, there is no standard for storing and retrieving data stored on an RFID tag. Hence it is important to understand the nature of the data on the tag and how processing can take place.

2.3 RFID Data Characteristics

In order to define any data model for RFID data, it is first important to understand the nature of RFID. RFID tags are read by interrogators continuously creating a stream of data. These readings could be taken at different time and location as in the SCM when items move along the conveyor belt for example. Hence, the literature is consulted to find out what needs to be accounted for in the emerging data model and the issues and solutions around it.

2.3.1 Voluminous RFID Data

Most literature on RFID data modelling is around capturing the voluminous data. This data could be in gigabytes of data in a moderate RFID deployment capturing the data continuously of its location and time (Derakhshan, Orlowska, & Li, 2007). The data may be read by multiple readers too. Thus the data may be in duplicates. Hence there is a need to clean such data for duplicates. However, to ease these issues Savant middleware takes care of most of the job before it sends data to the data server for extracting business intelligence. This concept is built around the data-on-network model. In case of data-on-tag, should these issues be considered locally? Moreover, Palmer (2004) stressed the need to filter streaming data close to the source. This could mean deleting duplicate readings at the site of capture. In case of the laundry bin project, the nature of the raw data should be considered before any processing is carried out. The interrogator or the microprocessor could filter the data before uploading into a hand held device like PDA to clean and filter data and upload the required data to the data warehouse server.

2.3.2 Erroneous and Missed Readings

Another factor related to cleansing RFID data is that some of the tags are not read or they could be erroneous. There is an observed read rate of 60-70% of tags by readers (Floerkemeier & Lampe, 2004) in most of RFID deployments. The problem not only relates to reliable manufacture of the tags, but also includes packaging considerations such as placement and tag orientation. Clarke et al (2006) in a study of shipping container loads comprising of cases loaded onto pallets packed into containers report varying error rates with the best being 74-79% of container loads with 100% of tags read accurately using UHF technology. Hence these factors have to be considered while processing data to retrieve any meaningful information.

Generally RFID interrogators can operate in one of two modes. Readers can be set to either read continuously or they can be set to read once. Hence the linen is counted only once when put into smart laundry bin. However, the ratio of missed readings could be improved if the read mode is continuous.

2.4 RFID Tag Characteristics

Generally, in order to have write functionality on an RFID tag, active technology would be necessary. However, a new generation of battery assistive passive RFID technology developed by Alien Technology now provides 4K bytes of read/write non-volatile memory. Of course, these particular tags would not withstand washing in a commercial laundry environment. However, this constraint is outside the scope of our investigation for the moment.

The EPC identification number occupies 96 bits or 8 bytes and therefore should provide applications with approximately 3192 bytes of space in which to store the data structure and the data itself.

2.5 RFID Data Management

After looking into the nature of the RFID data, many researchers have studied and given solutions to refine the data for processing like dealing with heterogeneous data management, aggregation and containment.

2.5.1 Heterogeneous Data Management

Many researchers have considered the issue of heterogeneous data management. For example, (Chamberlin & Robie, 2001) propose a 'quilt' framework that incorporates a universal query language and a universal markup language to manage data from many different sources such as semi-structured documents, databases and object repositories. (Haas & Miller, 1997) investigated the use of database middleware as a tool for managing data from heterogeneous data sources. More recently, researchers have applied heterogeneous data management techniques to data collected from various sensor network sources (Sanem, Adam, & al, 2006). Sanem et al (2006) discuss the concept of a virtual sensor within the context of a crane with three physical sensors to measure load pressures and much of the processing of the raw data from the physical sensors is done locally within the crane.

2.5.2 Aggregation and Containment

The next issue to consider is the importance of aggregation or containment (Wang & Liu, 2005) (Lin, Elmongui, Bertino, & Ooi, 2007). This builds the hierarchical relationship to determine what physical objects are contained within another (larger object). In Supply Chain Management System (SCMS) a pallet contains cases of items tagged at pallet, case and item level. This indicates logic information like transport details in the pallet could specify where the item is in the SCMS. A similar situation could be thought for a bin containing linen. This could imply that the linen is soiled. However, if the status – cleaned

/ soiled is stored in the linen tag there is no advantage of building an aggregation relationship. Aggregation could help in traceability of the item in the complete SCMS all the time. Although advantageous, if this is not required all the time in the laundry project, hence there is no need for the same.

After considering the characteristics of the RFID tag data, the focus is now on the management of data for the purpose of business intelligence.

2.6 Relational Database vs. Object Oriented Database

Currently most of the commercial applications use a relational database which is not very compatible with the object oriented programming languages (Gray, 2004). Hence, integrating the backend database with the front end programming language is required. (Nguyen, 2007) modelled the RFID data taking care of the time stamped events in an object relational approach making the best use of both relational and object oriented databases. Complex data structures can be defined well in object oriented database. However, building scripting queries is not easy. The aforementioned concept of aggregation is also easily implemented through inheritance in Object oriented concepts.

Figure 2. Object-oriented database for PDA interface (adopted from Steele, Ventsov, & Dillon, 2004)

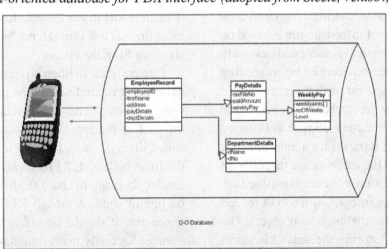

This could further help to build the interface for any PDA (Steele, Ventsov, & Dillon, 2004).

The top level objects have attributes and methods, for any further detail processing it could link to other objects and their methods. For example: the top level *EmployeeRecord* class have an object *PayDetails* object, and then this *PayDetails* object could link to *WeeklyPay* object. (Steele, Ventsov, & Dillon, 2004) proposed the object-oriented database architecture for mobiles for several reasons:

- Although object-oriented database can handle a large amount of data, aggregation helps in processing limited amounts of data.
- Aggregation also helps in limited display interface
- Integrates middle tier within the database

Although there were many advantages, the issue was the database schema or structure was known to the user through the interface.

2.6.1 Reading RFID Data into PDA

Reading RFID data into a PDA is very common in pervasive computing environment. A PDA is a handheld device which is easy to carry around and collect data anywhere in the environment. In most cases the data from the PDA is directly linked to wireless network and data transfer is done instantly. This type of infrastructure is based on EPC standard and needs expensive middleware to collect the data, filter and cleanse it before sending to the data warehouse for further processing.

On the contrary, researchers like (Schwieren & Vossen, 2007) have come up with PDA-based visitor information retrieval for a museum. The physical objects in the museum are tagged with RFID and through infra-red beacons or Bluetooth technology they can interact with a PDA loaded with information for that particular object. The PDA is capable of storing the data (Microsoft SQL Server Express) and there is no need for any

network infrastructure to connect to the backend. Whenever data needs to be updated in the PDA it can connect through WIFI hotspot or internet. Hence, the PDA maintains a copy of the required data for local access in the museum.

Having investigated the relevant literature, the design of the study will now be considered.

3. METHODOLOGY

The research approach taken in this study is design science (Hevner, 2004). Design Science is recognised in Information System (IS) literature as a problem-solving paradigm. The research involved building an artefact to illustrate the requirements for designing a standard for storing and accessing data on RFID tags. The requirements were recorded using a data model. The data model was populated and evaluated in a lab setting as a proof of concept. To help with exploring the requirements a case study is used.

4. CASE STUDY

The case study organisation is a commercial hospital laundry located in Australia. The business case for the RFID application is that the current inventory management practise of allowing five sets of linen for every bed serviced does not work if linen is lost in the system. It is estimated that most linen is lost through not being returned for cleaning from the client.

Currently, clean linen is replaced by the original order level and not by the number of soiled linen collected. The commercial laundry bears the cost of the lost linen. No manual count of soiled linen is made. In order to keep a track of the linen collected, RFID technology can be an ideal technology to count the linen as it requires no line of sight. Although RFID technology is expensive, it should be offset with the labour savings. Secondly, using the data-on-tag concept, value may be added by allowing accurate data on the number of times laundered and therefore information on the life of the linen, durability and throughput estimates for the system. Such added benefits should be evaluated against the cost of the system.

The laundry bin should be capable of doing some local data storage and processing. The main criterion is to bill the laundry clients for linen not returned and replenish lined supplies at the stock level returned rather than the stock level ordered. The system offers extra value to the laundry through keep track of the number of times each piece of linen is laundered allowing more efficient removal of worn linen from the system and costing of linen through the availability of more accurate business data.

The advantage of having a smart laundry bin is that the system does not rely on the laundry pick-up truck driver undertaking detailed processing using the PDA device. Wireless technology allows the PDA to automatically identify and

connect to the smart laundry bin when it comes in range and only requires the delivery driver to acknowledge each process through a very simple touch screen interface.

4.1 The Laundry Model

The requirements for the proposed smart laundry bin are summarised in a flow chart. (refer to Figure 3).

Through studying the full data flow model (Figure 3) several important aspects of the system can be identified: objects, receptacles, secondary storage and archive storage. Each of these is now described.

4.1.1 Object

An object is a physical item at different locations in the laundry system. It is identified electronically and has small memory storage to store information

Figure 3. Laundry flow chart - proposed

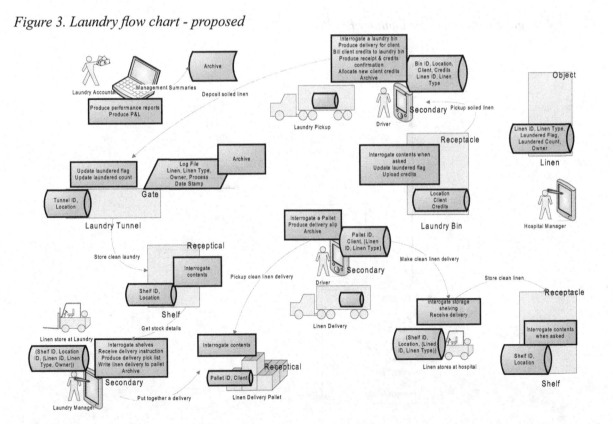

about it, for example linen. The electronic storage device is a RFID tag attached to the linen which is tough enough to withstand high temperature, detergents and water of the washing process.

4.1.2 Receptacle

A receptacle is a place where objects are collected temporally. Examples are laundry bins for storage of soiled linen. Receptacles have limited storage capabilities to store details of the bins. This is an RFID interrogator which has the ability to read the linen tags. It has additional functionality like updating some details in the linen tag (linen status – clean or soiled).

4.1.3 Secondary Storage

A secondary storage is a point where data is stored temporally when the receptacles are asked to interrogate the objects. Here some business pro-

cesses take place. It should be capable of storing a large set of functionality capabilities and larger memory storage. Examples can be PDA or tablet PC. A pickup person can then load the data from the bin into the handheld PDA and generate a receipt detailing the linen count and attach it to the respective bin.

4.1.4 Archive

At the end of the day the data from the PDA can be uploaded to the data warehouse for further processing at the enterprise level data archive. This could eliminate the need for the expensive middleware architecture.

5. DATA MODELLING APPROACH

As data is physically stored in the objects namely linen and bins, it does not need to be duplicated

Figure 4. Logical data model for Laundry Bin Project

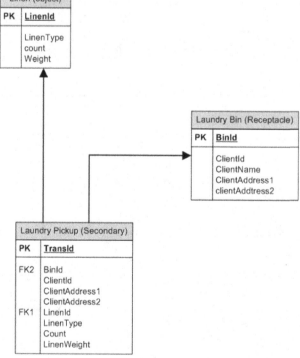

and stored in the enterprise database. This could lead to integrity issues and there might be varying data details at different levels. Hence data on the physical objects is read and manipulated whenever necessary. At pickup time, when linen data needs to be picked up by the PDA, new rows are created in the database based on the rows from the linen and bin tables (linen and bin are tables with a single row). This data is further used to process the linen count. As the system is not storing any individual's private data, it is not necessary to encrypt the data in the RFID tags.

The logical data model of objects (linen), receptacle (laundry bin) and secondary storage (PDA pickup) is projected in Figure 4.

6. EVALUATION

Using the data model (Figure 4) some sample data was generated that included duplicate readings. It was tested in SQL Server 2005 as this is widely used in the PDA database applications (see Figure 5, 6 & 7). Only the third table – Laundry Pickup was created to emulate the data representation in the secondary storage namely PDA. The primary keys were identified in each table. However there was no relationship built between the tables as this was found not necessary while processing the data. The data in different physical locations as in linen is brought together in the PDA database for temporarily processing of linen count in each bag and may be to upload this data into the data warehouse later. Any data update in the tag like linen status will take place in the physical tag. Hence the data is not conceptually brought together in a central database. If it were brought together in a central location, then there might be duplicate copies of the same piece of data – one in the centralised database and the other in the physical object leading to redundancy and data integrating issues.

The main processing was to count the linen which was checked through a SQL statement.

Figure 5. Linen table populated with sample data

Table - dbo.linen | Summary

	Linen_Id	Linen_Type	Laundered	count	owner
▶	1	FlatSht	False	1	aaa
	2	Pllw	False	0	aaa
	3	FlatSht	False	0	aaa
	4	Pllw	False	0	aaa
	5	Pllw	True	0	aaa
	6	Pllw	True	0	aaa
*	NULL	NULL	NULL	NULL	NULL

Figure 6. Bin Table populated with sample data

Table - dbo.bin | Summary

	bin_Id	client	credits
▶	1	aaa	100
	2	aaa	100
*	NULL	NULL	NULL

Figure 7. PickUp Table populated with sample data

Table - dbo.Pickup | Summary

	Trans_Id	Bin_Id	Client	Credits	Linen_Id	Linen_Type	Laundered	Count	owner
▶	1	1	aaa	100	1	FlatSht	False	0	aaa
	2	1	aaa	100	2	Pllw	False	0	aaa
	3	1	aaa	100	3	FlatSht	False	0	aaa
	4	2	aaa	100	4	Pllw	False	0	aaa
	5	1	aaa	100	2	Pllw	False	0	aaa
*	NULL	NULL	NULL	NULL	NULL	NULL	NULL	NULL	NULL

```
SELECT count (distinct linen_Id) "Linen Count"
from Pickup;
```

The keyword 'distinct' was used to eliminate any duplicate readings from the interrogator.

In order to investigate the size requirements for an SQL database table structure to be stored on a RFID tag, a SQL database table structure the linen table was created and populated with one row of data using MySQL. The resulting .opt file was 65 bytes. However, the .frm file was 8.46 KB. The result of this investigation shows that using the existing SQL framework, approximately 9 KB of read/write non-volatile memory would be needed for this particular application of data-on-tag storage. Therefore, even battery assisted passive RFID tags such as those made by Alien Technology do not have enough memory to be useful in this application.

7. DISCUSSION

Several issues were discovered in this smart laundry bin project. They are related to the RFID data nature, data model and application to the given case study.

7.1 Data redundancy

As RFID will be used in the linen, they will be read from a wider range by the different bin (readers). This could lead to redundancies at the reader level. The same tag could be read by multiple readers. One way of overcoming this issue is to keep a safe distance between the bins to avoid reading linen tags from other bins. To be surer of the final calculation, the pickup person could run a SQL query with the 'group by' clause on bin_Id. This will report the linen count in different bins avoiding duplicates. This could be,

SELECT bin_Id, count (distinct linen_Id) "Linen Count" from Pickup
    Group by bin_Id;

Hence a consolidated summary report could easily be generated on all the linen picked from the hospital.

7.2 Stock Taking

If all data about the linen is stored in the physical object, the data is lost along with the object. This raises the issue of how conceptually to account for the lost data. One possible solution could be to keep a master table about the linen at the central database. It could contain details like id, type etc. Transactional details like status and count is not maintained here.

A = {Records from master file linen}
B = {Records from the transaction file}

Then A − B = {Records from Master file and not in the transaction file}

However, there are instances when some linen may be still in the hospital shelves and may not be shown in the transaction file. According to the aforementioned query such objects would be reported as lost. The positive aspect of this particular method is that it gives a rough estimate of the type of linen (pillow case, flat sheet) collected back from the hospital. As the same linen is laundered and sent again to the hospital, there could be shortage of some certain types of linen which could be added by the laundry company.

7.3 Missed Readings

As RFID readings have a missed reading rate of 30%, the final count of linen collected may not be an accurate figure. One way to counter this problem could be to read in continuous mode and eliminate duplicate readings from the transaction file. Another alternative value adding approach would be to record the weight of each piece of linen on the linen tag and then have the smart bin add together the weights of each individual piece of linen and compare it with the total weight recorded in the bin. Field trials would be necessary to determine a more accurate read rate percentage and would depend on the composition of the smart bin itself and the surrounding environment.

7.4 Enterprise Level Computing

As data is physically stored in linen and bins, conceptually collating this data together at the central database is not easy. In case the same data is conceptually stored in central database, issues of redundancy and integrity arise. Hence data is thought to be kept at the tag level and through the transaction data, data manipulation will occur at enterprise level to extract business intelligence.

Another issue related to a separation of the smart bin entity from the enterprise level system is that look-ups involving access to the enterprise system will be difficult. Look-ups are a very traditional way to verify correct identification of laundry items and bins. One way to address this might be to read every tag more than once in a systematic way to ensure that the identification number has been read correctly. Another solution might involve implementing a check-sum algorithm to each identification number which then might provide a way to check that each identification number is valid. As the identification system is 'automatic' and does not involve a human entering the number, extra digits would not disadvantage the system and the length of the identification number is not constrained in the same way as a physical printed barcode.

7.5 Traceability and Visibility

If a data-on-tag approach is adopted, the status of the object is not known at the central database. There is no way to track each item instantly. This is in contrast with SCM applications, where, objects can be tracked through the system and the exact location of each object will be known.

8. CONCLUSION

RFID technology is proposed for the smart laundry bin. Moreover, writable tags are planned as they can write some data in the tag and local processing using SQL (such as checking the total weight and calculating the total number of items in the bin) can take place without the infrastructure of a network and middleware. This proposed smart laundry bin would be able to access RFID tagged linen without access to the network database and data in the linen is updated (clean or soiled) while the linen is processed. Hence there is no ambiguity of the linen status in the database and in reality.

Although the cost of writable tags is high, it is decreasing and eliminating the expensive middleware should offset the feasibility of the smart laundry bin concept. The data model involving the RFID data at different physical objects like

linen, bin and PDA is projected. Thus the count of soiled linen collected from the hospital is calculated close to source of collection. Later the transaction data captured at the PDA is sent to the data warehousing for enterprise level computing. All this can be helpful to bill the laundry clients efficiently taking care of lost linen. As writable tags are used with all relevant data written on it, it is a novel approach compared with the regular data-on-network approach.

REFERENCES

Chamberlin, D., & Robie, J. (2001). An XML Query Language for Heterogeneous Data Sources. *Lecture Notes in Computer Science* (pp. 1-25).

Chawanthe, S., Krishnamurthy, V., Ramachandra, S., & Sarma, S. (2004). Managing RFID data, Proceedings of the VLDB. (pp. 1189-1195).

Clarke, R. H., Twede, D., Tazelaar, J. R., & Boyer, K. K. (2006). Radio Frequency Identification (RFID) Performance: The Effect of Tag Orientation and Package Contents. *Packaging Technology and Science, 19*(1), 45-54.

Derakhshan, R., Orlowska, M. E., & Li, X. (2007). RFID Data Management: Challenges and Opportunities., *IEEE International Conference, Texas, USA,* (pp. 175-182).

Diekmann, T., Melski, A., & Schumann, M. (2007). Data-on-Network vs. Data-on-tag: Managing Data in Complex RFID Environments. *Proceedings of the 40th Annual Hawaii International Conference on System Sciences,* (pp. 224-233).

Floerkemeier, C., & Lampe, M. (2004). Issues with RFID usage in Ubiquitous Computing Applications. *Pervasive Computing: Second International Conference.*

Gray, J. (2004). The Next database Revolution SIGMOD, Paris, France. (pp. 1-4).

Haas, L. M., & Miller, R. J. (1997). Transforming Heterogeneous Data with Database middleware: Beyond Integration. *Bulletin of the IEEE Computer Society Technical Committee on Data engineering.*

Hardgrave, B. C., Armstrong, D. J., & Riemenschneider, C. K. (2007). RFID Assimilations hierarchy. *Proceedings of the 40th Hawaii International conference on System Sciences*, (pp. 1-10).

Harrison, M. (2003). EPC Information Service - Data Model and Queries. *White Paper, Auto-d Centre Institute for Manufacturing, University of Cambridge, United Kingdom.*, (pp. 1-20).

Hevner, A. R. (2004). Design Sciences in Information Systems Research. *MIS Quarterly*, (pp. 1-49).

Joseph, M. H. (2003). Toward network data independence. *SIGMOD Rec., 32*(3), 34-40.

Lin, D., Elmongui, H. G., Bertino, E., & Ooi, B. C. (2007). Data Management in RFID Applications. *DEXA*, (pp. 434-444).

Melski, A., Thoroe, L., Caus, T., & Schumann, M. (2007). Beyond EPC – Insights from Multiple RFID Case Studies on the storage of Additional Data on Tag. *International Conference on wireless Algorithms, Systems and Applications*, (pp. 281- 286).

Nguyen, T. (2007). A Data Model for EPC Information Services. *18th Data Engineering Workshop, Japan*, (pp. 1-8).

Ni, L. M., Liu, Y., & al, e. (2004). LANDMARC: Indoor Location Sensing Using Active RFID. *Wireless Networks, 10*, 701-710.

Palmer, M. (2004). Principles of Effective RFID Data Management. *Enterprise Systems*, 1-8.

Robert, H., & Clarke, D. T. J. R. T. K. K. B. (2006). Radio frequency identification (RFID) performance: the effect of tag orientation and package contents. *Packaging Technology and Science, 19*(1), 45-54.

Sanem, K., Adam, P., & al, e. (2006). Virtual Sensors: Abstracting Data from Physical Sensors. *Proceedings of the 2006 International Symposium on World of Wireless, Mobile and Multimedia Networks, IEEE Computer Society.*

Schwieren, J., & Vossen, G. (2007). Implementing Physical Hyperlinks for Mobile Applications Using RFID Tags. *11th International Databse Engineering and Applications Symposium, Banff, AB, Canada*, (pp. 154-162).

Steele, R., Ventsov, Y., & Dillon, T. (2004). An Object-Oriented Database-based Architecture for mobile enterprise Applications. *Proceedings of the International conference on Information Technology: Coding and Computing, IEEE computer society, 1*, 586-590.

Wang, F., & Liu, P. (2005). Temporal Management of RFID Data. *Proceedings of the 31st VLDB Conference, Trondheim, Norway* (pp. 1128-1139).

Weiser, M. (1993). Hot Topics - Ubiquitous Computing. *Computer, 26*, 71-72.

KEY TERMS

Aggregation: (Also known as containment) A hierarchical relationship to determine what physical objects are contained within another (larger object).

Data-on-Network Systems: Systems that specify minimal information on the tag, i.e. a unique identification, indexed to look up more details from a database via the enterprise network.

Data-on-Tag Systems: Systems where complete data of the object is saved on the tag.

Electronic Product Code (EPC): Uniquely identifies each RFID tag under the EPC scheme.

Heterogeneous Data Management: Management of data from a large number of sources such as semi-structured documents, databases and object repositories.

Middleware: Software that runs on a distributed network, collecting the RFID data read by the readers, cleansed before extracting meaningful information.

Personal Digital Assistant (PDA): A hand-held portable device used to collect data anywhere in the environment and linked to wireless network for instant data transfer.

ENDNOTE

[1] An implicit federated application designed to update data simultaneously across the storage medium (Christian & Matthias (2005).

Section V
Selected Readings

Chapter XII
An Agent–Based Library Management System Using RFID Technology

Maryam Purvis
University of Otago, New Zealand

Toktam Ebadi
University of Otago, New Zealand

Bastin Tony Roy Savarimuthu
University of Otago, New Zealand

ABSTRACT

The objective of this research is to describe a mechanism to provide an improved library management system using RFID and agent technologies. One of the major issues in large libraries is to track misplaced items. By moving from conventional technologies such as barcode-based systems to RFID-based systems and using software agents that continuously monitor and track the items in the library, we believe an effective library system can be designed. Due to constant monitoring, the up-to-date location information of the library items can be easily obtained.

INTRODUCTION

One of the primary objectives of a library is to provide a collection of information artefacts and enable easy and fast access to those artefacts. Most modern libraries provide open stack access for browsing and retrieving of the items available. This open access may lead to misplacement of items in various sections of large libraries. When an item is misplaced it cannot be reached by its potential users. It is tedious for the library staff to find and track a misplaced book that is needed by another user. In addition, it can be costly to locate the item, and possibly replace the item (when it is not possible to locate the item at the time that is needed). In this chapter, we describe an approach that can reduce the effort associated with finding such items.

RFID is an upcoming technology that facilitates easy object identification, in particular, when voluminous entities have to be tracked and monitored (such as products in the supply chain context, library items in a library). An item that is marked with an RFID tag can be read by a RFID reader. This information can be used in tracking and managing the tagged items. The cost of RFID tags (in particular, the passive ones) are low enough to make it feasible to be used for the identification of large quantities of items. Currently, more than 20 million books worldwide are embedded with RFID tags (Research Information, 2007) in more than 300 libraries (RFID Gazette, 2007).

Software agent systems are one of the well studied areas of artificial intelligence, as agents can be embedded with intelligent decision-making capabilities. Robots are physical embodiments of software agents. Software agents when embedded in a robot can be used for a variety of purposes such as planet exploration, handling nuclear wastes, and fire rescue. The study of collaboration using agents is important because they are indispensable for carrying out tasks in unmanned zones and industrial automation.

In our approach, the agents interact with each other in order to ensure up-to-date information in the central library database. They read the tag in the environment using a RFID reader, undertake appropriate processing and communicate the information to another agent. To provide inter-agent communication they can use languages such as FIPA (The Foundation for Intelligent Physical Agents (FIPA), 2007) ACL over WI-FI network. In this project, an agent is used to identify and obtain the location of a misplaced book.

BACKGROUND

Some researchers have worked in integrating agent-based systems with RFID technology for tracking and monitoring purposes (Mamei & Zambonelli, 2005). Our work is inspired by their approach in adopting the RFID technology with agent-based systems.

Related Work in the Context of Library Environment

In the previous works (Choi, et al., 2006; Molnar & Wagner, 2004) that have used RFIDs for library management system, most of the focus has been on automating the process of check-in and check-outs carried out at the circulation desks, automation of inventory management process and sorting returned items (RFID Sorting, 2007). The RFID technology has also been used in enabling antitheft functionality by requiring the gate sensors to check whether an item has been issued or not.

The authors of R-LIM system (Choi et al., 2006) describe how the position of tagged items in the library can be identified within a shelf, based on the shelf locator tags that indicate the relative position of the books in a particular rack of the bookshelf. In their approach, manual scanning (using a hand-held scanner) was employed to read the tags of the library items in a shelf. It was assumed that the library items are placed in their correct location. This may not be easily assumed in an open library stack where numerous patrons interact with the library artefacts. To ensure consistency, the library staffs need to periodically check the shelves for possible misplaced items. This is a tedious and time consuming operation. To our knowledge, not much work has been done that identifies the location of misplaced items in an automated manner.

In our system we have incorporated the idea of continuous monitoring of the library items which facilitates easier identification of misplaced items and their locations.

HIGH LEVEL DESCRIPTIONS OF APPLICATION AND ARCHITECTURE

We describe the design of an agent-based system that can be used for library book tracking. One of the common problems in a large library is that the books are often moved around and misplaced in different sections of a library. This problem can be solved by placing RFID tags on each book and using robotic agents to locate and track the books.

Assume that the library is made up of different floors. Each floor is partitioned into different reading zones. Each zone contains a certain number of bookshelves. Each shelf is made up of a number of racks where tagged books are kept. The tag embedded in each book contains information such as unique id, floor, zone, shelf, rack and availability details using a simple encryption mechanism.

In our system, there are different types of agents (shown in Figure 1), such as library service provider agent, floor agent, zone monitor agent, and tracker agent.

The book service provider agent is the agent to whom book tracking requests can be submitted. It performs the following tasks:

- Initializes the library items with appropriate location information
- Maintains the changes made to the location of library items
- Provides status information of the library items

Figure 1. Architecture of the RFID-based library system

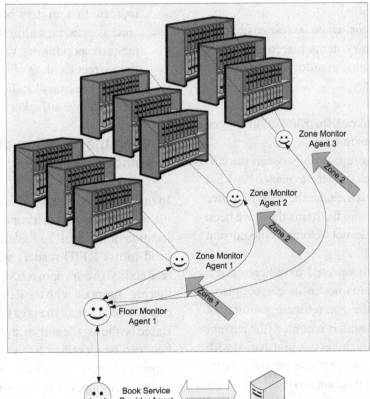

Figure 2. Scanning the books in a bookshelf using a robot equipped with a RFID reader

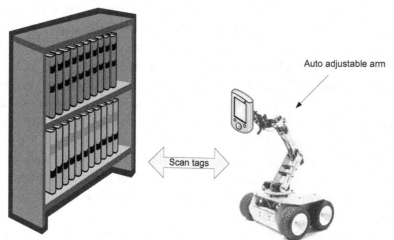

The floor agent resides at appropriate entry/exit points of a floor. The floor agent monitors when a book enters or leaves a floor. It updates the current floor information in the database while resetting the other attributes (zone, shelf, and rack). It also interacts with tracker agents assigned to that floor.

The zone monitor agent is responsible for monitoring the library items placed in shelves assigned to it. The zone monitor agent performs the following tasks:

a. Periodically takes a snapshot of the tagged items within its reach.
b. It finds the discrepancies between the currently read books and the expected book list for its zone. This includes the items that have been removed and the items that have been added which do not belong to the current zone.
c. The database is updated to indicate that a particular item is not in its correct place. In addition, the approximate position of the misplaced item is recorded (the current position). This includes the information with regard to the zone. For the removed items all the current position attributes are reset except the floor information. The misplaced

items are recorded in a log file called "misplaced-location.log" stored locally in the memory of zone agent. The log files are sent periodically to the service provider agent. Because the order in which the reader reads is not known, the zone agent can only indicate that an item belonging to another zone is present within its zone and obtain the corresponding tag values (which indicate the correct location of the misplaced item). To find the exact location of the misplaced book, we use a tracker agent.

Finding the Location of the Misplaced Item

In this scenario, we know only the existence of a misplaced item within a zone but not the current location of the item. To find this information, we need to use RFID readers with lower range of readability. In our approach, we use robotic agents that are equipped with the RFID readers and they can be used to scan the tags (shown in Figure 2). Based on the log file entries, a particular misplaced item can be identified by the robot. The robot is capable of moving back and forth across a shelf and it is equipped with an automatic adjustable arm which can read items in different (higher) racks. Shelves will be equipped with the beginning of the shelf and end of the shelf tags. The end shelf tags will have directional information which is used by the robot to locate the next shelf within a zone.

The tracker agent is capable of finding items misplaced across zones as well as within its current zone. The tracker agent locates an item that belongs to another zone, by reading each tag in its range and comparing it with the tag code of the target item (misplaced book recorded in the log file). After locating the item, it derives the location of the misplaced item by obtaining the location information from its neighbouring items. The current location of the misplaced item is stored in another log file called "found-location.log" and the database is updated accordingly.

In this process, the tracker agent is also checking the correct relative order of items that are being read. Whenever it finds an item that is out of order, it identifies it as a misplaced item and derives its location information based on its neighbourhood and stores it in the "found-location.log" file. This process ensures identification of items that are misplaced both within and across zones.

The library staffs periodically check the log files updated by the tracker agent and place the misplaced items in their correct location.

Operational Scenarios

Initial Configuration

All the library items are labeled (tagged) appropriately. All the items are recorded in the database. Whenever new items are added to the library, some adjustments to the neighbouring items may be required.

The library database consists of the following details associated with each item:

a. Call number
b. Unique identifier
c. Availability

d. Correct position (original location, as specified by the administrator)
    i.   Floor, Zone, Shelf, Rack
e. Current position (as indicated by the floor and the zone agents)
    i.   Floor, Zone, Shelf, Rack

When the items are initialized, the correct position and current position of an item are the same. When an item is moved from one location to another, the current position is updated. The correct position of an item remains the same (unless the administrator resets it to accommodate the growth of the library).

The database would have more details other than the above information such as due date and reserve status. The unique code, current position (in the encoded format) and the availability information are placed on the tag belonging to each library item.

Requesting a Book Scenario

When a request for locating the current position of an item is made, it may be an item that is in its original correct place. In this case, the user is informed of the item location details.

If the requested item is identified as a misplaced item, then the current zone is known. In this case, there could be two possibilities:

1. It can be found in the "found-location.log" file. In that case, the staff can fetch the item from the location and update the database, and the log-file.
2. Otherwise, the item details are found in the "misplaced-location.log" file. In this case the staff can use a hand-held reader to locate the item and update the relevant information such as database and log file. Alternatively, the tracker agent can be assigned to look for the location of the misplaced item.

It is possible that a misplaced book is in an unzoned area of the library floor such as a reading area. In this case, it is assumed that the library staff will collect all these books at the end of the day and place them in a designated shelf for further processing (to be placed in their correct location).

DESIGN CONSIDERATION AND IMPLEMENTATION

RFID Infrastructure

We are planning to use the RFID-chips conforming to ISO 15693 and avoid any proprietary tags belonging to one particular vendor. Our system uses two kinds of RFID readers. The long range RFID reader covers 3-5 meters while the short range reader used by the robotic agent covers 10-50 centimetres. A RFID tag can only be read if the reader has the appropriate authorizations.

Implementation Details of the Robotic Agent

We are using Garcia robot (Acroname Robotics, 2007) which is embedded with a RFID reader.

Each robot has an onboard processor called Stargate (Crossbow Technology Inc, 2006). The brainstem C development kit (Acroname Robotics, 2007) installed in the robot provides the API for the control of Garcia robot movement (moving forward, turning left and right). We are currently working on implementing a controller for the automatic arm adjustment (moving up and down).

Otago Agent Platform (OPAL) has been used to support multi-agent cooperation (Purvis et al., 2002). OPAL is a FIPA-compliant agent platform. Tracker agent is an OPAL agent which is made up of two components, namely Garcia robot controller and RFID reader. The instructions for the robot to perform certain operations can be issued using the FIPA ACL (The Foundation for Intelligent Physical Agents (FIPA), 2007) standard.

In our system, when a particular request is made for an item that is misplaced, then the service provider agent communicates this information to the tracker agent in order to find the current location of the item. For communication between zone monitor agent and tracker agent, we are using WIFI protocol.

Upon receiving a request for finding a particular book from a service provider agent, the tracker agent (which is an OPAL agent) instructs

Figure 3. Psuedocode for a tracker agent locating the position of a misplaced book

```
Find-tag(tag-code)
{
        Read till the-end-of-zone-tag
        {
                Read till the-end-of-shelf-tag
                {
                        Read till end-of-rack-tag
                        {
                                MessageToReaderAgent(readNextItem());
                                if (book found)
                                {
                                        ProcessInformation();
                                        Exit();
                                }
                        }
                        MessageToRobotAgent(goToNextRack());
                }
                MessageToRobotAgent(goToNextShelf());
        }
}
```

the Garcia robot to initiate a search using its RFID reader. In this process, when the end of rack tag is read, the robot agent is instructed to adjust the arm to reach to the next rack and also turns the robot around in order to be able to read the next rack. If the end of shelf tag is read, then the robot agent is directed to adjust the arm to its lower position and move to the next shelf using the directional information that is placed on the end of the shelf tag. When the requested book tag is found, the position of the book is calculated as described earlier.

Figure 3 shows the pseudo code that indicates the sequence of steps taken by a tracker agent when it tries to locate a misplaced book within a zone. In this code, the processInformation() method corresponds to the calculation of the current book position based on the neighbourhood and the update of the database and corresponding log files.

Communication Between Agents

The agents in our system can communicate with each other using FIPA ACL messages. The following interactions can take place in our system:

a. Library service provider agent can send a request for searching a book to a tracker agent;

b. In case a particular tracker agent is not available (or busy or unavailable due to charging or maintenance), the library service provider agent will send a request to the floor agent to find a replacement;

c. When a zone agent wants to update the database, it sends all the position data to the library service provider agent, which then updates the repository. Similarly, floor agent and tracker agent send the data to the library service provider agent.

Simulation and Testing of the Prototype System

In order to verify the operational correctness of the system, we are currently implementing a simulation system which is populated with a large number of books. We have parameterized the number of floors, zones, shelves and racks. The user requests are modeled based on the anonymous historic data of our local library. Based on this information, we measure the performance of the

Figure 4. System performance where agents are not collaborating

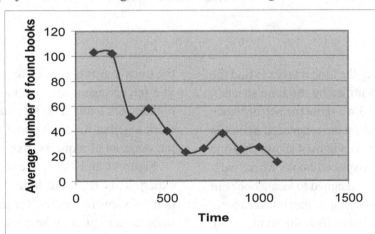

Figure 5. System performance where agents are collaborating

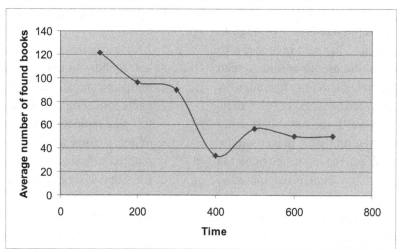

Figure 6. Agents participation where agents are not collaborating

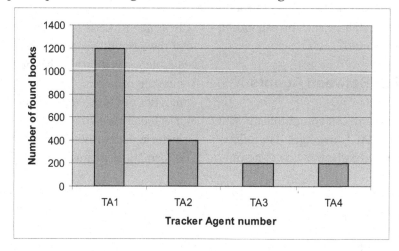

system by calculating the time it takes to find the misplaced books identified by the zone agents.

In Figures 4 and 5 we show the performance of the system in finding the misplaced books in two different scenarios. Figure 4 shows the time it takes to find the misplaced books where various tracker agents are assigned to locate books in specific zones (in this example, four tracker agents are assigned respectively to four different zones). Figure 5 shows the system performance where

the tracker agents cooperate with each other (an idle tracker agent may help another agent with higher work load). It is clear that when the agents work together the time that it takes to complete the same set of requests is shorter.

Figures 6 and 7 show the outcome of the same experiments from the individual tracker agent point of view. In Figure 7 the tracker agents' participations in finding the books are more evenly distributed, which resulted in a better overall system performance.

Figure 7. Agents participation where agents are collaborating

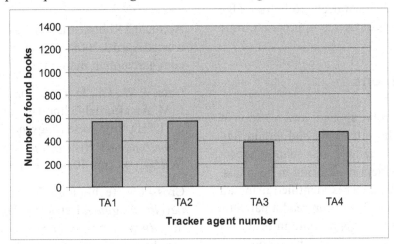

More simulation experiments will be designed to examine the system performance when different priorities are assigned for performing different tasks. In particular, we would like to explore an optimum time that has to be spent by the tracker agents to locate the misplaced books identified by the zone agents (using the long range RFID readers) as opposed to the time spent on locating the misplaced books within each zone (using the short range RFID readers by the tracker agents).

DISCUSSIONS

Issues with Use of RFID

Privacy is one of the important concerns of RFID systems. An adversary can attempt to read the library book details (such as the title, author of the book) which might reveal some personal information without the owner's consent. Molnar and Wagner discuss various methods that an adversary may use the tag information to reveal details about a person associated with certain tagged items. They describe how this can be achieved even when a unique identifier (such as barcode) is used by the process of association (linking different people reading the same book) or book hotlisting (where the barcode of known books are identified and tracked). By using a simple mechanism of access control and encoding, the information on the tag may be better protected. It is acknowledged that with the current limitation of the RFID tags in terms of the processing capability, the more sophisticated mechanisms such as use of hash functions and symmetric encryption may not be feasible (Molnar & Wagner, 2004).

Another issue is the fact that the adversary can bypass the security system by wrapping the library items in a metallic container.

Issues with Using Robotic Agents in the Library

The use of robotic agents in a library environment can interfere with the movements of the patrons of the library. This can be addressed if the robotic tasks are performed after the closing of the library. But this will increase the latency of the information that can be made available to the users. Alternatively, the robots can be assigned to designated paths which can be made known to the patrons.

The robotic agents may run out of power to operate. A mechanism needs to be provided so that it can be recharged at appropriate time intervals.

Other Applications

Our approach can be applied to a variety of applications that have tracking and monitoring requirements. For example, our robotic agents can be used for patient monitoring in hospitals. Assume that each patient is identified using an RFID tag. A robotic agent can read a patient's RFID tag and find the appropriate information about that patient (names of possible medication and the corresponding timing information for taking the medicine). The agent can then provide specialized service (such as dialysis) based on the information obtained. The agent can then communicate this information to the server as well as other robotic agents for further treatment relevant to the patient. The agents can request for and provide help when facing a heavy load.

CONCLUSION

In this work, we have described a mechanism for locating misplaced items in a library environment where the items are tagged using RFID technology. The communication infrastructure is facilitated by software agents. We have also used robotic agents to automate the tedious task associated with locating the position of the misplaced items. Our approach is promising, as it makes the misplaced items easily known due to the continuous monitoring. The proposed architecture enables the library administrative person to make more informed decision on allocation of the library resources (staff as well as robot trackers) based on the list of misplaced books identified by the RFID readers. We are currently working on the implementation details associated with our approach.

REFERENCES

Acroname Robotics. (2007). *Garcia manual*. Retrieved April 3, 2008, from http://www.acroname.com/garcia/man/man.html

Choi, J. W., Oh, D. I., & Song, I. Y. (2006). R-LIM: An affordable library search system based on RFID. In *Proceedings of the International Conference on Hybrid Information Technology (ICHIT'06)*, (pp. 103-108).

Crossbow Technology, Inc. (2006). *Stargate developers guide*. Retrieved April 3, 2008, from http://www.xbow.com/Support/Support_pdf_files/Stargate_Manual.pdf

Mamei, M., & Zambonelli, F. (2005). Spreading pheromones in everyday environments through RFID technology. In *Proceedings of the 2nd IEEE Symposium on Swarm Intelligence, (pp. 281-288)*. IEEE Press.

Molnar, D., & Wagner, D. (2004). *Privacy and security in library RFID: Issues, practices, and architectures*. New York: ACM Press.

Purvis, M., Cranefield, S., Nowostawski, M., & Carter, D. (2002). Opal: A multi-level infrastructure for agent-oriented software development. *Autonomous agents and multi-agent systems*. Bologna, Italy: ACM Press.

Research Information. (2007). *Radio-tagged books*. Retrieved April 3, 2008, from http://www.researchinformation.info/rimayjun04radio-tagged.html

RFID Gazette. (2007). *RFID applications for libraries*. Retrieved April 3, 2008, from http://www.rfidgazette.org/libraries/

The Foundation for Intelligent Physical Agents (FIPA). (2007). *Agent communication language specification*. Retrieved April 3, 2008, from http://www.fipa.org

This work was previously published in Intelligence Integration in Distributed Knowledge Management, edited by D. Król; N. Nguyen, pp. 171-181, copyright 2009 by Information Science Publishing (an imprint of IGI Global).

Chapter XIII
Semantic–Based Bluetooth–RFID Interaction for Advanced Resource Discovery in Pervasive Contexts

Tommaso Di Noia
Politecnico di Bari, Italy

Eugenio Di Sciascio
Politecnico di Bari, Italy

Francesco Maria Donini
Università della Tuscia, Italy

Michele Ruta
Politecnico di Bari, Italy

Floriano Scioscia
Politecnico di Bari, Italy

Eufemia Tinelli
Politecnico di Bari and Università degli Studi di Bari, Italy

ABSTRACT

We propose a novel object discovery framework integrating the application layer of Bluetooth and RFID standards. The approach is motivated and illustrated in an innovative u-commerce setting. Given a request, it allows an advanced discovery process, exploiting semantically annotated descriptions of goods available in the u-marketplace. The RFID data exchange protocol and the Bluetooth service discovery protocol have been modified and enhanced to enable support for such semantic annotation of products. Modifications to the standards have been conceived to be backward compatible, thus allowing the smooth coexistence of the legacy discovery and/or identification features. Also noteworthy is the introduction of a dedicated compression tool to reduce storage/transmission problems due to the verbosity of XML-based semantic languages.

INTRODUCTION AND MOTIVATION

Radio-frequency identification (RFID) is an increasingly widespread and promising wireless technology interconnecting via radio a transponder carrying data (*tag*) located on an object, and an interrogator (*reader*) able to receive the transmitted data. Tags usually contain a unique identification code, which can be used by readers to identify the associated object. Since low-cost tags can be fastened to objects unobtrusively, preserving their common functions, RFID de facto increases the "pervasiveness" of a computing environment. Current RFID applications focus on retrieving relevant attributes of the object the tag is clung to, via a networked infrastructure from a fixed information server. This identification process involves the code associated to the transponder exploited as index key. Nowadays, tags with larger memory capacity and on-board sensors enable new scenarios and further applications, not yet explored.

We believe that in the era of semantic technologies and mobile computing, there is room for more advanced and significant applications of RFIDs extended with structured descriptions, so that a good equipped with an RFID can semantically describe itself along its whole life-cycle. We therefore conceived a unified framework where a semantic-enhanced RFID-based infrastructure and an advanced Bluetooth service discovery—also endowed of semantic-based discovery features—are virtually "interconnected" at the application layer permitting innovative services in u-environments. In our mobile framework, tagged objects expose to a reader not simply a string code but a semantically annotated description. Such objects may hence describe themselves in a variety of scenarios (e.g., during supply chain management, shipment, storing, sale and post-sale), without depending on a centralized database. The exploitation of these annotations calls for discovery/interaction protocols that are able to effectively deal with rich and articulated descriptions. Therefore, a novel multi-protocol and interactive discovery mechanism has been designed. In this effort, we borrowed from ideas and technologies devised for the semantic Web initiative. To simply illustrate our proposal, we set our stage in a *u-marketplace* context[1], where objects endowed with RFID tags are dipped into an enhanced Bluetooth framework.

In particular, building on previous works that enhanced the basic discovery features of Bluetooth with semantic-based discovery capabilities (Ruta et al., 2006a), we propose an extension of EPCglobal specifications for RFID tag data standards, providing semantic-based value-added services. Coping with limited storage and computational capabilities of mobile and embedded devices, and with reduced bandwidth provided by wireless links, issues related to the verbosity of semantic annotation languages cannot be neglected. Compression techniques become essential to enable storage and transmission of semantically annotated information on mobile devices. We hence devised and exploited a novel efficient XML compression algorithm, specifically targeted for DIG 1.1 (Bechhofer et al., 2003) document instances. Benefits of compression apply to the whole ubiquitous computing environment, as decreasing data size means shorter communication delays, efficient usage of bandwidth and reduced battery drain for mobile devices in a Mobile ad hoc NETwork (MANET).

The remainder of the article is structured as follows. In the next section, relevant technological bricks of the proposed framework are surveyed. Section 3 outlines the framework, explaining the discovery process as well as proposed semantic-based enhancements to RFID standards. The compression algorithm for semantic annotations is outlined in section 4. Section 5 exemplifies the approach in a u-commerce scenario. Results on key performance measures to assess the feasibility of the proposed approach, are provided in section 6. Conclusion closes the article.

Basics

In this section, we survey relevant aspects of languages, technologies and protocols we use and adapt, concentrating on key features our proposal is based on. We assume the reader is familiar with at least basic elements of Semantic Web and ontologies (Berners-Lee et al., 2001; Horrocks et al., 2001; Martin et al., 2002; McGuinness et al., 2002; Shadbolt et al., 2006), of OWL (http://www.w3.org/TR/owl-features/) and related languages, such as Description Logics (DLs) (Borgida, 1995; Donini et al., 1996). We therefore move straightforwardly to analyze issues closely related to our proposal.

Exploiting Semantically Annotated Descriptions

Given a domain ontology $\mathcal{T}$, DL-based systems usually provide at least two basic reasoning services: *Concept satisfiability* and *concept subsumption*. Using subsumption, it is possible to establish if a description C is more specific than a description D, $\mathcal{T} \models C \sqsubseteq D$. If the previous relation holds, then we may say that information C associated to a given resource completely satisfies what has been requested in D, that is, a *full match* occurs. With concept satisfiability, the discovery of incompatible resources with respect to a request can be performed. If $D \sqcap C$ is not satisfiable with regards to the ontology $\mathcal{T}$, then C is not compatible with the request. Obviously, *full matches* cannot be deemed the one only useful, as they will be probably rare in a variety of contexts. Given a request and a set of resources, usually $C \not\sqsubseteq D$ and $D \sqcap C$ is satisfiable with regards to $\mathcal{T}$. That is, the resource does not completely satisfy the request but it is compatible with it. Hence, a metric is needed to establish "how much" the resource C is compatible with the request D or, equivalently, "how much" it is not specified in C to completely satisfy D, in order to make the subsumption relation $C \sqsubseteq D$ true. In Di Noia

et al. (2004) *rankPotential* algorithm was proposed to evaluate this measure. Given an $\mathcal{ALN}$ (attributive language with number restrictions) ontology $\mathcal{T}$ and two $\mathcal{ALN}$ concepts C and D both satisfiable in $\mathcal{T}$, *rankPotential*($C, D, \mathcal{T}$) computes a *semantic distance* of C from D with respect to the ontology $\mathcal{T}$.

If some requirements in the request D are in conflict with the resource C, *rankPotential* cannot be applied. Nevertheless, in looking for "not so much" unsatisfactory matches when recovering from an initial "no match", a partial match could still be useful. In Di Noia et al. (2004) the *rankPartial* algorithm was proposed for ranking incoherent pairs of descriptions. Given an ontology $\mathcal{T}$ and two concept expressions D and C, both satisfiable with respect to $\mathcal{T}$, if D is not compatible with C, that is, their conjunction is not satisfiable with respect to $\mathcal{T}$, then *rankPartial* returns a score measuring the semantic incompatibility of D and C.

Semantic-Based Bluetooth Service Discovery

Usually, resource discovery protocols involve a requester, a lookup or directory server and finally a resource provider. As a MANET is a volatile environment, a flexible resource discovery paradigm is needed to overcome difficulties due to the host mobility. Nevertheless, existing protocols for mobile applications use a simple string-matching, which is largely inefficient in advanced scenarios (Ruta et al., 2006b). With specific reference to the Bluetooth service discovery protocol (SDP), it is based on a 128 bit universally unique IDentifier (UUID) associated to single service classes. Resource matching in Bluetooth is hence strictly syntactic, and SDP manages only exact matches. In Ruta et al. (2006a) a framework has been proposed that allows the management of both syntactic and semantic discovery of resources, by integrating a semantic layer within the OSI Bluetooth stack at application level. The Bluetooth standard has been enriched by new functionalities which permitted to maintain a backward compatibility (handheld device connectivity), adding the support to discovery of semantically annotated resources. Unused classes of 128 bit UUIDs in the original Bluetooth standard were exploited to mark each specific ontology thus calling this identifier *OUUID* (ontology universally unique IDentifier). By means of the OUUID matching the context was identified and a preliminary selection of resource referring to the same request's ontology was performed. The fundamental assumption is that each resource is semantically annotated. A service provider stores annotations within resource records, labelled with unique 32-bit identifiers. Each record contains general information about a single semantic-enabled resource and it entirely consists of a list of resource attributes. In addition to the OUUID attribute, there are a *ResourceName* (a human-readable name for the resource), a *ResourceDescription* (expressed using DIG syntax) and a variable number of *ResourceUtilityAttr_i* attributes, that is, numerical values used according to specific applications. In Ruta et al. (2006a), by adding four SDP Protocol Data Units (PDUs) *SDP_OntologySearch* (request and response) and *SDP_SemanticServiceSearch* (request and response) to the original standard (exploiting not used PDU ID), together with the original SDP capabilities, further semantic-enabled discovery functionalities were introduced. The overall interaction was based on the original SDP in Bluetooth. No modifications were made to the original structure of transactions. In fact, a semantic-based micro-layer has been built over the standard SDP recycling its basic parameters, data structures and functions, just differently using the basic framework.

RFID Features

In our framework, we refer to RFID transponders compliant with EPCglobal standard for Class 1-Generation 2 UHF tags (Traub et al., 2005). Tag memory is divided in four logical banks (EPCglobal Inc., 2005a): **(1) *Reserved*.** It is optional; if present, it stores 32-bit kill and access to passwords; **(2) *Electronic product code (EPC)*.** It stores, starting from address 0: (i) 16 bits for a cyclic redundancy check (CRC) code; (ii) a 16-bit protocol control (PC) field, composed of 5 bits for identification code length, 2 bits reserved for future use and 9 bits of numbering system identification; (iii) an EPC field for the identification code; **(3) *Tag IDentification (TID)*.** It stores at least tag manufacturer and model identification codes. This bank may be enlarged to store other manufacturer or model-specific data (e.g., a tag serial number); **(4) *User*.** An optional bank that stores data defined by the user application. Memory organization is user-defined. EPCglobal air interface protocol is an *Interrogator-Talks-First* (ITF) protocol: tags only reply to reader commands. Here, we briefly outline basic protocol features.

An RFID reader can preselect a subset of the tag population currently in range, according to user-defined criteria, by means of a sequence of *Select* commands.

Select command sends a bit string to all tags in range. Each tag will compare it with the content of a memory area specified by the reader, then it will assert/de-assert one of its status flags according to the comparison result (match/no-match). Command structure is shown in Table 1; parameters are as follows: (i) *Target* determines which tag status flag will be modified by the Select command; (ii) *Action* tells how a tag is required

Table 1. Select command structure in RFID protocol

Opcode	Target	Action	MemBank	Pointer	Length	Mask	Truncate	CRC
1010_2	3 bits	3 bits	2 bits	bit vector	8 bits	1-255 bits	1 bit	16 bits

to modify the flag (assert, de-assert, do nothing) for either positive or negative match outcome (a three-bit field is thus required to encode the six cases); (iii) *MemBank* indicates what memory bank must be compared; (iv) *Pointer* is the address of the first bit of MemBank tag memory area that must be compared; (v) *Length* is the length of the bit string to be compared; (vi) *Mask* is the bit string to be compared with the content of the memory area selected by MemBank, Pointer and Length values; (vii) *Truncate* tells the tag to send only part of its EPC code in the following protocol step; (viii) *CRC,* used for command data integrity protection.

After this phase, the inventory loop begins. In each iteration, the reader isolates one tag in range, reads its EPC code and can access its memory content. Among available commands, only *Read* and *Write* are relevant for our purposes.

Read command allows reading from one of the four tag memory banks. Command structure is shown in Table 2; parameters are as follows: (i) *MemBank* indicates the bank data must be read from; (ii) *WordPtr* points to the first 16-bit memory word to be read; (iii) *WordCount* is the number of consecutive 16-bit memory words that must be read (if it is 0, then the tag will send data stored up to the end of the memory bank); (iv) *RN*, random number used as access transaction identifier between reader and tag; (v) *CRC.*

Write command allows a reader to write a 16-bit word to one of the four tag memory banks.

Command structure is similar to *Read*, as shown in Table 3.

Together with tag data and air interface protocol, the EPCglobal standard defines a support infrastructure for RFID applications, where a key role is played by *object naming service (ONS)* (EPCglobal Inc., 2005b). It is based on the domain name system adopted to solve symbolic Internet addresses. ONS allows retrieval of services related to a specific object using the EPC code stored within the tag as a URI. *EPCglobal network protocol parameter registry* is maintained by EPCglobal consortium and contains suffixes identifying all valid service types (e.g., *ws* for a Web service, *html* for a Web page of the manufacturer, *epcis* for a EPCglobal information service providing authoritative information about the object associated with an EPC code).

FRAMEWORK AND APPROACH

We designed a unified semantic-aware framework, comprising modified RFID- and Bluetooth-based infrastructures that are virtually "interconnected" at the application layer permitting innovative services in u-environments. Our framework introduces a proposed extension of EPCglobal standard, allowing a semantic-based object discovery. Protocols to read/write tags have been preserved maintaining original code-based access (so keeping a compatibility with legacy applica-

Table 2. Read command structure in RFID protocol

Opcode	MemBank	WordPtr	WordCount	RN	CRC
11000010$_2$	2 bits	bit vector	8 bits	16 bits	16 bits

Table 3. Write command structure in RFID protocol

Opcode	MemBank	WordPtr	Data	RN	CRC
11000011$_2$	2 bits	bit vector	16 bits	16 bits	16 bits

Figure 1. Infrastructure elements: semantic-enhanced RFID tags; air-interface EPCglobal RFID protocol; middleware stratum; Bluetooth SD protocol, hotspot enriched with semantic matchmaking capabilities.

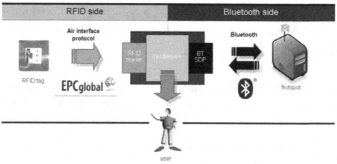

tions practically without modifications). A good can be easily and thoroughly described by means of a semantic annotated description stored within the tag it is associated with. Main elements of the proposed framework (see Figure 1) are: 1) goods equipped with semantic-enhanced RFID tags, 2) a middle tier component provided with an RFID reader and Bluetooth connectivity, 3) a hotspot enriched with semantic matchmaking capabilities. Two identification/discovery paradigms are involved: EPCglobal air interface protocol for RFID tags and semantic-enhanced Bluetooth Service Discovery Protocol. Interaction can be triggered by the user by means of either an implicit or an explicit request. The simplest—though not trivial, as obviously requests may change over time and during the product life-cycle—form of interaction is querying the tag (of the good) for some information, exploiting user's mobile handheld device. In implicit requests, the framework can be used to recognize choices the user performed so intercepting and interpreting them as a preliminary interaction aimed at discovery of goods similar or to be combined with the chosen one. In the first case, the user can directly interact with the hotspot, issuing requests to it via the semantic-enhanced Bluetooth SDP and waiting for replies. In the latter one, the user plays a more passive role as the "Environment" (in the sense of a pervasive and intelligent context, a

marketplace in our example scenario) is able to perceive modifications with regards to an earlier situation. RFID tags are required for hosting product features and to set a link between the *real* and the *digital* world, whereas the middle tier is a double-faced component. It listens for descriptions directly coming from the objects (by reading the tag memory content), issues requests to the service provider and finally records and displays results to the user. The RFID reader, scanning characteristics of a selected product, enables the further discovery phase which is aimed at identifying resources similar to the chosen one or to be combined with it. Via the semantic-based Bluetooth SDP and exploiting non-standard inference services outlined above, best matching resources of the marketplace will be discovered and returned to the user. Hence, the middleware integrates RFID and Bluetooth environments at the application layer: data coming from RFID tags are extracted, processed and reformatted. Furthermore, they are arranged to enable the interaction with the service provider (*hotspot*) via the semantic-enhanced Bluetooth SDP. The hotspot keeps track of resources within the marketplace and replies to a submitted request with the best matching products for similarity and association. To this aim, it is equipped with a DL reasoner able to provide previously introduced services. Such an approach may provide several benefits. Information about a product is structured and complete; it accurately follows the product history within the supply chain, being progressively built or updated during the good life cycle. This improves traceability of production and distribution, facilitates sales and post-sale services thanks to an advanced and selective discovery infrastructure.

Semantic-Enhanced EPCGlobal RFID Standard

In this subsection, we outline the proposed backward-compatible extensions to EPCglobal RFID standards enabling the framework described above. It is noteworthy that our semantic-enabled descriptions are expressed in DIG formalism (Bechhofer et al., 2003), a more compact syntactic variant of OWL.

Two reserved bits in the EPC area within each tag memory are exploited. The first one—at 15_h (10101_2) address—is exploited to indicate if the tag has a user memory (bit set) or not (bit cleared). The next one—at 16_h address—is asserted to mark semantic-enabled tags. In this manner, by means of a *Select* command (see Table 4), a reader can easily distinguish semantic-based tags. In particular, target and action parameters have the effect to assert the SL tag status flag only for semantic-enabled tags and de-assert it for remaining ones. The following inventory step will skip tags having SL flag de-asserted, thus allowing a reader to identify only semantic-enabled tags (protocol commands belonging to the inventory step have not been described, because they are used in the standard fashion).

The EPC standard for UHF-Class 1 tags impose the content of TID memory up to $1F_h$ bit is fixed. As said above, optional information could be stored in the TID memory. We use the TID memory area starting from 100000_2 address. There we store the identifier of the ontology (OUUID) with regards to the description contained within the tag is expressed. In order to make RFID systems

compliant with the ontology support system proposed in Ruta et al. (2006a), we define a bi-directional correspondence of OUUIDs stored in RFID transponders with those managed by Bluetooth devices. To retrieve the OUUID value stored within a tag, a reader will exploit a *Read* command with parameters as in Table 5.

Within the user memory bank, together with the semantically annotated description of the good the tag is clung to (opportunely compressed), there will be stored also contextual parameters (whose meaning depends on the specific application).

The extraction or the storing of a description within a tag can be performed by a reader through one or more read or write commands, respectively. Both commands are used in compliance with the standard air interface protocol. In Table 6, parameters of the read command for extracting a compressed description are reported.

In our approach, the ONS mechanism is considered as a supplementary system able to grant the ontology support. In case the reader does not manage the ontology the description within the tag refers to, it may need an Internet connection in order to retrieve the related DIG file, which will then remain stored for further usage on other goods of the same category. For this purpose, we use the ONS service and we hypothesize to register within the *EPCglobal Network Protocol Parameter Registry* a new service suffix, the *dig* one, that will contain the URL of the DIG file ontology. Of course the same can be done for OWL.

In case of EPC code families derived from the GS1 standard (formerly EAN.UCC) for barcode product identification, we assume that the pair of fields used for ONS requests—which refers to the manufacturer and to the merchandise class of the good—will correspond to a specific ontology. In fact, that pair exactly identifies the product category. Two goods with the same value for that field parameter will be surely homogeneous or even equal. Note that the vice versa is not verified, but this is not a concern for our purposes because ONS searches proceed only from the EPC code

Table 4. Select command parameters to detect semantic-enabled tags

Parameter	Target	Action	MemBank	Pointer	Length	Mask
Value	100_2	000_2	01_2	00010101_2	00000010_2	11_2
Description	SL flag	assert in case of match, deassert otherwise	EPC memory bank	initial address	number of bits to compare	bit mask

Table 5. Read command parameters to extract OUUID from TID memory bank

Parameter	MemBank	WordPtr	WordCount
Value	10_2	000000010_2	00001000_2
Description	TID memory bank	initial address	read up to 8 words (128 bits)

Table 6. Read command parameters to extract semantic annotations from the user bank

Parameter	MemBank	WordPtr	WordCount
Value	11_2	000000000_2	00000000_2
Description	User memory bank	initial address	read up to the end

toward the ontology. Hence we can surely have an unambiguous correspondence.

Deploying the Approach

In our case study framework, we hypothesize a "smart shopping cart" is equipped with a sensor and a tablet computer, which integrates an RFID reader and Bluetooth connectivity. When a customer picks up a product, the system assists him/her in discovering additional items, either similar or to be combined with the selected one. To this aim, a two-step discovery is performed, exploiting two different but related ontologies. In the first step, *rankPotential* algorithm is exploited to retrieve correspondences with the request. Resources analogous to the one selected by the user are identified, but at the same time, semantically incompatible goods are recognized. Their descriptions are submitted to the second matchmaking step. It exploits *rankPartial* over a differently modeled ontology allowing the

discovery of products to be associated with the chosen one. The hotspot will return two different lists of resource records, respectively, for objects in a potential correspondence with the request and in a partial one.

In advanced mobile scenarios, usually the match between a request and a provided resource involves not only the description of the resource itself but also data-oriented contextual properties. In fact, it would be quite strange to have a mobile commerce application without taking into account, for example, price or delivery time, among others. Hence, the overall match value should depend not only on the semantic distance between the description of the demand and of the resource, but also on those subsidiary values. An overall *utility function* has to combine them with semantic matchmaking results, in order to give a concrete match measure (Ruta et al., 2006b). In the proposed case study—referred to a u-commerce electronic product store—the utility function adopts three contextual parameters: price (in U.S.

dollars), estimated delivery time (in days), and product category, as shown in Table 7. They are exploited in a post-processing phase following the semantic-based matchmaking and aimed to better match discovery results with user needs.

The proposed utility function (whose formulation derives from common sense considerations) has two expressions, for potential and partial matches respectively:

$$f_{POT}(\cdot) = \frac{pot\_match}{2} + \frac{\tanh(\frac{t_R - t_O}{\beta})}{3} u(t_R - t_O)$$

$$+ (\frac{p_O}{p_R} - 0.5) \frac{(1+\alpha)p_R - p_O}{3(1+\alpha)p_R}$$

$$f_{PAR}(\cdot) = \frac{par\_match}{2} + \frac{\tanh(\frac{t_R - t_O}{\beta})}{6} u(t_R - t_O)$$

$$+ \frac{1-\gamma |c_R - c_O|}{3(2 + |c_R - c_O|)}$$

where *pot_match* and *par_match* are the potential and partial match values, p is price, t is delivery time and c is product category. The index R is referred to the request whereas the O one is referred to the supply and $u(\cdot)$ is the Heaviside step function. Parameters α, β, γ can be used to fine tune the utility function. Values we experimentally experienced with good results were $\alpha = 0.1$, $\beta = 10$, $\gamma = 0.2$. They have been determined by means of empirical tests through the comparison of system results with human users' judgment. The higher the utility value the better the obtained match. In both formulas, the leading term is represented by the semantic match.

The second term depends on the estimated delivery time and it is differently weighted in proposed formulas. In the first one (discovery of goods similar to the request), a late delivery is more penalized. On the other hand, partial matches refer to items that can be used together with the selected one (such as accessories or complements); therefore, a delay is less of a concern.

The last term is different in the two formulas. For potential matches, it is related to product price. The price imposed by the requester is increased with a factor α on the assumption that usually, the demander is willing to pay up to some more than what s/he originally specified, on the condition that s/he finds the requested item or something very similar. Supplies with a much lower price than requested (less than 50%) are penalized since they likely represent items in a different market segment. In the formula for partial matches, the last addend considers product category. Products in the same category are favored because they are presumably more suitable to be used together with the one selected by the user.

Coping with Verbose Descriptions

Languages at the heart of Semantic Web are based upon XML, whose known drawback is verbosity. Usually, this is not a concern for Internet-based applications (because link bandwidth and host memory capacity are enough for most practical purposes), but surely reduces efficiency of data storage and communication in mobile environments. Adapting ideas and techniques from the Semantic Web vision to ubiquitous scenarios requires coping with the limited storage and computational capabilities of mobile and embedded devices and with reduced bandwidth provided by wireless links. Here, we provide details about a novel efficient XML compression algorithm

Table 7. Product category contextual parameter

Product category	phones	computers	photo	audio/video	hobbies
Value	1	2	3	4	5

Figure 2. Structure of the proposed DIG compression tool

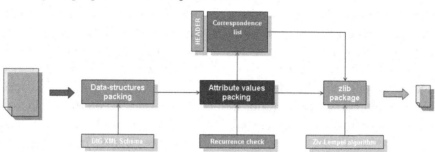

devised for the purposes of the framework presented in this article. It is specifically oriented to the packing of standard DIG 1.1 syntax. The XML Schema for DIG format contains 40 tags at most. A DIG is an XML document exposing specific characteristics. That is, no value is set for any tag; the value of tag attributes is within a well-defined finite set of values.

A basic distinction among various encoding techniques is in *fixed length* and *variable length* algorithms (Hamming, 1986). In the first case, having a specified alphabet, a fixed bit number is used to encode each symbol: in particular, we need $n = \log_2 k$ bits, with k alphabet symbols. A DIG file is encoded by means of ISO 8859-1 or UTF-8 encoding. In particular, each allowed character can be associated to 1 byte (special characters needing more than 1 byte in UTF-8 do not belong to the symbol set of DIG). Hence, in order to obtain a good compression rate, we must recur to a variable length coding algorithm: in this case the most efficient algorithm is the *Huffman* one (Huffman, 1952; Cover & Thomas, 1991). It requires having a *dictionary* containing the correspondences between each symbol and the bits sequence encoding it. This dictionary obviously varies according to the document. Although the Huffman algorithm could seem like a good choice to compress an ontology in DIG syntax, it does not work well with short semantically annotated DIG descriptions as the ones referred to resource metadata annotation. A resource description is usually a few hundred bytes long, so the Huffman

compression is sometimes inadequate because a description could be smaller than the dictionary itself. We propose a different DIG compression solution, particularly suitable for pervasive applications, whose structure is shown in Figure 2. We exploit the peculiarity of the DIG format having few, well-defined and limited tag elements and being mostly composed of empty XML elements. Three fundamental phases can be identified: **(1)** *data-structures packing*; **(2)** *attribute-values packing*; **(3)** *zlib packing*.

1. *Data-structures packing.* The proposed compression algorithm is based on two fundamental principles. First of all, pure data have to be divided from data structures; furthermore, data and data structures have to be separately encoded in order to obtain a more effective compression rate. Data structures are basically XML elements with possible related attributes, whereas data simply are attribute values. Recall that data structures in DIG syntax are fixed and well defined by means of the DIG XML Schema, whereas data are different from document to document. XML elements are encoded by associating an unambiguous 8-bit code to each structure in a static fashion. Consider that DIG files adopt an encoding which exploits one byte for each character: so an early size saving is performed. Note that the association between XML structures and corresponding code is fixed and invariable.

This is a further benefit because it is unnecessary to integrate within the compressed file a header containing the decoding table.

2. *Attribute-values packing.* In order to pack the attribute values, in the proposed approach, a further phase is introduced. Most recurrent words are identified in the previously distinguished data section. They will be encoded with a 16-bit sequence. The second compression stage allows to obtain a further size-saving especially in ontologies with recurrent concepts and roles. The second packing phase needs to build and maintain a header of the compressed file containing correspondences between each text string and the related 16-bit code. It is dynamically created and exclusively belongs to a specific DIG document instance. The provided header will be exploited in the decompression steps. Notice that assigned codes differ for the second byte, because the first octet is adopted as padding in order to distinguish the attribute value coding from the ASCII one. The use of this header could compromise compression performances for short files: recall that the size consumption for the header reduces saving obtained with compression. Hence, the encoding of all the string values of a DIG file without any a priori distinction must be avoided. Care has to be taken in the choice of attribute-value strings to encode. A correct compression procedure should properly take into account both the length of an attribute string and its number of occurrences within the file. The minimum length of strings to encode can be trivially established by comparing the size consumption needed to store correspondences *string–code* and the saving obtained with the encoding: in the proposed approach only text attributes with a length of at least three characters will be processed. Furthermore, in order to establish what attribute values (among remaining ones) have to be encoded, we must evaluate the number of occurrences of each attribute i (from now on *nr_occurences_i*). We fix a minimum optimum value *nr_occurences_min* and we will encode only i attribute values where *nr_occurences_i* > *nr_occurences_min*. We have performed statistical evaluations trying the compression of 72 sample ontologies and evaluating obtained compression rates varying *nr_occurences_min*. Results that show the best compression rates are produced by *nr_occurences_min* values within the range [2–8] with an average of 4.03 and a standard deviation in the range [0–0.3]. In the proposed approach, we set *nr_occurences_min* = 4, so we will encode only attribute strings with at least three characters recurring at least four times.

3. *Zlib packing.* The third and final compression step exploits *zlib* library. Although the *zlib* algorithm does not work well when it has to compress a partially encoded input (it is difficult to find more occurrences of the same sequence), the use of *zlib* in our approach resulted however useful especially for large files, where it produces the compression of words excluded by the previous compression steps and of the file header.

PROTOTYPE FRAMEWORK

U-commerce was chosen as a reference scenario for evaluating the effectiveness and feasibility of our object discovery framework and architecture.

A central role is played by the user interface component equipped with an integrated RFID reader as well as Bluetooth connectivity. The above logical framework can be adapted to different real scenarios with various physical devices involved. It will now be clarified and motivated in a consumer electronics store case study, where a "smart shopping cart" equipped with a tablet

Figure 3. Sequence diagram of a basic use case in our reference scenario

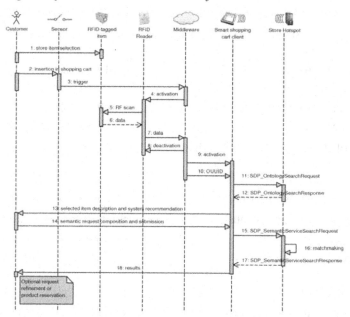

touchscreen, RFID reader and Bluetooth transceiver interacts with the store the hotspot at SDP level. The UML sequence diagram in Figure 3 shows the role played by these logical elements in a basic use case. We hypothesize that hotspot maintains semantic annotations and context values. Annotations of products in the marketplace refer to a consumer electronics ontology, marked with a specific identifier we indicate as $OUUID_E$. Interaction is triggered by inserting an item into the shopping cart, which is detected by a pressure sensor (also simulated in our current environment) and identified by the integrated RFID reader.

In the proposed object discovery framework, a session starts after the submission from client to server of the ontology identifier $OUUID_E$, in order to agree on the resource category to be adopted in upcoming requests. Semantic annotation describing the selected item will be exploited as basic user request to be adapted or updated for discovering further resources. Feature selection is performed by an intentional navigation of the reference ontology, represented as a hierarchy of elements. A tabbed panel allows easy navigation even in large ontologies. The user can concentrate

on his/her current focus and at the same time freely change the entry point through the upper tabs which record navigation history (Colucci et al., 2006). Pop-up menus and drag-and-drop are supported to further simplify user interaction.

Simulation Test Bed

A prototypical scenario was developed to validate the theoretical framework and to evaluate the feasibility and effectiveness of the proposed solution. IBM WebSphere RFID Tracking Kit (Chamberlain et al., 2006) was adopted as a development and simulation platform. It is a message-based service-oriented middleware for the integration of RFID systems and other mobile and embedded technologies in enterprise applications. It is based on OSGi (Open Service Gateway Initiative) Alliance open standard for platform-neutral, network-managed SOAs (Service Oriented Architectures) (OSGi Alliance, 2005).

The OSGi basic building block is the *bundle*, a self-contained software module whose lifecycle (install/start/update/restart/stop/uninstall) can be managed dynamically through a network. Bundle implementing EPCglobal RFID tag standards has been extended with support to semantic-based product descriptions: RFID tags and readers are software-simulated in our test bed.

Upon this infrastructure, WebSphere RFID Tracking Kit provides MBAF (MicroBroker application framework), a framework for event-based notification among software components. It adopts WebSphere MQTT (Message Queue Telemetry Transport), a lightweight publish-subscribe protocol for asynchronous message exchange. Components developed within MBAF are called *agents*. MBAF agents comply to OSGi bundle specifications and an agent behaves like a black box: it subscribes to messages representing events of interest. Upon message receipt, the agent processes its content and publishes zero or more new messages as a result. Overall application behavior is determined by the message flow among agents.

This service and message-oriented design fits well into ubiquitous computer paradigms, as it is aimed at maximizing modularity, flexibility and scalability. Such properties are essential in volatile and resource-constrained mobile environments, and benefits were noticeable in prototype testing and evolution. Simulation sessions with our prototype platform evidenced that semantic-

enhanced object discovery services can coexist with traditional RF identification and tracking applications. Test bed deployment and system components are represented in the UML diagram depicted in Figure 4 and the main elements are highlighted here. Both client and hotspot were deployed on notebook PCs running Microsoft Windows XP. WebSphere RFID Tracking Kit runs on client machine, integrating a Bluetooth communication interface with simulated RFID reader, sensors and an user interface by means of dedicated MBAF agents. Controller and configuration agents are added for supervising the application execution and managing system operating parameters, respectively. Hotspot hosts a J2SE runtime environment for running the service provider and a Linux Virtual Machine for running MAMAS-tng reasoner (Di Noia et al., 2004). The compression library implementing the algorithm described in the above section is included in both hosts as well as BlueCove[2], an open source Java Bluetooth library which was extended with support for semantic-based resource discovery. Both these components are deployed as standard Java archives in the hotspot, whereas they are encapsulated in OSGi bundles on the client node.

Figure 4. Test bed: HW?SW nodes and components

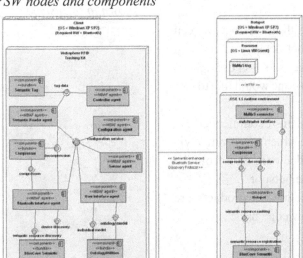

Example Scenario

Let us suppose Mary is looking for a new laptop computer. She notices a quite cheap notebook model, bundled with an office productivity suite. She puts it into the smart shopping cart. A sensor detects the event and the RFID reader is triggered. It reads data stored within the tag attached to the laptop package, then it is deactivated again. Extracted tag data consists of product EPC, ontology identifier $OUUID_E$, semantic-annotated description (stored as a compressed DIG expression) and contextual parameters. Let us suppose that tagged description corresponds to a notebook with Intel Centrino Core Duo CPU, 1 GB RAM, 80 GB hard disk drive, DVD writer and wireless LAN connectivity; it includes Microsoft Windows XP Home Edition OS and an office software suite. The price is $550, delivery time is 0 days and product category is 2. The equivalent expression in DL formalism with regards to $OUUID_E$ reference ontology is:

```
R:   notebook  ⊓∀has_CPU.Intel_centri-
     no_core_duo ⊓∀has_HDD.hard_disk_
     80_GB  ⊓∀has_disc_recorder.DVD_
     rec_16X_6X  ⊓∀has_ram.ram_1_GB
     ⊓∀has_cards.wireless_802_11_card
     ⊓∀has_OS.Windows_XP_Home_edition
     ⊓∀has_software.suite_office
```

As reported in Figure 5, the tablet touch screen shows the received product details for building further semantic-based requests. Let us suppose Mary likes her choice. Now she would like to find some basic accessories.

She confirms the system-recommended request (shown in Figure 6), which is submitted via the semantic-enhanced Bluetooth SDP from the smart shopping cart to the hotspot.

Let us suppose the following products are available in the store knowledge base:

S1: notebook with AMD Athlon XP-M CPU, 1 GB RAM, 80 GB hard disk drive, DVD writer and wireless LAN connectivity. It is bundled with Windows XP Professional and antivirus software. Price is $599; delivery time is 0 days; product category is 2:

```
notebook  ⊓∀has_CPU.AMD_Athlon_
XP_M ⊓∀has_HDD.hard_disk_80_GB
⊓∀has_disc_recorder.DVD_rec_
16X_6X  ⊓∀has_cards.wireless_
802_11_card ⊓∀has_ram.ram_1_GB
⊓∀has_OS.Windows_XP_Professional
⊓∀has_software.antiviruS
```

S2: notebook with Intel Centrino Core Duo CPU, 1 GB RAM, 80 GB hard disk drive, DVD writer and wireless LAN connectivity. It is bundled with Linux and an office suite. Price is $529; estimated delivery time is 1 day; product category is 2:

```
notebook  ⊓∀has_CPU.Intel_cen-
trino_core_duo ⊓∀has_HDD.hard_
disk_80_GB ⊓∀has_disc_recorder.
DVD_rec_16X_6X  ⊓∀has_cards.
wireless_802_11_card ⊓∀has_ram.
ram_1_GB 6 ...has_OS.Linux ⊓∀has_
software.suite_office
```

Figure 5. Product details are read via RFID and shown to the user

Figure 6. Graphical user interface for semantic request composition

S3: a desktop computer with Intel Pentium 4 CPU, 1 GB RAM, 250 GB hard disk drive, DVD writer, wireless LAN connectivity and an LCD display. It is bundled with Windows XP Home Edition and an office suite. Price is $499; delivery time is 0 days; product category is 2:

```
desktop _ computer  6  ...has _ CPU.
Intel _ Pentium _ 4  6  ...has _ HDD.
hard _ disk _ 250 _ GB 6 ...has _ dis-
play.LCD _ display 6 ...has _ disc _ re-
corder.DVD _ rec _ 16X _ 6X 6 ...has _
ram.ram _ 1 _ GB  6  ...has _ cards.
wireless _ 802 _ 11 _ card  6  ¼has _
OS.Windows _ XP _ Home _ edition  6
...has _ software.suite _ office
```

S4: a blue notebook bag. Price is $19; delivery time is 0 days; product category is 2:

```
notebook _ bag ⊓∀has _ color.blue
```

S5: a silver-colored UMTS mobile phone with dual display and miniSD memory card support. Price is $169; delivery time is 0 days; product category is 1:

```
mobile  phone ⊓∀has _ connectivity.
UMTS ⊓ =2 has _ display ⊓∀has _ dis-
play.LCD _ display  ⊓∀has _ memory _
card.mini _ sd
```

Hotspot performs the discovery and matchmaking processes as described in section 3 and returns results via Bluetooth SDP. Matchmaking results for this example are presented in Table 8. The second column shows whether each retrieved resource is compatible with request **R**. If so, the *rankPotential* computed result is shown, otherwise the *rankPartial* computed result is presented. In the last column, results of the overall utility function are reported. Note that **S2** is ranked as the best supply for similarity match, despite a longer delivery time than **S1**. This is due to a better *rankPotential* outcome. Among candidate resources for combination, category affinity favors **S4** over **S5**, while **S3** has a clearly poorer match. For each retrieved resource, a picture is returned along with matchmaking score, price and description, as displayed in Figure 7.

EXPERIMENTAL RESULTS

A thorough and significant experimental evaluation of all aspects of system performance requires a complete implementation of our framework into a testbed with real semantic-enabled RFID devices. That would only be possible through partnership agreements with device manufacturers/integrators. Therefore, analysis with our current PC-based simulation test bed focused on four groups of performance measures, that can provide valuable and reliable information about practical feasibility and efficiency of the proposed approach: 1) performance of the compression algorithm as a stand-alone tool; 2) impact of compression over Bluetooth system performance; 3) preliminary evaluation of access time of compressed semantic annotations on RFID tags with regards to tag scanning performance of EPCglobal RFID systems; 4) estimation of semantic matchmaking processing time.

The following subsections cover methods, results and discussion for each of the four analyses.

Table 8. Matchmaking results

Supply	Compatibility (Y/N)	*rankPotential* score	*rankPartial* score	$f(\cdot)$
S1: notebook with antivirus	Y	6		0.001
S2: notebook with office suite	Y	3		0.236
S3: desktop computer	N		79	0.166
S4: notebook bag	N		26	0.502
S5: UMTS phone	N		23	0.443

Figure 7. Retrieved results are shown to the user

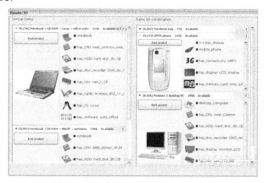

Compression Algorithm

Performance evaluation of the proposed algorithm has been carried out estimating three fundamental parameters: **(1)** compression rate; **(2)** turnaround time; **(3)** memory usage.

Two stand-alone tools were developed in C language implementing our compression and decompression algorithms, named *DIG Compressor* and *DIG Decompressor*, respectively. Currently, Windows and Linux platforms are supported, leveraging the freely available *zlib* compression library. Tests for compression rate and running time were performed using a PC equipped with an Intel Pentium 4 CPU (3.06 GHz clock frequency), 512 MB RAM at 266 MHz and Windows XP operating system. Tests for memory usage were performed on a PC running Gentoo GNU/Linux with 2.6.19 kernel version and *Valgrind* profil-

ing toolkit (Nethercote & Seward, 2007). This second PC was equipped with a Pentium M CPU (2.00 GHz clock frequency) and 1 GB RAM at 533 MHz.

1. The compression rates achieved by the proposed algorithm were tested with 70-DIG documents of various size. Our aim was to evaluate them for both smaller instance descriptions and larger ontologies. Figure 8 shows average compression rates and standard deviations for different size ranges of DIG input data. Overall, the average compression rate is 92.58±3.58%. As expected, higher compression rates were achieved for larger documents. Even for very short DIG files (less than 2 KB), however, average compression rate is 87.05±2.80, which is surely satisfactory for our purposes. A comparative evaluation was carried out using *XMill* general purpose XML compressor (Liefke & Suciu, 2000) and *gzip* generic compressor[3] as benchmarks. Testing the compression rate, the proposed tool allowed to obtain the smallest resulting files, as shown in Figure 9. It should be noticed that our algorithm performed significantly better for small DIG documents. This is a very encouraging result, since mobile scenarios usually deal with small XML annotations of available resources.

2. In order to evaluate turnaround time, each test was run ten times consecutively,

Figure 8. Compression rates obtained by the proposed algorithm

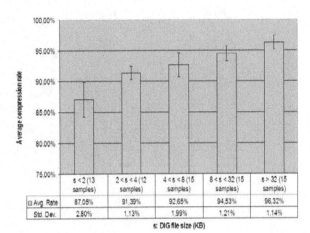

and the average of the last eight runs was taken. Results are presented in Figure 10. It can be noticed that processing times are comparable for documents up to 80 kB. For larger documents DIG Compressor has higher turnaround times than other tools, though absolute values are still quite acceptable. Such an outcome suggests further work should be put into optimizing the implementation for execution speed.

3. Finally, memory usage analysis was performed using *Massif* tool of *Valgrind* debugging/profiling toolkit. Massif measures stack and heap memory profile throughout the life of a process. For our comparison, only the memory occupancy peak was considered. Results are reported in Table 9.

DIG compressor memory usage is only slightly higher than the one of gzip, with high correlation (r = 0.96) between the two value sets. This result could be expected, since our algorithm relies on Ziv-Lempel compression in its last phase. On the contrary, XMill showed a more erratic behavior. Outcomes can be reputed as good because memory-efficient implementations of zlib

Figure 9. Compression rates in gzip, XMill and DIG compressor

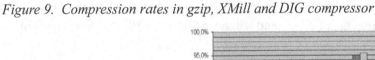

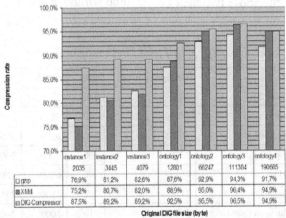

Figure 10. Turnaround time in gzip, XMill and DIG compressor

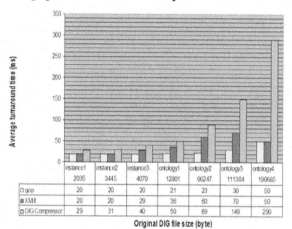

	instance1	instance2	instance3	ontology1	ontology2	ontology3	ontology4
	2035	3445	4079	12801	66247	111384	190685
□ gzip	20	20	20	21	23	30	50
■ XMill	20	20	29	36	60	70	50
□ DIG Compressor	29	31	40	50	89	149	290

Original DIG file size (byte)

library are currently available for all major mobile platforms.

Impact of Compression Over Bluetooth Performance

Like other wireless networking technologies, throughput of data transfer between two Bluetooth nodes is influenced mostly by: (1) fading due to obstacles and physical distance between nodes (Zanella et al., 2002), and (2) interference from other electromagnetic sources in range (Haartsen & Zürbes, 1999). In particular, Bluetooth operates in the unlicensed 2.45 GHz band also used by IEEE 802.11 wireless LANs, which are widespread in home and business environments. It is therefore important to take the above two factors into proper account when investigating the impact of data compression on Bluetooth application performance in ubiquitous computing scenarios. Since, in our approach a domain ontology is typically two or three orders of magnitude larger than individual resource annotations, ontology transfer from hotspot to a client was chosen as performance measure. The consumer electronics store ontology developed for the case study was used: original document size is 187 kB, whereas compressed size is 9.5 kB. Bluetooth transfer time of the uncompressed ontology was compared to the sum of (i) hotspot compression, (ii) transfer and (iii) client decompression time for the same resource. Tests were repeated at three client/hotspot distances (1 m, 5 m and 10 m) and both with and without a 802.11b/g WLAN (composed of an

Table 9 Memory usage peak (kB) in gzip, XMill and DIG compressor

DIG document	Original size (B)	gzip	XMill	DigCompressor
Playstation_2_Slim.dig	2035	220	2700	290
Kodak_P880_camera.dig	3445	200	4500	250
Asus_A3FP_Notebook.dig	4079	200	6500	250
Toy_ontology.dig	12801	200	4000	240
Rent_ontology.dig	66247	200	6500	250
clothing_ontology.dig	111384	202	4500	250
electronic_products_ontology.dig	190685	210	4000	260

Figure 11. Ontology transfer time via Bluetooth (data compression disabled and enabled)

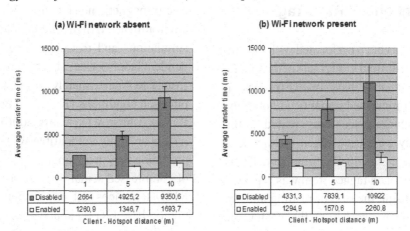

Figure 12. Hotspot encoding, Bluetooth transmission and client decoding times for a compressed ontology in various environmental conditions

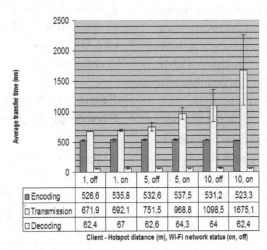

access point and a terminal) actively operating in the same room, for six different environmental conditions. Each ontology transfer test was run ten times consecutively; average values and standard deviations were then calculated.

Figure 11 summarizes results. Reported transfer time when compression is enabled, comprises the time spent in encoding and decoding of ontological data. Compression produces a significant speedup in all cases. At the same time, when compression is enabled, the system is much more resilient to performance degradation due to longer communication distance and interference by an active Wi-Fi network.

In Figure 12, the overall transfer time is dissected into its three components. Note that data compression occupies a significant share of total time (23.1% to 41.8%), while decompression is almost negligible. As expected, transmission time accounts for much of total variability and is affected by environmental conditions, while compression and decompression times are substantially constant.

Access Time of Simulated Semantic-Enhanced RFID Tag

This evaluation has been performed with the aim of providing a preliminary judgment of the impact that our approach may have on RFID system performance. Compressed semantic annotations of 40 different marketplace items created for the above case study were used. Their mean size is 266±104 B (range 91-440 B). Simulated RFID data access from each tagged item was repeated 100 times, recording the sum of reading and decompression time. For each item, the mean value was then considered.

Results are reported in Figure 13. The average access time is 2.02±0.36 ms, corresponding to a theoretical tag read rate of approximately 500 tags/s. Since tests were run on a software-simulated RFID platform, exact numerical values are not as significant as their order of magnitude. The latter can be sensibly compared to performance of RFID systems compliant with EPCglobal standards for Class 1 Generation 2 UHF RFID systems.

RFID performance in the field highly depends on the application, environmental conditions (electromagnetic noise, RFID reader density) and local regulations affecting the available bandwidth. Alien Technology RFID equipment manufacturer claimed maximum tag read rates of 1000 tags/s in environments with good insulation from electromagnetic noise and 50-100 tags/s in noisy environments (Alien Technology, 2005). Early simulations and tests by universities and independent laboratories estimated read rates ranging from 7 to approximately 100 tags/s in typical application conditions (Kawakita & Mistugi, 2006; Ramakrishnan & Deavours, 2006). Our simulation results are fully compatible with such data, thus providing very preliminary evidence that adoption of compressed semantic resource annotations on RFID tags does not impair performance of semantic-based RFID applications in the field with regards to to traditional ones. The latter, in turn, will not suffer any direct performance degradation from the newly introduced features, as they will read the EPC only. Finally, access time showed a moderate positive correlation ($r = 0.60$) with annotation size. This may suggest that structure of a DIG annotation also has an impact over the decompression.

Semantic Matchmaking Processing Computation

A semantic-enhanced Bluetooth simulated test bed embedded in *ns-2 Network Simulator[4]* has been used to assess semantic matchmaking processing times. Three ontologies of different

Figure 13. RFID tag reading and decompression time for 40 resource descriptions

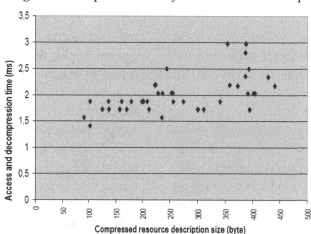

levels of complexity were examined, and five different demands for each one were submitted to MAMAS-tng reasoning engine. Average response times were recorded. Figure 14 shows the average response time, the number of concepts and the ratio of these two values for each ontology.

It can be noticed that, for the most complex ontologies, semantic matchmaking time dominates the other system performance measures shown in previous subsections. This problem was also pointed out by Ben Mokhtar et al. (2006), who devised optimizations to reduce online reasoning time in a semantic-based mobile service discovery protocol. The main proposed optimizations were offline pre-classification of ontology concepts and concept encoding: both solutions, however, are viable in matchmaking schemes based on pure subsumption (and therefore able to provide only binary yes/no answers), but are not directly applicable to our matchmaking scheme. Also note that, due to the large amount of time required by the matchmaker computation, RFID reading times have a relative importance within the overall performance evaluation. From this point of view, the differences between tag reading time interval in a practical deployment of the system and in the simulated one are un-influential in an extensive evaluation of the approach.

RELATED WORK

Smart identification technologies and techniques have been discussed in many recent research proposals in the field of ubiquitous computing. In De

et al. (2004), a pervasive architecture for tracking mobile objects in real time is presented, aimed at supply chain and B2B transaction management. A global and persistent IT infrastructure is necessary in order to interface RFID systems within partner organizations through the Internet. These requirements make the approach less suitable for B2C and C2C scenarios especially in MANET contexts. An XML formalism named Physical Markup Language (PML) is used to describe objects and processes. However, it does not exploit any semantics of resource descriptions and only allows string-matching discovery.

Römer et al. (2004) present two frameworks (respectively based on Jini and UDDI service discovery protocols) for ubiquitous computing applications using smart identification technologies. Core design abstractions such as object location, neighborhood, composition, history and context make them flexible. Nevertheless, as admitted by the authors, scalability issues are present. A further limitation is that semantics of object properties and capabilities is not explicit, but it is encapsulated in either Java classes or Web services.

A key usability issue of mobile and ubiquitous computing solutions is to assist the user in timely and unobtrusive ways, without either being inappropriate or altering his/her habits. In our framework, interaction is started implicitly, that is, by user actions in the real world. Schmidt et al. (2000) focus on implicit *Human-Computer Interaction* (HCI) in pervasive computing. The authors introduce a wearable RFID solution enabling operations on an information system simply by picking up or using an operation-related

Figure 14. Performance evaluation of semantic matchmaking

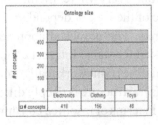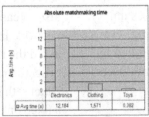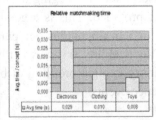

tagged object. The proposed system has been also integrated with SAP R/3 in a case study. Since no semantic information is associated to tags, however, RFID is used merely as a bridge towards the centralized information infrastructure. Interaction patterns are quite unnatural in some cases, because real-world objects are used to start even those tasks that need explicit HCI (e.g., editing a document in a word processor).

In Siegemund and Florkemeier (2003), interaction patterns between users endowed with GSM phones and everyday objects are investigated. Exploited objects are augmented through active RFID transponders equipped with on-board sensors, modest computing capabilities and Bluetooth connectivity. An infrastructure enabling a hybrid implicit-explicit HCI model is implemented. In order to minimize user involvement, an "invisible" pre-selection based on contextual conditions is performed. Elected objects send *interaction stubs* to the GSM terminal of the user. Basically, stubs are SMS templates to issue commands to objects or to ask their status. Authors claim that proposed interaction patterns are perceived as natural, nevertheless sending SMS messages to special objects requires too much user attention, thus altering normal relationships between people and everyday things. The need for a costly communication link such as GSM is an open issue.

In Kawakita et al. (2004), a support system aimed at enhancing information exchange within a conference room is presented. RFID-enabled badges are given to the meeting attendants, everyone having a remotely stored profile. Each room has an RFID reader. A location- and time-aware middleware tracks participants while entering or exiting meetings. Upon this basic infrastructure, location-based instant messaging and file sharing services are provided. This is a good example of implicit HCI in ubiquitous computing, even though the applicability is somewhat limited by the preliminary explicit profiling of both users and conference events.

Data compression of XML-based ontological languages is another major problem tackled in our proposal. Gzip (along with its library version *zlib*) is perhaps the most popular universal compression tool. It is based on a variant of the LZ77 algorithm (Ziv & Lempel, 1977). Among general purpose compression algorithms and tools, the *PAQ* family (Mahoney, 2005) shows the best compression rates. It is based on two fundamental ideas which evolve upon classic Huffman encoding algorithm: *context mixing* and *arithmetic coding*. A major drawback of PAQ algorithms is their huge processing and memory requirements, which currently are far beyond the capabilities of mobile computing devices.

By exploiting structural peculiarities of XML, better compression rates can be achieved than most general purpose tools. *XMill* (Liefke & Suciu, 2000) is an efficient XML compressor. Its approach is based upon the separation of XML content into different *containers*, which are stored sequentially in the output file. Each container is compressed by a specialized module. XMill performances are better than generic compressors only for medium and large XML documents.

CONCLUSION AND FUTURE WORK

In this article, we proposed a fully unified framework integrating RFID technologies with enhanced Bluetooth SDP supporting formal semantics. Objects tagged with RFID transponders carry a semantically annotated description so permitting to implement an advanced object discovery. Thanks to the semantic-enhanced SDP in Bluetooth, it is possible to exploit reasoning services from everywhere in the marketplace also in case of the lack of dependable and stable network links. The proposed approach aims to avoid the need for stable Internet connections in order to make the framework really "mobile", as a Bluetooth infrastructure is deeply different from a fixed one in terms of resource consumption and required support, therefore more suitable for giving a *non-invasive* structure to fully decentralized volatile environments. This is a good feature in sight of a future work in the mobility direction aimed to make the reasoner resident on mobile devices. Some slight modifications to the EPCglobal standard have allowed to support ontology-based data as well as non-standard inference services, while keeping total compatibility with legacy applications. The framework includes a compression tool based on an efficient algorithm specifically aiming at size reduction of document instances expressed in various ontological languages. The complete framework has been implemented within a message-oriented commercial middleware in order to test the feasibility and the usability of the proposed solutions.

Current limits of the proposed approach and tool emerge because the time spent in performing the overall discovery and ranking procedure is still somewhat high to be definitively acceptable (even if it has to be traded off with a far higher quality of the discovery with regards to traditional approaches). Future work is aimed to an optimization of the reasoner features for a dedicated utilization in pervasive and ubiquitous applications.

A real-world, practical application of the proposed framework has to face concrete difficulties of the modification of a closed standard as the EPCglobal currently is, and furthermore exhaustive preliminary studies have to be performed in order to test the feasibility of the approach in case of multiple readings (in those cases the collision phenomenon must be taken into account, although it is not expected to be a real problem). Finally, privacy and security issues have to be faced in order to make the proposed approach ready for a real-world commercial exploitation.

REFERENCES

Alien Technology. (2005). *EPCglobal Class 1 Gen 2 RFID Specification*. Whitepaper. Morgan Hill, CA: Alien Technology Corporation.

Baader, F., Horrocks, I., & Sattler, U. (2003). Description logics as ontology languages for the semantic Web. *Lecture Notes in Artificial Intelligence*. Springer.

Bechhofer, S., Möller, R., & Crowther, P. (2003). The DIG description logic interface. *Proceedings of the 16th International Workshop on Description Logics (DL'03)*.

Ben Mokhtar, S., Kaul, A., Georgantas, N., & Issarny, V. (2006). Efficient semantic service discovery in pervasive computing environments. *Proceedings of the ACM/IFIP/USENIX 7th International Middleware Conference, Middleware '06*.

Berners-Lee, T., Hendler, J., & Lassila, O. (2001). The semantic Web. *Scientific American, 248*(4), 34-43.

Borgida, A. (1995). Description logics in data management. *IEEE Transactions on Knowledge and Data Engineering, 7*(5), 671-682.

Brachman, R., & Levesque, H. (1984). The tractability of subsumption in Frame-based description languages. *4th National Conference on Artificial Intelligence – AAAI-84* (pp. 34-37).

Chamberlain, J., Blanchard, C., Burlingame, S., Chandramohan, S., Forestier, E., Griffith, G, et al. (2006). *IBM WebSphere RFID handbook: A solution guide*, 1st ed. IBM International Technical Support Organization.

Colucci, S., Di Noia, T., Di Sciascio, E., Donini, F., Ragone, A., & Rizzi, R. (2006). A semantic-based fully visual application for matchmaking and query refinement in b2c e-marketplaces. *8th International conference on Electronic Commerce, ICEC 06* (pp. 174-184).

Cover, T., & Thomas, J. (1991). *Elements of information theory*. John Wiley and Sons Inc.

De, P., Basu, K., & Das, S. (2004). An ubiquitous architectural framework and protocol for object tracking using RFID tags. *The First Annual International Conference on Mobile and Ubiquitous Systems, Networking and Services, MOBIQUITOUS 2004* (pp. 174-182).

Di Noia, T., Di Sciascio, E., Donini, F., & Mongiello, M. (2004). A system for principled matchmaking in an electronic marketplace. *International Journal of Electronic Commerce, 8*(4), 9-37.

Donini, F., Lenzerini, M., Nardi, D., & Schaerf, A. (1996). Reasoning in description logics. In: G. Brewka (Ed.), *Principles of knowledge representation: Studies in logic, language and information* (pp. 191-236). CSLI Publications.

EPCglobal Inc. (2005a). *EPC Radio-Frequency Identity Protocols Class-1 Generation-2 UHF RFID Protocol for Communications at 860 MHz-960 MHz.* January 2005.

EPCglobal Inc. (2005b). *Object Naming Service (ONS - ver. 1.0).* October 2005.

Haartsen, J., & Zürbes, S. (1999). *Bluetooth voice and data performance in 802.11 DS WLAN environment.* Ericsson Sig Publication.

Hamming, R. (1986). *Coding and information theory.* Prentice Hall.

Horrocks, I., van Harmelen, F., Patel-Schneider, P., Berners-Lee, T., Brickley, D. (2001). *DAML+OIL specifications.* Retrieved May 01, 2007 from http://www.daml.org/2001/03/daml+oil-index.html.

Huffman, D. (1952). A method for the construction of Minimum Redundancy Codes. *IRE,* 1098-1101.

Kawakita, Y., Wakayama, S., Hada, H., Nakamura, O., & Murai, J. (2004). Rendezvous enhancement for conference support system based on RFID. *International Symposium on Applications and the Internet Workshops, SAINT2004* (pp. 280-286).

Kawakita, Y., & Mistugi, J. (2006). Anti-collision performance of Gen2 Air Protocol in Random Error Communication Link. *International Sympo-sium on Applications and the Internet Workshops, SAINTW'06* (pp. 68-71).

Liefke, H., & Suciu D. (2000). XMill: An efficient compressor for XML data. *SIGMOD Rec., 29*(2), 153-164.

Mahoney, M. (2005). *Adaptive weighing of context models for lossless data compression.* Florida Tech. Technical Report, CS-2005-16.

Martin, D., Burstein, M., Hobbs, J., Lassila, O., McDermott, D. (n.d.). *OWL-S: Semantic markup for Web services.* Retrieved May 01, 2007 from http://www.daml.org/services/owl-s/1.1/overview/.

McGuinness, D., Fikes, R., Hendler, J., & Stein, L. (2002). DAML+OIL: An ontology language for the semantic Web. *IEEE Intelligent Systems, 17*(5), 72-80.

Nethercote, N., & Seward J. (2007). Valgrind: A framework for heavyweight dynamic binary instrumentation. *Conference on Programming Language Design and Implementation - PLDI 07.* ACM SIGPLAN.

OSGi Alliance. (2005). *About the OSGi service platform* (rev. 4.1). San Ramon, CA: OSGi Alliance.

Ramakrishnan, K., & Deavours, D. (2006). Performance benchmarks for passive UHF RFID tags. *Proceedings of the 13th GI/ITG Conference on Measurement, Modeling, and Evaluation of Computer and Communication Systems.* Nurenberg, Germany.

Römer, K., Schoch, T., Mattern, F., & Dübendorfer, T. (2004). Smart identification frameworks for ubiquitous computing applications. *Wireless Networks, 10*(6), 689-700.

Ruta, M., Di Noia, T., Di Sciascio, E., & Donini, F. (2006a). Semantic-enhanced Bluetooth discovery protocol for M-Commerce applications. *International Journal of Web and Grid Services, 2*(4), 424-452.

Ruta, M., Di Noia, T., Di Sciascio, E., Donini, F., & Piscitelli, G. (2006b). Advanced resource discovery protocol for semantic-enabled M-commerce. *Encyclopaedia of Mobile Computing and Commerce (EMCC)*. Hershey, PA: Idea Group.

Schmidt, A., Gellersen, H., & Merz, C. (2000). Enabling implicit human computer interaction: A wearable RFID tag reader. *The 4th International Symposium on Wearable Computers* (pp. 193-194).

Siegemund, F., & Florkemeier, C. (2003). Interaction in pervasive computing settings using Bluetooth-enabled active tags and passive RFID technology together with mobile phones. *Proceedings of the 1st IEEE International Conference on Pervasive Computing and Communications, PerCom 2003* (pp. 378-387).

Shadbolt, N., Hall, W., & Berners-Lee, T. (2006). The semantic Web revisited. *IEEE Intelligent Systems, 21*(3), 96-101.

Traub, K., Allgair, G., Barthel, H., Bustein, L., Garrett, J., et al. (2005). *EPCglobal architecture framework*. Technical report, EPCglobal Inc., July 2005.

Zanella, A., Tonello, A., & Pupolin S. (2002). On the impact of fading and inter-piconet interference on Bluetooth performance. *The 5th International Symposium on Wireless Personal Multimedia Communications, 1*, 218-222.

Ziv, J., & Lempel, A. (1977). A universal algorithm for sequential data compression. *IEEE Transactions on Information Theory, 23*(3), 337-343.

ENDNOTES

[1] *i.e.,* an ubiquitous environment where mobile peer users—both buyers and sellers—can submit their advertisements, browse through available ads and be assisted in finding the best available counterparts to meet their needs so beginning a commercial transaction.

[2] http://sourceforge.net/projects/bluecove/

[3] http://www.gzip.org/

[4] http://www.isi.edu/nsnam/ns/

This work was previously published in International Journal on Semantic Web & Information Systems, Vol. 4, Issue 1, edited by A. Sheth, pp. 50-74, copyright 2008 by IGI Publishing, formerly known as Idea Group Publishing (an imprint of IGI Global).

Chapter XIV
Facing the Challenges of RFID Data Management

Indranil Bose
University of Hong Kong, Hong Kong

Chun Wai Lam
University of Hong Kong, Hong Kong

ABSTRACT

Radio frequency identification (RFID) has generated vast amounts of interest in the supply chain, logistics, and the manufacturing area. RFID can be used to significantly improve the efficiency of business processes by providing automatic data identification and capture. Enormous data would be collected as items leave a trail of data while moving through different locations. Some important challenges such as false read, data overload, real-time acquisition of data, data security, and privacy must be dealt with. Good quality data is needed because business decisions depend on these data. Other important issues are that business processes must change drastically as a result of implementing RFID, and data must be shared between suppliers and retailers. The main objective of this article is focused on data management challenges of RFID, and it provides potential solutions for each identified risk.

INTRODUCTION

According to the definition provided by the *RFID Journal,* "Radio frequency identification (RFID) is a generic term that is used to describe a system that transmits the identity of an object or person wirelessly in the form of a unique serial number, using radio waves. It's grouped under the broad category of automatic identification technolo-

gies." RFID is much more advantageous than the barcode and other smart card technologies. When a large quantity of items are moved from one place to another place, the individual reading and processing of tags is time consuming when using barcode. RFID can deal with those items with the design and mapping of generic IDs of individual products. In Malaysia the government's commitment to drive the use of RFID has led to the successful adoption of chip-based credit cards. The Veterinary Services Department of Malaysia has decided to tag all 2.5 million livestock animals with economic value such as cattle, goat, and pigs by 2008 (Businessweek, 2007). It is expected that the RFID technology will grow very fast over the next three years. The global RFID market, which would include services, software, readers, and tags, will grow from $2.8 billion in 2006 to $8.1 billion by 2010 (The Economist, 2007).

RFID has a wide range of applications including warehouse resources management system (Chow, Choy, Lee, & Lau, 2006), integrated inventory management system (Saygin, 2007), retail management system (Sellitto, Burgess, & Hawking, 2007), real-time food traceability system (Connolly, 2007; Folinas, 2006; Kelepouris, 2007; Regattieri, Gamberi, & Manzini, 2007; Kempfer, 2007), product lifecycle management system (Harrison, McFarlane, Parlikad, & Wong, 2005; Parlikad & McFarlane, 2007), health care environment management system (Janz, Pitts, & Otondo, 2005), library resources management system (Yu, 2007), and shop-floor automation and factory information system (Qiu, 2007). Popular retailers like Wal-Mart, Gillette, Marks & Spencer, Tesco, Target, and Home Depot have already adopted the RFID technology. Using RFID data, Wal-Mart can predict the sales of a given item on a store-by-store basis and find out the reason why some products did not sell well. RFID allows Wal-Mart to sit down with its partners and plan how best to move products (Roberti, 2004). Gillette investigated the manner in which its tagged products were delivered from factory to customer store in its packaging and distribution center. Benefits reported by these stores appear to be directly related to the availability of the RFID data that are more accurate and timely than what was previously available, thereby allowing stock inventory to be better managed (Roberti, 2005a).

RFID data that is collected during the manufacturing process includes process start and finish time, product location, equipment location, labor location, equipment working status, stock keeping units (SKU), staff members' identities, and quantity of goods received. In retail industry, date of manufacture, product ingredients, temperature history, number of operation cycles, total time in operation, and details of maintenance would be recorded. Apart from the manufacturing and retail industry, RFID also plays an important role in the health care industry. Verichip is marketing its human-implantable RFID chip for medical use. The chip, which is the size of a grain of rice, can be injected into a person's arm. The pertinent medical records can be saved in the chip with a 16-digit code. Verichip expected the sales resulting from RFID chips to increase from $27.3 million in 2006 to $36 million in 2008 (Marcial, 2007).

Venture Development Corp. surveyed 100 chief technology officers and found that data management and monitoring was rated as one of the most important issues in the implementation of RFID systems (Li, Visich, Khumawala, & Zhang, 2006; O'Connor, 2004). Conventional systems, such as bar code printers and readers, are designed for human processing and are restricted to low transaction volumes. On the contrary, RFID can automate these processes and has the potential to generate much more data. RFID increases the volume of data substantially, as items leave a trail of data while moving through different locations. It is known that Wal-Mart's in-store RFID implementation will generate about 7.5 terabytes of RFID data a day. This overwhelming amount of data calls for newer and efficient data management approaches (Kasturi, 2005).

The reliability, quality, and management of the data must be sufficient because business decisions are made with these data. RFID technology entails risks with regard to data management, which can have an important influence on the result of implementing the technology. Another important issue is that business processes must change drastically as a result of implementing RFID because it is a completely new way of doing business. The main focus of this article would be to discuss the risks involved in data management and the solutions that can be adopted to lessen these risks.

RFID SYSTEM ARCHITECTURE

An RFID system consists of three main components, namely, tag, antenna, and reader. An RFID tag consists of a microchip attached to an antenna. Tags are either active or passive. Passive tags derive the power from the field generated by the reader. An RFID antenna is connected to the RFID reader. The antenna activates the RFID tag and transfers data by emitting wireless pulses. The RFID reader handles the communication between the information system and the RFID tag. The signals transfer to the host computer and pass through to the electronic product code (EPC) network. After that, the data is stored in the database server or other business application systems. There is an important tool called RFID middleware which consists of a set of software components that act as a bridge between the RFID system components (i.e., tags and readers) and the host application software. In other words, middleware tools are used to manage RFID data by routing it between tag/readers and the systems within the businesses. Middleware solutions filter duplicate, incomplete, and erroneous data that it receives. After digesting all data from the various sources, middleware forwards only the meaningful events to the enterprise systems. The tasks of the RFID middleware include data filtering, classification, data normalization, and aggregation of data transmitted between tags and readers for integration with the host application (Bhuptani & Moradpour, 2005; Goyal & Krishna, 2005; Shah, 2006). The detailed functions of the middleware are described in the following sections.

Data Filtering and Classification

Tag data needs to be cleansed to remove duplicate messages. Filtering and alerts may need to be raised based on certain predefined rules for data collection. Data filtering would mainly divide into low-level data and semantic data filtering. Low-level data filtering cleans the raw RFID data, and semantic data filtering extracts data on demand or interprets semantics from RFID data. The data classification can be done by the periodic batch program, which will pull all transaction data from the RFID application and dump it into a staging table in the middleware. A processor will periodically scan the staging table for any new transactions. This processor will match each record in the staging table with the history table. The purpose of this matching is to filter out duplicate transaction records and reduce network traffic (Goyal & Krishna, 2005). An example of data filtering and classification is the purchase order (PO) receiving process and advanced shipment notifications (ASNs). In an RFID supply chain, the transaction using the RFID will start with the supplier placing the tag on the pallet for the buyer. While the tagged pallet is stored in the warehouse, an ASN which contains the tag and pallet information would be sent to the buyer. The data will include shipment number, vendor name and location, number of containers, transaction date, quantity, and item description, and would be sent through the ASN to the buyer. When the pallets arrive at the receiving site, the reader at the dock will read the tag information. The data will be transmitted by the middleware for further identification and filtering. Then the filtered transaction will be classified according to tag ID, reader ID, location, and PO number, and will become a formal PO transaction (Goyal & Krishna, 2005).

Data Normalization

In the absence of standards, reader data formats and communication protocols for a host are usually proprietary. To function in a multi-vendor environment, the RFID middleware software is responsible for translating various reader data formats into a normalized format for easier integration at the host application level. The Physical Markup Language (PML), which is a standard technology based on the eXtensible Markup Language (XML), helps to transform and model the selected data (Folinas, 2006; Harrison et al., 2005; McMeekin et al., 2006). The host application receives processed and normalized data sent from the tag, via the reader and the RFID middleware software. The host application typically is a previously existing software system in an enterprise. Those systems can include a manufacturing execution system (MES), supply chain management (SCM) system, warehouse management system (WMS), and enterprise resource planning system (Bhuptani & Moradpour, 2005; Kleist, Chapman, Sakai, & Jarvis, 2004; Sellitto et al., 2007; Vijayaraman & Osky, 2006; Warden, 2005).

Data Integration

The RFID middleware can make it much easier to integrate retail data. Forecasts and orders become more accurate (Asif & Mandviwalla, 2005; RFID Journal, 2007). Collaborative planning, forecasting, and replenishment (CPFR), enterprise resource planning (ERP), warehouse management systems (WMS), and transportation management systems (TMS) allow companies to optimize forecasts, productions, and warehouse transportation. A combination of these systems with the RFID technology will result in more frequent and less costly data reads, thereby significantly enhancing their productivity (Twist, 2005). This would help to have the right product in the right place at the right time. Inventory is only needed for inappropriate information. RFID would provide better, faster, and more accurate information for allocation of resources and optimization of manufacturing process. High capital investment of RFID technology can be minimized through the backend integration of the enterprise applications. An enterprise application integration-based RFID middleware developed by Goyal and Krishna

(2005) provided a two-way integration between an RFID application and any business application. The RFID integration mainly maintained a channel of communication between the business application and the RFID application. Also, the data needed to transfer and move from the RFID application to a schema, which will be used by the middleware to process and then submit for further processing to the business applications. Another important function of data integration is mapping of the classified data to the business application it should hit and interfacing the data to the business application in a format that is acceptable to that application.

Example of Middleware

Siemens RFID middleware, developed by the Integrated Data Systems Department of Siemens Corporate Research, is a good example of RFID middleware. Siemens RFID middleware enables semantic RFID data filtering and automatic data transformation, supports RFID object tracking and monitoring, and can be adapted to different RFID-enabled applications. The Siemens RFID middleware consists of event managers and a data server (Wang & Liu, 2005). Event managers are the front end of the system. These include reader adapter, filter, and writer. Reader adapter is the component that interacts with the RFID readers. A reader adapter can control the reading frequency and also receive data from the reader. The filter is the data filtering component to detect the duplicate and error data from raw RFID data. The writer would format the data with PML and send them to different targets.

After event managers filter and normalize the data, the data would be forwarded to the RFID data server, which includes the components of RFID data manager, RFID data store, product data store, and RFID data archive. RFID data manager is the key component of the RFID data server in an RFID data management system. It consists of three layers: semantic data processing layer, query layer, and decision-making layer. The semantic data processing layer provides high-level semantic data processing including automatic data transformation and semantic filtering. The query layer provides RFID object tracking and monitoring support. The decision-making layer provides low inventory alerts and trend analysis. The RFID data store stores RFID data for RFID object tracking, monitoring, decision making, and data retrieval. The product data store stores the static data such as product description and product model. In the RFID data archive, non-active data are archived into historical partitions. Finally, the RFID data server provides an application integration layer to integrate the system with other applications. Figure 1 shows the whole RFID system architecture and the corresponding RFID middleware system.

CHALLENGES AND SOLUTIONS

Before discussing the challenges of data management for RFID systems, the framework for data processing must be investigated. The framework consists of five stages for data flow, namely, data collection, data preprocessing, data analysis, data evaluation, and data integration and usage.

Data is a measurement of reality that may consist of measurements or observations. Those measurements or observations comprise numbers, words, or images. When the data becomes organized, it becomes information. Data collection, which refers to the process of preparing and collecting business data, usually takes place in the early stage of a project. A formal data collection process is necessary as it ensures that the data gathered is both well defined and accurate. Data

Figure 1. RFID system architecture and middleware system

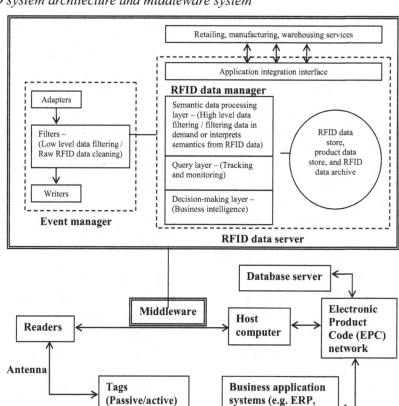

preprocessing is the act of processing data before the syntactic analysis. Preprocessing is also used in data mining before data is filtered, analyzed, and a model is constructed. Data analysis is the act of transforming data with the aim of extracting useful information. During the process of analysis, one or more models will be used. Data evaluation is the systematic determination of quality, merit, worth, and significance of data. Data integration is the act to allow the movement of data from one device or software to another. For example, RFID data could be transferred to an Enterprise Resources Planning system. Data integration allows companies to optimize forecasts, production, and warehouse transportations. Thus, these five stages are important in management of data for the RFID information system. Figure 2 shows the model of an RFID data management system.

Data Collection

Real-Time Acquisition of Data

Although accurate information can be obtained for all tagged parts close to real time for most of the supply chain systems, most current tools can-

not handle the amount and the real-time aspects of those data (Ranky, 2006). The manufacturing companies track the number of pallets shipped out hourly and daily, and upload the information in batch mode, possibly every few hours or every shift. As RFID technologies become more ubiquitous, real-time transmission of data poses additional challenges in the ability of managers to process the information in a timely manner (Angeles, 2005). The challenge lies in processing such voluminous data and making timely decisions that are tied to the manufacturing execution systems (Saygin, 2007).

In the wireless manufacturing (WM) technology, RFID has played an important role in the collection and synchronization of the real-time field data from manufacturing workshops. It is crucial that the real-time shop-floor information visibility and traceability enable the implementation of just-in-time manufacturing to reduce the shop-floor work in process inventories and to smoothen their flows (Huang, Zhang, & Jiang, 2007).

In logistics management and supply chain management, the critical issues are to integrate the inventory, distribution, and sales data, and to make the integrated logistics information available to the

Figure 2. The model of an RFID data management system

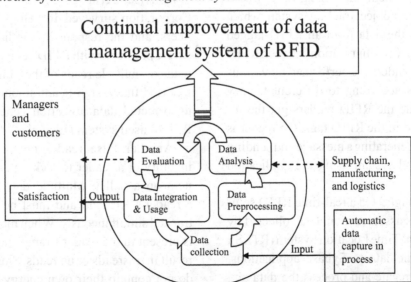

organization in real time. The key point of logistic information integration is the real-time acquisition and recognition of distribution information. Compared to traditional approaches for logistics data capture and identification (e.g., bar code), RFID technology enables real-time automatic data capture, data identification, and information interchange; therefore, merchandise tracking, product sorting, and distribution data collection and analysis can be efficiently accomplished (Hou & Huang, 2006). As the RFID-enabled supply chain is able to get real-time information from all interfaces in the supply chain accurately and quickly, this facilitates aggregation of forecasts upstream into the supply chain and provides more accurate forecasts at the store and supplier level (Pagarkar, Natesan, & Prakash, 2005).

One of the feasible solutions is to develop operational data management architectures. Operational data management architectures are common in the financial industry. For example, trading systems collect market data in real time, execute trading strategies heuristically, identify trading opportunities, and forward the results to traders for action (Palmer, 2004). Actually, different solutions have been proposed by different companies and researchers for the efficient tracking and monitoring of real-time data.

Chen, Chen, Chen, and Chang (2007) have proposed an RFID object tracking system which is able to track the data from an RFID-tagged object efficiently. Communication between RFID tags and RFID readers are performed by various RFID protocols according to different factory standards. While the RFID readers get the information stored in the RFID tags, the reader is responsible for generating a message and sending it to the backend system using the application layer protocol.

Sybase has suggested a real-time RFID solution which takes asset location data collected by AeroScout's Real Time Location System (RTLS). RTLS feeds that data to Sybase applications, which then aggregate and process the data and

deliver it to mobile devices such as smart phones and PDAs (Collins, 2004).

False Read

RFID has the advantage that the RFID tags can be read without human intervention and without line of sight, and this enables bulk reading. However, if the data itself is inaccurate, RFID does not provide any value (Tellkamp, Angerer, Fleisch, & Corsten, 2005). False reads is the result of radio waves being distorted, deflected, absorbed, and interfered with (Angeles, 2005). Extreme temperature ranges, labeling standards, and packaging constraints are some of the potential causes affecting the radio waves transmission (Sellitto et al., 2007). As RFID systems are extremely susceptible to environmental noise, environmental factors such as reflective surfaces (e.g., swinging metal doors) or leaky protective devices (e.g., carrying cases with ill-fitting lids) can make the false read problem much worse by misdirecting RFID signals. In other words, although an RFID reader obtains the data from the tag, it does not mean that the reading is part of the true data flow or business process. The false read problem in turn can significantly affect the reliability of reporting, decision support, and other information systems (Janz et al., 2005). Venture Development Corporation surveyed 100 chief technology officers, and the respondents indicated there are severe problems with RFID devices sending false reads or multiple reads of the same tag. It is also reported that a significant amount of noise and uncorrected data are often generated from an RFID-based system (Li et al., 2006).

Another false read problem concerns the inability of a reader to pick up data from every item on a pallet. Multiple tags are present in a reader's RF field and must be identified and tracked simultaneously. When more than one tag is present in the reader's range, tag collision can result in misreads or no reads. Since passive tags do not contain their own energy source, power consumption constraints are also imposed. In fact, the accuracy of some readers can fall below 90% (Asif & Mandviwalla, 2005). Moreover, the range of most readers drops drastically if the pallets have metal foil packaging or high water content because both these substances absorb radio waves. For example, the reader cannot read a tag behind a can of soda because the aluminum and the contents of the can block the signal transmission (Lin & Brown, 2006).

However, innovative solution strategies are being proposed to handle these problems. Efficient anti-collision algorithms are being developed, including time-division-multiple-access (TDMA), phase-jitter-modulation (PJM), and frequency and time-division-multiple-access (FTDMA). The anti-collision function requires cooperation between the tags and readers to minimize the risk of many tags responding all at one time (Asif & Mandviwalla, 2005). In some cases, the algorithm may be as simple as each tag waiting a random amount of time before responding to a reader's request (Bhuptani & Moradpour, 2005). Progress is also being made in attempts to produce more power-efficient chip design and efficient error-correcting-code (ECC) schemes. It is also critical that business rules are well defined so as to separate useful data from unwanted data (Evans, 2004). Lin and Brown (2006) suggested that the accuracy could be improved by reading pallets as they rotate during the packaging process. This allows the reader to get signals from the tags at different angles. Besides, readers must be properly installed and potential electromagnetic interference or barriers must be eliminated to ensure data accuracy.

Data Preprocessing

Data Explosion

RFID technology would increase the volume of data substantially, as items leave a trail of data while moving through different locations (Kant-

ers, 2007; Vijayaraman & Osky, 2006). Firms that have tracked pallets and cases with RFID tags would show an increase of at least 30% in the data that needed to be processed (Angeles, 2005). The costs associated with storing RFID-generated data and the data-generating capabilities of RFID hardware and software would then increase (Janz et al., 2005; Lin & Brown, 2006). At the same time, more time will be needed to process the data (Lin & Brown, 2006). Database administrators need to be able to deal with the potential stress on the databases, both in terms of speed and volume involved in processing RFID applications. Angeles (2005) has estimated that tracking all items from production to point of sale for a manufacturing process would require 3,000 database transactions per second on the low end and upwards of 30,000 on the high end. If each product has 1,000 bytes of data associated with it, the RFID system would generate 10 terabytes of data per year. If the data is stored for five years, a 50-terabyte database will be needed.

For the food industry in the UK, food retailers will face the problem of inability to handle and make effective use of the data captured by RFID systems. Since the retail systems will collect a massive and continuous stream of real-time data, the storage and transmission of this data will impose severe strains on existing data management and storage structures and strategies (Jones, Clarke-Hill, Comfort, Hillier, & Shears, 2005). Besides, a field research conducted by Wal-Mart, the Auto-ID Center, and the key suppliers at Wal-Mart's pilot distribution center in Oklahoma resulted in the generation of 30 times more data, as products were tracked through the supply chain (Li et al., 2006).

One of the feasible solutions for the data explosion is the use of data warehouses. A data warehouse is adapted to store data extracted from different sources of a manufacturing process. The data such as process start time/finish time, equipment working status, equipment location, Stock Keeping Unit (SKU), staff members' identities, and quantity of goods received can be recorded and properly stored using a data warehouse. Moreover, the process information such as the process progress and staff members' responsibility would also be recorded (Chow, Choy, & Lee, 2007).

Data explosion could also be handled through pipeline processing. Once you have a Savant concentrator architecture in place, pipelines could be set up to handle the streams of data. Pipelines separate streams of EPC data to handle load and coordinate the data streams after they have been captured (Palmer, 2004). The Auto-ID Center at MIT developed a a software program named 'Savant' to manage the enormous amount of data expected to be generated by RFID readers. The filtering, collecting, and reporting layer , is essential in order to deploy large quantities of RFID tags and readers without overwhelming the network capacity (Asif & Mandviwalla, 2005; Harrison et al., 2005; Palmer, 2004).

Another possible solution is to determine the level of granularity for data collection. The granularity of data collection should be driven by business requirements and not by the technical limitations. It should be up to the business managers to define what constitutes a business event. The frequency of read or write events should be adjusted to the business needs (Evans, 2004). Only goods that need to be recalled such as fresh perishable produce or meat or high-value items such as expensive electronic gadgets or luxury designer goods may require a more detailed record of their movements through the purchase experience (Angeles, 2005). This will help to reduce the burden on the network and on data storage systems.

Data Analysis

Data Mining

After a vast amount of data is gathered from the activities along the supply chain, this data must be warehoused and mined to identify patterns that can lead to better control of the supply chain. The feasible solution is data mining. Data mining is a process that uses data analysis tools to discover relationships in data or potentially useful information that may be used to make valid predictions. Another objective of data mining is to discover hidden facts contained in databases.

Ngai, Cheng, Au, and Lai (2007) have proposed an RFID-integrated m-commerce framework for the container depot management support system (CDMSS). The data are gathered and stored in the data analysis module of the CDMSS for data mining. Useful business information are extracted from the data and this enables better decision making. Using online analytical processing (OLAP) technology with RFID technology, instant decisions can be made based on the data collected from the RFID-integrated m-commerce framework. Different popular data mining techniques such as discriminant analysis (DA), decision trees (DT), and artificial neural networks (ANNs) can be used to enhance the data analysis process.

Data Evaluation

Data Quality Assessment

Data obtained from the RFID readers only describe the events, activities, transactions, and numbers. Without organization of those numbers, they would not make much sense. Turban, Mclean, Wetherbe, Bolloju, and Davison (2002) have said:

Information is data that have been organized so that they have meaning and value to the recipient. The recipient interprets the meaning and draws conclusions and implications. Data processed by an application program represent a more specific use and a higher value added than simple retrieval from a database.

Actually, the data quality characteristics are rather subjective. Data quality attributes such as accuracy, completeness, timeliness, consistency, and relevancy can be intuitively defined by people. Accuracy represents data that is correct; completeness relates to an all-encompassing value allowing a task at hand to be addressed; the timeliness dimension reflects the creation and removal dates of the data; consistency ensures product quality standards; and relevancy is associated with how the data is used in a specific task. Only if all these data quality attributes are satisfied, then RFID will be beneficial for businesses.

Data Security and Privacy

RFID chips embedded in retail products without the knowledge of the customers who buy those products could remain in products for indefinite periods and so can be potentially traceable beyond the limited scope of their original purpose (Angeles, 2007). Use of RFID in supply chain applications before the point of sale is of no concern to consumers because there are no privacy implications. However, the use of RFID after the point of sale has privacy implications (Dobson & Todd, 2006). If the RFID tags are not removed or deactivated when the customer leaves a store, the customer can be monitored via the radio signals that continue to emit from their purchases.

Moreover, if the unique product information on an RFID tag is linked to some identifiable customer information, such as a credit card number, which may in turn offer access to further personal data such as address, income, and even the credit rating, then this allows the retailer to build up detailed profiles of their customers. This suggests that a widespread network of RFID receivers could be constantly observing, processing, and evaluating consumers' behaviors and purchases. There is the possibility that retailers may sell personalized data to other commercial organizations for illegal purposes (Jones, Clarke-Hill, Hillier, Shears, & Comfort, 2004). Finally, the linking of personal identification data with a unique product code would also mean that individuals would have the possibility of being physically stalked without their knowledge or consent (Jones et al., 2004).

Ayoade (2006) has proposed the Authentication Processing Framework (APF) to provide assurance to RFID users that the information stored in the tag is secure in the sense that only authenticated readers of the APF have access to the tag. The data received by the reader from the tag is encrypted, and this data can only be decrypted by using the decryption key from the APF. Moreover, for preventing the tags from being cloned, a heuristic Jigsaw encoding scheme is proposed. This simple scheme helps encrypt an EPC code into a pseudo-EPC code. The pseudo-EPC code looks like a random code, and an attacker is not able to reverse it into a valid EPC code in a short period of time. Attackers, even with same RFID reader, can only make cloned tags with these pseudo-EPCs. Such encryption is able to protect EPC data on passive RFID tags (Wong, Hui, & Chan, 2006).

Inventory control requires a radio signal strong enough to track inventory across a warehouse. However, for contactless purchases of retail products, the signal that just extends a few inches from the card reader can be used. Each purchase is separately encoded. Identity thieves cannot steal radio signals and use data to make subsequent illicit purchases (Ward, 2007). Finally, deployment of RFID tag-embedded products must be accompanied by the effective enforcement of privacy legislation, voluntary self- and co-regulation, and codes of conduct (Reid, 2007).

Data Integration and Usage

RFID Data Integration with Existing Business Processes

Business processes must change drastically as a result of implementing RFID, so enterprises must carefully consider RFID before implementing it. Methodology such as Analytic Hierarchy Process (AHP) can be used to assist organizations in judging if the RFID technology is suitable for them (Lin & Lin, 2007). The framework for evaluating RFID adoption is shown in Figure 3.

Companies interested in adopting RFID should reexamine how supply chain decisions are made. This will require a deep understanding of how RFID impacts supply chain dynamics. For example, as organizations migrate to RFID, they may have to consider an environment made up of both barcodes and RFID tags at the case or palette level (Brown & Russell, 2007). Systems integration is not just about sending the filtered data into the ERP systems. It requires solutions to help the end users understand the data, and link it with the systems and processes. Servers that form the backbone of the information technology infrastructure for the company would require understanding of what is being collected from the edge devices in order to automate the analytical

and feedback processes. Spieß, Bornhövd, Lin, Haller, and Schaper (2007) suggested the Smart Item Infrastructure (SII), which provides the solution for RFID data integration with the business process automation. The business process bridging layer, one of the five layers of SII, describes the services to aggregate and transfer data from the RFID to business-relevant information, thereby reducing the amount of data being sent to the enterprise application systems.

Data Sharing

Retailers using RFID would be most interested in attaining faster processes, higher visibility of flows, and a decrease in errors and discrepancies, so that they can maximize the profit. Data sharing would be the key to this challenge. Sharing the data with suppliers would allow them to track

Figure 3. A framework for evaluation of RFID adoption

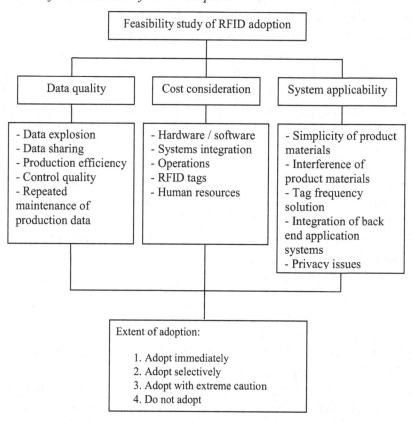

shelf availability more accurately and reduce the chance of stockouts.

The first step in data sharing is the exchange of RFID raw data. The retailer provides feedback to the supplier on the status of the incoming delivery. After that, the exchange of RFID data within a business context should be implemented between partners. At this stage partners start using RFID to understand its business significance and identify achievable business benefits. Retailers and suppliers can benefit greatly from RFID, but RFID data sharing is a major process change which is needed to make the most out of it (RFID Journal, 2007). One of the examples for data sharing is sharing of EPC data of Target and Wal-Mart beginning with 13 manufacturers. The pilot represents a major advance toward the goal of using EPC data to track goods throughout the entire supply chain (Roberti, 2005b).

All the challenges in the management of RFID data and their corresponding potential solutions that are discussed in this section are summarized in Table 1.

FUTURE RESEARCH DIRECTIONS

Many new research questions can be posed from the listing of challenges and solutions for RFID data management. At present the problem of false read is a major issue for RFID tags. An important research question in this area is: what is the optimal amount of time the tag should be exposed to the reader so that the reading is accurate and at the same time the process of movement of the tagged item is not substantially delayed? Another important research idea that requires further exploration is: for a basket of items that are individually tagged, what should be the optimal sequence in which the tags should be read? Associated with the false read problem, is the difficult issue of detection of outliers in tag readings? How can an operations manager determine whether a reading is spurious. In addition to

his or her intuition and domain knowledge, what mathematical and pattern matching techniques can be used to determine the correctness of the reading. When transporting a basket of different products from the distribution center to the retail outlet, numerous readings will be generated at different points of time. Decision rules must be developed for filtering this data. However, more research needs to be done to ascertain if those decision rules should be of a generic nature or if they should be dependant on the characteristics of the product. The filtered data on the tagged products is likely to be stored in a data warehouse that will receive such data from a number of points of data capture. What should be the most appropriate schema to be used in the data warehouse so as to maintain the integrity and concurrency of the temporal data arriving from multiple sources at different times? The data stored in the data warehouse needs to be of sufficient quality so that they can be of use subsequently. But existing metrics for assessment of data quality may not be sufficient for assessment of RFID-related data. More importantly, researchers will have to define different data quality metrics for different applications using RFID. For example, the data quality metrics used in retail outlets may be different from those used in the supply chain. The summarized data from the data warehouse will be amenable to data analysis. This raises a number of research questions in the area of data mining. What kind of patterns should analysts hope to discover from this data—clusters, sequences, association rules, or outliers? Will popular standalone methods of data mining like decision trees, neural networks, K-means clustering, and so forth be sufficient, or will there be a need to develop specialized or hybrid algorithms specially tailored to RFID data? Privacy issues related to RFID tags have been discussed in this article. But a generic approach that disables all tags after the point of sale may not always be appropriate. Some customers may be inclined to reveal the movements of some products of some marketing companies in return

Table 1. Challenges and proposed solutions for the management of RFID data

Challenges	Proposed Solutions
Real-time acquisition of data	• Operational data management architecture is needed. • RFID object tracking system that is able to keep maintenance and efficient tracking of the data from an RFID-tagged object is proposed. • A real-time RFID solution is suggested by Sybase.
False read	• Efficient anti-collision algorithms are being developed, including time-division-multiple-access, phase-jitter-modulation, and frequency and time-division-multiple-access. • Progress is made in attempts to produce more power-efficient chip designs and efficient error-correcting-code schemes. • The accuracy could be improved by reading pallets as they rotate during the packaging process. It allows the reader to get signals from the tags at different angles and obtain the best view. • Potential electromagnetic interference or barriers must be eliminated to ensure data accuracy.
Data explosion	• Data warehousing is adapted to store data extracted from different sources of a manufacturing process. • Pipelines could be set up to handle the streams of data. • The Auto-ID Center at MIT developed a software program named 'Savant' to manage the enormous amount of data expected to be generated by RFID readers. • The level of granularity for data collection must be determined.
Data mining	• An RFID-integrated m-commerce framework for the Container Depot Management Support System has been proposed. • Different popular data mining techniques such as discriminant analysis, decision trees, and artificial neural networks can be used.
Data security and privacy	• Authentication Processing Framework is proposed. • For preventing the tags from being cloned, a heuristic Jigsaw encoding scheme is proposed. • For contactless purchases of retail products, the signal that just extends a few inches from the card reader can be used.
Data integration with existing business processes	• An environment made up of both barcodes and RFID tags at the case or palette level should be considered. • Analytic Hierarchy Process can be used to assist organizations in judging if they are suitable to adapt the RFID system. • Smart Item Infrastructure, which provides the solution for the RFID data integration with the business process automation, is proposed.
Data sharing	• Exchange of RFID raw data. • RFID data within a business context should be shared between partners.

for monetary rewards, but not the movement of all products of all companies. Organizations will have to find a systematic way to do selective disablement of tags based on customers' preferences and will have to maintain a list of tags of particular products of some companies that are not disabled. Integration of the RFID information system with the enterprise information system is a major challenge in itself. However, researchers must answer whether a phased or a big-bang approach should be adopted for the implementation of the integration project, keeping in mind the physical and human resources of the organization. Finally, benefits of RFID can be achieved through sharing of data related to movement of items. However, all participants in the supply chain may not be willing to share business-critical data as that may lead to eroding their power and profit. Researchers must decide on the optimal dynamics of data revelation and sharing between the various parties.

CONCLUSION

In this article we have discussed the existing challenges for data management of RFID, and put forward several suggested solutions for the successful business implementation of RFID. For the false read problem, technical tests of specific cases must be performed to reduce the problems of tags collisions and absorption by packaging material. Apart from data filtering, business rules must be set up to govern data collection and storage. While RFID would generate a massive amount of data, the first step in a successful data management strategy is to ensure that only meaningful data is collected for the backend applications and data repositories. It is critical that there are well-defined business rules to separate duplicate or unwanted data from useful data. This will help in reducing the burden on the network and on data storage systems (Evans, 2004). When linking RFID technology to existing enterprise applications, the changes in infrastructure need to be done in a way that minimizes cost. Also, use of RFID may lead to privacy issues, especially after the point of sale, and there is a need to handle this in a very careful manner, keeping in mind the preferences of the customers.

More and more companies are expected to implement RFID technology in the near future. Although RFID poses many challenges to current data management systems, this technology is much more advantageous than the barcode and other smart card technologies. Several potential solutions have been suggested to address the various challenges related to real-time acquisition of data, false read, data explosion, data mining, data security and privacy, data integration with existing business processes, and data sharing. Some specific research questions related to these challenges that need to be explored further have been listed in the previous section. In the future, it is foreseeable that data management will continue to remain a major concern for worldwide adoption of RFID.

REFERENCES

Angeles, R. (2007). An empirical study of the anticipated consumer response to RFID product item tagging. *Industrial Management & Data Systems, 107,* 461-483.

Angeles, R. (2005). RFID technologies: Supply-chain applications and implementation issues. *Information Systems Management, 22,* 51-65.

Asif, Z., & Mandviwalla, M. (2005). Integrating the supply chain with RFID: A technical and business analysis. *Communications of the Association for Information Systems, 15,* 393-427.

Ayoade, J. (2006). Security implications in RFID and authentication processing framework. *Computers & Security, 25,* 207-212.

Bhuptani, M., & Moradpour, S. (2005). *RFID field guide: Deploying radio frequency identification systems.* New York: Prentice Hall.

Brown, I., & Russell, J. (2007). Radio frequency identification technology: An exploratory study on adoption in the South African retail sector. *International Journal of Information Management.*

Businessweek. (2007, April 25). *Asia RFID market need gov't boost.* Retrieved from *http://www. businessweek.com/globalbiz/content/apr2007/ gb20070425_369568.htm?chan=search*

Chen, J.L., Chen, M.C., Chen, C.W., & Chang, Y.C. (2007). Architecture design and performance evaluation of RFID object tracking systems. *Computer Communications.*

Chow, H.K.H., Choy, K.L., & Lee, W.B. (2007). A dynamic logistics process knowledge-based system—an RFID multi-agent approach. *Knowledge Based Systems, 20,* 357-372.

Chow, H.K.H., Choy, K.L., Lee, W.B., & Lau, K.C. (2006). Design of a RFID case-based resource management system for warehouse operations.

Expert System with Applications, 30, 561-576.

Collins, J. (2004, August 23). *Sybase initiates RFID solution.* Retrieved from *http://www.rfid-journal.com/article/articleview/1093/1/1/*

Connolly, C. (2007). Sensor trends in processing and packaging of food and pharmaceuticals. *Sensor Review, 27,* 103-108.

Dobson, T., & Todd, E. (2006). Radio frequency identification technology. *Computer Law & Security Report, 22,* 313-315.

Evans, N.D. (2004, June 28). *Planning for RFID data.* Retrieved from *http://www.rfidjournal. com/article/articleview/1004/1/82/*

Folinas, D. (2006). Traceability data management for food chains. *British Food Journal, 108,* 622-633.

Goyal, K., & Krishna, D. (2005). *RFID middleware—integration to the entire supply chain.* RFID Journal White Paper.

Harrison, M., McFarlane, D., Parlikad, A.K., & Wong, C.Y. (2005). *Information management in the product lifecycle—the role of networked RFID.* Auto-ID Center White Paper.

Hou, J.L., & Huang, C.H. (2006). Quantitative performance evaluation of RFID applications in the supply chain of the printing industry. *Industrial Management & Data Systems, 106,* 96-120.

Huang, G.Q., Zhang, Y.F., & Jiang, P.Y. (2007). RFID-based wireless manufacturing for walking-worker assembly islands with fixed-position layouts. *Robotics and Computer-Integrated Manufacturing, 23,* 469-477.

Janz, B.D., Pitts, M.G., & Otondo, R.F. (2005). Information systems and health care II: Back to the future with RFID: Lessons learned—some old, some new. *Communications of the Association for Information Systems, 15,* 132-148.

Jones, P., Clarke-Hill, C., Comfort, D., Hillier, D., & Shears, P. (2005). Radio frequency identification and food retailing in the UK. *British Food Journal, 107,* 356-360.

Jones, P., Clarke-Hill, C., Hillier, D., Shears, P., & Comfort, D. (2004). Radio frequency identification in retailing and privacy and public policy issues. *Management Research News, 27,* 46-56.

Kanters, R.H.L. (2007). *Data management risks of radio frequency identification (RFID).* Unpublished Masters Thesis, Tiburg University, The Netherlands.

Kasturi, R. (2005). *Tapping the RFID data flood.* Retrieved from *http://www.intelligententerprise. com/showArticle.jhtml?articleID=163100818*

Kelepouris, T. (2007). RFID-enabled traceability in the food supply chain. *Industrial Management & Data Systems, 107,* 183-200.

Kempfer, L.M. (2007). A dollop of RFID. *Material Handling Management, 62,* 40-41.

Kleist, R.A., Chapman, T.A., Sakai, D.A., & Jarvis, B.S. (2004). *RFID labeling: Smart labeling concepts & applications for the consumer packaged goods supply chain.* Printronix.

Li, S., Visich, F.K., Khumawala, B.M., & Zhang, C. (2006). Radio frequency identification technology: Applications, technical challenges and strategies. *Sensor Review, 26,* 193-202.

Lin, K., & Lin, C. (2007). Evaluating the decision to adopt RFID systems using analytic hierarchy process. *Journal of American Academy of Business, 11,* 72-78.

Lin, P.P., & Brown, K.F. (2006). Radio frequency identification and how to capitalize on it. *The CPA Journal, 76,* 34-37.

Marcial, G.G. (2007, May 28). *VeriChip is I.D.'d as a winner.* Retrieved from *http://www.business-week.com/magazine/content/07_22/b4036093. htm?chan=search*

McMeekin, T.A., Baranyi, J., Bowman, J., Dalgaard, P., Kirk, M., Ross, T., Schmid, S., & Zwietering, M.H. (2006). Information systems in food safety management. *International Journal of Food Microbiology, 112,* 181-194.

Ngai, E.W.T., Cheng, T.C.E., Au, S., & Lai, K. (2007). Mobile commerce integrated with RFID technology in a container depot. *Decision Support Systems, 43,* 62-76.

O'Connor, M.C. (2007, January 8). *Michelin shrinks its e-tire pressure monitor.* Retrieved from *http://www.rfidjournal.com/article/articleview/2950/1/1/*

O'Connor, M.C. (2006a). *Warehouse management systems that handle RFID data.* Retrieved from *http://www.rfidjournal.com/magazine/article/2259*

O'Connor, M.C. (2006b, August 18). *Apparel & footwear summit attracts wide audience.* Retrieved from *http://www.rfidjournal.com/article/articleview/2599/1/1/*

O'Connor, M.C. (2004, November 30). *RFID users want clear data.* Retrieved from *www.rfidjournal.com/article/articleview/1232/1/1/*

Pagarkar, M., Natesan, M., & Prakash, B. (2005). *RFID in integrated order management systems: RFID, VMI and CPFR in integrated order management systems for retail supply chains.* RFID Journal White Paper.

Palmer, M. (2004, February 2). *Build an effective RFID architecture.* Retrieved from *http://www.rfidjournal.com/article/articleview/781/1/82/*

Parlikad, A.K., & McFarlane, D. (2007). RFID-based product information in end-of-life decision making. *Control Engineering Practice.*

Qiu, R.G. (2007). RFID-enabled automation in support of factory integration. *Robotics and Computer-Integrated Manufacturing.*

Ranky, P.G. (2006). An introduction to radio frequency identification (RFID) methods and solutions. *Assembly Automation, 26,* 28-33.

Reid, A.S. (2007). Is society smart enough to deal with smart cards? *Computer Law & Security Report, 23,* 53-61.

Regattieri, A., Gamberi, M., & Manzini, R. (2007). Traceability of food products: General framework and experimental evidence. *Journal of Food Engineering, 81,* 347-356.

RFID Journal. (2007, February). *EPC/RFID data sharing: Enter a new era of supply chain collaboration between retailers and suppliers.* Retrieved from *http://www.rfidjournal.com/whitepapers/download/209*

RFID Journal. (2003, September 22). *Tesco deploys class 1 EPC tags.* Retrieved from *http://www.rfidjournal.com/article/articleview/587/1/1/*

RFID Journal. (2002a, October 24). *CD tracking project deemed a hit.* Retrieved from *http://www.rfidjournal.com/article/articleview/98/1/1/*

RFID Journal. (2002b, June 24). *Learning from Prada.* Retrieved from *http://www.rfidjournal.com/article/view/425*

Roberti, M. (2005a, October 31). *The serendipity effect.* Retrieved from *http://www.rfidjournal.com/article/articleview/1960/1/2/*

Roberti, M. (2005b, October, 17). *Target, Wal-Mart share EPC data.* Retrieved from *http://www.rfidjournal.com/article/articleview/1928/1/1/*

Roberti, M. (2004, April 30). *Wal-Mart begins RFID rollout.* Retrieved from *http://www.rfidjournal.com/article/articleview/926/1/1*

Saygin, C. (2007). Adaptive inventory management using RFID data. *International Journal of Advanced Manufacturing Technology, 32,* 1045-1051.

Sellitto, C., Burgess, S., & Hawking, P. (2007). Information quality attributes associated with RFID-derived benefits in the retail supply chain. *International Journal of Retail & Distribution Management, 35*, 69-87.

Shah, S. (2006). *Semantics and Internet of things.* RFID Journal White Paper.

Spieß, P., Bornhövd, C., Lin, T., Haller, S., & Schaper, J. (2007). Going beyond auto-ID: A service-oriented smart items infrastructure. *Journal of Enterprise Information Management, 20*, 356-370.

Tellkamp, C., Angerer, A., Fleisch, E., & Corsten, D. (2005). *From pallet to shelf: Improving data quality in retail supply chains using RFID.* Auto ID Center White Paper.

The Economist. (2007, June 7). *Radio silence.* Retrieved from *http://www.economist.com/search/displaystory.cfm?story_id=9249278&CFID=15975447&CFTOKEN=95269337#top*

Turban, E., Mclean, E., Wetherbe, J., Bolloju, N., & Davison, R. (2002). *Information technology management: Transforming business in the digital economy.* New York: John Wiley & Sons.

Twist, D.C. (2005). The impact of radio frequency identification on supply chain facilities. *Journal of Facilities Management, 3*, 226-239.

Vijayaraman, B.S., & Osyk, B.A. (2006). An empirical study of RFID implementation in the warehousing industry. *International Journal of Logistics Management, 17*, 6-20.

Wang, F., & Liu, P. (2005). *Temporal management of RFID data* (pp. 1128-1139). Siemens Corporate Research.

Ward, M. (2007). The price of speed. *National Petroleum News, 99*, 28-32.

Warden, T. (2005). *The RFID software conundrum.* RFID Journal White Paper.

Wong, K.H.M., Hui, P.C.L., & Chan, A.C.K. (2006). Cryptography and authentication on RFID passive tags for apparel products. *Computers in Industry, 57*, 342-349.

Yu, S.C. (2007). RFID implementation and benefits in libraries. *The Electronic Library, 25*, 54-64.

This work was previously published in International Journal of Information Systems and Supply Chain Management, Vol. 1, Issue 4, edited by J. Wang, pp. 1-19, copyright 2008 by IGI Publishing, formerly known as Idea Group Publishing (an imprint of IGI Global).

Chapter XV
A Mobile Computing Framework for Passive RFID Detection System in Health Care

Masoud Mohammadian
University of Canberra, Australia

Ric Jentzsch
Compucat Research Pty Limited, Australia

INTRODUCTION

The cost of health care continues to be a world wide issue. Research continues into ways and how the utilization of evolving technologies can be applied to reduce costs and improve patient care, while maintaining patient's lives. To achieve these needs requires accurate, near real time data acquisition and analysis. At the same time there exists a need to acquire a profile on a patient and update that profile as fast and as possible. All types of confidentiality need to be addressed no matter which technology and application is used. One possible way to achieve this is to use a passive detection system that employs wireless radio frequency identification (RFID) technology. This detection system can integrate wireless networks for fast data acquisition and transmission, while maintaining the privacy issue. Once this data is

obtained, then up to date profiling can be integrated into the patient care system. This article discussed the use and need for a passive RFID system for patient data acquisition in health care facilities such as a hospital. The development of profile data is assisted by a profiling intelligent software agent that is responsible for processing the raw data obtained through RFID and database and invoking the creation and update of the patient profile.

BACKGROUND

Health is on everyone's agenda whether they are old or young. Millions of hours of lost time is recorded each week by employers' whose staff are in need of health care. It is and has been known that more research into applications and

Figure 1. Data repositories for patient and doctors

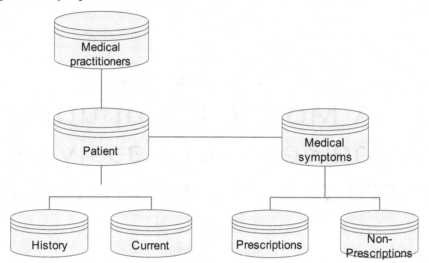

innovative architectures is needed. To this end the use of Radio Frequency Identification (RFID), a relatively new technology and is showing itself to be a viable and promising technology as an aid to health care (Finkenzeller, 1999; Glover & Bhatt, 2006; Hedgepeth, 2007; Lahiri, 2005; Schuster, Allen, & Brock, 2007; Shepard, 2005). This technology has the capability to penetrate and add value to nearly every area of health care. It can be used to lower the cost of some services as well as improving service to individuals and the health care provider. Although many organizations are developing and testing the possible use of RFIDs, the real value of RFID is achieved in conjunction with the use of intelligent software agents. Thus the issue becomes the integration of these two great technologies for the benefit of assisting health care services.

To begin with, let us look at data collection. In health care, we can collect data on the patients, doctors, nurses, institution itself, drugs and prescriptions, diagnosis, and many other areas. It would not be feasible to do all of these nor would all of these be able to effectively use RFID. Thus for our perspective we will concentrate on a subset with the understanding that all areas could, directly or indirectly, benefit from

the use of RFID and intelligent software agents in a health care and hospital environment.

In this research, we begin to look at the architecture of integrating intelligent software agents technology with RFID technology, in particular in managing patients' health care data in a hospital environment.

An intelligent software agent can continuously profile a patient based on their medical history, current illness, and on going diagnostics. The RFID provides the passive vehicle to obtain the data via its monitoring capabilities. The intelligent software agent provides the active vehicle in the interpretation profiling of the data and reporting capacity. There are certain data that is stored about each patient in a hospital. The investigation of this data provides an analysis that describes the patient's condition, is able to monitor their status, and cross reflect on why the patient was admitted to the hospital. Using this information an evolving profile of each patient can be constructed and analysed.

Using the data and analysis this will allow us to assist in deciding what kind of care he/she requires, the effects of ongoing care, and how to best care for this patient using available resources (doctors, nurses, beds, etc.) for the patient. The software agent is used to build a profile of each patient as they are admitted to the health care institution. Although not shown in the illustration, an additional profile for each doctor can be developed that practices in the hospital can be developed. If this is done, then the patient and doctor profile can be correlated to obtained the availability of the best doctor to suit the patient. However, this will require an additional data repository, as shown in Figure 1.

The patient profiling is useful in a variety of situations:

- The profile provides a personalized service based on the patient and not on symptoms or illness. to a particular patient. For example, by identifying the services that the patient requires this will allow us to target that which will be directed to speeding up their recovery progress;

- A good profile will assist the medical facilities in trying to prevent the need for the patient to return to the hospital any sooner than necessary;

- Disambiguating patient's diagnostic based on patient profile may help in assisting in matching a doctor's specialization to the right patient;

- When a patient needs to re-enter a hospital, a past profile can make it easier to match the patient's needs to a relevant available doctor;

- Presenting information about the patient on an on-going, continuous basis for the doctors means that current up to date information is available rather than information that needs to be searched for and compiled before it is useful; and

- Providing tailored and appropriate care to reduce health care costs.

Profiling is being done in many business operations today. Often profiling is combined with personalization, and user modeling for many e-commerce applications such as those by IBM, ATG Dynamo, BroadVision, Amazon, and Garden (18). However, there is very little in the way of the use of such systems in hospital and very little in health care in this perspective has been reported. It must be remember that there are different definitions of personalization, user modeling, and profiling. In e-commerce the practice of tracking information about consumers' interests by monitoring their movements online is considered profiling or user modeling. This can be done without using any personal information, but simply by analyzing the content, URL's, and other information about a user's browsing path/click-stream. Many user models try to predict the user's preference in a narrow and specific domain. This works well as long as that domain remains relatively static and, as such, the results of such work may be limited.

In this research, profiling is a technique whereby a set of characteristics of a particular class of person, patient, is inferred from their past and data-holdings are then searched for individuals with a close fit to symptom characteristics. One of the main aims of profiling and user modeling is to provide information recipients with correct and timely response for their needs. This entails an evolving profile to ensure that as the dynamics of that which is being monitored change, the profile and model reflects these updates as appropriate.

There are several ways in which a patient's visit to a hospital can be recorded. A patient's visit may simply be classified as a regular visit. This may be for a check up, for tests, or at the request of a doctor. A patient might be at the hospital because of an emergency or an ad hoc appointment due to lack of other facilities being available. Of course there are a whole set of patients that visit the hospital for reasons that are less well defined. In each situation, the needs of the patients are different.

The patient's profile can assist the attending doctor in being aware of the particular patient's situation. This provides the attending doctor with information that is needed without waiting for the patient's regular doctor. The regular doctor may be unavailable and therefore the profile of the patient can be matched with the available doctor suitable to the needs of the patient. The patient to doctor assignment is a type of scheduling issue and is not going to be discussed in this article.

However, in an emergency visit, there is no assigned doctor for such a patient. The doctor in emergency section of the hospital will provide information about a patient after examination and a patient profile then can be created. In this case, the intelligent agent can assist the patient by matching the profile of the patient with the doctors suitable to the needs of the patient. Also the doctors can be contacted in a speedier manner as they are identified and their availability is known.

An appointment visit is very similar to a regular visit but it may happen only once and therefore the advantages mentioned for regular patients applies here.

We will endeavor to describe several of these, but will expand on one particular potential use of RFIDs in managing patient health data. First let us provide some background on RFIDs and present some definitions. We will discuss the environment that RFIDs operate in and their relationship to other available wireless technologies such as the IEEE 802.11b, IEEE 802.11g, IEEE 802.11n, and so forth, in order to fulfill their requirements effectively and efficiently.

This research is divided into four main sections. Section two is based on the patient to doctor profiling and intelligent software agents. The third section is a RFID background; this will provide a good description of RFIDs and their components. This section discusses several practical cases of RFID technology in and around hospitals. It will also list three possible applicable cases assisting in managing patients' medical data. The final section discusses the important

issue of maintaining patients' data security and integrity and relates that to RFIDs.

PATIENT TO DOCTOR PROFILING

A profile represents the extent to which something exhibits various characteristics. These characteristics are used to develop a linear model based on the consensus of multiple sets of data, generally over some period of time. A patient or doctor profile is a collection of information about a person based on the characteristics of that person. This information can be used in a decision analyze situation between the doctor, domain environment, and patient. The model can be used to provide meaningful information for useful and strategic actions. The profile can be static or dynamic. The static profile is kept in prefixed data fields where the period between data field updates is long such as months or years. The dynamic profile is constantly updated as per evaluation of the situation. The updates may be performed manually or automated. The automated user profile building is especially important in real time decision-making systems. Real time systems are dynamic. These systems often contain data that is critical to the user's decision making process. Manually updated profiles are at the need and discretion of the relevant decision maker.

The profiling of patient doctor model is base on the patient/doctor information. These are:

- The categories and subcategories of doctor specialization and categorization. These categories will assist in information processing and patient/doctor matching.
- Part of the patients profile based on symptoms (past history problems, dietary restrictions, etc.) can assist in prediction of the patient's needs specifically.
- The patients profile can be matched with the available doctor profiles to provide

Figure 2. Agent profiling model using RFID

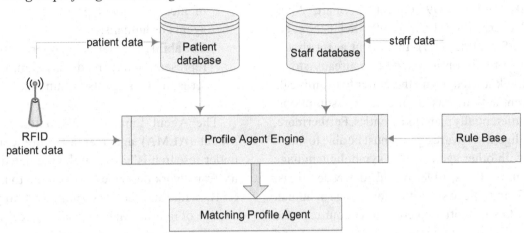

doctors with information about the arrival of patients as well as presentation of the patients profile to a suitable, available doctor.

A value denoting the degree of association can be created form the above evaluation of the doctor to patient's profile. The intelligent agent based on the denoting degrees and appropriate, available doctors can be identified and allocated to the patient.

In the patient/doctor profiling, the agent will make distinctions in attribute values of the profiles and match the profiles with highest value. It should be noted that the agent creates the patient and doctor profiles based on data obtained from the doctors and patient namely:

- Explicit profiling occurs based on the data entered by hospital staff about a patient.
- Implicit profiling can fill that gap for the missing data by acquiring knowledge about the patient from its past visit or other relevant databases if any and then combining all these data to fill the missing data. Using legacy data for complementing and updating the user profile seems to be a better choice than implicit profiling. This approach capitalizes on user's personal

history (previous data from previous visit to doctor or hospital).

The proposed agent architecture allows user profiling and matching in such a time intensive important application. The architecture of the agent profiling systems using RFID is given in Figure 2.

PROFILE MATCHING

Profile matching done is based on a vector of weighted attributes. To get this vector, a rule based systems can be used to match the patient's attributes (stored in patient's profile) against doctor's attributes (stored in doctor's profile). If there is a partial or full match between them, then the doctor will be informed (based on their availability from the hospital doctor database).

INTEGRATION OF INTELLIGENT SOFTWARE AGENTS AND RFID TECHNOLOGIES

Intelligent software agent technology has been used in order to provide the needed transformation of RIFD passive data collection into an active organizational knowledge assistant (Finkenzeller, 1999; Glover & Bhatt, 2006; Hedgepeth, 2007; Lahiri, 2005; Schuster et al., 2007; Shepard, 2005). Intelligent agent should be able to act on new data and already stored profile/knowledge and thereafter to examine its current actions based on certain assumptions, and inferentially plans its activities. Furthermore, intelligent software agents must be able to *interact* with other agents using symbolic language (Bigus & Bigus, 1998; Wooldridge & Jennings, 1995) and able to substitute for a range of human activities in a situated context. (In our case the activities are medical/patient assignment and the context is a hospital environment)

Context driven Intelligent software agents' activities are also dynamic and under continuous development in an historical time related environment (Bigus & Bigus, 1998; Wooldridge & Jennings, 1995).

Medical and hospital patient applied ontology's describing the applied domain are necessary for the semantic communication and data understanding between RFID inputs and knowledge bases inference engines so that profiling of both patients and doctors can be achieved (Gruber, 1993; Guarino, Carrara, & Giaretta, 1994).

The integration of RFID capabilities and intelligent agent techniques provides promising development in the areas of performance improvements in RFID data collection, inference, knowledge acquisition, and profiling operations.

By using mediated activity theories, an RIFD agent architecture could be modeled according to the following characteristics:

- The ability to use patient/doctor profile in natural language, ACL, or symbolic form as communicative tools mediating agents cooperative activities.
- The ability to use subjective and objective properties required by intelligent software agents to perform bidirectional multiple communication activities.

- The ability to internalize representations of medical/patient profile patterns from agents or humans.
- The ability to externalize internally stored representations of medical assignment patterns to other agents or humans.

The Agent Language Mediated Activity Model (ALMA) agent architecture currently under research is based on the mediated activity framework described and is able to provide RFID with the necessary framework to profile a range of internal and external medical/patient profiling communication activities performed by wireless multi-agents.

RFID DESCRIPTION

RFID or Radio Frequency Identification is a progressive technology that has been said to be easy to use and well suited for collaboration with intelligent software agents. Basically an RFID can:

- Be read-only;
- Volatile read/write; or
- Write once/read many times
- RFID are:
  ○ Noncontact and
  ○ Non line-of-sight operations.

Being noncontact and non line-of-sight will make RFIDs able to function under a variety of environmental conditions and while still providing a high level of data integrity (Finkenzeller, 1999; Glover & Bhatt, 2006; Hedgepeth, 2007; Lahiri, 2005; Schuster et al., 2007; Shepard, 2005).

MAIN COMPONENTS

A basic RFID system consists of four components:

1. The RFID tag (sometimes referred to as the transponder);
2. A coiled antenna;
3. A radio frequency transceiver; and
4. Some type of reader for the data collection.

Basically there are three components as often components are combined such as the transponder or transceiver or the antenna.

Transponders

The reader emits radio waves in ranges of anywhere from 2.54 centimeters to 33 meters. Depending upon the reader's power output and the radio frequency used and if a booster is added that distance can be somewhat increased. When RFID tags (transponders) pass through a specifically created electromagnetic zone, they detect the reader's activation signal. Transponders can be online or off-line and electronically programmed with unique information for a specific application or purpose. A reader decodes the data encoded on the tag's integrated circuit and passes the data to a server for data storage or further processing.

Coiled Antenna

The coiled antenna is used to emit radio signals to activate the tag and read or write data to it.

Antennas are the conduits between the tag and the transceiver that controls the system's data acquisition and communication. RFID antennas are available in many shapes and sizes. They can be built into a doorframe, book binding, DVD case, mounted on a tollbooth, embedded into a manufactured item such as a shaver or software case (just about anything) so that the receiver tags the data from things passing through its zone (Finkenzeller, 1999; Glover & Bhatt, 2006; Hedgepeth, 2007; Lahiri, 2005; Schuster et al., 2007; Shepard, 2005).

Transceiver

Often the antenna is packaged with the transceiver and decoder to become a reader. The decoder device can be configured either as a handheld or a fixed-mounted device. In large complex, often chaotic environments, portable or handheld transceivers would prove valuable.

TYPES OF RFID TRANSPONDERS

RFID tags can be categorized as active, semi-active, or passive. Each has and is being used in a variety of inventory management and data collection applications today. The condition of the application, place and use determines the required tag type.

Figure 3. Semi-passive tag

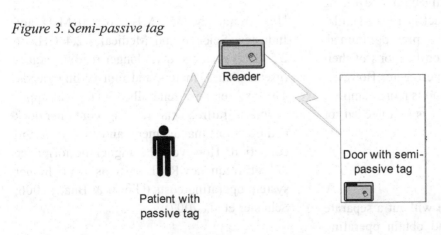

Active Tags

Active RFID tags are powered by an internal battery and are typically read / write. Tag data can be rewritten and/or modified as the need dictates. An active tag's memory size varies according to manufacturing specifications and application requirements; some tags operate with up to 5 megabyte of memory. For a typical read/write RFID work-in-process system, a tag might give a machine a set of instructions, and the machine would then report its performance to the tag. This encoded data would then become part of the tagged part's history. The battery-supplied power of an active tag generally gives it a longer read range. The trade off is greater size, greater cost, and a limited operational life that has been estimated to be a maximum of 10 years, depending upon operating temperatures and battery type (Finkenzeller, 1999; Glover & Bhatt, 2006).

Semi-Active Tags

The semi-active tag comes with a battery. The battery is used to power the tags circuitry and not to communicate with the reader. This makes the semi-active tag more independent than the passive tag, and it can operate in more adverse conditions. The semi-active tag also has a longer range and more capabilities than a passive tag (Shepard, 2005). Linear barcodes that reference a database to get product specifications and pricing are also data devices that act is a very similar way. Semi-passive tags are preprogrammed, but can allow for slight modifications of their instructions via the reader/interrogator. However, it is bigger, weighs more, and is more complete than a passive tag. A reader is still needed for data collection.

Passive Tags

Passive RFID tags operate without a separate external power source and obtain operating power generated from the reader. Passive tags, since they have no power source embedded, are consequently much lighter than active tags, less expensive, and offer a virtually unlimited operational lifetime. However, the trade off is that they have shorter read ranges, than active tags, and require a higher-powered reader.

Read-only tags are typically passive and are programmed with a unique set of data (usually 32 to 128 bits) that cannot be modified. Read-only tags most often operate as a data device that utilizes a database for all data storage (Finkenzeller, 1999; Shepard, 2005).

Range

RFID systems can be distinguished by their deployment and frequency range. RFID tags generally operate in two different types of frequencies that make them adaptable for nearly any application. These frequency ranges are:

Low Frequency Range (Short Range)

Low-frequency (30 KHz to 500 KHz) systems have short reading ranges and lower system costs. They are most commonly used in security access, asset tracking, and animal identification applications (Glover & Bhatt, 2006; Hedgepeth, 2007; Lahiri, 2005).

High Frequency Range (Long Range)

High-frequency (850 MHz to 950 MHz and Industry, Science and Medical - 2.4 GHz to 2.5 GHz) systems, offer longer reading ranges (greater than 33 meters) and high reading speeds. These systems are generally used for such applications as railroad car tracking, container dock and transport management, and automated toll collection. However, the higher performance of high-frequency RFID systems incurs higher system operating costs (Glover & Bhatt, 2006; Schuster et al., 2007).

Hospital Environment

In hospitals, systems need to use rules and domain knowledge that is appropriate to the situation. One of the more promising capabilities of intelligent software agents is their ability to coordinate information between the various resources.

In a hospital environment, in order to manage patient medical data we need both types; fixed and handheld transceivers. Also, transceivers can be assembled in ceilings, walls, or doorframes to collect and disseminate data. Hospitals have become large complex environments.

In a hospital, nurses and physicians can retrieve the patient's medical data stored in transponders (RFID tags) before they stand beside a patient's bed or as they are entering a ward.

Given the descriptions of the two types and their potential use in hospital patient data management we suggest that:

- It would be most useful to embed a passive RFID transponder into a patient's hospital wrist band;
- It would be most useful to embed a passive RFID transponder into a patient's medical file (there are several versions and perspectives that we can take no this).

Doctors should have PDAs equipped with RFID or some type of personal area network device. Either would enable them to retrieve some patient's information whenever they are near the patient, instead of waiting until the medical data is pushed to them through the hospital server (there are several versions and perspectives that we can take no this):

- *Active RFID tags* are more appropriate for the continuous collection of the patient's medical data. Since the patient's medical data needs to be continuously recorded to an active RFID tag and an associated

reader needs to be employed. Using an active RFID means that the tag will be a bit bulky because of the needed battery for the write process and there is a concern with radio frequency admissions. Thus, it is felt that an active tag would not be a good candidate for the patient wrist band. However, if the patient's condition is to be continuously monitored, the collection of the data at the source is essential. The inclusion of the tag in the wrist band is the only way to recorder the medical data on a real-time base using the RFID technology. As more organizations get into the business of manufacturing RFIDs and the life and size of batteries decrease, the tag size will decrease and this may be a real possible use.

- *Passive RFID tags* can be also used as well. These passive tags can be embedded in the doctors PDA, which is needed for determining their locations whenever the medical staff requires them. Also, passive tags can be used in patients' wrist bands for storage of limited amount of data- on off-line bases, for example, date of hospital admission, medical record number, and so forth.

After examining both ranges, we can suggest the following:

- *Low frequency range tags* are suitable for the patients' band wrist RFID tags. Since we expect that the patients' bed will not be too far from a RFID reader. The reader might be fixed over the patient's bed, in the bed itself, or over the door-frame. The doctor using his/her PDA would be aiming to read the patient's data directly and within a relatively short distance.
- *High frequency range tags* are suitable for the physician's tag implanted in their PDAs. As physicians use to move from one

location to another in the hospital, data on their patients could be continuously being updated.

One final point in regards to the range of RFIDs: until 2002, the permissible radio frequency range was not regulated, that is, it still operated in some low frequency ranges (30- 500 KHz) and in the free 2.45 GHz ISM band of frequency. The IEEE's 802.11b and IEEE's 802.11g (WiFi) wireless networks also operate in the same range (actually there are many other wireless application that operate in that range). This band of frequency is crowded. Where equipment in a hospital is often in the ISM band of frequency, there may be some speed of transmission degradation. The IEEE 802.11n builds upon previous 802.11 standards by adding MIMO (multiple-input multiple-output). MIMO uses multiple transmitter and receiver antennas to allow for increased data throughput via spatial multiplexing and increased range by exploiting the spatial diversity. Note that 802.11n draft 2.0 has been released but the certification of products is still in progress. What this means is that even though 802.11n has greater benefits then previous standards, it is still a draft. The full version is not expected until 2008; thus; products may take several years to be compliant and incorporate that into RFIDs (Hedgepeth, 2007).

Shapes of RFID Tags

RFID tags come in a wide variety of shapes and sizes. Animal tracking tags that are inserted beneath the animal's skin can be as small as a pencil lead in diameter and about one centimeter in length. Tags can be screw-shaped to identify trees or wooden items, or credit card shaped for use in access applications. The antitheft hard plastic tags attached to merchandise in stores are RFID tags (Glover & Bhatt, 2006). Manufacturers can create the shape that is best for the application, including flexible shaped tags that act like and resemble human skin. RFID tags can be flexible and do not have to be rigid.

Transceivers

The transceivers/interrogators can differ quite considerably in complexity, depending upon the type of tags being supported and the application. T\he overall function of the application is to provide the means of communicating with the tags and facilitating data transfer. Functions performed by the reader may include quite sophisticated signal conditioning, parity error checking, and correction. Once the signal from a transponder has been correctly received and decoded, algorithms may be applied to decide whether the signal is a repeat transmission, and may then instruct the transponder to cease transmitting or temporarily cease asking for data from the transponder. This is known as the "Command Response Protocol" and is used to circumvent the problem of reading multiple tags over a short time frame. Using interrogators in this way is sometimes referred to as "Hands Down Polling." An alternative, more secure, but slower tag polling technique is called "Hands Up Polling." This involves the transceiver looking for tags with specific identities, and interrogating them in turn. A further approach may use multiple transceivers, multiplexed into one interrogator, but with attendant increases in costs (Glover & Bhatt, 2006; Hedgepeth, 2007; Lahiri, 2005; Schuster et al., 2007).

Hospital patient data management deals with sensitive and critical information (patient's medical data). *Hands Down polling* techniques in conjunction with multiple transceivers that are multiplexed with each other, form a wireless network. The reason behind this choice is that, we need high speed for transferring medical data from medical equipment to or from the RFID wrist band tag to the nearest RFID reader, and then through a wireless network or a network of RFID transceivers or LANs to the hospital server. From there it is a short distance to be transmitted to the doctor's PDA, a laptop, or desktop through a WLAN IEEE 802.11b, 802.11g, or 802.11n, or wired LAN which operates at the 5.2 GHz band with a maximum data transfer rate exceeding 104 Mbps.

The "Hand Down Polling" techniques, as previously described, provides the ability to detect all detectable RFID tags at once (i.e., in parallel). Preventing any unwanted delay in transmitting medical data corresponding to each RF tagged patient.

RFID TRANSPONDER PROGRAMMERS

Transponder programmers are the means, by which data is delivered to write once, read many (WORM) and read/write tags. Programming can be carried out off-line or online. For some systems re-programming may be carried out online, particularly if it is being used as an interactive portable data file within a production environment, for example. Data may need to be recorded during each process. Removing the transponder at the end of each process to read the previous process data, and to program the new data, would naturally increase process time and would detract substantially from the intended

flexibility of the application. By combining the functions of a transceiver and a programmer, data may be appended or altered in the transponder as required, without compromising the production line.

We conclude from this section that RFID systems differ in type, shape, and range; depending on the type of application, the RFID components shall be chosen. Low frequency range tags are suitable for the patients' band wrist RFID tags. Since we expect that a patients' bed is not too far from the RFID reader, which might be fixed on the room ceiling or door-frame. High frequency range tags are suitable for the physician's PDA tag. As physicians use to move from on location to another in the hospital, long read ranges are required. On the other hand, transceivers which deal with sensitive and critical information (patient's medical data) need the Hands Down polling techniques. These multiple transceivers should be multiplexed with each other forming a wireless network.

PRACTICAL CASES USING RFID TECHNOLOGY

This section explains in details three possible applications of the RFID technology in three applicable cases. Each case is discussed step-by-

Figure 4. Acquisition of patient data

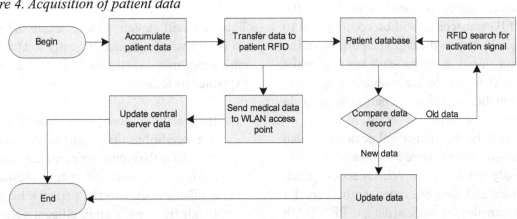

step then represented by a flowchart. Those cases cover issues as acquisition of Patient's Medical Data, locating the nearest available doctor to the patients location, and how doctors stimulate the patient's active RFID tag using their PDAs in order to acquire the medical data stored in it.

Case I: Acquisition of Patient's Medical Data

Case one will represent the method of acquisition and transmission of medical data. This process can be described in the following points as follows:

1. A biomedical device equipped with an embedded RFID transceiver and programmer will detect and measure the biological state of a patient. This medical data can be an ECG, EEG, BP, sugar level, temperature or any other biomedical reading.

   After the acquisition of the required medical data, the biomedical device will write-burn this data to the RFID transceiver's EE-PROM using the built in RFID programmer. Then the RFID transceiver with its antenna will be used to transmit the stored medical data in the EEPROM to the EEPROM in the patient's transponder (tag) which is around his/her wrist. The data received will be updated periodically once new fresh readings are available by the biomedical device. Hence, the newly sent data by the RFID transceiver will be accumulated to the old data in the tag. The purpose of the data stored in the patient's tag is to make it easy for the doctor to obtain medical information regarding the patient directly via the doctor's PDA, tablet PC, or laptop.

2. Similarly, the biomedical device will also transfer the measured medical data wirelessly to the nearest WLAN access point. Since high data rate transfer rate is crucial in transferring medical data, IEEE 802.11b

or g is recommended for the transmission purpose.

3. The wirelessly sent data will be routed to the hospitals main server; to be then sent (pushed) to:

   i. Other doctors available throughout the hospital so they can be notified of any newly received medical data.

   ii. To an online patient monitoring unit or a nurse's workstation within the hospital.

   iii. Or the acquired patients' medical data can be fed into an expert (intelligent) software system running on the hospital server. To be then compared with other previously stored abnormal patterns of medical data, and to raise an alarm if any abnormality is discovered.

4. Another option could be using the in-built-embedded RFID transceiver in the biomedical device to send the acquired medical data wirelessly to the nearest RFID transceiver in the room. Then the data will travel simultaneously in a network of RFID transceivers until reaching the hospital server.

Case II: Locating the Nearest Available Doctor to the Patients Location

This case will explain how to locate the nearest doctor who is needed urgently to attend an emergency medical situation. This case can be explained as follows:

1. If a specific surgeon or physician is needed in a specific hospital department, the medical staff in the monitoring unit (e.g., nurses) can query the hospital server for the nearest available doctor to the patient's location. In our framework an intelligent agent can

Figure 5. Locating nearest doctor

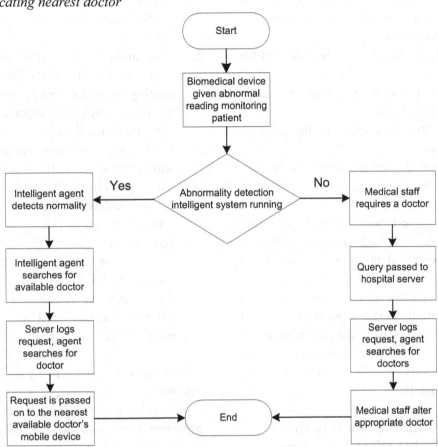

perform this task.

2. The hospital server traces all doctors' locations in the hospital through detecting the presences of their wireless mobile device; for example, PDA, tablet PC, or laptop in the WLAN range.

3. Another method that the hospital's server can use to locate the physicians is making use of the RFID transceivers built-in the doctor's wireless mobile device. Similarly to the access points used in WLAN, RFID transceivers can assist in serving a similar role of locating doctor's location. This can be described in three steps, which are:

   i. The fixed RFID transceivers throughout the hospital will send a stimulation signal to detect other free RFID transceivers—which are in the doc-

tors PDAs, tablets , r laptops, and so forth.

   ii. All free RFID transceivers will receive the stimulation signal and reply back with an acknowledgement signal to the nearest fixed RFID transceiver.

   iii. Finally, each free RFID transceiver cell position would be determined by locating to which fixed RFID transceiver range it belongs to or currently operating in.

4. After the hospital server located positions of all available doctors, it determines the nearest requested physician (pediatrics, neurologist, and so forth) to the patient's location.

5. Once the required physician is located, an alert message will be sent to his\her PDA,

tablet PC or laptop indicating the location to be reached immediately. This alert message could show:

    i.   The building, floor, and room of the patient (e.g., 3C109).

    ii. Patient's case (e.g., heart stroke, arrhythmia, etc.)

    iii. A brief description of the patient's case.

6.   If the hospital is running an intelligent agent as described in the proposed framework on its server, the process of locating and sending an alert message can be automated. This is done through comparing the collected medical data with previously stored abnormal patterns of medical data, then sending an automated message describing the situation. This system could be used instead of the staff in the patient monitoring unit or the nurse's workstation where nurses observe and then send an alert message manually.

Case III: Doctors Stimulate the Patient's Active RFID Tag Using their PDAs in Order to Acquire the Medical Data Stored in it

This method can be used in order to get rid of medical files and records placed in front of the patient's bed. Additionally, it could help in preventing medical errors- reading the wrong file for the wrong patient and could be considered as an important step towards a paperless hospital.

This case can be described in the following steps:

1.   The doctor enters into the patient's room or ward. The doctor wants to check the medical status of a certain patient. So instead of picking up the "hard" paper medical file, the doctor interrogates the patient's RFID wrist

tag with his RFID transceiver equipped in his\her PDA, tablet PC, or laptop, and so forth.

2.   The patient's RFID wrist tag detects the signal of the doctor's RFID transceiver coming from his\her wireless mobile device and replies back with the patient's information and medical data.

3.   If there was more than one patient in the ward possessing RFID wrist tags, all tags can respond in parallel using Hands Down polling techniques back to the doctor's wireless mobile device.

4.   Another option could be that the doctor retrieving only the patient's number from the *passive* RFID wrist tag. Then through the WLAN the doctor could access the patient's medical record from the hospital's main server.

RFID technology has many potential important applications in hospitals, and the discussed three cases are a real practical example. Two important issues can be concluded from this section: WLAN is preferred for data transfer; given that IEEE's wireless networks have much faster speed and coverage area as compared to RFID transceivers\transponders technology. Yet, RFID technology is the best for data storage and locating positions of medical staff and patients as well.

The other point is that we need a RFID transceiver & programmer embedded in a biomedical device for data acquisition and dissemination, and only a RFID transceiver embedded in the doctor's wireless mobile device for obtaining the medical data. With the progress the RFID technology is currently gaining, it could become a standard as other wireless technologies (Bluetooth, for example), and eventually manufacturers building them in electronic devices; biomedical devices for our case.

MAINTAINING PATIENTS' DATA SECURITY AND INTEGRITY

Once data is transmitted wirelessly, security becomes a crucial issue. Unlike wired transmission, wirelessly transmitted data can be easily sniffed out leaving the transmitted data vulnerable to many types of attacks. For example, wireless data could be easily eavesdropped on using any mobile device equipped with a wireless card. In worst cases wirelessly transmitted data could be intercepted and then possibly tampered with, or in best cases, the patient's security and privacy

would be compromised. Hence emerges the need for data to be initially encrypted from the source.

In this section, a discussion on how to apply encryption for the designed wireless framework for hospital is considered. Suggesting exactly where data needs to be encrypted and\or decrypted depending on the case that is being examined does this.

First a definition of the type of encryption that would be used in the design of the security (encryption\decryption) framework is discussed, followed by a flowchart demonstrating the framework in a step-by-step process.

Figure 6. Functional flow

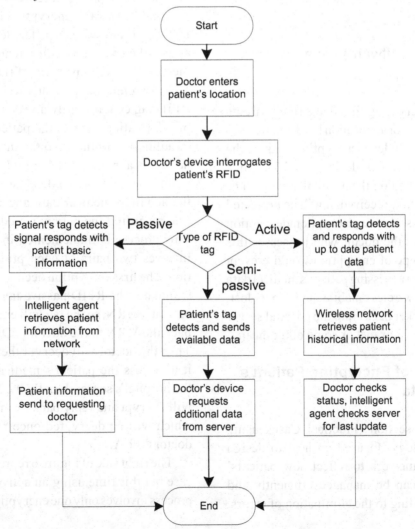

Layers of Encryption

Two main layers of encryption are recommended. They are:

Physical (Hardware) Layer Encryption

This means encrypting all collected medical data at the source or hardware level before transmitting it. Thus, we insure that the patient's medical data would not be compromised once exposed to the outer world on its way to its destination. So even if a person with a malicious intent and also possessing a wireless mobile device steps into the coverage range of the hospitals' WLAN, this intruder will gain actually nothing since all medical data is encrypted, making all intercepted data worthless.

Application (Software) Layer Encryption

This means encrypting all collected medical data at the destination or application level once receiving it. Application level encryption runs on the doctor's wireless mobile device (e.g., PDA, tablet PC, or laptop) and on the hospital server. Once the medical data is received, it will be protected by a secret pass-phrase (encryption\decryption key) created by the doctor who possesses this device. This type of encryption would prevent any person from accessing patient's medical data if the doctor's wireless mobile device gets lost, or even if a hacker hacks into the hospital server via the Internet, intranet or some other mean.

Framework of Encrypting Patient's Medical Data

The previous section (Practical Cases using RFID Technology) focused on how to design a wireless framework to reflect how patients' medical data can be managed efficiently and effectively leading to the elimination of errors, delays, and even paperwork. Similarly, this section will focus on the previously discussed framework from a security perspective, attempting to increase security and data integrity.

i.   Acquisition of Patients' Medical Data
ii. Doctors stimulating the patient's active RFID tag using their wireless mobile devices in order to acquire the medical data stored in it.

While the third case which was about locating the nearest available doctor to the patients location, is more concerned about locating doctors than transferring patient's data, so it is not discussed here.

The lower part of Figure 6 represents the physical (hardware) encryption layer. This part is divided into two sides. The left side demonstrates the case of a doctor acquiring patient's medical data via a passive RFID tag located in a band around the patient's wrist. The passive RFID tag contains only a very limited amount of information such as the patients name, date of admission to the hospital and above all his/her medical record number (MRN), which will grant access to the medical record containing the acquired medical data and other information regarding the patient's medical condition. This process is implemented in six steps, and involves two pairs of encryption and decryption. The first encryption occurs after the doctor stimulates the RFID passive tag to acquire the patient's MRN, so the tag will encrypt and reply back the MRN to the doctors PDA for example. Then the doctor will decrypt the MRN and use it to access the patient's medical record from the hospital's server. Finally the hospital server will encrypt and reply back the medical record, which will be decrypted once received by the doctors' PDA.

The right side of Figure 6 represents a similar case but this time using an active RF tag. This process involves only one encryption and decryption. The encryption happens after the doctor stimulates the active RFID tag using his PDA which has an in-equipped RFID transceiver, so the tag replies with the medical data encrypted. Then the received data is decrypted through the doctors' PDA.

The upper part of Figure 6 represents the application encryption layer, requiring the doctor to enter a pass-phrase to decrypt and then access the stored medical data. Whenever the doctor wants to access patient's medical data, the doctor simply enters a certain pass-phrase to grant access to either wireless mobile device or a hospital server depend where the medical data actually resides.

CHOOSING LEVEL OF SECURITY FOR THE WIRELESSLY-TRANSMITTED MEDICAL DATA

Securing medial data seems to be uncomplicated, yet the main danger of compromising such data comes from the people managing it, for example, doctors, nurses, and other medical staff. For that, we have seen that even though the transmitted medical data is initially encrypted from the source, doctors have to run application level encryption on their wireless mobile devices in order to protect this important data if the devices gets lost, left behind, robbed, and so forth. Nevertheless, there is a compromise. Increasing security through using multiple layers, and increasing length of encryption keys decreases the encryption\decryption speed and causes unwanted time delays, whether we were using application or hardware level of encryption. As a result, this could delay medical data sent to doctors or online monitoring units.

Figure 6 represents the case of high and low level of security in a flowchart applied to the previously discussed two cases in the last report.

At the end of this section, we conclude that there are two possible levels of encryption, software level (application layer) or hardware level (physical layer), depending on the level of security required. Both physical (hardware) layer and application layer encryption are needed in maintaining collected medical data on hospital servers and doctors wireless mobile devices.

Encrypting medical data makes the process of data transmission slower while sending data unencrypted is faster. We have to have a compromise between speed and security. For our case, medical data has to be sent as fast as possible to medical staff, yet the security issue has the priority.

CONCLUSION

Managing patients' data wirelessly (paperless) can prevent errors, enforce standards, make staff more efficient, simplify record keeping, and improve patient care. In this research report, both passive and active RFID tags were used in acquiring and storage of medical data, and then linked to the hospitals' server via a wireless network Moreover, three practical applicable RFID cases discussed how the RFID technology can be put in use in hospitals, while at the same time maintaining the acquired patients' data security and integrity.

This research in the wireless medical environment introduces some new ideas in conjunction to what is already available in RFID technology and wireless networks. Linking both technologies to achieve the research main goal, delivering patients medical data as fast and secure as possible, to pave the way for future paperless hospitals.

Finally, as reported by Frost and Sullivan, the high cost of radio frequency identification (RFID) technology is a deterrent for health care providers, though RFID has great benefits to hospitals in tracking patients, monitoring patients, assisting in health care administration, and reducing medical costs. With the reduction in cost of radio frequency identification (RFID) technology, increased use of RFID technology in health care in monitoring patients and assisting in health care administration is expected.

REFERENCES

Bigus, J. P., & Bigus, J. (1998). *Constructing intelligent software agents with Java – a programmers guide to smarter applications*. Wiley. ISBN: 0-471-19135-3.

Finkenzeller, K. (1999). *RFID handbook*. John Wiley and Sons Ltd.

Glover, B., & Bhatt, H. (2006). *RFID essentials*. O'Reilly Media, Inc. ISBN: 10-0596009445.

Gruber, T.R. (1993). A translation approach to portable ontology specifications. *Knowledge Acquisition, 5,* 199-220.

Guarino, N., Carrara, M., & Giaretta, P. (1994). An ontology of meta-level categories. Journal of knowledge representation and reasoning. In *Proceedings of the Fourth International Conference (KR94)*, Morgan Kaufmann, San Mateo, CA.

Hedgepeth, W. O. (2007). *RFID metrics: Decision making tools for today's supply chains.* Boca Raton, FL: CRC Press. ISBN: 9780849379796.

Lahiri, S. (2005). *RFID sourcebook*. IBM Press. ISBN: 10-0131851373.

Odell, J. (Ed.). (2000, September). *Agent technology*. OMG Document 00-09-01, OMG Agents interest Group.

RFID Australia. (2003). *Why use RFID*. Retrieved February 15, 2008, from http://www.rfid-australia.com/files/htm/rfid%20brochure/page4.html

Schuster, E. W., Allen, S. J., & Brock D. L. (2007). *Global RFID: The value of the EPCglobal network for supply chain management*. Berlin; New York: Springer. ISBN: 9783540356547.

Shepard, S. (2005). *RFID: Radio frequency identification*. New York: McGraw-Hill. ISBN: 0071442995.

Wooldridge, M., & Jennings, N. (1995). Intelligent software agents: Theory and Practice. *The Knowledge Engineering Review,* 10(2), 115-152.

Chapter XVI
Intelligent Agents Framework for RFID Hospitals

Masoud Mohammadian
University of Canberra, Australia

Ric Jentzsch
Compucat Research Pty Ltd., Canberra, Australia

ABSTRACT

When dealing with human lives, the need to utilize and apply the latest technology to help in saving and maintaining patients' lives is quite important and requires accurate, near-real-time data acquisition and evaluation. At the same time, the delivery of a patient's medical data needs to be as fast and as secure as possible. One possible way to achieve this is to use a wireless framework based on radio-frequency identification (RFID). This framework can integrate wireless networks for fast data acquisition and transmission while maintaining the privacy issue. This chapter discusses the development of an agent framework in which RFID can be used for patient data collection. The chapter presents a framework for the knowledge acquisition of patient and doctor profiling in a hospital. The acquisition of profile data is assisted by a profiling agent that is responsible for processing the raw data obtained through RFID and a database of doctors and patients.

INTRODUCTION

The use and deployment of radio-frequency identification (RFID) is a relatively new area and it has been shown to be a promising technology (Glover & Bhatt, 2006; Lahiri, 2005; Shepard, 2004). This technology has the capability to penetrate and add value to nearly every field, lowering costs while improving service to individuals and businesses. Although many organizations are developing and testing the deployment of RFIDs, the real value of RFID implementation is achieved in conjunction with the use of intelligent systems and intelligent agents. The real issue is how intelligent-agent technologies can be integrated with RFID to be used to achieve the best outcome in business and services areas.

In this research, a new method for integrating intelligent-agent technologies with RFIDs in managing patients' healthcare data in a hospital environment is given. Knowledge acquisition and profiling of patients and doctors in a hospital are assisted by a profiling agent that is responsible for processing the raw data obtained through RFID data that are stored in a hospital database. There are several perspectives for profiling that could be used in a healthcare and hospital environment.

An intelligent agent can assist in profiling patients based on their illness and ongoing diagnostics as reported by the RFIDs. There are certain data and knowledge about each patient in the hospital. This knowledge could be the description of what the patient's symptoms are, monitoring status, and why the patient was admitted to the hospital. Using this information, an evolving profile of each patient can be built.

This data and knowledge can assist in deciding what kind of care he or she requires, the effects of ongoing care, and how to best care for this patient using available resources (doctors, nurses, beds, etc.). The intelligent agent will build a profile of each patient. Along with a profile of each patient, a profile for each doctor can also be developed. Then the patient and doctor profiles can be correlated to find the best doctor to suit the patient.

The patient-doctor profiling can be useful in several situations:

- Providing personalized services to a particular patient, for example, by identifying the services that a patient requires and hence speeding his or her recovery progress in or even out of the hospital.
- Disambiguating a patient's diagnostic based on the patient profile and matching this profile to the available doctor's profile. This may help in matching doctors with the suitable specialization to a patient.

- Providing speedy, reliable reentry of patients into the hospital by having the patients allocated to visit the relevant doctors.
- Presenting information in a way suitable to the doctor's needs, for example, presenting the information about the patients on a continuous basis for the doctors.
- Providing tailored and appropriate care to assist in cost reduction.

Personalization, user modeling, and profiling have been used for many e-commerce applications by IBM, ATG Dynamo, BroadVision, Amazon, and Garden. However, the use of such systems in hospital and personal care and profiling has not been reported. It should be noted that the definitions of personalization, user modeling, and profiling that these companies discuss are not quite the same as our intended meanings.

Many user models try to predict the user's preference in a narrow and specific domain. This works well as long as that domain remains relatively static and as such the results may be limited.

One of the main aims of profiling and user modeling is to provide users with correct and timely responses for their needs. This entails an evolving profile to ensure that as the dynamics of the user and real world change, the profile and user model reflects these changes.

A patient's visit to the hospital can simply be classified as a regular visit, an emergency visit, or an ad hoc appointment (on a need basis). In each of these situations, the needs of the patients are different. During a regular visit, the patient visits the hospital at a regular interval and usually a doctor is assigned to that patient. The patient's profile can assist the patient in a situation where the assigned doctor suddenly becomes unavailable. In this situation, the profile of the patient can be matched with the available doctors with suitable specializations for the needs of the patient. The patient-doctor assignment here is a kind of timetabling problem as we know the profile of the patient and doctors as well as the available doctors. Timetabling of doctors is out of the scope of this research study.

However, in an emergency visit, there is no assigned doctor for such a patient. The doctor in the emergency section of the hospital will provide information about a patient after examination, and a patient profile then can be created. In this case, the intelligent agent can assist the patient by matching the profile of the patient with the doctors suitable for the needs of the patient. Also, the doctors can be contacted in a speedier manner as they are identified and their availability is known.

An appointment visit is very similar to a regular visit, but it may happen only once and therefore the advantages mentioned for regular patients apply here.

We will endeavor to describe several of these, but will expand on one particular potential use of RFIDs in managing patient health data. First some background on RFIDs will be presented in this chapter including some definitions. We will discuss the environment that RFIDs operate in and their relationship to other available wireless technologies such as the IEEE (Institute of Electrical and Electronics Engineers) 802.11b, IEEE 802.11g, and so forth in order to fulfill their requirements effectively and efficiently.

This research is divided into five main sections. The following is based on the patient-doctor profiling and intelligent agents. Then the chapter gives an RFID background that will provide a good description of RFIDs and their components. This section discusses several practical cases of RFID technology in and around hospitals. It lists three possible applicable cases assisting in managing patients' medical data. Next we discuss the important issue of maintaining patients' data security and integrity, and relate that to RFIDs. Finally, the conclusion and further research directions are given.

PATIENT-DOCTOR PROFILING

A profile represents the extent to which something exhibits various characteristics. These characteristics are used to develop a linear model based on the consensus of multiple sets of data, generally over some period of time. A patient or doctor profile is a collection of information about a person based on the characteristics of that person. This information can be used in a decision situation between the doctor, domain environment, and patient. The model can be used to provide meaningful information for useful and strategic actions. The profile can be static or dynamic. The static profile is kept in prefixed data fields where the period between data-field updates is long, such as months or years. The dynamic profile is constantly updated as per evaluation of the situation. The updates may be performed manually or automated. The automated user-profile building is especially important in real-time decision-making systems. Real-time systems are dynamic. These systems often contain data that are critical to the user's decision-making process. Manually updated profiles are at the need and discursions of the relevant decision maker.

The profiling of patients and doctors is based on the patient-doctor information:

- The categories and subcategories of doctor specialization and categorization. These categories will assist in information processing and patient-doctor matching.
- Part of the patient's profile is based on symptoms (past history problems, dietary restrictions, etc.) and can assist in the prediction of the patient's needs specifically.
- The patient's profile can be matched with the available doctor profiles to provide doctors with information about the arrival of patients as well as presentation of the patient's profile to a suitable available doctor.

A value denoting the degree of association can be created from the above evaluation of the doctor-patient profile. The intelligent-agent based on the denoting degrees can identify (and allocate) an appropriate available doctor to the patient.

In the patient-doctor profiling, the intelligent agent will make distinctions in attribute values of the profiles and match the profiles with the highest value. It should be noted that the intelligent agent creates the patient and doctor profiles based on data obtained from the doctors and patient using the following:

- Explicit profiling based on the data entered by hospital staff about a patient.
- Implicit profiling by filling that gap for the missing data by acquiring knowledge about the patient from his or her past visit or other relevant databases if any, and then combining all these data to fill in the missing data. Using legacy data for complementing and updating the user profile seems to be a better choice than implicit profiling. This approach capitalizes on the user's personal history (previous data from previous visits to the doctor or hospital).

The proposed intelligent-agent system architecture allows user profiling and matching in such a time-intensive and important application.

The architecture of the intelligent-agent profiling system using RFID is given in Figure 1.

INTEGRATION OF INTELLIGENT AGENTS, RFID TECHNOLOGIES, AND PROFILE MATCHING

Intelligent agents have been used in order to provide the needed transformation of RIFD passive data collection into an active organizational knowledge assistant. An intelligent agent should be able to act on new data and already stored profile knowledge and thereafter examine its current actions based on certain assumptions. It then inferentially plans its activities. Furthermore, intelligent agents must be able to interact with other agents if required (Bigus & Bigus, 1998; Watson, 1997; Wooldridge & Jennings, 1995) and be able to substitute for a range of human activities in a situated context. In our case, the activities are medical patient assignment and the context is a hospital environment. The integration of RFID capabilities and intelligent-agent techniques provides promising development in the areas of performance improvements in RFID data collection, inference and knowledge acquisition, and profiling operations.

Profile matching is based on a vector of weighted attributes. To get this vector, a rule-

Figure 1. Intelligent-agents profiling model using RFID

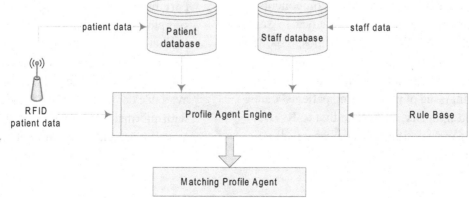

based system can be used to match the patient's attributes (stored in the patient's profile) against a doctor's attributes (stored in the doctor's profile). If there is a partial or full match between them, then the doctor will be informed based on his or her availability from the hospital doctor database. The matching is done through the rule-based system by examining the attributes of the patient profile and matching them using the rules already created to the doctor's profile based on the availability of doctors. Figure 1 displays the integration of intelligent agents, RFID technologies, and the profile-matching module.

RFID Description

RFID is a progressive technology that has been said to be easy to use and is well suited for collaboration with intelligent agents. Basically, an RFID can be read only, volatile read and write, or write once and read many (WORM) times. RFIDs are non-contact and non-line-of-sight operations. Being non-contact and non-line-of-sight will make RFIDs able to function under a variety of environmental conditions while still providing a high level of data integrity (Glover & Bhatt, 2006; Lahiri, 2005; Shepard, 2004). A basic RFID system consists of four components. These are the RFID tag (sometimes referred to as the transponder), a coiled antenna, a radio-frequency transceiver, and some type of reader for the data collection.

The RFID tag (transponder) emits radio waves in ranges of anywhere from 2.54 centimeters to 33 meters. Depending upon the reader's power output and the radio frequency used, and if a booster is added, that distance can be somewhat increased. When RFID tags pass through a specifically created electromagnetic zone, they detect the reader's activation signal. Transponders can be online or off line and electronically programmed with unique information for a specific application or purpose. A reader decodes the data encoded on the tag's integrated circuit and passes the data to a server for data storage or further processing.

RFID tags can be categorized as active, semi-active, or passive. Each has and is being used in a variety of inventory-management and data-collection applications today. The condition of the application, place, and use determines the required tag type.

Active RFID tags are powered by an internal battery and are typically read-write. Tag data can be rewritten and/or modified as the need dictates. An active tag's memory size varies according to manufacturing specifications and application requirements; some tags operate with up to 5 megabytes of memory. For a typical read-write RFID work-in-process system, a tag might give a machine a set of instructions, and the machine would then report its performance to the tag. This encoded data would then become part of the tagged part's history. The battery-supplied power of an active tag generally gives it a longer read range. The trade-off is greater size, greater cost, and a limited operational life that has been estimated to be a maximum of 10 years, depending upon operating temperatures and battery type.

The semi-active tag comes with a battery. The battery is used to power the tag's circuitry and not to communicate with the reader. This makes the semi-active tag more independent than the passive tag, and it can operate in more adverse conditions. The semi-active tag also has a longer range and more capabilities than a passive tag. Linear bar codes that reference a database to get product specifications and pricing are also data devices that act in a very similar way. Semi-passive tags are preprogrammed, but can allow for slight modifications of their instructions via the reader or interrogator. However, they are bigger, weigh more, and are more complete than passive tags. A reader is still needed for data collection.

Passive RFID tags operate without a separate external power source and obtain operating power generated from the reader. Passive tags have no power source embedded in them and are consequently much lighter than active tags, less expensive, and offer a virtually unlimited operational lifetime. However, the trade-off is that they have shorter read ranges than active tags, and require a higher powered reader. Read-only tags are typically passive and are programmed with a unique set of data (usually 32 to 128 bits) that cannot be modified.

RFID systems can be distinguished by their deployment and frequency range. RFID tags generally operate in two different types of frequencies that make them adaptable for nearly any application. These frequency ranges are as follows.

Low-frequency (30 KHz to 500 KHz) systems have short reading ranges and lower system costs. They are most commonly used in security access, asset tracking, and animal-identification applications.

High-frequency (850 MHz to 950 MHz, or in industry, science, and medical applications, 2.4 GHz to 2.5 GHz) systems offer longer reading ranges (greater than 33 meters) and high reading speeds. These systems are generally used for such applications as railroad-car tracking, container dock and transport management, and automated toll collection. However, the higher performance of high-frequency RFID systems incurs higher system-operating costs.

The coiled antenna is used to emit radio signals to activate the tag and read or write data to it. Antennas are the conduits between the tag and the transceiver that controls the system's data acquisition and communication. RFID antennas are available in many shapes and sizes. They can be built into a door frame, mounted on a tollbooth, or embedded into a manufactured item such as a shaver or software case so that the receiver tags the data from things passing through its zone. Often, the antenna is packaged with the transceiver and decoder to become a reader. The decoder device can be configured either as a handheld or a fixed-mounted device. In large, complex, often chaotic environments, portable or handheld transceivers would prove valuable.

RFID for Hospital Environment

In hospitals, systems need to use rules and domain knowledge that is appropriate to the situation. One of the more promising capabilities of intelligent agents is their ability to coordinate information between the various resources.

In a hospital environment, in order to manage patient medical data, there is a need for both types: fixed and handheld transceivers. Transceivers can be assembled in ceilings, walls, or door frames to collect and disseminate data. Hospitals have become large complex environments.

Nurses and physicians can retrieve the patient's medical data stored in transponders (RFID tags) before they enter a ward or patient's room.

Given the descriptions of the two types of RFID tags and their potential use in hospital patient data management, we suggest the following:

- It would be most useful to embed a passive RFID transponder into a patient's hospital wristband.

Figure 2. Semi-passive tag

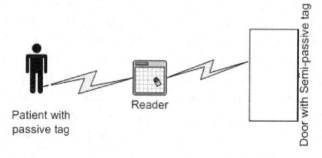

Patient with
passive tag

Reader

Door with Semi-passive tag

- It would be most useful to embed a passive RFID transponder into a patient's medical file.
- Doctors should have PDAs (personal digital assistants) equipped with RFID or some type of personal area network device. Either would enable them to retrieve some patient information whenever they are near the patient instead of waiting until the medical data is pushed to them through the hospital server.
- Active RFID tags are more appropriate for the continuous collection of patient medical data since the patient's medical data need to be continuously recorded to an active RFID tag and an associated reader needs to be employed. Using an active RFID means that the tag will be a bit bulky because of the needed battery for the write process, and there is a concern about radio-frequency emissions. Thus, it is felt that an active tag would not be a good candidate for the patient wristband. However, if the patient's condition is to be continuously monitored, the collection of the data at the source is essential. The inclusion of the tag in the wristband is the only way to record the medical data on a real-time basis using the RFID technology. As more organizations get into the business of manufacturing RFIDs and the life and size of batteries decrease, the tag size will decrease and this may be a real possible use.
- Passive RFID tags can be used as well. These passive tags can be embedded in the doctors PDA, which is needed for determining their locations whenever the medical staff requires them. Also, passive tags can be used in patients' wristbands for storage of limited amount of data on an off-line basis, for example, information such as the date of hospital admission, medical record number (MRN), and so forth.

Low-frequency-range tags are suitable for the patients' wristband RFID tags since it is expected that the patients' bed will not be too far from an RFID reader. The reader might be fixed over the patient's bed, in the bed itself, or over the door frame. The doctor using his or her PDA would be aiming to read the patient's data directly and within a relatively short distance. High-frequency-range tags are suitable for the physician's tag implanted in the PDA. As physicians move from one location to another in the hospital, data on their patients could be continuously being updated.

Finally, the transceivers and interrogators can differ quite considerably in complexity, depending upon the type of tags being supported and the application. The overall function of the application is to provide the means of communicating with the tags and facilitating data transfer. Functions performed by the reader may include quite sophisticated signal conditioning and parity error checking and correction. Once the signal from a transponder has been correctly received and decoded, algorithms may be applied to decide whether the signal is a repeat transmission, and may then instruct the transponder to cease transmitting or temporarily cease asking for data from the transponder. This is known as the command-response protocol and is used to circumvent the problem of reading multiple tags over a short time frame. Using interrogators in

Figure 3. Patient and outpatient

Inpatient   In Ward   Outpatient

this way is sometimes referred to as hands-down polling. An alternative, more secure but slower tag polling technique is called hands-up polling. This involves the transceiver looking for tags with specific identities, and interrogating them in turn. A further approach may use multiple transceivers multiplexed into one interrogator.

Hospital patient data management deals with sensitive and critical information (patients' medical data). Hands-down polling techniques in conjunction with multiple transceivers that are multiplexed with each other form a wireless network. The reason behind this choice is that there is a need for high-speed transfer of medical data from medical equipment to or from the RFID wristband tag to the nearest RFID reader and then through a wireless network or a network of RFID transceivers or LANs (local area networks) to the hospital server. From there it is a short distance to be transmitted to the doctor's PDA, a laptop, or a desktop through a WLAN (wireless LAN) IEEE 802.11b or 803.11g, or a wired LAN, which operates at the 5.2 GHz band with a maximum data transfer rate of 54 Mbps.

The hand-down polling techniques, as previously described, provide the ability to detect all detectable RFID tags at once (i.e., in parallel), preventing any unwanted delay in transmitting medical data corresponding to each RF tagged patient.

Transponder programmers are the means by which data are delivered to WORM and read-write tags. Programming can be carried out off line or online. For some systems, re-programming may be carried out online, particularly if it is being used as an interactive portable data file within a production environment, for example. Data may need to be recorded during each process. Removing the transponder at the end of each process to read the previous process data and to program the new data would naturally increase process time and would detract substantially from the intended flexibility of the application. By combining the functions of a transceiver and a programmer, data may be appended or altered in the transponder as required without compromising the production line.

Practical Cases using RFID Technology

This section explains in detail three possible applications of the RFID technology in three applicable cases. Each case is discussed step by step and then represented by a flowchart. These cases cover issues of the acquisition of a patient's medical data, locating the nearest available doctor to the patient's location, and how doctors stimulate the patient's active RFID tag using their PDAs in order to acquire the medical data stored in it.

Figure 4. Acquisition of patient data

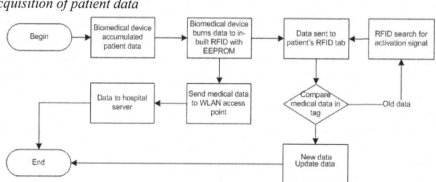

Figure 5. Locating nearest doctor

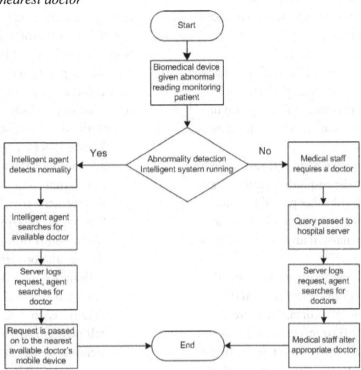

Case 1: Acquisition of Patient's Medical Data

Case 1 will represent the method of acquisition and transmission of medical data. This process can be described in the following points as follows:

- A biomedical device equipped with an embedded RFID transceiver and programmer will detect and measure the biological state of a patient. This medical data can be an ECG (electrocardiogram), EEG (electroencephalogram), BP (blood pressure), sugar level, temperature, or any other biomedical reading.

- After the acquisition of the required medical data, the biomedical device will write this data to the RFID transceiver's EEPROM (electronically erasable programmable read-only memory) using the built-in RFID programmer. Then the RFID transceiver with its antenna will be used to transmit the stored medical data in the EEPROM to the EEPROM in the patient's transponder (tag) that is around his or her wrist. The data received will be updated periodically once new fresh readings are available by the biomedical device. Hence, the newly sent data by the RFID transceiver will be accumulated with the old data in the tag. The purpose of the data stored in the patient's tag is to make it easy for the doctor to obtain medical information regarding the patient directly via the doctor's PDA, tablet PC (personal computer), or laptop.

- Similarly, the biomedical device will also transfer the measured medical data wirelessly to the nearest WLAN access point. Since a high data-transfer rate is crucial in transferring medical data, IEEE 802.11b is recommended for the transmission purpose.

- The wirelessly sent data will then be routed to the hospital's main server to be sent (pushed) to the following:
  - Other doctors available throughout the hospital so they can be notified of any newly received medical data.
  - An online patient-monitoring unit or a nurse's workstation within the hospital.
  - An expert (intelligent) software system running on the hospital server to be then compared with other previously stored abnormal patterns of medical data and to raise an alarm if any abnormality is discovered.
- Another option could be using the embedded RFID transceiver in the biomedical device to send the acquired medical data wirelessly to the nearest RFID transceiver in the room. Then the data will travel simultaneously in a network of RFID transceivers until reaching the hospital server.

Case 2: Locating the Nearest Available Doctor to the Patient's Location

This case will explain how to locate the nearest doctor, who is needed urgently, to attend an emergency medical situation. This case can be explained as follows:

- If a specific surgeon or physician is needed in a specific hospital department, the medical staff in the monitoring unit (e.g., nurses) can query the hospital server for the nearest available doctor to the patient's location. In our framework, an intelligent agent can perform this task.
- The hospital server traces all doctors' locations in the hospital through detecting the presence of their wireless mobile device, for example, PDA, tablet PC, or laptop in the WLAN range.

- Another method that the hospital's server can use to locate the physicians is making use of the RFID transceivers built into the doctor's wireless mobile device. Similar to the access points used in WLAN, RFID transceivers can assist in serving a similar role of locating a doctor's location. This can be described in three steps.
  - The fixed RFID transceivers throughout the hospital will send a stimulation signal to detect other free RFID transceivers, which are in the doctors' PDAs, tablets, laptops, and so forth.
  - All free RFID transceivers will receive the stimulation signal and respond back with an acknowledgement signal to the nearest fixed RFID transceiver.
  - Finally, each free RFID transceiver cell position would be determined by locating to which fixed RFID transceiver range it belongs to or currently is operating with.
- After the hospital server locates the positions of all available doctors, the RFID determines the nearest requested (condition evaluation) physican (pediatries, neuologist, etc...) to the patient's location.
- Once the required physician is located, an alert message will be sent to his or her PDA, tablet PC, or laptop indicating the location to be reached immediately. This alert message would show the following.
  - Case profile over application period
  - The building, floor, and room of the patient (e.g., 3C109).
  - The patient's case (e.g., heart stroke, arrhythmia, etc.).
  - A brief summary description of the patient's case.
- If the hospital is running an intelligent agent on its server as described in our proposed framework, the process of locating and sending an alert message can be automated. This is done through comparing the col-

lected medical data with previously stored abnormal patterns of medical data, then sending an automated message describing the situation. This system could be used in the patient-monitoring unit or the nurse's workstation, who observe and then send an alert message manually.

Case 3: Doctors Stimulate a Patient's Active RFID Tag using Their PDAs in Order to Acquire the Medical Data Stored in It

This method can be used in order to get rid of medical files and records placed in front of the patient's bed. Additionally, it could help in preventing medical errors (reading the wrong file for the wrong patient) and could be considered an important step toward a paperless hospital.

This case can be described in the following steps:

- The doctor enters the patient's room or ward. The doctor wants to check the medical status of a certain patient. Instead of picking up the hard-copy paper medical file, the doctor interrogates the patient's RFID wrist tag with his or her RFID transceiver equipped in a PDA, tablet PC, laptop, or so forth.
- The patient's RFID wrist tag detects the signal of the doctor's RFID transceiver coming from his or her wireless mobile device and replies back with the patient's information and medical data.
- If there was more than one patient in the ward possessing RFID wrist tags, all tags can respond in parallel using hands-down polling techniques back to the doctor's wireless mobile device.
- Another option could be that the doctor retrieves only the patient's number from the passive RFID wrist tag. Then, through the WLAN, the doctor could access the patient's medical record from the hospital's main server.

RFID technology has many potential important applications in hospitals, and the three cases discussed are real practical examples. Two important issues can be concluded from this section. WLAN is preferred for data transfer given that IEEE's wireless networks have much faster speed and greater coverage area as compared to RFID transceiver and transponder technology. Yet, RFID technology is the best for data storage and locating positions of medical staff and patients as well.

Here there is a need for the RFID transceiver and programmer to be embedded in biomedical devices for data acquisition and dissemination. A RFID transceiver embedded in a doctor's wireless mobile device enables the doctor to obtain medical data. With the progress of the RFID technology, it could become a standard as other wireless technologies (Bluetooth, for example) and eventually manufacturers will be building them in electronic devices, or biomedical devices, in our case.

Maintaining Patients' Data Security and Integrity

Once data are transmitted wirelessly, security becomes a crucial issue. Unlike in wired transmission, wirelessly transmitted data can be easily sniffed out, leaving the transmitted data vulnerable to many types of attacks. For example, wireless data could be easily eavesdropped on using any mobile device equipped with a wireless card. In worst cases, wirelessly transmitted data could be intercepted and then possibly tampered with, or in best cases, the patient's security and privacy F be compromised. Hence emerges the need for data to be initially encrypted from the source.

This section of the chapter discusses how we could apply encryption to the designed wireless framework that was explained in the previous section, suggesting exactly where data need to be encrypted and\or decrypted depending on the case that is being examined.

Figure 6. Functional flow

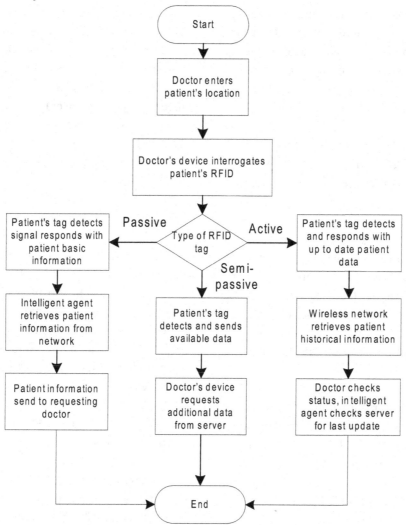

Next, a definition of the type of encryption that would be used in the design of the security (encryption or decryption) framework will be discussed, and this will be followed by a flowchart demonstrating the framework in a step-by-step process. There are two layers of encryption that are recommended to be used.

- **Physical:** (hardware) layer encryption means encrypting all collected medical data at the source or hardware level before transmitting them. This ensures that the patient's medical data would not be compromised once

exposed to the outer world on its way to its destination. Even if a person with a malicious intent and also possessing a wireless mobile device steps into the coverage range of the hospitals' WLAN, this intruder will gain actually nothing since all medical data are encrypted, making all intercepted data worthless.

- **Application:** (software) layer encryption means encrypting all collected medical data at the destination or application level once receiving it. Application-level encryption runs on the doctor's wireless mobile device (e.g., PDA, tablet PC, or laptop) and on the hospital server. Once the medical data are received, they will be protected by a secret password (encryption or decryption key) created by the doctor who possesses this device. This type of encryption would prevent any person from accessing the patient's medical data if the doctor's wireless mobile device gets lost, or even if a hacker hacks into the hospital server via the Internet, intranet, or some other means.

Framework of Encrypting a Patient's Medical Data

The previous section (practical cases using RFID technology) focused on how to design a wireless framework to reflect how a patient's medical data can be managed efficiently and effectively leading to the elimination of errors, delays, and even paperwork. Similarly, this section will focus on the previously discussed framework from a security perspective, attempting to increase security and data integrity during the acquisition of a patient's medical data and when doctors stimulate the patient's active RFID tag using their wireless mobile devices in order to acquire the medical data stored in it. The third case on locating the nearest available doctor to the patient's location is more concerned about locating doctors than transferring a patient's data and it is not discussed here.

The lower part of Figure 6 represents the physical (hardware) encryption layer. This part is divided into two sides. The left side demonstrates the case of a doctor acquiring a patient's medical data via a passive RFID tag located in a band around the patient's wrist. The passive RFID tag contains only a very limited amount of information such as the patient's name, date of admission to the hospital, and above all his or her MRN, which will grant access to the medical record containing the acquired medical data and other information regarding the patient's medical condition. This process is implemented in six steps, and involves two pairs of encryption and decryption. The first encryption occurs after the doctor stimulates the RFID passive tag to acquire the patient's MRN, so the tag will encrypt and reply back with the MRN to the doctors PDA, for example. Then the doctor will decrypt the MRN and use it to access the patient's medical record from the hospital's server. Finally, the hospital server will encrypt and reply back with the medical record, which will be decrypted once received by the doctor's PDA.

The right side of Figure 6 represents a similar case, but this time using an active RFID tag. This process involves only one encryption and decryption. The encryption happens after the doctor stimulates the active RFID tag using a PDA that has an equipped RFID transceiver, so the tag replies with the medical data encrypted. Then the received data is decrypted through the doctor's PDA. The upper part of Figure 6 represents the application encryption layer requiring the doctor to enter a password to decrypt and then access the stored medical data. So, whenever the doctor wants to access a patient's medical data, he or she simply enters a certain password to get access to either the wireless mobile device or a hospital server, depending on where the medical data actually resides.

Securing medial data seems to be uncomplicated, yet the main danger of compromising such data comes from the people managing it, for example, doctors, nurses, and other medical staff. We have seen that even though the transmitted medical data are initially encrypted from the source, doctors have to run application-level encryption on their wireless mobile devices in order to protect the important data if the device gets lost, left behind, stolen, and so forth. Nevertheless, there is a compromise. Increasing security through using multiple layers and increasing the length of encryption keys decreases the encryption-decryption speed and causes unwanted time delays, whether we are using application- or hardware-level encryption. As a result, this could delay medical data being sent to doctors or online monitoring units. Figure 6 represents the case of high and low levels of security in a flowchart applied to the previously discussed two cases.

We conclude that there are two possible levels of encryption: the software level (application layer) or hardware level (physical layer) depending on the level of security required. Both physical-layer and application-layer encryption are needed in maintaining collected medical data on hospital servers and doctors' wireless mobile devices. Encrypting medical data makes the process of data transmission slower, while sending data unencrypted is faster. Here there is a need to compromise between speed and security. For medical data, it has to be sent as fast as possible to medical staff, yet the security issue has the priority.

CONCLUSION

Managing patients' data wirelessly (paperless) can prevent errors, enforce standards, make staff more efficient, simplify record keeping, and improve patient care. In this chapter, both passive and active RFID tags were used in acquiring and storing medical data, and in linking to the hospital's server via a wireless network. Moreover, three practical applicable RFID cases were discussed and it was explained how the RFID technology can be put in use in hospitals while at the same time maintaining the acquired patient data's security and integrity.

This research in the wireless medical environment introduces some new ideas in conjunction with what is already available in the RFID technol-

ogy and wireless networks. The aim here is to link both technologies with each other to achieve the research's main goal, which is delivering patient medical data as fast and secure as possible to pave the way for future paperless hospitals.

REFERENCES

Bigus, J. P., & Bigus, J. (1998). *Constructing intelligent agents with Java: A programmers guide to smarter applications.* New York: Wiley. (ISBN:0-471-19135-3)

Glover, B., & Bhatt, H. (2006). *RFID essentials.* O'Railly Media Inc. (ISBN:0-596-0094-4)

Kaptelinin, V. (1992). Human computer interaction in context: The activity theory perspective. In *Proceedings of the East-West Human Computer Interaction Conference*, St. Petersburg, Russia.

Lahiri, H. (2005). *RFID sourcebook.* New York: IBM Press. (ISBN:0-131-8513-73)

Odell, J. (Ed.). (2000). *Agent technology* (OMG Document 00-09-01). OMG Agents interest Group.

Shepard, S. (2004). *RFID.* McGraw-Hill. (ISBN: 0-071-4429-95)

Watson, M. (1997). *Intelligent Java applications for the Internet and intranets.* Morgan Kaufmann. (ISBN: 1-55860-420-0)

Wooldridge, M., & Jennings, N. (1995). Intelligent agents: Theory and practice. *The Knowledge Engineering Review, 10*(2), 115-152. (ISBN: 0-269-888-9)

This work was previously published in Web Mobile-Based Applications for Healthcare Management, edited by L. Al-Hakim, pp. 316-334, copyright 2007 by IRM Press (an imprint of IGI Global).

Chapter XVII
Radio Frequency Identification (RFID) Technology

David C. Wyld
Southeastern Louisiana University, USA

INTRODUCTION

We are in the midst of what may become one of the true technological transformations of our time. RFID (radio frequency identification) is by no means a new technology. RFID is fundamentally based on the study of electromagnetic waves and radio, pioneered in the 19th century work of Faraday, Maxwell, and Marconi. The idea of using radio frequencies to reflect waves from objects dates back as far as 1886 to experiments conducted by Hertz. Radar was invented in 1922, and its practical applications date back to World War II, when the British used the IFF (Identify Friend or Foe) system to identify enemy aircraft (Landt, 2001). Stockman (1948) laid out the basic concepts for RFID. However, it would take decades of development before RFID technology would become a reality. Since 2000, significant improvements in functionality, decreases in both size and costs, and agreements on communication standards have combined to make RFID technology viable for commercial and governmental purposes. Today, RFID is po-

sitioned as an alternative way to identify objects with the ubiquitous bar code.

BACKGROUND

Automatic identification, or Auto-ID, represents a broad category of technologies that are used to help machines identify objects, humans, or animals. Auto-ID is a means of identifying items and gathering data on them without human intervention or data entry. As can be seen in Figure 1, RFID a type of Auto-ID technology. Sometimes referred to as dedicated short-range communication (DSRC), RFID is "a wireless link to identify people or objects" (d'Hont, 2003, p. 1). RFID is, in reality, a subset of the larger radio frequency (RF) market, which encompasses an array of RF technologies, including the following:

- Cellular phones
- Digital radio
- The Global Positioning System (GPS)
- High-definition television (HDTV)
- Wireless networks (Malone, 2004)

Figure 1. The family of automatic identification technologies

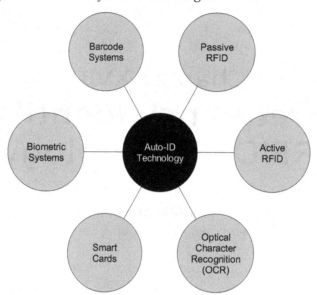

RFID is a technology that already surrounds us. If you have an Exxon/Mobil SpeedPass™ in your pocket, you are using RFID. If you have a toll tag on your car, you are using RFID. If you have checked out a library book, you have likely encountered RFID. If you have been shopping in a department store or an electronics retailer, you have most certainly encountered RFID in the form of an EAS (electronic article surveillance) tag.

RFID TECHNOLOGY

To best understand the power of radio frequency identification, it is first useful to compare RFID with bar-code technology, which is omnipresent today. The specific differences between bar-code technology and RFID are summarized in Table 1. The principal difference lies in the potential of RFID to provide unique identifiers for objects. While the bar code and the UPC (Universal Product Code) have become all pervading and enabled a host of applications and efficiencies (Brown, 1997), they only identify an object as belonging to a particular class, category, or type. Due to

its structure (as shown in Figure 2), a bar code cannot uniquely identify a specific object: It can identify only the product and its manufacturer. Thus, a bar code on any one package of sliced meat in a grocery store is the same as on any other of a particular type or size from a particular firm. Likewise, the bar code on a case or pallet of military supplies cannot tell one shipment from another. The two technologies also differ in the way in which they read objects. With bar coding, the reading device scans a printed label with optical laser or imaging technology. However, with RFID, the reading device scans, or interrogates, a tag using radio frequency signals.

There are three necessary elements for an RFID system to work. These are tags, readers, and the software necessary to link to a larger information processing system. In a nutshell, the technology works as follows. The tag is the unique identifier for the item it is attached to. The reader sends out a radio signal, and the tag responds to identify itself. The reader then converts the radio waves returned from the tag into data that can be passed on to an information processing system to filter, categorize, analyze, and enable action based on the identifying information.

Table 1. RFID and bar codes compared

Bar-Code Technology	RFID Technology
• Bar codes require line of sight to be read.	• RFID tags can be read or updated without line of sight.
• Bar codes can only be read individually.	• Multiple RFID tags can be read simultaneously.
• Bar codes cannot be read if they become dirty or damaged.	• RFID tags are able to cope with harsh and dirty environments.
• Bar codes must be visible to be logged.	• RFID tags are ultrathin, can be printed on a label, and can be read even when concealed within items.
• Bar codes can only identify the type of item.	• RFID tags can identify a specific item.
• Bar-code information cannot be updated.	• Electronic information can be overwritten repeatedly on RFID tags.
• Bar codes must be manually tracked for item identification, making human error an issue.	• RFID tags can be automatically tracked, eliminating human error.

There are three essential components that combine to form an RFID tag. These are the chip, the antenna, and the packaging that contains them. An RFID tag has an integrated circuit (IC) that contains the unique identifying data about the object to which is it is attached. One of the identifiers, but not the only one, that can be used to identify the item uniquely with an RFID tag is the EPC (Electronic Product Code). The IC is attached to a small antenna, which most commonly is a small coil of wires. The third element is the packaging of the tag that protects the IC and the antenna. RFID tags can take on a variety of forms for specific applications, including smart labels, keys or key fobs, watches, smart cards, disks and coins (which can be attached to an item with a fastening screw), and implantable glass transponders (for animal or human use). Hitachi has developed the mu-chip, a very tiny (0.4 mm²) RFID tag that is the size of a grain of rice (Anonymous, 2004).

There are two basic categories of tags: passive and active. A summary of the differences between the two general categories is presented in Table 2. Passive tags are already very familiar to us as we see simple examples of such in the form of the EAS tags used throughout the retail industry. Without a power source, a passive tag is only able to transmit information when it is within range of an RFID reader. Passive tags function through a process known as energy harvesting, wherein

Figure 2. Anatomy of a bar code

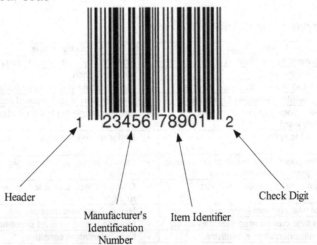

Header

Manufacturer's Identification Number

Item Identifier

Check Digit

energy from the reader is gathered by the tag, stored momentarily, and then transmitted back to the reader at a different frequency.

RFID readers have three essential components. These are the antenna, transceiver, and decoder. RFID readers can differ quite considerably in their complexity, form, and price, depending upon the type of tags being supported and the functions to be fulfilled. Readers can be large and fixed, or small handheld devices. However, the read range for a portable reader will be less than the range that can be achieved using a fixed reader. The reader, either continuously (in the case of a fixed-position reader) or on demand (as with a handheld reader), sends out an electromagnetic wave to inquire if there are any RFID tags present in its active read field. When the reader receives any signal from a tag, it passes that information on to the decoding software and processes it for forwarding to the information system it is a part of. Recently, it has been forecast that as soon as 2007, RFID reading capabilities will soon be capable of being integrated into cell phones, PDAs (personal digital assistants), and other electronic devices (Thomas, 2005).

In brief, the science of a passive RFID system works as follows. The reader sends out electromagnetic waves, and a magnetic field is formed when the signal from the reader couples with the tag's antenna. The passive RFID tag draws its power from this magnetic field, and it is this power that enables the tag to send back an identifying response to the query of the RFID reader. Singel (2004) likened passive RFID to a "high-tech version of the children's game 'Marco Polo.'" In a passive RFID system, the reader sends out a signal on a designated frequency, querying if any tags are present in its read field (the equivalent of yelling out "Marco" in a swimming pool). If a chip is present, the tag takes the radio energy sent out by the reader to power itself up and respond with the electronic equivalent of kids yelling "Polo" to identify their position.

All of this happens almost instantaneously. In fact, today's RFID readers are capable of reading tags at a rate of up to 1,000 tags per second.

Smart labels are a particularly important form of passive RFID tag. A smart label is an adhesive label that is human and quite often machine readable with a bar code. However, the label is also embedded with an ultrathin RFID tag inlay. Smart labels combine the functionality of passive RFID tags with the convenience of a printed label. Looking ahead, analysts have predicted that the vast majority of all RFID tags will come in the form of smart labels. In fact, it has been estimated that smart labels will constitute 99.5% of the trillion tags forecast to be in use a decade from now (Anonymous, 2005).

Table 2. Differentiating passive and active RFID tags

Passive Tags	Active Tags
• Operate without a battery	• Powered by an internal battery
• Less expensive	• More expensive
• Unlimited life (because of no battery)	• Finite lifetime (because of battery)
• Less weight (because of no battery)	• Greater weight (because of battery)
• Lesser range (up to 3-5 meters, usually less)	• Greater range (up to 100 meters)
• Subject to noise	• Better noise immunity
• Derive power from the electromagnetic field generated by the reader	• Internal power to transmit signal to the reader
• Require more powerful readers	• Can be effective with less powerful readers
• Lower data transmission rates	• Higher data transmission rates
• Less tags can be read simultaneously	• More tags can be read simultaneously
• Greater orientation sensitivity	• Less orientation sensitivity

An active tag functions in the same manner as its passive counterpart, but it contains a fourth element: an internal battery that continuously powers the tag. As such, the tag is always on and transmitting the information. The active tag is only readable, however, when it is in the reading field of an RFID reader. However, the battery significantly boosts the effective operating range of the tag. Thus, while a passive tag can only be read at a range of a few yards, active tags can be read at a distance of 10 to 30 yards. However, the useful life of an active tag is limited by the life of the onboard battery (typically 5 years at present). Furthermore, due to the need for a battery, active tags will always cost more and weigh more than a passive tag.

RFID tags are intentionally designed to not be the repository of item information. Rather, through a coding system known as EPC, the tag serves as an electronic license plate for each tagged item, directing the user via the Internet to the database where complete descriptive information about the item is housed (Aitoro, 2005). As can be seen in Figure 3, there are four elements that comprise the 96-bit-capacity Electronic Product Code. These are the following.

1. **Header (or Version):** This section identifies the length of the EPC number including the code type and version in use (up to 8 bits).
2. **EPC Manager (or Manufacturer):** This section identifies the company or entity responsible for managing the next two EPC elements (up to 28 bits).
3. **Object Class (or Product):** This section identifies the class of the item (for example, the stock-keeping unit [SKU] or consumer unit; up to 24 bits).
4. **Serial Number:** This section identifies a unique serial number for all items in a given object class (up to 36 bits).

With the 96-bit EPC structure, manufacturers should not have to worry about running out of EPC numbers for many decades. In fact, the EPC data structure can generate approximately 33 trillion different unique combinations, which according to Helen Duce of Cambridge University, would be enough to label all of the atoms in the universe (as cited in Anonymous, 2003). According to projections from the National Research Council's Committee on Radio Frequency Identification Technologies (2004), this will allow for the billions of people on earth to have billions of tags each.

Table 3 outlines some of the present and emerging RFID applications. Over time, RFID will likely supplement, rather than supplant, barcode technology for tracking items in supply chain management and other applications in organizations. They are by no means mutually exclusive technologies. Indeed, some of the most creative and cost-beneficial applications may come from combining RFID and bar codes together, where

Figure 3. The electronic product code

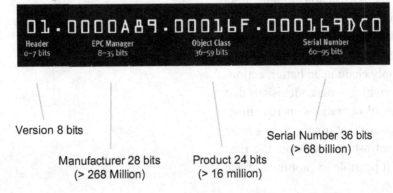

Table 3. RFID applications

Traditional RFID Applications	Emerging RFID Applications
• Security/Access Control	• Warehouse Management
• Electronic Article Surveillance	• Supply Chain Management
• Asset/Fleet Management	• Reverse Logistics
• Mass Transit	• Shipment Tracking
• Library Access	• Asset Tracking
• Toll Collection	• Retail Management
• Animal Identification	• Document Tracking
	• Anticounterfeit
	• Advance Access Control
	• Mass Transit Monthly and Single Trip
	• Airline Baggage Handling
	• Aircraft Parts and Tools
	• Health Care Applications
	• Regulatory Compliance
	• Payments

RFID tags and labels may be used to identify large groups of items and bar codes remain the tracking device for individual items.

FUTURE TRENDS

There are five principal drivers behind the recent upswing of interest across the American economy, and indeed globally, in RFID. These are depicted in Figure 4.

First, as we have come to expect with all electronics, the costs and size of the technology have sharply decreased, and concomitantly, the capabilities and applications of it have rapidly increased. Thus, the increased accessibility of RFID tags and labels have made it possible today

to have them be utilized in new, innovative ways. Second, emerging open, common standards in RFID technology will enable greater data sharing and collaboration between supply chain partners. Third, with increased competitive pressures and customer expectations, organizations throughout the supply chain need better, actionable information on which to make decisions that can impact successful operations in real time. Fourth, the investments that organizations have made in their IT infrastructures over the past decade now make it possible to capture and use this information.

The final reason is simply that leading-edge organizations have recognized these four drivers of RFID technology and created a fifth driver by mandating its use in their inbound supply chains and seeking to integrate RFID into their internal

Figure 4. The driving forces behind RFID

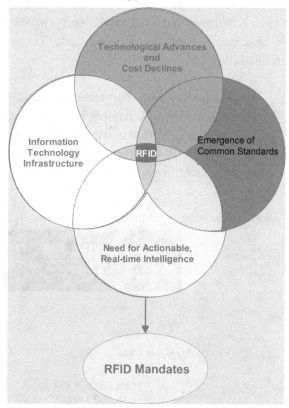

Figure 5.

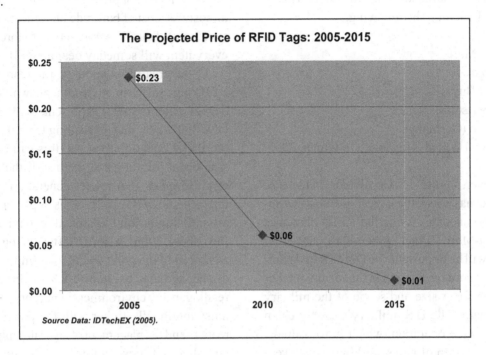

Figure 6.

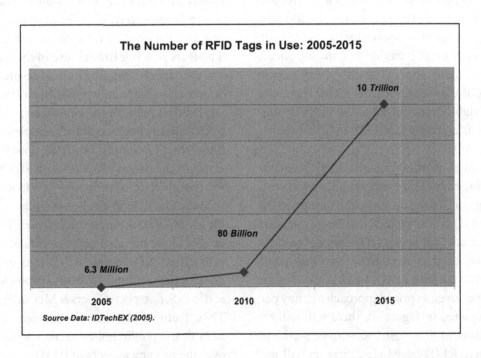

operations. These mandates include those of major retailers, including the following.

- Wal-Mart
- Target
- Best Buy
- Albertson's
- Metro (Germany)
- Tesco (United Kingdom; Goodman, 2005)

However, it is the U.S. Department of Defense (DoD) that has issued the largest and most sweeping RFID mandate. While the RFID mandates from Wal-Mart, Target, Albertson's, and other retailers will be important, the DoD's RFID mandate is far more reaching than that of any retailer due to the sheer size and scope of the military supply chain. The U.S. military's supply chain is a worldwide operation, which moves almost $29 billion worth of items worldwide each year (Sullivan, 2005). The military supply chain is not just bullets, bombs, and uniforms as it involves a wide panoply of goods, the majority of which are consumer goods as well. The DoD's directive will ultimately affect approximately 60,000 suppliers, which are not necessarily the Lockheeds and Boeings of the world, but mostly small businesses, many employing only a few people (Wyld, 2005). As such, the DoD's RFID mandate has been rightly categorized as the likely tipping point for widespread use of RFID in supply chains (Roberti, 2003).

The forces working against RFID's ascension are threefold. These surround issues of cost, technology, and privacy. First, the unit price for passive RFID tags is projected to steeply decline over the next decade as cost efficiencies in production take hold and volumes grow from millions of tags today to trillions of tags by 2015 (see Figure 5). However, even as prices approach a penny per tag (as depicted in Figure 6), there will still be applications for low-cost, non-mission-critical items where RFID-based identification will not

be cost effective or practical in comparison to the almost free cost of bar-code identification (Webster, 2006). Thus, it is impractical to forecast that every item will someday bear an RFID tag.

In the area of technology, the read rates for RFID tags suffer in environments where a great deal of water or metal is present. With a need to have 100% accuracy in reading tagged items for the RFID equation to work, this can be a very significant limitation to the use of the technology. However, the newest generation of RFID tag technology (GEN 2) seems to perform better around liquids and in metallic environments (Swedberg, 2006). Also, RFID technology has not advanced to the point where it is simply a matter of plug and play to obtain 100% accuracy in tag reading in any environment. Thus, organizations must continually tinker with the positioning of readers and the placement of tags and smart labels on pallets, cartons, and items to obtain optimal accuracy with their RFID systems.

Finally, there are serious concerns over the privacy aspects of RFID. As O'Shea (2003) reminds us, RFID is a technological tool, and "as with all technology, it can be used to manipulate our world or be abused for unwarranted control." The fears of a Big Brother use of the technology and the data generated by it are widespread. These apprehensions are only inflamed by references to the Biblical mark of the beast (Jones, 2005) and to Orwellian popular culture examples, such as in the movies *A Beautiful Mind* and *Minority Report*. Fears of the privacy aspects of RFID has led to the introduction of proposed legislation, both at the state and federal levels, to regulate or prohibit the use of RFID at the consumer level (Trebilcock, 2006). There has also been an escalating outcry over efforts to integrate RFID into state-issued driver's licenses and ID cards (Lipowicz, 2006) and in U.S. passports (Evers & McCullagh, 2006). Thus, there will be a continuing need for debate in both the public policy arena and in industry over the privacy aspects of RFID.

CONCLUSION

In the end, the current push for RFID may be a small part of a larger mosaic. Indeed, futurist Paul Saffo foresees that much of the focus on RFID today is on doing old things in new ways, but the truly exciting proposition is the new ideas and new ways of doing things that will come from RFID. Building upon the previously discussed ideas of RFID as making possible "an Internet of things" (Schoenberger, 2002) or a "wireless Internet of artifacts" (Gadh, 2004), Saffo sees RFID as making possible what he terms "the sensor revolution." This is based on viewing RFID as a media technology, making possible what he categorizes as "'smartifacts' or intelligent artifacts, that are observing the world on our behalf and increasingly manipulating it on our behalf" (as cited in O'Connor, 2005). Saffo thus stresses the importance of thinking outside the box on RFID and looking beyond today's problems to find "unexpected applications," which is where "the greatest potential for RFID lies" (as cited in O'Connor). Indeed, Saffo urges people to take a 20-year perspective on RFID, according to which we are in the early stages of "a weird new kind of media revolution" in that "RFID will make possible new companies that do things we don't even dream about" (as cited in Van, 2005, p. B1).

If we indeed take the long view of history, we can see that some of today's biggest industries, most pedestrian technologies, and most indispensable parts of our lives come from sparks of imagination on how to use a technology in unimagined ways. Indeed, we have seen bar coding itself used in applications far beyond the supply chain functions it was created for (Brown, 1997). Thus, we are still in the early stages of this technological revolution, and we should be mindful of the advice of U.S. Undersecretary of Defense Alan Estevez (2005), who observed, "The real value of RFID lies not in what it can do today but in what it will do in the future."

FUTURE RESEARCH DIRECTIONS

At this early stage in the widespread use of RFID technology, there are far more questions than answers, far more pilots than implementations, far more interested observers than users of RFID, and far more skeptics than enthusiasts among the general public about the value and integrity of the technology. Indeed, we are early on in the life span of RFID technology. In fact, many leading industry experts expect full-fledged implementation of RFID to take 10 to 15 years, or more.

There will be a great need for a continuing academic research agenda as the RFID revolution moves forward. This research will generally fall into three categories.

1. "Nuts-and-Bolts" Research
2. "Big-Picture" Research
3. "Ramifications and Permutations" Research

Of course, all of these areas are interdependent, and none can or even should be conducted in isolation of the others. One of the hallmarks of the development of RFID to date has been the openness of companies, executives, and academics to share their research, lessons learned, and best-practice findings. Hopefully, this will continue to be a hallmark of this area of technology.

The first area of research will be perhaps the most active in the short term, and this will fall in what can be best described as nuts-and-bolts research. For the next 5 to 10 years, and perhaps longer, there will be a great need for basic research into just how to make RFID technology work in various settings. This will involve such fundamental questions as the following.

- How and where should tags be applied to pallets, cases, and individual items to maximize their readability?
- How should individual readers be positioned to maximize their ability to scan tags, and

how should arrays of readers be stationed to best ensure coverage of a specific type of area?

- What can be done to mitigate the effects of metals, water, and other environmental conditions on the ability to read tags?
- What are the environmental consequences of RFID tags, and what measures will need to be taken in the future to mitigate the pollution and landfill problems that might be created through widespread use?

Certainly, much of this research is being conducted by individual organizations, and hopefully, companies and governmental agencies will continue to be open in sharing both their best practices and lessons learned with the wider RFID community, both through presentations and written reports and case studies as they have been in the formative stages of the RFID revolution. If such research begins to be held as being proprietary, then the rising tide for RFID will be held back.

There is a great need for academic work as well in this area of RFID research. At this early point, even if corporate and governmental interests wanted university involvement, there are very few true RFID experts in academia and few schools that have placed emphasis to date on such research. Right now, perhaps the leading center for such research is housed at the University of Arkansas. Certainly, other entrepreneurial-minded universities with similar capabilities in their business, engineering, and even public administration programs will follow suit in the near future.

The second category of research will address the impact RFID can and will have on the big picture of organizations, both in the private and public sectors. This will focus on how RFID has and will affect organizations, both in terms of their internal systems, operations, and capabilities, and with their interorganizational relationships. In the latter regard, research should focus not only on supply chain relationships, but how real-time data

sharing impacts areas such as service delivery, finance and payments, and customer service. This research should be carried out by discipline specialists in the following areas.

- Strategic Management
- Marketing
- Health Care Administration
- Supply Chain Management
- Public Administration
- Engineering
- Communications

Again, there is great need for cross-disciplinary research and communication as concepts, theories, models, and cases from one area may apply equally well, if not better, in different application areas.

The final area of research should be in what can be categorized as the ramifications and permutations of the technology, examining RFID's impact on society, business, law, privacy, and ethics. Less applied than either of the prior two areas, this may be the toughest category of research to find funding and support for. However, it may well be the most important area of research. This area should draw upon the wealth of many disciplines, including, but by no means limited to, the following.

- Law
- Ethics
- Psychology
- Sociology
- Anthropology
- Computer Science
- Information Management
- Strategic Management
- Health Care Administration

The area would encompass research into how RFID technology is challenging and changing the boundaries, norms, and laws in specific areas of business, government, and society. It may at times be controversial and may bring to light varying perspectives on the impact of this new technology on all of us.

REFERENCES

Aitoro, J. (2005, February 25). The government and RFID. *VARBusiness*. Retrieved June 8, 2005, from http://www.varbusiness.com/sections/governmentvar/govt.jhtml?articleId=60403591

Anonymous. (2003). Pushing the envelope. *Management Today*, p. 39.

Anonymous. (2004). Micro tracker. *Technology Review, 107*(3), 18.

Anonymous. (2005, March 23). RFID unites the supply chain. *Business Process Management Today*. Retrieved March 30, 2005, from http://bpm-today.newsfactor.com/scm/story.xhtml?story_title=RFID-Unites-the-Supply-Chain&story_id=31672&category=scm#storystart

Brown, S. (1997). *Revolution at the checkout counter*. Cambridge: Harvard University Press.

Committee on Radio Frequency Identification Technologies, National Research Council. (2004). *Radio frequency identification technologies: A workshop summary*. Retrieved April 30, 2005, from http://www.nap.edu/catalog/11189.html

d'Hont, S. (2003). *The cutting edge of RFID technology and applications for manufacturing and distribution*. Retrieved July 10, 2003, from http://www.ti.com/tiris/docs/manuals/whtPapers/manuf_dist.pdf

Estevez, A. F. (2005). RFID vision in the DOD supply chain. *Army Logistician*. Retrieved May 7, 2005, from http://www.almc.army.mil/alog/rfid.html

Evers, J., & McCullagh, D. (2006, August 5). Researchers: E-passports pose security risk. *CNET*. Retrieved August 17, 2006, from http://news.com.com/Researchers+E-passports+pose+security+risk/2100-7349_3-6102608.html?tag=st.ref.goo

Gadh, R. (2004, August 11). The state of RFID. *Computerworld*. Retrieved August 30, 2004, from http://www.computerworld.com/mobiletopics/mobile/story/0,10801,95179,00.html

Goodman, B. (2005, March 17). Is RFID taking off, or just taking its time? *Integrating the Enterprise*. Retrieved March 24, 2005, from http://www.itbusinessedge.com/content/3Q/3qpub2-20050317.aspx

IDTechEx. (2005, April 10). *RFID market to reach $7.26Bn in 2008*. Retrieved April 18, 2005, from http://www.idtechex.com/products/en/articles/00000169.asp

Jones, J. (2005, April 3). Is the RFID chip the mark of the beast? *Political Gateway*. Retrieved April 8, 2005, from http://www.politicalgateway.com/main/columns/read.html?col=323

Landt, J. (2001). *Shrouds of time*. Retrieved August 1, 2003, from http://www.aimglobal.org/technologies/rfid/resources/shrouds_of_time.pdf

Lipowicz, A. (2006, January 19). Group objects to driver's license RFID. *Washington Technology*. Retrieved April 17, 2006, from http://www.washingtontechnology.com/news/1_1/daily_news/27794-1.html

Malone, R. (2004). Reconsidering the role of RFID. *Inbound Logistics*. Retrieved September 11, 2004, from http://www.inboundlogistics.com/articles/supplychain/sct0804.shtml

O'Connor, M. (2005, April 13). RFID and the media revolution. *RFID Journal*. Retrieved April 20, 2005, from http://www.rfidjournal.com/article/articleview/1508/1/1/

O'Shea, P. (2003). RFID comes of age for tracking everything from pallets to people. *ChipCenter*. Retrieved July 12, 2003, from http://www.chipcenter.com/analog/ed008.htm

Roberti, M. (2003, October 6). The tipping point. *RFID Journal.* Retrieved October 26, 2003, from http://www.rfidjournal.com/article/articleprint/607/-1/2/

Schoenberger, C. (2002, March 18). RFID: The Internet of things. *Forbes.* Retrieved September 18, 2003, from http://www.mindfully.org/Technology/RFID-Things-Forbes18mar02.htm

Singel, R. (2004, October 21). American passports to get chipped. *Wired.* Retrieved December 12, 2004, from http://www.wired.com/news/privacy/0,1848,65412,00.html

Stockman, H. (1948, October). Communication by means of reflected power. *Proceedings of the Institute of Radio Engineers* (pp. 1196-1204).

Sullivan, L. (2004, October 25). IBM shares RFID lessons. *InformationWeek.* Retrieved November 9, 2004, from http://www.informationweek.com/shared/printableArticle.jhtml?articleID=51000091

Swedberg, C. (2006, April 19). University of Kansas' tag for metal, liquids. *RFID Journal.* Retrieved May 7, 2006, from http://www.rfidjournal.com/article/articleview/2275/1/1/

Thomas, L. (2005, January 26). RFID cell phones? Maybe in 2007. *Mobile Magazine.* Retrieved January 30, 2005, from http://www.mobilemag.com/content/100/102/C3673/

Trebilcock, B. (2006, July 25). RFID goes to Washington. *Modern Materials Handling.* Retrieved August 3, 2006, from http://www.mmh.com/article/CA6355944.html

Van, J. (2005, April 16). RFID spells media revolution, futurist says. *Chicago Tribune,* p. B1.

Webster, J. (2006, January 2). RFID: Cost and complexity continue to block enterprise use. *Computerworld,* Retrieved February 28, 2006, from http://www.computerworld.com/managementtopics/management/story/0,10801,107308,00.html?source=NLT_EB&nid=107308

Wyld, D. C. (2005, February 24). Supporting the "warfighter." *RFIDNews.* Retrieved March 1, 2005, from http://www.rfidnews.org/library/2005/02/24/supporting-the-warfighter/

FURTHER READING

Anonymous. (2007, January 18). Social Security Administration uses Intermec RFID technology to improve data collection accuracy, reduce labor costs. *MSN/Money.* Retrieved January 19, 2007, from http://news.moneycentral.msn.com/provider/providerarticle.aspx?Feed=BW&Date=20070118&ID=6354695

Best, J. (2004, October 8). Senior management "clueless" about RFID. *Silicon.com.* Retrieved December 30, 2004, from http://news.zdnet.co.uk/business/management/0,39020654,39169620,00.htm

Best, J. (2005, January 25). 2015: RFID is all over. Make way for super RFID. *Silicon.com.* Retrieved February 2, 2005, from http://networks.silicon.com/lans/print.htm?TYPE=story&AT=39127336-39024663t-40000017c

Clarke, R. (2005). Assessing readability problems with RFID systems. *RFID Product News.* Retrieved March 12, 2005, from http://www.rfidproductnews.com/issues/2005.01/feature/readability.php

Collins, J. (2005, April 8). Consumers more RFID-aware, still wary: A recent survey finds that more U.S. consumers have heard about RFID, but worries about privacy remain. *RFID Journal.* Retrieved April 15, 2005, from http://www.rfidjournal.com/article/articleview/1491/1/1/

Committee on Radio Frequency Identification Technologies, National Research Council. (2004). *Radio frequency identification technologies: A workshop summary.* Retrieved April 30, 2005, from http://www.nap.edu/catalog/11189.html

Douglas, R. (2005, February 14). Bar codes vs. RFID. *London Globe and Mail*. Retrieved February 16, 2005, from http://www.globetechnology.com/servlet/story/RTGAM.20050111.gtflbarcodejan11/BNStory/Technology/

Fox, R., & Rychak, L. (2004). *The potential and challenges of RFID technology*. Retrieved June 9, 2004, from http://www.mintz.com/publications/detail/264/Communications_Advisory_The_Potential_and_Challenges_of_RFID_Technology/

Government Accountability Office (GAO). (2005). *Report to Congressional requesters: Information security. Radio frequency identification technology in the federal government*. Retrieved June 1, 2005, from http://www.gao.gov/new.items/d05551.pdf

Greenemeier, L. (2004, December 13). Uncle Sam's guiding hand: Government mandates increasingly translate directly into IT initiatives, setting the top priorities at many companies. *InformationWeek*. Retrieved December 29, 2004, from http://www.informationweek.com/story/showArticle.jhtml?articleID=55301001

Grosso, B. (2004, November 15). Intelligent objects versus unhappy objects. *RFID Buzz*. Retrieved December 30, 2004, from http://www.rfidbuzz.com/news/2004/intelligent_objects_versus_unhappy_objects.html

Hardgrave, B., & Miller, R. (2006). The myths and realities of RFID. *International Journal of Global Logistics & Supply Chain Management, 1*(1). Retrieved August 6, 2006, from http://spears.okstate.edu/msis/ijglscm/articles/volume01/number01/Hardgrave-Miller%20Article%20.pdf

Harrop, P. (2006, August 23). The price-sensitivity curve for RFID. *Smart Labels Analyst*. Retrieved September 1, 2006, from http://www.idtechex.com/products/en/articles/00000488.asp

Hasson, J. (2004, September 27). The next big thing for government. *Federal Computer Week*. Retrieved December 20, 2004, from http://www.fcw.com/fcw/articles/2004/0927/news-next-thing-09-27-04.asp

Hesseldahl, A. (2004, July 29). A hacker's guide to RFID. *Forbes*. Retrieved September 11, 2004, from http://www.forbes.com/2004/07/29/cx_ah_0729rfid_print.html

Jones, J. (2005, April 3). Is the RFID chip the mark of the beast? *Political Gateway*. Retrieved April 8, 2005, from http://www.politicalgateway.com/main/columns/read.html?col=323

Kuchinskas, S. (2005, January 12). RFID tags a booming biz. *Internetnews.com*. Retrieved January 16, 2005, from http://www.internetnews.com/wireless/article.php/3458331

Maenza, T. (2005). Supply chain visibility exposes weak links, hidden costs. *Insights*. Retrieved June 6, 2005, from http://www.unisys.com/commercial/insights/insights__compendium/supply__chain__visibility__exposes__weak__links__hidden__costs.htm

Microsoft. (2006, May 15). *White paper: RFID in the retail industry*. Retrieved June 18, 2006, from http://www.microsoft.com/industry/retail/businessvalue/rfidoverview.mspx

Moore, J. (2005, April 18). RFID's positive identification. *Federal Computer Week*. Retrieved April 20, 2005, from http://www.fcw.com/article88603-04-18-05-Print

O'Connor, M. C. (2005, April 13). RFID and the media revolution: Renowned futurist Paul Saffo predicts that RFID's biggest impact will come from surprising applications. *RFID Journal*. Retrieved April 20, 2005, from http://www.rfidjournal.com/article/articleview/1508/1/1/

O'Connor, M. C. (2006a, July 28). DOD getting Gen 2-ready: The Department of Defense is expanding its RFID requirements and infrastructure while it takes steps toward transitioning its requirements to support the EPC UHF Gen 2 standard. *RFID Journal*. Retrieved December 13, 2006, from http://www.rfidjournal.com/article/articleview/2530/1/1/

O'Connor, M. C. (2006b, August 16). Will China's RFID standards support EPC protocols, systems? China has yet to release its much-anticipated RFID standards; some observers say it has produced too little, too late. *RFID Journal*. Retrieved December 1, 2006, from http://www.rfidjournal.com/article/articleview/2593/

Ricadela, A. (2005, January 24). Sensors everywhere: A "bucket brigade" of tiny, wirelessly networked sensors someday may be able to track anything, anytime, anywhere. *Information-Week*. Retrieved February 1, 2005, from http://www.informationweek.com/story/showArticle.jhtml?articleID=57702816

Rothfeder, J. (2004, August 1). What's wrong with RFID? *CIO Insight*. Retrieved September 5, 2004, from http://www.cioinsight.com/print_article/0,1406,a=133044,00.asp

Saffo, P. (2002, April 15). Smart sensors focus on the future. *CIO Insight*. Retrieved July 6, 2003, from http://www.cioinsight.com/print_article/0,3668,a=25588,00.asp

Schoenberger, C. R. (2002, March 18). RFID: The Internet of things. *Forbes*. Retrieved September 18, 2003, from http://www.mindfully.org/Technology/RFID-Things-Forbes18mar02.htm

Shepard, S. (2005). *RFID: Radio frequency identification*. New York: McGraw-Hill.

Sirico, L. (2005, February 3). Numbers that please the palate. *RFID Operations*. Retrieved February 12, 2005, from http://www.rfidoperations.com/newsandviews/20050203.html

Sullivan, L. (2005, June 20). Where's RFID going next? Supply-chain projects spurred development. Now chips are turning up in ever-more-innovative uses. *InformationWeek*. Retrieved June 21, 2005, from http://www.informationweek.

com/story/showArticle.jhtml?articleID=164900910&tid=5978

A summary of RFID standards. (2006). *RFID Journal*. Retrieved August 18, 2006, from http://www.rfidjournal.com/article/articleprint/1335/-1/1

Swedberg, C. (2006, April 19). University of Kansas' tag for metal, liquids. *RFID Journal*. Retrieved May 7, 2006, from http://www.rfidjournal.com/article/articleview/2275/1/1/

Van Osten, E. (2006). Fast forward: The past, present, and future of Metro's experimental future store. *RFID Product News*. Retrieved August 30, 2006, from http://www.rfidproductnews.com/issues/2006.07/ff.php

Wasserman, E. (2005, July 18). Agencies affirm privacy policies for RFID: A panel of government officials explained how agencies are trying to build privacy safeguards into potential U.S.-issued RFID-enabled IDs. *RFID Journal*. Retrieved September 10, 2005, from http://www.rfidjournal.com/article/articleview/1747/1/1/

Welsh, W. (2005, March 21). Growin' on empty: RFID's many uses outpace available funds. *Washington Technology*. Retrieved April 11, 2005, from http://www.washingtontechnology.com/news/20_6/statelocal/25834-1.html

Wikipedia. (2006). *Radio frequency identification*. Retrieved August 8, 2006, from http://en.wikipedia.org/wiki/RFID

Wyld, D. C. (2005). *RFID: The right frequency for government*. The IBM Center for the Business of Government. Retrieved November 1, 2005, from http://www.businessofgovernment.org/pdfs/WyldReport4.pdf

Wyld, D. C. (2006a). Better than advertised: The early results from Wal-Mart's RFID efforts are in, and the technology may be outperforming even some of the most optimistic forecasts for improving retail...And the best is yet to come. *Global Identification*, pp. 10-13.

Wyld, D. C. (2006b). Delivering at the "moment of truth" in retail: How RFID can reduce out-of-stocks and improve supply chain performance to store shelves, benefiting both retailers and product manufacturers. *Global Identification*, pp. 50-53.

Wyld, D. C. (2006c). The National Animal Identification System: Ensuring the competitiveness of the American agriculture industry in the face of mounting animal disease threats. *Competition Forum*, pp. 110-115.

Wyld, D. C. (2006d). Sports 2.0: A look at the future of sports in the context of RFID's "weird new media revolution." *The Sport Journal*. Retrieved November 4, 2006, from http://www.thesportjournal.org/2006Journal/Vol9-No4/Wyld.asp

Wyld, D. C., & Jones, M. A. (in press). RFID is no fake: The adoption of radio frequency identification technology in the pharmaceutical supply chain. *International Journal of Integrated Supply Management*.

Zappone, C. (2006, July 13). E-passports: Ready or not here they come. The state department expresses confidence in "e-passports" while technologists fret about their security risks. *CNN/Money*. Retrieved November 30, 2006, from http://money.cnn.com/2006/07/13/pf/rfid_passports/

KEY TERMS

Active Tag: An active tag is a type of RFID tag that has its own power supply (battery or external power) and, when interrogated by a reader, the tag emits its own signal. Active tags have far greater read distances than passive tags, and they can be combined with sensors to provide information on the environment and condition of the item. They are also more expensive than passive tags and, due to the battery, have a limited life span.

Automatic Identification (Auto-ID): Auto-ID is a broad term encompassing technologies used to help machines identify objects. A host of technologies fall under the automatic-identification umbrella, including bar codes, biometrics, smart cards, voice recognition, and RFID.

Electronic Product Code (EPC): An EPC is a unique number, stored in the chip on an RFID tag, that identifies an item in the supply chain, allowing for tracking of that item.

Frequency: Frequency is the number of repetitions of a complete wave within 1 second; 1Hz equals one complete waveform in 1 second, and 1KHz equals 1,000 waves in a second.

Passive Tag: A passive tag is a type of RFID tag that does not have its own power supply. Instead, the tag draws power from the reader, which sends out electromagnetic waves that induce a current in the tag's antenna. Without an onboard power source, passive tags have a lesser read range than active tags. However, they cost less than active tags and have an unlimited life span.

Radio Frequency Identification (RFID): RFID is an automatic identification technology that uses radio waves to identify objects.

Semipassive Tag: This type of tag is similar to an active tag in that there is an onboard battery, which is used to run the microchip's circuitry and boost the effective read range of the tag. It is also called a battery-assisted tag.

Smart Label: This is a printed label that contains printed information, a bar-code identifier, and an RFID tag. It is considered to be smart because of its ability to communicate with an RFID reader.

This work was previously published in Handbook of Research on Public Information Technology, edited by G. Garson; M. Khosrow-Pour, pp. 425-440, copyright 2008 by Information Science Reference, formerly known as Idea Group Reference (an imprint of IGI Global).

Compilation of References

A wearable augmented reality testbed for navigation and control, built solely with commercial-off-the-shelf (COTS) hardware. Paper presented at the Augmented Reality, 2000. (ISAR 2000). *Proceedings. IEEE and ACM International Symposium.*

Aalto, L., Göthlin, N., Korhonen, J., & Ojala, T., (2004). Bluetooth and WAP Push Based Location-Aware Mobile Advertising System. *International Conference On Mobile Systems, Applications And Services,* Proceedings of the 2nd international conference on Mobile systems, applications, and services, Boston, MA, USA, 2004 (pp 49 - 58).

ABIResearch. (2006). RFID End-User Survey. *ABIResearch.* Retrieved November 13, 2007, from http://www.abiresearch.com

Acroname Robotics. (2007). *Garcia manual.* Retrieved April 3, 2008, from http://www.acroname.com/garcia/man/man.html

Adam, S., Hari, B., Michel, G., & Nissanka, P. (2004). *Tracking moving devices with the cricket location system.* Paper presented at the Proceedings of the 2nd international conference on Mobile systems, applications, and services, Boston, MA, USA.

ADPC. (2000). Community Based Disaster Management (CBDM): Trainers Guide Module 4: Disaster Management. *Asian Disaster Preparedness Center (ADPC) Bangkok, Thailand.*

Agarwala, A., Hertzmann, A., Salesin, D., & Seitz, S. (2004). Keyframe-based tracking for rotoscoping and animation. *Proceedings of the SIGGRAPH Conference,* (pp. 584-591).

Aitoro, J. (2005, February 25). The government and RFID. *VARBusiness.* Retrieved June 8, 2005, from http://www.varbusiness.com/sections/governmentvar/govt.jhtml?articleId=60403591

Alexandra, D. (2003). Woolworths counts on RFID for security's sake. *Logistics Management, 42*(9), 61.

Alien Technology. (2005). *EPCglobal Class 1 Gen 2 RFID Specification.* Whitepaper. Morgan Hill, CA: Alien Technology Corporation.

Allen, L. G. (1991). Automatic Identification: How Do You Choose It & Where Do You Use It? *Automation, 38*(7), 30-33.

Altus, D. E., Mathews, R. M., Xaverius, P. K., Engelman, K. K., & Nolan, B. A. D. (2000). Evaluating an electronic monitoring system for people who wander. *American Journal of Alzheimer's Disease and Other Dementias, 15*(2), 121-125.

Amft, O., Stager, M., Lukowicz, P., & Troster, G., (2006) Analysis of Chewing Sounds for Dietary Monitoring. *Pervasive 2006* (pp. 56-72). Springer-Verlag Berlin Heidelberg

Ammenwerth, E., Brender, J., Nykanen, P., Prokosch, H. U., Rigby, M., & Talmon, J. (2004). Visions and strategies to improve evaluation of health information systems: Reflections and lessons based on the HS-EVAL workshop in Innsbruck. *International Journal of Medical Informatics, 73,* 479-491.

Anastasi, G., Bandelloni, R., Conti, M., Delmastro, F., Gregori, E. & Mainetto, G. (2003). Experimenting an Indoor Bluetooth-Based Positioning Service. *Distributed*

Computing Systems Workshops, 2003. Proceedings. 23rd International Conference, May 2003 (pp 480- 483).

Angeles, R. (2005). RFID technologies: Supply-chain applications and implementation issues. *Information Systems Management, 22,* 51-65.

Angeles, R. (2007). An empirical study of the anticipated consumer response to RFID product item tagging. *Industrial Management & Data Systems, 107,* 461-483.

Anonymous. (2004). Active RFID System Frequencies. Retrieved December 21, 2007, from http://www. idtechex.com

Anonymous. (2007). Automatic Identification and Data Capture Technologies - An overview. Retrieved January, 29, 2007, from http://www.aimglobal.org/technologies/aidc_overview.asp

Anonymous. (2006). Avetana OBEX-1.4. Retrieved March 2, 2006, from http://sourceforge.net/ projects/avetanaobex/

Anonymous. (1993). Bar code technology increases efficiency for off-site records storage firm. *Managing Office Technology, 38*(11), 65-67.

Anonymous. (2006). BlueCove. Retrieved March 2, 2006, from http://sourceforge.net/ projects/bluecove/

Anonymous. (2007). *Electromagnetic compatibility and Radio spectrum Matters (ERM)*: European Telecommunications Standards Institution.

Anonymous. (2007). *An Engineering Discussion Paper on Spectrum Allocations for Short Range Devices*: New Zealand Ministry of Economic Development.

Anonymous. (2007). GPS Applications Exchange. *National Aeronautics and Space Administration*. Retrieved January 19, 2008, from http://gpshome.ssc.nasa.gov/

Anonymous. (2006). How do 2D barcodes work? *Who, What, Why?* Retrieved April 20, 2008, from http://news.bbc.co.uk/

Anonymous. (2002). JavaTM APIs for BluetoothTM Wireless Technology (JSR-82). Specification Version 1.0a, JavaTM 2 Platform, Micro Edition (2002).

Anonymous. (2004). Micro tracker. *Technology Review, 107*(3), 18.

Anonymous. (2006). The official Bluetooth Web site. Retrieved January 18, 2006, from http://www. bluetooth.com/bluetooth/

Anonymous. (2003). Pushing the envelope. *Management Today*, p. 39.

Anonymous. (2004). *Radio Frequency ID*. Retrieved November 1, 2004, from wiki.lianza.org.nz

Anonymous. (2004). *RFID - Tracking every step you take*. Retrieved February 12, 2008, from www.istart.co.nz

Anonymous. (2005, March 23). RFID unites the supply chain. *Business Process Management Today*. Retrieved March 30, 2005, from http://bpm-today.newsfactor.com/scm/story.xhtml?story_title=RFID-Unites-the-Supply-Chain&story_id=31672&category=scm#story-start

Anonymous. (2003). Specification of the Bluetooth System. Wireless connections made easy, specification Volume 0, Covered Core Package version: 1.2.

Anonymous. (2007). *Tracient Technologies helps Mini Tankers NZ deliver to its customers*. Retrieved February 12, 2008, from www.istart.co.nz

Arulampalam, M. S., Maskell, S., Gordon, N., & Clapp, T. (2002). A tutorial on particle filters for online nonlinear/non-Gaussian bayesian tracking. *IEEE Transation on Signal Processing, 50*(2), 174-188.

Asif, Z., & Mandviwalla, M. (2005). Integrating the supply chain with RFID: A technical and business analysis. *Communications of the Association for Information Systems, 15,* 393-427.

Associates, K. S. (1993). *Efficient Consumer Response: Enhancing Consumer Value in the Grocery Industry*. Washington DC.

Atkinson, W. (2004). Web-Based RFID: Hype or Glimpse of the Future? *Apparel, 45*(6), 24-28.

Atmanand. (2003). Insurance and Disaster Management: The Indian Context. *Disaster Prevention and Management, 12*(4), 286-304.

Auckland District Health Board. (2002). *Proposed Strategic Plan for the Auckland District Health Board 2002-07.* Auckland.

Avidan, S. (2005). Ensemble tracking. *Proceedings of the IEEE Conference on Computer Vision and Pattern Recognition, 2,* 494 – 501.

Ayalew, G., McCarthy, U., McDonnell, K., Butler, F., McNulty, P. B., & Ward, S. M. (2006). Electronic Tracking and Tracing in Food and Feed Traceability. *LogForum, 2*(2), 1-17.

Ayoade, J. (2006). Security implications in RFID and authentication processing framework. *Computers & Security, 25,* 207-212.

Ayoade, J. (2006, May). Security implications in the RFID and Authentication Processing Framework. *Journal of Computers and Security.*

Ayoade, J., Takizawa, O., & Nakao, K. (2005). A Prototype System of the RFID Authentication Processing Framework. Keynote Speaker at IWWST 2005 3rd International Workshop in Wireless Security Technologies, London, United Kingdom.

Baader, F., Horrocks, I., & Sattler, U. (2003). Description logics as ontology languages for the semantic Web. *Lecture Notes in Artificial Intelligence.* Springer.

Bacheldor, B. (2007). *ASD Healthcare Deploys RFID Refrigerated Drug Cabinets.* Retrieved December 20, 2007, from www.rfidjournal.com

Bacheldor, B. (2007). *AT&T Debuts Managed RTLS for Health Care Organisations.* Retrieved December 20, 2007, from www.rfidjournal.com

Bacheldor, B. (2007). *Local Hospital Spearheads Mexico's Digital-Hospital Initiative.* Retrieved February 12, 2008, from www.rfidjournal.com

Bacheldor, B. (2007). *N.J. Medical Center Uses LF Tags to Protect Patient Records.* Retrieved February 12, 2008, from www.rfidjournal.com

Bacheldor, B. (2007). *RFID Documents Surgery at Huntsville Hospital.* Retrieved February 12, 2008, from www.rfidjournal.com

Bacheldor, B. (2008). *RFID Take Root in Bangladesh.* Retrieved February 12, 2008, from www.rfidjournal.com

Bacheldor, B. (2007). *UMass Med Centre Finds Big Savings Through Tagging.* Retrieved December 20, 2007, from www.rfidjournal.com

Bahl, P. & Padmanabhan, V. (2000). Radar: An in-building RF_based user location and tracking system. *INFOCOM 2000. Nineteenth Annual Joint Conference of the IEEE Computer and Communications Societies. Proceedings.* IEEE Volume 2, (pp 775-784).

Bahl, P., & Padmanabhan, V. N. (2000). *RADAR: An in-building user location and tracking system.* Paper presented at the Proceedings of the IEEE Infocom 2000.

Bandara, U., Hasegawa, M., Inoue, M., Morikawa, H., & Aoyama, T., (2004). Design and Implementation of a Bluetooth Signal Strength Based Location Sensing System. *Mobile Networking Group,* Nat. Inst. of Inf. & Commun. Technol., Yokosuka, Japan; Radio and Wireless Conference, 2004 IEEE 2004 (pp 319- 322).

Barthel, H. (2006). *Regulatory Status for Using RFID in the UHF Spectrum.* Brussels: GS1.

Bassen, H. (2002). Electromagnetic Interference of Medical Devices and Implications for Patient Safety. *International Journal of Bioelectromagnetism, 4*(2), 169-172.

Bates, D. W., Cullen, D. J., & Laird, N. (1995). Incidence of Adverse Drug Events and Potential Adverse Drug Events. *Journal of the American Medical Association, 1995*(274), 29-34.

Baw, A,. (2006). *Delivering fixed-mobile convergence (FMC) services to the enterprise.* Technology Marketing Corporation, One Technology Plaza, Norwalk.

Bechhofer, S., Möller, R., & Crowther, P. (2003). The DIG description logic interface. *Proceedings of the 16th International Workshop on Description Logics (DL'03).*

Bednarz, A. (2004). RFID joins wireless lineup at UPS. *Network World, 21*(38), 8.

Behringer, R., Behringer, R., Tam, C., McGee, J., Sundareswaran, S. A. S. S., & Vassiliou, M. A. V. M. (2000). *A wearable augmented reality testbed for navigation and control, built solely with commercial-off-the-shelf (COTS) hardware:*

Bell, S. (2004). *Kiwi firms radio in RFID progress.* Retrieved April 12, 2004, from www.computerworld.co.nz

Ben Mokhtar, S., Kaul, A., Georgantas, N., & Issarny, V. (2006). Efficient semantic service discovery in pervasive computing environments. *Proceedings of the ACM/IFIP/USENIX 7th International Middleware Conference, Middleware '06.*

Bernardi, P., Demartini, C., Gandino, F., Montrucchio, B., Rebaudengo, M., & Sanchez, E.R. (2007). Agri-food traceability management using a RFID system with privacy protection. *The 21st International Conference on Advanced Networking and Applications* (pp. 68-75).

Berners-Lee, T., Hendler, J., & Lassila, O. (2001). The semantic Web. *Scientific American, 248*(4), 34-43.

Berthon, A. (2000, July). Security in RFID. Retrieved from http://www.nepc.sanc.org.sg/html/techReport/NN327.doc.

Bhattacharyya, A. (1943). On a measure of divergence between two statistical populations defined by probability distributions. *Bulletin of the Calcutta Mathematical Society, 35,* 99–109.

Bhuptani, M., & Moradpour, S. (2005). *RFID Field Guide - Deploying Radio Frequency Identification Systems.* NJ: Prentice Hall.

Bigus, J. P., & Bigus, J. (1998). *Constructing intelligent agents with Java: A programmers guide to smarter applications.* New York: Wiley. (ISBN:0-471-19135-3)

Bigus, J. P., & Bigus, J. (1998). *Constructing intelligent software agents with Java – a programmers guide to smarter applications.* Wiley. ISBN: 0-471-19135-3.

Blau, J. (2006). RFID on all goods is 15 years away, says Metro. *Computerworld* Retrieved November 16, 2006, from http://www.computerworld.co.nz

Booth-Thomas, C. (2003). *The See-It-All Chip.*

Borgida, A. (1995). Description logics in data management. *IEEE Transactions on Knowledge and Data Engineering, 7*(5), 671-682.

Brachman, R., & Levesque, H. (1984). The tractability of subsumption in Frame-based description languages. *4th National Conference on Artificial Intelligence – AAAI-84* (pp. 34-37).

Broder, C. (2004). *Hospitals Wade into Asset-Tracking Technology.* Retrieved October 30, 2004, from www.ihealthbeat.com

Brown, I., & Russell, J. (2007). Radio frequency identification technology: An exploratory study on adoption in the South African retail sector. *International Journal of Information Management.*

Brown, S. (1997). *Revolution at the checkout counter.* Cambridge: Harvard University Press.

Buchanan, A., & Fitzgibbon, A. (2006). Interactive feature tracking using K-D trees and dynamic programming. *Proceedings of the IEEE Conference on Computer Vision and Pattern Recognition, 1,* 626 – 633.

Burger, K. A., (2007). M-Commerce Hot Spots, Part 2: Scaling Walled Gardens. E-Commerce Times. Retrieved May 9, 2008, from http://www.ecommercetimes.com/story/57161.html

Burkett, T. (1993). Bar code implementation. *Quality, 32*(3), 28.

Burrough, T.E., Desikan, R., Waterman, B.M., Gilin D, & McGill, J. Development and validation of the diabetes quality of Life brief clinical inventory. Diabetes Spectrum. 2004;17(1):41-49.

Businessweek. (2007, April 25). *Asia RFID market need gov't boost.* Retrieved from http://www.businessweek.com/globalbiz/content/apr2007/gb20070425_369568.htm?chan=search

Canadian Task Force on Preventive Health Care. (1997). *Levels of Evidence - Research Design Rating.* Retrieved October 1, 2004, from www.ctfphc.org

Carter, J. R., & Ragatz, G. L. (1991). Supplier Bar Codes: Closing the EDI Loop. *International Journal of Purchasing and Materials Management, 27*(3), 19.

Chamberlain, J., Blanchard, C., Burlingame, S., Chandramohan, S., Forestier, E., Griffith, G, et al. (2006). *IBM WebSphere RFID handbook: A solution guide,* 1ˢᵗ ed. IBM International Technical Support Organization.

Chamberlin, D., & Robie, J. (2001). An XML Query Language for Heterogeneous Data Sources. *Lecture Notes in Computer Science* (pp. 1-25).

Chamberlin, D., & Robie, J. (2001). An XML Query Language for Heterogeneous Data Sources. *Lecture Notes in Computer Science* (pp. 1-25).

Chao, H. M., Hsu, C. M., & Miaou, S. G. (2002). A Data-Hiding Technique With Authentication, Integration, and Confidentiality for Electronic Patient Records. *IEEE Transactions on Information Technology in Biomedicine, 6*(1), 46-53.

Chassin, M. R. (1998). Is healthcare ready for sigma six quality. *Milbank Quarterly, 76*(4).

Chawanthe, S., Krishnamurthy, V., Ramachandra, S., & Sarma, S. (2004). Managing RFID data, Proceedings of the VLDB. (pp. 1189-1195).

Chawanthe, S., Krishnamurthy, V., Ramachandra, S., & Sarma, S. (2004). Managing RFID data, Proceedings of the VLDB. (pp. 1189-1195).

Chen, J.L., Chen, M.C., Chen, C.W., & Chang, Y.C. (2007). Architecture design and performance evaluation of RFID object tracking systems. *Computer Communications.*

Cheng, Y. (1995). Mean Shift, Mode Seeking, and Clustering. Mean Shift, Mode Seeking, and Clustering. *IEEE Transaction on Pattern Analysis and Machine Intelligence, 17*(8), 790-799.

Choi, J. W., Oh, D. I., & Song, I. Y. (2006). R-LIM: An affordable library search system based on RFID. In *Proceedings of the International Conference on Hybrid Information Technology (ICHIT'06),* (pp. 103-108).

Chow, H.K.H., Choy, K.L., & Lee, W.B. (2007). A dynamic logistics process knowledge-based system—an RFID multi-agent approach. *Knowledge Based Systems, 20,* 357-372.

Chow, H.K.H., Choy, K.L., Lee, W.B., & Lau, K.C. (2006). Design of a RFID case-based resource management system for warehouse operations. *Expert System with Applications, 30,* 561-576.

Cisco Systems (2007). *Generating new revenue with fixed mobile convergence.* Viewed 24 September, 2007,

Clarke, R. H., Twede, D., Tazelaar, J. R., & Boyer, K. K. (2006). Radio Frequency Identification (RFID) Performance: The Effect of Tag Orientation and Package Contents. *Packaging Technology and Science, 19*(1), 45-54.

Clarke, R. H., Twede, D., Tazelaar, J. R., & Boyer, K. K. (2006). Radio Frequency Identification (RFID) Performance: The Effect of Tag Orientation and Package Contents. *Packaging Technology and Science, 19*(1), 45-54.

Classen, D. C., Pestotnik, S. L., Evans, R. S., Lloyd, J. F., & Burke, J. P. (1997). Adverse Drug Events in Hospitalized Patients: Excess Length of Stay, Extra Costs, and Attributable Mortality. *Journal of the American Medical Association, 277,* 301-306.

Collins, A., Brown, J. S., & Newman, S. E. (1989). Cognitive apprenticeship: Teaching the crafts of reading, writing, and mathematics. In L. B. Resnick (Ed.), *Knowing, learning, and instruction: Essays in honor of Robert Glaser* (pp. 453-494). Hillsdale, NJ: Lawrence Erlbaum Associates.

Collins, J. (2004). *Healthy RFID Rivalry for Hospitals.* Retrieved September 9, 2004, from www.rfidjournal.com

Collins, J. (2004). New Two-Frequency RFID System. *RFID Journal.* Retrieved April 2, 2007, from http://www.rfidjournal.com

Collins, J. (2004). Self-checkout gets RFID upgrade. *RFID Journal*, August 25, 2004 from http:/www.rfid-journal.com/ article/view/1082.

Collins, J. (2004, August 23). *Sybase initiates RFID solution.* Retrieved from *http://www.rfidjournal.com/ article/articleview/1093/1/1/*

Collins, J. (2005). Test Detect RFID-Radar Interference. Retrieved December 21, 2007, from http://www.rfidjournal.com

Colucci, S., Di Noia, T., Di Sciascio, E., Donini, F., Ragone, A., & Rizzi, R. (2006). A semantic-based fully visual application for matchmaking and query refinement in b2c e-marketplaces. *8th International conference on Electronic Commerce, ICEC 06* (pp. 174-184).

Comaniciu, D., Ramesh, V., & Meer, P. (2000). Real-time tracking of non-rigid objects using mean shift. *Proceedings of the IEEE Conference on Computer Vision and Pattern Recognition, 2,* 142-149.

Committee on Radio Frequency Identification Technologies, National Research Council. (2004). *Radio frequency identification technologies: A workshop summary.* Retrieved April 30, 2005, from http://www.nap.edu/catalog/11189.html

Connolly, C. (2007). Sensor trends in processing and packaging of food and pharmaceuticals. *Sensor Review, 27,* 103-108.

Consolvo, S., Froehlich, J., Harrison, B., Klasnaja, P., La-Marca, A., Landay, J., Legrand, L., Libby, R., McDonald, D., Smith, I., & Toscos, T. (2008). Activity Sensing in the Wild: A Field Trial of UbiFit Garden. *Proc. Of CHI 2008.* Florence, Italy

Cooper, A. (1995).The Myth of Metaphor. *Visual Basic Programmer's Journal.*

Corsten, D. & Gruen, T.W. (2004). Stock-Outs Cause Walkouts. *Harvard Business Review,* 26-28

Coursey, D., (2002), "Bluetooth vs. WiFi: Why it's NOT a death match". Retrieved February 10, 2006, from http://reviews-zdnet.com.com/4520-6033_16-4207317.html

Cover, T., & Thomas, J. (1991). *Elements of information theory.* John Wiley and Sons Inc.

Crossbow Technology, Inc. (2006). *Stargate developers guide.* Retrieved April 3, 2008, from http://www.xbow.com/Support/Support_pdf_files/Stargate_Manual.pdf

Curry, R. G., Trejo Rinoco, M., & Wardle, D. (2002). *The Use of Information and Communication Technology (ICT) to Support Independent Living for Older and Disabled People.* 2008, from http://www.rehabtool.com/forum/discussions/ictuk02.pdf

Cutter, S. L. (2003). GI Science, Disaster, and Emergency Management. *Transactions in GIS, 7*(4), 439-445.

Cyganik, K. A. (2003). Disaster preparedness in Virginia Hospital Center-Arlington after Sept 11, 2001. *Disaster Management and Response, 1*(3), 80-86.

Cyganik., K. (2003). Disaster preparedness in Virginia Hospital Center-Arlington after Sept 11, 2001. *Disaster Management and Response, 1*(3), 80-86.

d'Hont, S. (2003). *The cutting edge of RFID technology and applications for manufacturing and distribution.* Retrieved July 10, 2003, from http://www.ti.com/tiris/docs/manuals/whtPapers/manuf_dist.pdf

David, M., & David, W. (2004). *Privacy and security in library RFID: issues, practices, and architectures.* Paper presented at the Proceedings of the 11th ACM conference on Computer and communications security, Washington DC, USA.

Davis, P., Lay-Yee, R., Briant, R., Ali, W., Scott, A., & Schug, S. (2003). Adverse events in New Zealand public hospitals II: preventability and clinical context. *New Zealand Medical Journal, 116*(1183).

De, P., Basu, K., & Das, S. (2004). An ubiquitous architectural framework and protocol for object tracking using RFID tags. *The First Annual International Conference on Mobile and Ubiquitous Systems, Networking and Services, MOBIQUITOUS 2004* (pp. 174-182).

Deare, S. (2004). *Hospitals Ga-Ga Over RFID.* Retrieved October 30, 2004, from www.pcworld.idg.com.au

Department of Internal Affairs, Dog Control (Microchip Transponder) Regulations 2005, (2005).

Derakhshan, R., Orlowska, M. E., & Li, X. (2007). RFID Data Management: Challenges and Opportunities. , *IEEE International Conference, Texas, USA*, (pp. 175-182).

Derakhshan, R., Orlowska, M. E., & Li, X. (2007). RFID Data Management: Challenges and Opportunities. , *IEEE International Conference, Texas, USA*, (pp. 175-182).

Dhem, J. F., & Feyt, N. (2001). Hardware and Software Symbiosis Helps Smart Card Evolution. *IEEE Micro, 21*(6), 14-25.

DHS (2006). The use of RFID for Human Identification: A draft Report from DHS Emerging Applications and Technology Subcommittee to the Full Data Privacy and Integrity Advisory Committee, version 1.0

Di Noia, T., Di Sciascio, E., Donini, F., & Mongiello, M. (2004). A system for principled matchmaking in an electronic marketplace. *International Journal of Electronic Commerce, 8*(4), 9-37.

Diekmann, T., Melski, A. Schumann, M. (2007). Data-on-Network vs. Data-on-Tag: Mananging Data in Complex RFID Environments. *Proceedings of the 40th Hawaii International Conference on System Sciences*. IEEE

Diekmann, T., Melski, A., & Schumann, M. (2007). Data-on-Network vs. Data-on-tag: Managing Data in Complex RFID Environments. *Proceedings of the 40th Annual Hawaii International Conference on System Sciences*, (pp. 224-233).

Diekmann, T., Melski, A., & Schumann, M. (2007). Data-on-Network vs. Data-on-tag: Managing Data in Complex RFID Environments. *Proceedings of the 40th Annual Hawaii International Conference on System Sciences*, (pp. 224-233).

Dobson, T., & Todd, E. (2006). Radio frequency identification technology. *Computer Law & Security Report, 22*, 313-315.

Donini, F., Lenzerini, M., Nardi, D., & Schaerf, A. (1996). Reasoning in description logics. In: G. Brewka (Ed.), *Principles of knowledge representation: Studies in logic, language and information* (pp. 191-236). CSLI Publications.

Doughty, K., Lewis, R., & McIntosh, A. (2000). The design of a practical and reliable fall detector for community and institutional telecare. *Journal of Telemedicine and Telecare, 6*(Supp. 1), S150-154.

Drucker, P. (1989). *The New Realities*. New York: Harper & Row.

Easton, B. (2002). The New Zealand health reforms of the 1990s in context. *Applied Health Economics and Health Policy, 1*(2), 107-112.

Edwards, J. (2008). RFID Is a Winner in the Sports Arena. *RFID Journal*. Retrieved April 26, 2008, from http://www.rfidjournal.com

Eeden, H. v. (2004). Europe Needs New RFID Regulations. *RFID Journal* Retrieved December 21, 2007, from http://www.rfidjournal.com

Ekman, S. (1992). Bar Coding Fixed Asset Inventories. *Management Accounting, 74*(6), 58.

Engelbrecht, J., Hunter, I., & Whiddet, R. (2007). Further Evidence of How Technology Availability Doesn't Guarantee Usage. *Health Care and Informatics Review.*

Engels, D. W., & Sarma, S. E. (2005). *Standardization Requirements within the RFID Class Structure Framework*. MA: Auto-ID Labs.

England, I., Stewart, D., & Walker, S. (2000). Information technology adoption in health care: when organisations and technology collide. *Australian Health Review, 23*(3), 176-185.

EPCglobal (2005). EPCTM Radio-Frequency Identity protocols Class-1 Generation-2 UHF RFID Protocol for Communications at 860 MHz - 960 MHz. Version 1.0.9.

EPCGlobal (2007). *EPC Standards Overview*. Retrieved November 23, 2007, from http://www.epcglobalinc.org/standards.

EPCglobal Inc. (2005a). *EPC Radio-Frequency Identity Protocols Class-1 Generation-2 UHF RFID Protocol for Communications at 860 MHz-960 MHz*. January 2005.

EPCglobal Inc. (2005b). *Object Naming Service (ONS - ver. 1.0)*. October 2005.

Estevez, A. F. (2005). RFID vision in the DOD supply chain. *Army Logistician*. Retrieved May 7, 2005, from http://www.almc.army.mil/alog/rfid.html

Evans, N.D. (2004, June 28). *Planning for RFID data*. Retrieved from *http://www.rfidjournal.com/article/articleview/1004/1/82/*

Evers, J., & McCullagh, D. (2006, August 5). Researchers: E-passports pose security risk. *CNET*. Retrieved August 17, 2006, from http://news.com.com/Researchers+E-passports+pose+security+risk/2100-7349_3-6102608.html?tag=st.ref.goo

Finkenzeller, K. (1999). *RFID handbook*. John Wiley and Sons Ltd.

Finkenzeller, K. (2003). *RFID Handbook - Fundamentals and Applications in Contactless Smart Cards and Identification* (2nd ed.). Chichester: Wiley.

Fixed Mobile Convergence Conference (FMCC), 2007.

Fleisch, E. (2001). *Business Perspectives on Ubiquitous Computing* (M-Lab Working Paper No. 4). St Gallen: University of St Gallen.

Floerkemeier, C., & Lampe, M. (2004). Issues with RFID usage in Ubiquitous Computing Applications. *Pervasive Computing: Second International Conference.*

Floerkemeier, C., & Lampe, M. (2004). Issues with RFID usage in Ubiquitous Computing Applications. *Pervasive Computing: Second International Conference.*

Folinas, D. (2006). Traceability data management for food chains. *British Food Journal, 108*, 622-633.

Fry, E. A., & Lenert, L. A. (2005). MASCAL: RFID Tracking of Patients, Staff and Equipment to Enhance Hospital Response to Mass Casualty Events.

Gadh, R. (2004, August 11). The state of RFID. *Computerworld*. Retrieved August 30, 2004, from http://www.computerworld.com/mobiletopics/mobile/story/0,10801,95179,00.html

Gandino, F., Montrucchio, B., Rebaudengo, M., & Sanchez, E.R. (2007). Analysis of an RFID-based Information System for Tracking and Tracing in an Agri-Food Chain. *The 1st Annual RFID Eurasia Conference.*

Garskof, J. (2004). The Many Faces Of RFID Tech: Luggage, cellphones, casino chips. The "smart tag" is starting to live up to its potential.(Headlines/Trends; radio frequency identification). . *Popular science.*

Gavin, C., David, D., Greg, G., Lyle, G., Jeff, S., & Joseph, T. (2003). *Auto-ID in the Box: The Value of Auto-ID Technology in Retail Stores*. Cambridge, USA: Massachusetts Institute of Technology.

Gibson, B. J., Mentzer, J. T., & Cook, R. L. (2005). Supply chain management: the pursuit of a consensus definition. *Journal of Business Logistics, 26*(2), 17-25.

Gibson, J. F., Bilderbeek, P. & Vestergaard L. (2005). *Fixed-Mobile Convergence: Unifying the communications experience*, An IDC Whitepaper, pp. 1-43.

Gillespie, L. G., Robertson, M. C., Lamb, S. E., Cumming, R. G., & Rowe, B. H. (2006). *Interventions for preventing falls in elderly people*. (Publication. Retrieved 31st January 2007, from Cochrane Database of Systematic Reviews.

Glover, B., & Bhatt, H. (2006). *RFID essentials*. O'Railly Media Inc. (ISBN:0-596-0094-4)

Glover, B., & Bhatt, H. (2006). *RFID essentials*. O'Reilly Media, Inc. ISBN: 10-0596009445.

Golan, E., Krissoff, B., Kuchler, F., Nelson, K., Price, G. & Calvin, L. (2003). Traceability in the US Food Supply: Dead End or Superhighway? *Choices, 18*(2), 17-20.

Goodhue, D. L., & Thompson, R. L. (1995). Task-Technology Fit and Individual Performance. *MIS Quarterly,, 19*(2), 213-236.

Goodman, B. (2005, March 17). Is RFID taking off, or just taking its time? *Integrating the Enterprise*. Retrieved March 24, 2005, from http://www.itbusinessedge.com/content/3Q/3qpub2-20050317.aspx

Goyal, K., & Krishna, D. (2005). *RFID middleware—integration to the entire supply chain.* RFID Journal White Paper.

Grabner, H., & Bischof, H. (2006). On-line boosting and vision. *Proceedings of the IEEE Conference on Computer Vision and Pattern Recognition, 1*, 260 - 267.

Grasso, J. (2004). The EPCglobal Network. *EPCglobal* Retrieved December 21, 2007, from http://www.epcglobalus.org

Gray, J. (2004). The Next database Revolution SIGMOD, Paris, France. (pp. 1-4).

Gray, J. (2004). The Next database Revolution SIGMOD, Paris, France. (pp. 1-4).

Greco, P. J., & Eisenberg, J. M. (1993). Changing physicians practices. *New England Journal of Medicine, 329*, 1271-1274.

Greengard, S. (2004). *A Healthy Dose of RFID.* Retrieved September 8, 2004, from www.rfidjournal.com

Grimley, D., Prochaska, J.O., Velicer, W.F., Vlais, L.M., & DiClemente, C.C., (1994). The transtheoretical model of change. In T.M. Brinthaupt & R.P. Lipka, *Changing the self: Philosophies, techniques, and experiences. SUNY series, studying the self* (p. 201 – 227). Albany, NY: State University of New York Press

Gruber, T.R. (1993). A translation approach to portable ontology specifications. *Knowledge Acquisition, 5*, 199-220.

Guarino, N., Carrara, M., & Giaretta, P. (1994). An ontology of meta-level categories. Journal of knowledge representation and reasoning. In *Proceedings of the Fourth International Conference (KR94)*, Morgan Kaufmann, San Mateo, CA.

Gunes, A. E., & Kovel, J. B. (2000). Using GIS in Emergency Management Operations. *Urban Plng. and Devel, 126*(3), 136-149

Haartsen, J., & Zürbes, S. (1999). *Bluetooth voice and data performance in 802.11 DS WLAN environment.* Ericsson Sig Publication.

Haas, L. M., & Miller, R. J. (1997). Transforming Heterogeneous Data with Database middleware: Beyond Integration. *Bulletin of the IEEE Computer Society Technical Committee on Data engineering.*

Haas, L. M., & Miller, R. J. (1997). Transforming Heterogeneous Data with Database middleware: Beyond Integration. *Bulletin of the IEEE Computer Society Technical Committee on Data engineering.*

Hallberg, J., Nilsson, M. & Synnes, K. (2003). Positioning with Bluetooth. *Telecommunications, 2003. ICT 2003. 10th International Conference. March 2003,* Volume 2, (pp 954- 958).

Hamming, R. (1986). *Coding and information theory.* Prentice Hall.

Hardgrave, B. C., Armstrong, D. J., & Riemenschneider, C. K. (2007). RFID Assimilations hierarchy. *Proceedings of the 40th Hawaii International conference on System Sciences,* (pp. 1-10).

Hardgrave, B. C., Armstrong, D. J., & Riemenschneider, C. K. (2007). RFID Assimilations hierarchy. *Proceedings of the 40th Hawaii International conference on System Sciences,* (pp. 1-10).

Hardgrave, B.C., Waller, M., Miller, R. (2005). *Does RFID Reduce Out of Stocks? A Preliminary Analysis.* Tech. report, Information Technology Research Center, University of Arkansas.

Harrell R. (2007). *Fixed Mobile Convergence: Understanding the Landscape,* 2007

Harrison, M. (2003). EPC Information Service - Data Model and Queries. *White Paper, Auto-d Centre Institute for Manufacturing, University of Cambridge, United Kingdom.,* (pp. 1-20).

Harrison, M. (2003). EPC Information Service - Data Model and Queries. *White Paper, Auto-d Centre Institute for Manufacturing, University of Cambridge, United Kingdom.,* (pp. 1-20).

Harrison, M., McFarlane, D., Parlikad, A.K., & Wong, C.Y. (2005). *Information management in the product lifecycle—the role of networked RFID.* Auto-ID Center White Paper.

Health Information Strategy Action Committee. (2007, 30th January 2007). *Action Zone 7 - Chronic Care and Disease Management: An Initial View*. Retrieved 1st July 2007, 2007, from http://www.moh.govt.nz/moh.nsf/pagescm/532

Health Information Strategy Steering Committee. (2005). *Health Information Strategy for New Zealand 2005*. Wellington: Ministry of Health.

Hedgepeth, W. O. (2007). *RFID metrics: Decision making tools for today's supply chains*. Boca Raton, FL: CRC Press. ISBN: 9780849379796.

Hedquist, U. (2007). *Orion Health teams with Oracle and Intel in Spain*. Retrieved February 12, 2008, from www.computerworld.co.nz

Heeks, R., Mundy, D., & Salazar, A. (1999). Why Health Care Information Systems Succeed or Fail. In A. Armoni (Ed.), *Health Care Information Systems: Challenges of the Next Millenium*: Idea Group Publishing.

Heinen, M. G., Coyle, G. A., & Hamilton, A. V. (2003). Barcoding makes its mark on daily practice. *Nursing Management, Oct 2003*, 18-20.

Helal, S., Mann, W. H., King, J., Kaddoura, Y., & Jansen, E. (2005). The Gator Tech Smart House: a programmable pervasive space. *Computer, 38*(3), 50-60.

Herper, M. (2004). *Tiny Chips Could Combat Counterfeit Pills*. Retrieved August 1, 2004, from www.forbes.com

Hevner, A. R. (2004). Design Sciences in Information Systems Research. *MIS Quarterly*, (pp. 1-49).

Hevner, A. R. (2004). Design Sciences in Information Systems Research. *MIS Quarterly*, (pp. 1-49).

Hevner, A.R., Salvatore, T.M. Park, J. & Ram, S. (2004). Design Science in Information Systems Research. *MIS Quarterly 28*(1), 75-105.

Hightower, J., Vakili, C., Borriello, C. & Want, R. (2001). Design and Calibration of the SpotON AD-Hoc Location Sensing System. University of Washington, Department of Computer Science and Engineering, Seattle. Retrieved January 19, 2008, from http://www.cs.washington.edu/homes/jeffro/pubs/hightower2001design/hightower2001design.pdf

Hightower, J., Vakili, C., Borriello, G., & Want, R. (2001). Design and Calibration of the SpotON Ad-Hoc Location Sensing System. *University of Washington* Retrieved April 26, 2008, from http://seattle.intel-research.net/people/jhightower//pubs/hightower2001design/hightower2001design.pdf

Hills, D. & Mercouroff, N. (2005). *Using Fixed/Mobile Convergence to Competitive Advantage*. Retrieved from http://www1.alcatel-lucent.com/com/en/appcontent/apl/T0512-FMC-EN_tcm172-521331635.pdf

Holbrook, P. R. L. D. R. G. B. S., Born, J. Hurtado, R. E., & Buczkiewicz, R. T. (2004). USA Patent No. 6,674,364.

Honey, M., Øyri, K., Newbold, S., Coenen, A., Park, H., Ensio, A., et al. (2007). *Effecting change by the use of emerging technologies in healthcare: A future vision for u-nursing in 2020*. Paper presented at the Health Informatics New Zealand (HINZ), 6th Annual Forum., Rotorua.

Horrocks, I., van Harmelen, F., Patel-Schneider, P., Berners-Lee, T., Brickley, D. (2001). *DAML+OIL specifications*. Retrieved May 01, 2007 from http://www.daml.org/2001/03/daml+oil-index.html.

Hou, J.L., & Huang, C.H. (2006). Quantitative performance evaluation of RFID applications in the supply chain of the printing industry. *Industrial Management & Data Systems, 106*, 96-120.

Houliston, B. (2005). *Integrating RFID Technology into a Drug Administration System*. Paper presented at the Health Informatics NZ Conference, Auckland, New Zealand.

Huang, E. M. and Mynatt, E. D. (2003). Semi-public displays for small, co-located groups. In *Proceedings of the ACM Conference on Human Factors in Computing Systems, CHI 2003* (pp. 49-56).

Huang, G.Q., Zhang, Y.F., & Jiang, P.Y. (2007). RFID-based wireless manufacturing for walking-worker assembly islands with fixed-position layouts. *Robotics and Computer-Integrated Manufacturing, 23,* 469-477.

Huffman, D. (1952). A method for the construction of Minimum Redundancy Codes. *IRE,* 1098-1101.

Iacovou, I. C., Benbasat, I., & Dexter, A. S. (1995). Electronic Data Interchange and Small Organizations. *MISQ, 19*(4).

IDTechEx. (2005, April 10). *RFID market to reach $7.26Bn in 2008.* Retrieved April 18, 2005, from http://www.idtechex.com/products/en/articles/00000169.asp

Institute of Medicine. (2001). *Crossing the Quality Chasm: A New Health System for the 21st Century.* Washington DC: National Academies Press.

Intel OpenCV library. http://www.sourceforge.net/projects/ opencvlibrary.

Intille, S. S. (2003). Ubiquitous Computing Technology for Just-in-Time Motivation of Behavior Change (Position Paper). In *Proceedings of the UbiHealth Workshop' 2003.*

Isard, M., & Blake, A. (1998). CONDENSATION--conditional density propagation for visual tracking. *International Journal of Computer Vision, 28*(1):5-28.

Jackson, G., & Rea, H. (2007). Future hospital trends in New Zealand. *The New Zealand Medical Journal, 120*(1264).

Janz, B.D., Pitts, M.G., & Otondo, R.F. (2005). Information systems and health care II: Back to the future with RFID: Lessons learned—some old, some new. *Communications of the Association for Information Systems, 15,* 132-148.

Japsen, B. (2008, 2 January 2008). *Technology cuts risk of surgical sponges.* Retrieved February 12, 2008, from www.chicagotribune.com

Jilovec, N. (2004). *EDI, UCCnet & RFID - Synchronizing the Supply Chain.* Colorado: 29th Street Press.

Johnson, J. A., & Bootman, J. L. (1995). Drug-related Morbidity and Mortality: A Cost of Illness Model. *Archives of Internal Medicine, 155,* 1949-1956.

Johnston, M. (2007). Wired for saving lives. *Weekend Herald, August 25,* p. B4.

Jones, A. K., Dontharaju, S., Tung, S., Hawrylak, P. J., Mats, L., Hoare, R., et al. (2006). Passive active radio frequency identification tags. *International journal of Radio Frequency Technology and Applications, 1*(1), 52-73.

Jones, J. (2005, April 3). Is the RFID chip the mark of the beast? *Political Gateway.* Retrieved April 8, 2005, from http://www.politicalgateway.com/main/columns/read.html?col=323

Jones, P., Clarke-Hill, C., Comfort, D., Hillier, D., & Shears, P. (2005). Radio frequency identification and food retailing in the UK. *British Food Journal, 107,* 356-360.

Jones, P., Clarke-Hill, C., Hillier, D., Shears, P., & Comfort, D. (2004). Radio frequency identification in retailing and privacy and public policy issues. *Management Research News, 27,* 46-56.

Jonietz, E. (2004). *Making Medicine Modern.* Retrieved August 1, 2004, from www.technologyreview.com

Jonker, C., Geerlings, M. I., & Schmand, B. (2000). Are memory complaints predictive for dementia? A review of clinical and population-based studies. *International Journal of Geriatric Psychiatry, 15*(11), 983-991.

Joseph, M. H. (2003). Toward network data independence. *SIGMOD Rec., 32*(3), 34-40.

Joseph, M. H. (2003). Toward network data independence. *SIGMOD Rec., 32*(3), 34-40.

Juels A. (2004) *Minimalist Cryptograhy for Low-Cost RFID tags.* The Fourth International Conference on Security, Colombia.rsa.com

Juels A., Rivest R.L. & Szydlo M. (2003). *The Blocker Tag: Selective Blocking of RFID Tags for Consumer Privacy.* CCS'03, Washington, DC, USA, October 27-31]

Juels, A., Rivest, R. L., & Szydlo, M. (2003). *The Blocker Tag: Selective Blocking of RFID Tags for Consumer Privacy*. Paper presented at the Tenth International Conference on Computer and Communication Security, Washington, DC.

Kanters, R.H.L. (2007). *Data management risks of radio frequency identification (RFID)*. Unpublished Masters Thesis, Tiburg University, The Netherlands.

Kaptelinin, V. (1992). Human computer interaction in context: The activity theory perspective. In *Proceedings of the East-West Human Computer Interaction Conference*, St. Petersburg, Russia.

Kärkkäinen, M. (2003). Increasing efficiency in the supply chain for short shelf life goods using RFID tagging. *International Journal of Retail & Distribution Management, 10*(31), 529-536.

Kasturi, R. (2005). *Tapping the RFID data flood*. Retrieved from *http://www.intelligententerprise.com/showArticle.jhtml?articleID=163100818*

Katz, J. (2006). Bar Codes: Alive and Well. *Industry Week, 255*(7), 14.

Kawakita, Y., & Mistugi, J. (2006). Anti-collision performance of Gen2 Air Protocol in Random Error Communication Link. *International Symposium on Applications and the Internet Workshops, SAINTW'06* (pp. 68-71).

Kawakita, Y., Wakayama, S., Hada, H., Nakamura, O., & Murai, J. (2004). Rendezvous enhancement for conference support system based on RFID. *International Symposium on Applications and the Internet Workshops, SAINT2004* (pp. 280-286).

Kearney, A. (2004). RFID/EPC: Managing the Transition (2004-2007).

Kelepouris, T. (2007). RFID-enabled traceability in the food supply chain. *Industrial Management & Data Systems, 107*, 183-200.

Kelley, D. (2001). Authentication as the Foundation for eBusiness *Security Focus*.

Kelly, C. (1999). Simplifying disasters: developing a model for complex non-linear events *Australian Journal of Emergency Management, 14*(1), 25-27.

Kempfer, L.M. (2007). A dollop of RFID. *Material Handling Management, 62*, 40-41.

Kim, K. K., & Michelman, J. E. (1990). An Examination of Factors for the Strategic Use of Information Systems in the Healthcare Industry. *MIS Quarterly, 14*(2), 201-215.

Kleiner, A., Prediger, J., & Nebel, B. (2006). RFID Technology-based Exploration and SLAM for Search and Rescue.

Kleist, R.A., Chapman, T.A., Sakai, D.A., & Jarvis, B.S. (2004). *RFID labeling: Smart labeling concepts & applications for the consumer packaged goods supply chain*. Printronix.

Kondratova, I. (2003). *Voice and multimodal access to AEC project information*. Paper presented at the The 10th ISPE International Conference on Concurrent Engineering: The Vision for Future Generations in Research and Applications, Portugal.

Kotanen, A., Hännikäinen, M., Leppäkoski, H. & Hämäläinen T. (2003). Experiments on Local Positioning with Bluetooth. *Information Technology: Coding and Computing [Computers and Communications], 2003. Proceedings. ITCC 2003. International Conference.*

Kranendonk, A. & Rackebrandt, S. (2002). *Optimising availability - getting products on the shelf!* Official ECR Europe Conference, Barcelona.

Lacharite, R. (1991). Rethinking Bar Coding: Turning Preconceptions into System Tools. *ARMA Records Management Quarterly, 25*(2), 3.

Lacy, S. (2005). RFID: Plenty of Mixed Signals. *BusinessWeek Online, January 31, 2005*.

Lahiri, H. (2005). *RFID sourcebook*. New York: IBM Press. (ISBN:0-131-8513-73)

Lahiri, S. (2005). *RFID sourcebook*. IBM Press. ISBN: 10-0131851373.

Lakoff, G., Johnson, M. (1981). *Metaphors We Live By*. Chicago: The University of Chicago Press.

Landt, J. (2001). *Shrouds of time*. Retrieved August 1, 2003, from http://www.aimglobal.org/technologies/rfid/resources/shrouds_of_time.pdf

Landt, J. (2001). Shrouds of Time. *The history of RFID* Retrieved 19 January, 2006, from http://www.aimglobal.org/technologies/rfid/resources/shrouds_of_time.pdf

Landt, J. (2005). The History of RFID. *Potentials, IEEE, 24*(4), 8- 11.

Lau, L. (2003). *Pen Based Computers in Health Care*. Unitec New Zealand, Auckland.

Lave, J. & Wenger, E. (1991). *Situated Learning: Legitimate Peripheral Participation*. New York: Cambridge University Press

Lazar, L. D., & Moss, H. K. (2005). *Radio Frequency Identification Technology: An Introduction*. Paper presented at the Proceedings of the 2005 Southern Association for Information Systems Conference, Savannah.

Leape, T., Bates, D. W., & Cullen, D. J. (1995). Systems Analysis of Adverse Drug Events. *Journal of the American Medical Association, 274*, 35-43.

Lee, Y.M., Cheng, F., & Leung, Y.T. (2004). Exploring the impact of RFID on supply chain dynamics. *Proceedings of the 2004 Winter Simulation Conference*.

Lefebvre, L.A., Lefebvre, E., Bendavid, Y., Wamba, S.F., & Boeck, H. (2006). RFID as an Enabler of B-to-B e-Commerce and its Impact on Business Processes: A Pilot Study on a Supply Chain in the Retail Industry. *The 39th Annual Hawaii International Conference on System Sciences*. 6, 104a-104a.

Levantis, T. & Gani, A. *Tourism Demand and the Nuisance of Crime*. Retrieved from http://www.emeraldinsight.com/Insight/ViewContentServlet?Filename=/published/emeraldfulltextarticle/pdf/0060270718.pdf#search=%22crime%20deterrent%20in%20the%20south%20pacific%20region%22

Li, S., Visich, F.K., Khumawala, B.M., & Zhang, C. (2006). Radio frequency identification technology: Applications, technical challenges and strategies. *Sensor Review, 26,* 193-202.

Li, S., Visich, J. K., Khumawala, B. M., & Zhang, C. (2006). Radio frequency identification technology: applications, technical challenges and strategies. *Sensor Review, 26*(3).

Liefke, H., & Suciu D. (2000). XMill: An efficient compressor for XML data. *SIGMOD Rec., 29*(2), 153-164.

Lin, D., Elmongui, H. G., Bertino, E., & Ooi, B. C. (2007). Data Management in RFID Applications. *DEXA,* (pp. 434-444).

Lin, D., Elmongui, H. G., Bertino, E., & Ooi, B. C. (2007). Data Management in RFID Applications. *DEXA,* (pp. 434-444).

Lin, J., Mamykina, L., Delajoux, G., Lindtner, S., & Strub, H. (2006). Fish'n'Steps: Encouraging Physical Activity with an Interactive Computer Game, UbiComp'06, Springer-Verlag Berlin Heidelberg

Lin, K., & Lin, C. (2007). Evaluating the decision to adopt RFID systems using analytic hierarchy process. *Journal of American Academy of Business, 11,* 72-78.

Lin, P.P., & Brown, K.F. (2006). Radio frequency identification and how to capitalize on it. *The CPA Journal, 76,* 34-37.

Lionel, M. N., Yunhao, L., Yiu Cho, L., & Abhishek, P. P. (2004). LANDMARC: indoor location sensing using active RFID. *Wirel. Netw., 10*(6), 701-710.

Lipowicz, A. (2006, January 19). Group objects to driver's license RFID. *Washington Technology*. Retrieved April 17, 2006, from http://www.washingtontechnology.com/news/1_1/daily_news/27794-1.html

Littlejohns, P., Wyatt, J. C., & Garvican, L. (2003). Evaluating computerised health information systems: hard lessons still to be learnt. *British Medical Journal, 326,* 860-863.

Loebbecke, C., (2005). RFID Technology and Applications in the Retail Supply Chain: The Early Metro Group Pilot. *The 18th Bled eConference eIntegration in Action.*

Loftus, R., (2005). Traceability of biotech-derived animals: application of DNA technology. *Scientific and Technical Review The Office International des Epizooties, 2005, 24*(1), 231-242.

Love, J., Mariam, & Vogel, C. (1998). White Paper on Disaster Management. *Journal.* Retrieved from http://www.local.gov.za/DCD/policydocs/wpdm/wpdm_app.html

Mahmoud, Q., (2003), Wireless Application Programming with J2ME and Bluetooth. Retrieved February 11, 2006, from http://developers.sun.com/techtopics/mobility/midp/articles/ bluetooth1/

Mahoney, M. (2005). *Adaptive weighing of context models for lossless data compression.* Florida Tech. Technical Report, CS-2005-16.

Malkary, G. (2005). *Healthcare without Bounds: Trends in RFID.* Menlo Park, CA: Spyglass Consulting Group.

Malone, R. (2004). Reconsidering the role of RFID. *Inbound Logistics.* Retrieved September 11, 2004, from http://www.inboundlogistics.com/articles/supplychain/sct0804.shtml

Mamei, M., & Zambonelli, F. (2005). Spreading pheromones in everyday environments through RFID technology. In *Proceedings of the 2nd IEEE Symposium on Swarm Intelligence, (pp. 281-288).* IEEE Press.

Mamykina, L., Mynatt E.D., & Kaufman, D. (2006) Investigating Health Management Practices of Individuals with Diabetes. In Nielsen-Bohlman et al (Eds.), *Proceedings of the ACM SIGCHI conference on Human factors in computing systems, CHI'06*, Montreal, Canada/

Mamykina, L., Mynatt, E.D., Davidson, P.R., & Greenblatt D. (2008). MAHI: Investigation of Social Scaffolding for Reflective Thinking in Diabetes Management. In *Proceedings of ACM SIGCHI Conference on Human Factors in Computing, CHI 2008.*

Man, M. (2007). All About 2D Bar Codes. *Socket Communications Technology Brief.* Retrieved April 20, 2008, from http://www.socketmobile.com

Manitoba-Health-Disaster-Management. (2002). Disaster Management Model for the Health Sector: Guideline for Program Development.

Marcial, G.G. (2007, May 28). *VeriChip is I.D.'d as a winner.* Retrieved from *http://www.businessweek.com/magazine/content/07_22/b4036093.htm?chan=search*

Martin, D., Burstein, M., Hobbs, J., Lassila, O., McDermott, D. (n.d.). *OWL-S: Semantic markup for Web services.* Retrieved May 01, 2007 from http://www.daml.org/services/owl-s/1.1/overview/.

Mason, B. (2005). *Bar Code Scanner Demand Remains Strong* (Press Release). Massachusetts: Venture Development Corporation.

Massload. (2007). RFID-Brochure. Retrieved March 30, 2007, from http://www.massload.com/Brochure-RFID.pdf

Mathie, A. Z. (1997). Doctors and change. *Journal of Management in Medicine, 11*(6), 342-356.

Matsuo, Y., Hamasaki, M., Takeda, H., Mori, J., Bollegala, D., Nakamura, Y., et al. (2006). *Spinning Multiple Social Networks for Semantic Web.* Paper presented at the Association for the Advancement of Artificial Intelligence, Boston.

May, C., Harrison, R., Finch, T., MacFarlane, A., Mair, F., Wallace, P., et al. (2003). Understanding the normalization of telemedicine services through qualitative evaluation. *Journal of the American Medical Informatics Association, 10*(6), 596-604.

May, E. L. (2003). The case for bar coding: Better information, better care and better business. *Healthcare Executive, 18*(5), 8-13.

Mayer, K. N. (1993). Total Contingency Planning for Disasters: Managing Risk, Minimizing Loss, Ensuring Business Continuity.

McGinity, M. (2000). RFID: Not Your Father's Bar Code. *IEEE Distributed Systems Online.*

McGuinness, D., Fikes, R., Hendler, J., & Stein, L. (2002). DAML+OIL: An ontology language for the semantic Web. *IEEE Intelligent Systems, 17*(5), 72-80.

McMeekin, T.A., Baranyi, J., Bowman, J., Dalgaard, P., Kirk, M., Ross, T., Schmid, S., & Zwietering, M.H. (2006). Information systems in food safety management. *International Journal of Food Microbiology, 112,* 181-194.

McPherson, K., Parry, D., & Symonds, J. (2007, 4th December 2007). *Radio Frequency Identification (RFID) for Assisted Living: Testing the Aura Object Location (AOL) Model.* Paper presented at the 18th Australasian Conference on Information Systems, Toowoomba, Queensland, Australia.

Meissner, A., Luckenbach, T., Risse, T., Kirste, T., & Kirchner, H. (2002). Design Challenges for an Integrated Disaster Management Communication and Information System. *The First IEEE Workshop on Disaster Recovery Networks (DIREN 2002).*

Melski, A., Thoroe, L., Caus, T., & Schumann, M. (2007). Beyond EPC – Insights from Multiple RFID Case Studies on the storage of Additional Data on Tag. *International Conference on wireless Algorithms, Systems and Applications,* (pp. 281- 286).

Melski, A., Thoroe, L., Caus, T., & Schumann, M. (2007). Beyond EPC – Insights from Multiple RFID Case Studies on the storage of Additional Data on Tag. *International Conference on wireless Algorithms, Systems and Applications,* (pp. 281- 286).

Merry, A., & Webster, C. (2004). Bar Codes and the Reduction of Drug Administration Error in Anesthesia. *Seminars in Anesthesia, Perioperative Medicine and Pain, 23,* 260-270.

Merry, A., Webster, C., Weller, J., Henderson, S., & Robinson, B. (2002). Evaluation in an anaesthetic simulator of a prototype of a new drug administration system designed to reduce error. *Anaesthesia, 57,* 256-263.

Meyera, H. J., Chansueb, N., & Monticellia, F. (2005). Implantation of Radio Frequency Identification Device (RFID) Microchip in Disaster Victim Identification (DVI). *Forensic Science International, 157*(2-3).

Michael, K., & McCathie, L. (2005). The Pros and Cons of RFID in Supply Chain Management. *Mobile Business, 2005. ICMB 2005. International Conference.*

Michahelles, F., Matter, P., Schmidt, A., & Schiele, B. (2003). Applying wearable sensors to avalanche rescue. *Computers and Graphics, 27*(6), 839-847(839).

Mihailidis, A., Carmichael, B., & Boger, J. (2004). The use of computer vision in an intelligent environment to support aging-in-place, safety, and independence in the home. *IEEE Transactions on Information Technology in Biomedicine, 8*(3), 238-247.

Ministry of Economic Development. (2007). *SMEs in New Zealand: Structure and Dynamics.* Wellington: Ministry of Economic Development.

Ministry of Health (2008a). Every Day in New Zealand: DVD. Wellington: Ministry of Health.

Ministry of Health. (2003a). *Guidelines for Capital Investment.* Wellington: Ministry of Health.

Ministry of Health. (2003b). *New Zealand Health and Disability Sector Overview.* Wellington: Ministry of Health.

Ministry of Health. (2006). A Day in the Life statistics. In DayInTheLife.xls (Ed.). Wellington, New Zealand.

Ministry of Health. (2007). *Health Expenditure Trends in New Zealand 1994-2004.* Wellington: Ministry of Health.

Ministry of Health. (2008b). *Statement of Intent 2008-11.* Retrieved September 26, 2008, from www.moh.govt.nz

Molnar, D., & Wagner, D. (2004). *Privacy and security in library RFID: Issues, practices, and architectures.* New York: ACM Press.

Morrissey, J. (2003). An info-tech disconnect. *Modern Healthcare, 33,* 6.

Morrissey, J. (2004). Capital crunch eats away at IT. *Modern Healthcare, 34*, 32.

Mullen, D., & Moore, B. (2005). Automatic Identification and Data Collection: What the future holds. In S. Garfinkel & B. Rosenberg (Eds.), *RFID Applications, Security, and Privacy* (pp. 3-13). NJ: Addison-Wesley.

Mustapha, I. M. S. F.-r. A. S. a. (2003). Technological disaster's criteria and models. *Disaster Prevention and Management, 12*(4), 305-311.

Mynatt, E. D., Rowan, J., Craighill, S., & Jacobs, A. (2001). Digital family portraits: supporting peace of mind for extended family members. In *Proceedings of the SIGCHI Conference on Human Factors in Computing Systems* (pp. 333-340). Seattle, Washington, United States.

Nethercote, N., & Seward J. (2007). Valgrind: A framework for heavyweight dynamic binary instrumentation. *Conference on Programming Language Design and Implementation - PLDI 07*. ACM SIGPLAN.

New Zealand Veterinary Association. (2002). *Annual Report*. Retrieved November 1, 2004, from www.vets. org.nz

Ngai, E.W.T., Cheng, T.C.E., Au, S., & Lai, K. (2007). Mobile commerce integrated with RFID technology in a container depot. *Decision Support Systems, 43*, 62-76.

Nguyen, H. T., Ji, Q., & Smeulders, A. W. M. (2006). Robust multi-target tracking using spatio-temporal context. *Proceedings of the IEEE Conference on Computer Vision and Pattern Recognition, 1*, 578 - 585.

Nguyen, T. (2007). A Data Model for EPC Information Services. *18th Data Engineering Workshop, Japan*, (pp. 1-8).

Nguyen, T. (2007). A Data Model for EPC Information Services. *18th Data Engineering Workshop, Japan*, (pp. 1-8).

Ni, L. M., Liu, Y. H., Lau, Y. C., & Patil, A. P. (2004). LANDMARC: Indoor Location Sensing Using Active RFID. *Wireless Networks, 10*, 701-710.

Ni, L. M., Liu, Y., & al, e. (2004). LANDMARC: Indoor Location Sensing Using Active RFID. *Wireless Networks, 10*, 701-710.

Ni, L. M., Liu, Y., & al, e. (2004). LANDMARC: Indoor Location Sensing Using Active RFID. *Wireless Networks, 10*, 701-710.

Ni, L. M., Liu, Y., Lau, C. Y. & Patil, A. (2003). LANDMARC: Indoor Location Sensing Using Active RFID. *percom, p. 407, First IEEE International Conference on Pervasive Computing and Communications (PerCom'03)*.

Ni, L. M., Liu, Y., Lau, Y. C., & Patil, A. P. (2003). *LANDMARC: indoor location sensing using active RFID*. Paper presented at the Pervasive Computing and Communications, 2003. (PerCom 2003). *Proceedings of the First IEEE International Conference*.

Nielsen-Bohlman, L., Panzer, A.M., & Hindig, D.A. (Eds.) (2004). *Health Literacy: A Prescription to End Confusion*. Washington, D.C.: The National Academic Press.

Nikitin, P.V., Rao, K.V.S., and Lazar, S., (2007). An Overview of Near Field UHF RFID. *IEEE International Conference on RFID 2007*.

Nilsson, M. & Hallberg, J., (2002). Positioning with Bluetooth, IrDA and RFID. Master thesis Lulea University of Technology, Department of Computer Science and Electrical Engineering.

NJE Consulting (2006). *RFID Technical Information*. Retrieved from http://www.nje.ca/Index_RFIDTechnical.htm

Nortel (2006). *Why Nortel for fixed-mobile convergence?* Viewed 03 October, 2007

NZ Health Information Service. (2004). *National Health Index FAQ*. Retrieved August 31, 2004, from www. nzhis.govt.nz

O'Connor, M. (2005, April 13). RFID and the media revolution. *RFID Journal*. Retrieved April 20, 2005, from http://www.rfidjournal.com/article/articleview/1508/1/1/

O'Connor, M.C. (2004, November 30). *RFID users want clear data.* Retrieved from *www.rfidjournal.com/article/articleview/1232/1/1/*

O'Connor, M.C. (2006, August 18). *Apparel & footwear summit attracts wide audience.* Retrieved from *http://www.rfidjournal.com/article/articleview/2599/1/1/*

O'Connor, M.C. (2007, January 8). *Michelin shrinks its e-tire pressure monitor.* Retrieved from *http://www.rfidjournal.com/article/articleview/2950/1/1/*

O'Connor, M.C. (2006). *Warehouse management systems that handle RFID data.* Retrieved from *http://www.rfidjournal.com/magazine/article/2259*

O'Shea, P. (2003). RFID comes of age for tracking everything from pallets to people. *ChipCenter.* Retrieved July 12, 2003, from http://www.chipcenter.com/analog/ed008.htm

Odell, J. (Ed.). (2000). *Agent technology* (OMG Document 00-09-01). OMG Agents interest Group.

Odell, J. (Ed.). (2000, September). *Agent technology.* OMG Document 00-09-01, OMG Agents interest Group.

Ortiz, S., (2006). Is Near-Field Communication Close to Success? *Computer, 39*(3), 18-20.

OSGi Alliance. (2005). *About the OSGi service platform* (rev. 4.1). San Ramon, CA: OSGi Alliance.

Paciga, M., & Lutfiyya, H., (2005). Herecast:An Open Infrastructure for Location-Based Services Using WiFi. *Wireless And Mobile Computing, Networking And Communications, 2005.* (WiMobapos 2005), IEEE International Conference, Volume 4, Aug. 2005 (pp 21 – 28).

Pagarkar, M., Natesan, M., & Prakash, B. (2005). *RFID in integrated order management systems: RFID, VMI and CPFR in integrated order management systems for retail supply chains.* RFID Journal White Paper.

Palmer, M. (2004). Principles of Effective RFID Data Management. *Enterprise Systems,* 1-8.

Palmer, M. (2004). Principles of Effective RFID Data Management. *Enterprise Systems,* 1-8.

Palmer, M. (2004, February 2). *Build an effective RFID architecture.* Retrieved from *http://www.rfidjournal.com/article/articleview/781/1/82/*

Pare, G., Jaana, M., & Sicotte, C. (2007). Systematic Review of Home Telemonitoring for Chronic Diseases: The Evidence Base. *J Am Med Inform Assoc, 14*(3), 269-277.

Paric Limited. (2006). Paric homepage. Retrieved 1st December 2006, 2006, from http://www.paric.co.nz/

Parlikad, A.K., & McFarlane, D. (2007). RFID-based product information in end-of-life decision making. *Control Engineering Practice.*

Perry, R. W. (1991). Managing Disaster Response Operations. *Emergency Management International City/Country Management Association, Washington, DC 201-223 Drabek.*

Peterson, D. M., & Perry, R. W. (1999). The Impact of Disaster Excercises on Participants. *Disaster Prevention and Management, 8*(4), 241-254.

Pettigrew, A., Ferlie, E., & McKee, L. (1992). *Shaping Strategic Change.* London: Sage.

Pink, B. (2004). *District Health Board Deficit Decreases.* Retrieved November 1, 2004, from www.stats.govt.nz

Pisello, T. (2004). The Three Rs of RFID: Rewards, Risk, and ROI from http://www.ism.co.at/analyses/RFID/Three_Risks.html

Porikli, F. (2005). Integral histogram: a fast way to extract histograms in Cartesian spaces. *Proceedings of the IEEE Conference on Computer Vision and Pattern Recognition, 1,* 829 - 836.

Porter, J. D., Billo, R. E., & Mickle, M. H. (2006). Effect of active interference on the performance of radio frequency identification systems. *International journal of Radio Frequency Technology and Applications, 1*(1).

Position Statement on the use of RFID on consumer products (2003, November). Retrieved from http://www.spychips.org/jointrfid_position_paper.html

Prabhu, B. S., Su, X., Ramamurthy, H., Chu, C., & Gadh, R. (2004). WinRFID: A Middleware for the Enablement of Radio Frequency Identification (RFID) Based Applications.

Prashant, S., & Huosheng, H. (2005). *Techniques used for Location-based Services: A survey.* University of Essex.

Prince, K., Morán, H., & McFarlane, D. (2004). *Auto-ID Use Case: Food Manufacturing Company Distribution.* Cambridge University, UK.

Priyantha, B., N., Chakraboorty, A., & Balakrishnan, H., (2000). The Cricket location-support system. *Proc. of the Sixth Annual ACM International Conference on Mobile Computing and Networking* (MOBICOM), August 2000.

Proc, J. (2006). Decca Navigator System. Retrieved February 4, 2008, from http://www.jproc.ca/ hyperbolic/decca.html

Proc, J. (2006). LORAN. Retrieved February 4, 2008, from http://www.jproc.ca/hyperbolic/ loran_a.html

Proc, J. (2006). Omega Navigation System. Retrieved February 6, 2008, from http://www.jproc.ca/ hyperbolic/omega.html

Purvis, M., Cranefield, S., Nowostawski, M., & Carter, D. (2002). Opal: A multi-level infrastructure for agent-oriented software development. *Autonomous agents and multi-agent systems.* Bologna, Italy: ACM Press.

Qiu, R.G. (2007). RFID-enabled automation in support of factory integration. *Robotics and Computer-Integrated Manufacturing.*

Quan, T., & Tran, E. D. M. (2005). The Aware Home - Memory Mirror. Retrieved 1st December 2006, 2006, from http://www-static.cc.gatech.edu/fce/ahri/projects/ Memory_Mirror.pdf

Quarterly, M. K. (2003). *Why Retail Wants Radio Tags.*

Ramakrishnan, K., & Deavours, D. (2006). Performance benchmarks for passive UHF RFID tags. *Proceedings of the 13th GI/ITG Conference on Measurement, Modeling, and Evaluation of Computer and Communication Systems.* Nurenberg, Germany.

Ranky, P.G. (2006). An introduction to radio frequency identification (RFID) methods and solutions. *Assembly Automation, 26,* 28-33.

Raza, N., Bradshaw, V., & Hague, M. (1999). Applications of RFID technology. *RFID Technology (Ref. No. 1999/123), IEE Colloquium.*

Reddy, M., & Dourish, P. (2002). *A Finger on the Pulse: Temporal Rhythms and Information Seeking in Medical Work.* Paper presented at the ACM Conference on Computer-Supported Co-operative Work, New Orleans, Louisiana.

Regattieri, A., Gamberi, M., & Manzini, R. (2007). Traceability of food products: General framework and experimental evidence. *Journal of Food Engineering, 81,* 347-356.

Reid, A.S. (2007). Is society smart enough to deal with smart cards? *Computer Law & Security Report, 23,* 53-61.

Research Information. (2007). *Radio-tagged books.* Retrieved April 3, 2008, from http://www.researchinformation.info/rimayjun04radiotagged.html

RFID Australia. (2003). *Why use RFID.* Retrieved February 15, 2008, from http://www.rfid-australia. com/files/htm/rfid%20brochure/page4.html

RFID Gazette. (2007). *RFID applications for libraries.* Retrieved April 3, 2008, from http://www.rfidgazette. org/libraries/

RFID Journal (n.d.). *RFID Journal frequency asked questions.* Retrieved from http://www.rfidjournal.com

RFID Journal. (2002, October 24). *CD tracking project deemed a hit.* Retrieved from *http://www.rfidjournal. com/article/articleview/98/1/1/*

RFID Journal. (2002, June 24). *Learning from Prada.* Retrieved from *http://www.rfidjournal.com/article/ view/425*

RFID Journal. (2003, September 22). *Tesco deploys class 1 EPC tags*. Retrieved from *http://www.rfidjournal. com/article/articleview/587/1/1/*

RFID Journal. (2007, February). *EPC/RFID data sharing: Enter a new era of supply chain collaboration between retailers and suppliers*. Retrieved from *http://www. rfidjournal.com/whitepapers/download/209*

Richardson, B. (1994). Socio-Technical Disasters: Profile and Prevalence. *Disaster Prevention and Management, 3*(4), 41-69.

Robert, H., & Clarke, D. T. J. R. T. K. K. B. (2006). Radio frequency identification (RFID) performance: the effect of tag orientation and package contents. *Packaging Technology and Science, 19*(1), 45-54.

Robert, H., & Clarke, D. T. J. R. T. K. K. B. (2006). Radio frequency identification (RFID) performance: the effect of tag orientation and package contents. *Packaging Technology and Science, 19*(1), 45-54.

Roberti, M. (2003). *Singapore Fights SARS with RFID*. Retrieved August 1, 2004, from www.rfidjournal.com

Roberti, M. (2003, October 6). The tipping point. *RFID Journal*. Retrieved October 26, 2003, from http://www. rfidjournal.com/article/articleprint/607/-1/2/

Roberti, M. (2004). New ETSI RFID Rules Move Forward. *RFID Journal*. Retrieved December 21, 2007, from http://www.rfidjournal.com

Roberti, M. (2004, April 30). *Wal-Mart begins RFID rollout*. Retrieved from *http://www.rfidjournal.com/article/articleview/926/1/1*

Roberti, M. (2005a, October 31). *The serendipity effect*. Retrieved from *http://www.rfidjournal.com/article/articleview/1960/1/2/*

Roberti, M. (2005b, October, 17). *Target, Wal-Mart share EPC data*. Retrieved from *http://www.rfidjournal. com/article/articleview/1928/1/1/*

Roberti, M. (2006). SmartCode Offers 5-Cent EPC Tags. *RFID Journal*. Retrieved April 26, 2008, from http://www.rfidjournal.com

Roberts, C. (2006). Radio Frequency Identification (RFID). *Journal of Computers and Security*.

Rogers, E. M. (1995). *Diffusion of Innovations*. New York: The Free Press.

Römer, K., Schoch, T., Mattern, F., & Dübendorfer, T. (2004). Smart identification frameworks for ubiquitous computing applications. *Wireless Networks, 10*(6), 689-700.

Rosenal, T., Paterson, R., Wakefield, S., Zuege, D., & Lloyd-Smith, G. (1995). *Physician involvement in hospital information system selection: a success story*. Paper presented at the Eighth World Conference on Medical Informatics, Vancouver, Canada.

Rosenberg J D. (2006). *SIP and fixed mobile convergence: Realizing the component architecture*.

Ross, D. A., & Blasch, B. B. (2002). Development of a Wearable Computer Orientation System. *ACM Personal and Ubiquitous Computing, 6*(1), 49-63.

Ruta, M., Di Noia, T., Di Sciascio, E., & Donini, F. (2006a). Semantic-enhanced Bluetooth discovery protocol for M-Commerce applications. *International Journal of Web and Grid Services, 2*(4), 424-452.

Ruta, M., Di Noia, T., Di Sciascio, E., Donini, F., & Piscitelli, G. (2006b). Advanced resource discovery protocol for semantic-enabled M-commerce. *Encyclopaedia of Mobile Computing and Commerce (EMCC)*. Hershey, PA: Idea Group.

Sanem, K., Adam, P., & al, e. (2006). Virtual Sensors: Abstracting Data from Physical Sensors. *Proceedings of the 2006 International Symposium on World of Wireless, Mobile and Multimedia Networks, IEEE Computer Society*.

Sanem, K., Adam, P., & al, e. (2006). Virtual Sensors: Abstracting Data from Physical Sensors. *Proceedings of the 2006 International Symposium on World of Wireless, Mobile and Multimedia Networks, IEEE Computer Society*.

SAP. (2003). *SAP Auto-ID Infrastructure*.

Sarma, S. (2001). *Towards the 5-cent Tag*. MA: Auto-ID Labs.

Sarma, S. (2005). A History of the EPC. In S. Garfinkel & B. Rosenberg (Eds.), *RFID Applications, Security, and Privacy* (pp. 37-55). NJ: Addison-Wesley.

Satoh, I. (2005). *A location model for pervasive computing environments*.

Sawicki, E. & Wells, N. (2006). *Advanced Guide to Linux Networking and Security*.

Saygin, C. (2007). Adaptive inventory management using RFID data. *International Journal of Advanced Manufacturing Technology, 32,* 1045-1051.

Schmidt, A., Gellersen, H., & Merz, C. (2000). Enabling implicit human computer interaction: A wearable RFID tag reader. *The 4th International Symposium on Wearable Computers* (pp. 193-194).

Schoenberger, C. (2002, March 18). RFID: The Internet of things. *Forbes*. Retrieved September 18, 2003, from http://www.mindfully.org/Technology/RFID-Things-Forbes18mar02.htm

Schuerenberg, B. K. (2007). *Bar Codes vs RFID: A Battle Just Beginning*. Retrieved October 2, 2007, from www.healthdatamanagement.com

Schuster, E. W., Allen, S. J., & Brock D. L. (2007). *Global RFID: The value of the EPCglobal network for supply chain management*. Berlin; New York: Springer. ISBN: 9783540356547.

Schwartz D. (2005). *InFocus: Why wireline carriers will be the early adopters of fixed mobile convergence*.

Schwieren, J., & Vossen, G. (2007). Implementing Physical Hyperlinks for Mobile Applications Using RFID Tags. *11th International Databse Engineering and Applications Symposium, Banff, AB, Canada,* (pp. 154-162).

Schwieren, J., & Vossen, G. (2007). Implementing Physical Hyperlinks for Mobile Applications Using RFID Tags. *11th International Databse Engineering and Applications Symposium, Banff, AB, Canada,* (pp. 154-162).

Sellitto, C., Burgess, S., & Hawking, P. (2007). Information quality attributes associated with RFID-derived benefits in the retail supply chain. *International Journal of Retail & Distribution Management, 35,* 69-87.

Shadbolt, N., Hall, W., & Berners-Lee, T. (2006). The semantic Web revisited. *IEEE Intelligent Systems, 21*(3), 96-101.

Shah, S. (2006). *Semantics and Internet of things*. RFID Journal White Paper.

Sharma, A., Citurs, A., & Konsynski, B. (2007). *Strategic and Institutional Perspectives in the Adoption and Early Integration of Radio Frequency Identification (RFID)*. Paper presented at the Proceedings of the 40th Hawaii International Conference on System Sciences - 2007, Hawaii

Sheffi, Y. (2004). RFID and the Innovation Cycle. *The International Journal of Logistics Management, 15*(1).

Shepard, S. (2005). *Radio Frequency Identification*. NY: McGraw-Hill.

Shepard, S. (2004). *RFID*. McGraw-Hill. (ISBN: 0-071-4429-95)

Shepard, S. (2005). *RFID: Radio frequency identification*. New York: McGraw-Hill. ISBN: 0071442995.

Siegemund, F., & Florkemeier, C. (2003). Interaction in pervasive computing settings using Bluetooth-enabled active tags and passive RFID technology together with mobile phones. *Proceedings of the 1st IEEE International Conference on Pervasive Computing and Communications, PerCom 2003* (pp. 378-387).

Singel, R. (2004, October 21). American passports to get chipped. *Wired*. Retrieved December 12, 2004, from http://www.wired.com/news/privacy/0,1848,65412,00.html

Singh, R., Gmdetto, M., Guainazzo, M., Angiati, D., & Ragazzoni, S., C., (2004). A novel positioning system for static location estimation employing WLAN in indoor environment. *Personal, Indoor and Mobile Radio Communications, PIMRC 2004*. 15th IEEE International Symposium Volume 3 (pp 1762 - 1766).

Smith, J. R., Fishkin, K. P., Jiang, B., Mamishev, A., Philipose, M., Rea, A. D., et al. (2005). RFID-based techniques for human-activity detection. *Communications of the ACM, 48*(9), 39-44.

Smucker, T. (2006). *Making the GS1 Vision a Reality* (Annual Report). Brussels: GS1.

Sokol, B., & Shah, S. (2004). *RFID in Healthcare*. Retrieved October 30, 2004, from www.rfidjournal.com

Soon, C. B., & Gutierrez, J. (2008, May 18-20). *Where is New Zealand at with Radio Frequency Identification in the Supply Chain? - A Survey Result.* Paper presented at the Proceedings of 2008 International Conference on Information Resources Management, Niagara Falls, Canada.

Soon, C. B., & Gutierrez, J. A. (2008). Effects of the RFID Mandate on Supply Chain Management. *Journal of Theoretical and Applied Electronic Commerce Research, 3*(1), 81-91.

Spieβ, P., Bornhövd, C., Lin, T., Haller, S., & Schaper, J. (2007). Going beyond auto-ID: A service-oriented smart items infrastructure. *Journal of Enterprise Information Management, 20,* 356-370.

Stanford, V. (2003). Pervasive Computing Goes the Last Hundred Feet with RFID Systems. *Pervasive Computing, 2*(2), 9-14.

Stasko, J., Miller, T., Pousman, Z., Plaue, C., & Ullah, O. (2004). Personalized Peripheral Information Awareness through Information Art, In *Proceedings of UbiComp '04* (pp. 18-35). Nottingham, U.K

Statistics New Zealand. (2005). *National Population Projections 2004(base) – 2051.* Retrieved 28th November 2005, 2005, from http://www2. stats.govt.nz/domino/external/pasfull/pasfull.nsf/ 7cf46ae26dcb6800cc256a62000a2248/c2567ef00247c 6acc256f6b00095c46?OpenDocument

Statistics New Zealand. (2006, October 2007). *The 2006 New Zealand Disability Survey.* Retrieved 1st May 2008, 2008, from http://www.stats.govt.nz/NR/rdonlyres/ 799A77CC-4DF6-445C-96DA-F5A266538A72/0/ 2006disabilitysurveyhotp.pdf

Stauffer, H. B. (1991). Smart enabling system for home automation. *IEEE Transactions on Consumer Electronics, 37*(2), xxix-xxxv.

Steele, R., Ventsov, Y., & Dillon, T. (2004). An Object-Oriented Database-based Architecture for mobile enterprise Applications. *Proceedings of the International conference on Information Technology: Coding and Computing, IEEE computer society, 1,* 586-590.

Stefanov, D. H., Bien, Z., & Bang, W.-C. (2004). The smart house for older persons and persons with physical disabilities: structure, technology arrangements, and perspectives. *IEEE Transactions on Neural Systems and Rehabilitation Engineering, 12*(2), 228-250.

Stocking, B. (1985). *Initiative and Inertia.* London: Nuffield Provincial Hospital Trust.

Stockman, H. (1948, October). Communication by means of reflected power. *Proceedings of the Institute of Radio Engineers* (pp. 1196-1204).

Stoutenburg, A. (2007). *Overview of FMC architecture & challenges.* Viewed 12 October 2007.

Strassner, M., & Schoch, T. (2002). *Today's Impact of Ubiquitous Computing on Business Processes.* Paper presented at the First International Conference on Pervasive Computing, Zurich, Switzerland.

Stringleman, H. (2003). *Electronic identification comes a step closer.* Retrieved November 1, 2004, from www. country-wide.co.nz

Sullivan, L. (2004, October 25). IBM shares RFID lessons. *InformationWeek.* Retrieved November 9, 2004, from http://www.informationweek.com/shared/print-ableArticle.jhtml?articleID=51000091

Suzuki, R., Ogawa, M., Otake, S., Izutsu, T., Tobimatsu, Y., Iwaya, T., et al. (2006). Rhythm of daily living and detection of atypical days for elderly people living alone as determined with a monitoring system. *Journal of Telemedicine and Telecare, 12*(4), 208-214.

Swedberg, C. (2006). China Endorses ISO 18000-7 433 MHz Standard. *RFIDJournal* Retrieved July 29, 2007, from http://www.rfidjournal.com/

Swedberg, C. (2007). EC Spectrum Decision Expected to Boost UWB RFID Adoption. *RFID Journal*. Retrieved December 29, 2007, from http://www.rfidjournal.com

Swedberg, C. (2008). *Italian Hospital Uses RFID to Document Patient Location, Treatment*. Retrieved February 12, 2008, from www.rfidjournal.com

Swedberg, C. (2008). RFID Fuels Gas Tank Sercurity. *RFID Journal*. Retrieved April 26, 2008, from http://www.rfidjournal.com

Swedberg, C. (2006, April 19). University of Kansas' tag for metal, liquids. *RFID Journal*. Retrieved May 7, 2006, from http://www.rfidjournal.com/article/articleview/2275/1/1/

Swedberg, C. (2008). U.S. FDA Seeks Research for Medical Device Tracking System. *RFID Journal*. Retrieved April 26, 2008, from http://www.rfidjournal.com

Symonds, J., Parry D., & Briggs J. (2007, June 8-10 2007.). *An RFID-based system for assisted living: Challenges and Solutions*. Paper presented at the ICMCC 2007 Event: Empowering the Patient. , Amsterdam.

Tafte, E.R. (2001). *The Visual Display of Quantitative Information*. Cheshire, Connecticut: Graphics Press.

Tang, F., Brennan, S., Zhao, Q., & Tao, H. (2007). Co-tracking using semi-supervised support vector machines. *In IEEE International Conference on Computer Vision*.

Telecare Knowledge Network. (2007, 1st June 2007). *Telecare Knowledge Network*. Retrieved 1st July 2007, 2007, from http://www.tkn.port.ac.uk/

Tellkamp, C., Angerer, A., Fleisch, E., & Corsten, D. (2005). *From pallet to shelf: Improving data quality in retail supply chains using RFID*. Auto ID Center White Paper.

The Economist. (2007, June 7). *Radio silence*. Retrieved from *http://www.economist.com/search/displaystory.cfm?story_id=9249278&CFID=15975447&CFTOKEN=95269337#top*

The European Parliament and The Council (2002). Article 18. Regulation (EC) No 178/2002 Of The European Parliament And Of The Council of 28 January 2002. *UE: Official Journal of the European Communities*.

The Foundation for Intelligent Physical Agents (FIPA). (2007). *Agent communication language specification*. Retrieved April 3, 2008, from http://www.fipa.org

Thomas, L. (2005, January 26). RFID cell phones? Maybe in 2007. *Mobile Magazine*. Retrieved January 30, 2005, from http://www.mobilemag.com/content/100/102/C3673/

Thuraisingham, B. (2004). Secure Sensor Information Management and Mining. *Signal Processing Magazine, IEEE 21*(3), 14-19.

Timing New Zealand. (2004). *Winning Time Timing System*. Retrieved November 1, 2004, from www.poprun.co.nz

Tornatzky, L., Eveland, J. D., Boylan, M. G., & Hetzner, W. A. (1990). The Process of Technological Innovation. *Lexington, MA*.

Traub, K., Allgair, G., Barthel, H., Bustein, L., Garrett, J., et al. (2005). *EPCglobal architecture framework*. Technical report, EPCglobal Inc., July 2005.

Trebilcock, B. (2006, July 25). RFID goes to Washington. *Modern Materials Handling*. Retrieved August 3, 2006, from http://www.mmh.com/article/CA6355944.html

Turban, E., Mclean, E., Wetherbe, J., Bolloju, N., & Davison, R. (2002). *Information technology management: Transforming business in the digital economy*. New York: John Wiley & Sons.

Turner, B. A. (1976). The Organizational and Interorganizational Development of Disasters. *Administrative Science Quarterly, 21*(3), 378-397.

Tuscaloosa. (2003). Tuscaloosa County Emergency Management Cycle. Retrieved June 4, 2007, from http://www.tuscoema.org/cycle.html

Tversky, B., Kugelmass, S., & Winter, A. (1991). Cross-Cultural and Developmental Trends in Graphic Production. *Cognitive Psychology, 23*, 515-557.

Twist, D. C. (2005). The impact of radio frequency identification on supply chain facilities. *Journal of Facilities Management, 3*(3), 226-239.

UK Audit Commission. (2004, 12th Feburary 2004). *Assistive Technology Independence and Well-being 4.* Retrieved 1 November 2006, 2006, from http://www.audit-commission.gov.uk/reports/NATIONAL-REPORT.asp?CategoryID=&ProdID=BB070AC2-A23A-4478-BD69-4C19BE942722

UK Department of Health. (2005, 2nd March 2007). Our health, our care, our say. Retrieved 1st July 2007, 2007, from http://www.dh.gov.uk/en/Publicationsandstatistics/Publications/PublicationsPolicyAndGuidance/DH_4127453

Ukkonen, L., Schaffrath, M., Kataja, J., Sydanheimo, L., & Kivikoski, M. (2006). Evolutionary RFID tag antenna design for paper industry applications. *International journal of Radio Frequency Technology and Applications, 1*(1), 107-122.

Van, J. (2005, April 16). RFID spells media revolution, futurist says. *Chicago Tribune*, p. B1.

Varshney, U. (2001). Location Management Support for Mobile Commerce Applications. *International Workshop on Mobile Commerce, 2001.* Proceedings of the 1st international workshop on Mobile commerce, New York, NY, USA, ACM, 2001. (pp 1-6).

Vijayaraman, B. S., & Osyk, B. A. (2006). An empirical study of RFID implementation in the warehousing industry. *The International Journal of Logistics Management, 17*(1), 6-20.

Vijayaraman, B.S., & Osyk, B.A. (2006). An empirical study of RFID implementation in the warehousing industry. *International Journal of Logistics Management, 17*, 6-20.

Violino, B. (2006). APL Reaps Double Benefits From Real-Time Visibility [Electronic Version]. *RFID Journal.* Retrieved December 28, 2006 from http://www.rfidjournal.com.

Walker, J. (2003). What You Need To Know About RFID in 2004. *Forrester Research.* Retrieved December 20, 2003, from http://www.forrester.com

Walker, J., Spivey Overby, C., Mendelsohn, T., & Wilson, C. P. (2003). *What You Need to Know About RFID in 2004.* Retrieved February 9, 2004, from www.forrester.com

Wallace, P. (2004). The Health of Nations. *The Economist, 372,* 1-18.

Wallston, BS, Wallston, KA, Kaplan, GD, & Maides, SA. (1976). Development and validation of the health locus of control (HLC) scale. *J Consult Clin Psychol 44*(4), 580-585.

Walter, E. J. (1988). Bar Code Boom Extending thru Industry. *Purchasing World, 32*(2), 39.

Wang, F., & Liu, P. (2005). *Temporal management of RFID data* (pp. 1128-1139). Siemens Corporate Research.

Wang, F., & Liu, P. (2005). Temporal Management of RFID Data. *Proceedings of the 31st VLDB Conference, Trondheim, Norway* (pp. 1128-1139).

Wang, F., & Liu, P. (2005). Temporal Management of RFID Data. *Proceedings of the 31st VLDB Conference, Trondheim, Norway* (pp. 1128-1139).

Wang, Y., Jia, X., & Lee, K., H., (2003). *An indoors wireless positioning system based on wireless local area network infrastructure.* Paper presented at SatNav 2003, The 6th International Symposium on Satellite Navigation Technology Including Mobile Positioning & Location Services Melbourne, Australia 22–25 July 2003.

Want, R. (2006). An Introduction to RFID Technology. *IEEE CS and IEEE ComSoc.*

Want, R., (2006). An introduction to RFID technology. *IEEE Pervasive Computing, 5*(1), 25-33.

Want, R.., Fishkin, K.P., Gujar, A. & Harrison, B.L. (1999). *Bridging Physical and Virtual Worlds with Electronic Tags.* CHI 99 Pittsburgh P.A., USA, 15-20 May

Ward, M. (2007). The price of speed. *National Petroleum News, 99,* 28-32.

Warden, T. (2005). *The RFID software conundrum.* RFID Journal White Paper.

Wasserman, E. (2007). Europe Embraces EPC - Slowly. *RFID Journal.* Retrieved December 21, 2007, from http://www.rfidjournal.com

Wasserman, E. (2007). *A Healthy ROI.* Retrieved October 12, 2007, from www.rfidjournal.com

Watson, M. (1997). *Intelligent Java applications for the Internet and intranets.* Morgan Kaufmann. (ISBN: 1-55860-420-0)

WAVE Advisory Board. (2001). *From Strategy to Reality: The WAVE Project.*

Webster, C., Merry, A., Gander, P. H., & Mann, N. K. (2004). A prospective, randomised clinical evaluation of a new safety-orientated injectable drug administration system in comparison with conventional methods. *Anaesthesia, 59,* 80-87.

Webster, J. (2006, January 2). RFID: Cost and complexity continue to block enterprise use. *Computerworld,* Retrieved February 28, 2006, from http://www.computerworld.com/managementtopics/management/story/0,10801,107308,00.html?source=NLT_EB&nid=107308

Wei, Y., Sun, J., Tang, X., & Shum, H. (2007). Interactive offline tracking for color objects. *In IEEE International Conference on Computer Vision.*

Weinstein, R. (2005). RFID: A Technical Overview and Its Application to the Enterprise. *IT Professional Magazine, 7*(3), 27-33.

Weiser, M. (1993). Hot Topics - Ubiquitous Computing. *Computer, 26,* 71-72.

Wessel, R. (2007). European EPC Competence Center Releases UHF Tag Study. *RFID Journal.* Retrieved July 16, 2007, from http://www.rfidjournal.com

Wessel, R. (2007a). *German Hospital Expands Bed-Tagging Project.* Retrieved February 12, 2008, from www.rfidjournal.com

Wessel, R. (2007b). *RFID Synergy at a Netherlands Hospital.* Retrieved October 31, 2007, from www.rfidjournal.com

Wikipedia. (2008). List of Disasters. Retrieved February 1, 2008, from http://en.wikipedia.org/wiki/List_of_natural_disasters_by_death_toll

Wikipedia (n.d.). Retrieved from http://en.wikipedia.org/wiki/Automated_identification_and_data_capture

Wikipedia (2006). Wikipedia. *Journal.* Retrieved from http://en.wikipedia.org/wiki/List_of_wars_and_disasters_by_death_toll

Wilson, R. M., Runciman, W. B., Gibberd, R. W., Harrison, B. T., Newby, L., & Hamilton, J. (1995). The quality in Australian health care study. *Medical Journal of Australia, 163,* 458-471.

Wong, K.H.M., Hui, P.C.L., & Chan, A.C.K. (2006). Cryptography and authentication on RFID passive tags for apparel products. *Computers in Industry, 57,* 342-349.

Wooldridge, K, Graber, A, Brown, A, & Davidson, P. (1992). The relationship between health beliefs, adherence, and metabolic control of diabetes. *Diabetes Educator, 18*(6), 495-450

Wooldridge, M., & Jennings, N. (1995). Intelligent agents: Theory and practice. *The Knowledge Engineering Review, 10*(2), 115-152. (ISBN: 0-269-888-9)

Wooldridge, M., & Jennings, N. (1995). Intelligent software agents: Theory and Practice. *The Knowledge Engineering Review, 10*(2), 115-152.

Wright, D. (2003). *Business Case for Clinical Information System - Phase 1.* Auckland: Waitemata District Health Board.

Wu, H., Chellappa, R., Sankaranarayanan, A. C., & Zhou, S. K. (2007). Robust visual tracking using time-reversibility constraint. *In IEEE International Conference on Computer Vision.*

Wyld, D. C. (2005, February 24). Supporting the "warfighter." *RFIDNews.* Retrieved March 1, 2005, from http://www.rfidnews.org/library/2005/02/24/supporting-the-warfighter/

Xiaojun, D., Junichi, I. & Sho, H., (2004). Unique Features of Mobile Commerce. *Journal of Business Research.*

Xiong, R. & Donath, J. (1999). PeopleGarden: creating data portraits for users. In *Proceedings of the 12th Annual ACM Symposium on User interface Software and Technology* (Asheville, NC, United States, November 07 - 10, 1999). UIST '99, pp. 37-44.

Yu, S.C. (2007). RFID implementation and benefits in libraries. *The Electronic Library, 25,* 54-64.

Zanella, A., Tonello, A., & Pupolin S. (2002). On the impact of fading and inter-piconet interference on Bluetooth performance. *The 5ᵗʰ International Symposium on Wireless Personal Multimedia Communications, 1,* 218-222.

Zhen-hua, D., Jin-tao, L., & Bo, F. (2007). Radio Frequency Identification in Food Supervision. *The 9th International Conference on Advanced Communication Technology.* 542-545.

Zhu, W., Wang, D., & Sheng, H. (2005). Mobile RFID technology for improving M-Commerce. *e-Business Engineering, 2005. ICEBE 2005. IEEE International Conference.*

Ziv, J., & Lempel, A. (1977). A universal algorithm for sequential data compression. *IEEE Transactions on Information Theory, 23*(3), 337-343.

Zlatanova, S., Oosterom, P., & Verbree, E. (2004). *3D Technology for Improving Disaster Management: Geo-DBMS and Positioning.* Paper presented at the XXth ISPRS congress.

About the Contributors

Judith Symonds is a senior lecturer at AUT University, Auckland, New Zealand. Judith serves as the editor-in-chief of the *International Journal of Advanced Pervasive and Ubiquitous Computing (IJAPUC)*. Judith holds a PhD in rural systems management from the University of Queensland (2005, Australia). Judith has published in international refereed journals, book chapters and conferences, including the Australian Journal of Information Systems and the *Journal of Cases on Information Technology*. She currently serves on editorial boards for the *Journal of Electronic Commerce in Organisations* and the *International Journal of E-Business Research*. Her current research interests include data management in pervasive and ubiquitous computing environments.

John Ayoade obtained his PhD degree in information systems under Japanese Government Scholarship from the Graduate School of Information Systems in the University of Electro-Communications, Tokyo, Japan. He has research and teaching experience from research institutes and universities around the globe. His research work focuses on IT emerging technologies (pervasive computing, RFID, computer network security and mobile communications). He has presented and published papers in many international conferences and journals in the USA, Japan, Canada, U.K, Australia, New Zealand and Korea. He is presently an assistant professor in the School of Information Technology and Communications, American University of Nigeria.

David Parry is a senior lecturer in the Auckland University of Technology School of Computing and Mathematical Sciences New Zealand. His PhD thesis was concerned with the use of fuzzy ontologies for medical information retrieval. He holds degrees from Imperial College and St. Bartholomew's Medical College, London and the University of Otago, New Zealand. His research interests include internet-based knowledge management and the Semantic Web, health informatics, the use of radio frequency ID in healthcare and information retrieval.

* * *

Ashir Ahmed. After completing master's of information technology and six years of work as a software developer/analyst; Ashir Ahmed is currently doing PhD in the area of emergency management from Monash University, Australia. So far, he has three published conference papers. In addition to emergency management his other interest areas includes radio frequency identification (RFID), project management and database systems.

Professor Olaf Diegel, director of Creative Industries Research Institute, AUT University. Professor Olaf Diegel is both an educator and a practitioner of engineering product development with an excellent track record of developing innovative product solutions. At AUT, he is director of the Creative Industries Research Institute, an interdisciplinary institute that crosses over between engineering, art & design, computers and communications. In his consulting practice he develops a wide range of products for New Zealand and international companies. Over the past 10 years he has developed over 40 commercialized new products including innovative new theatre lighting products, security and marine products and several home health monitoring products. He has received numerous New Zealand and international product development awards, and helped to firmly put New Zealand on the world innovation map.

Tommaso Di Noia (t.dinoia@poliba.it) is an assistant professor in information technology engineering at Technical University of Bari (Politecnico di Bari). He got his PhD from Technical University of Bari. His main scientific interests include: Description Logics - theoretical and practical aspects; resource matchmaking; knowledge representation systems for electronic commerce; automatic (Web) services discovery and composition; knowledge representation systems and applications for the Semantic Web. He co-authored papers which received the best paper award at conferences ICEC-2004, IEEE CEC-EEE-2006 and ICEC-2007.

Eugenio Di Sciascio (disciascio@poliba.it) received the master's degree with honours from University of Bari, and the PhD from Politecnico di Bari (Technical University of Bari). He is currently full professor of information technology engineering at Technical University of Bari, and leads the research group of SisInfLab, the Information Systems Laboratory of Technical University of Bari. Formerly, he has been an assistant professor at University of Lecce and associate professor at Technical University of Bari. His research interests include multimedia information retrieval, knowledge representation and e-commerce. He is involved in several national and European research projects related to his research interests. He co-authored papers that received best paper awards at conferences ICEC-2004, IEEE CEC-EEE-2006 and ICEC-2007.

Francesco Maria Donini (donini@unitus.it) is a full professor at the Università della Tuscia–Viterbo, Italy. Formerly, he was an assistant professor at the Università La Sapienza, Rome, and associate professor at Politecnico di Bari. His PhD thesis was on description logics; he has subsequently worked on many aspects of knowledge representation in artifi cial intelligence, both on theoretical issues and practical applications. His research interests range from description logics to non-monotonic reasoning, abduction, algorithms, and complexity of reasoning in KR formalisms to their application in a variety of practical contexts. He co-authored papers that won awards at the IJCAI-1991, ICEC-2004, and IEEE CEC EEE -2006 conferences.

Toktam Ebadi, B.E., is a PhD student at the University of Otago, Dunedin, New Zealand. Her research interests are in the areas of distributed computing, collaborative decision-making and Multi agent robotic systems.

Filippo Gandino received the MS degree in computer engineering from Politecnico di Torino, Italy, in 2005. He is currently a PhD student at the Department of Computer Engineering of Politecnico di Torino. His research interests include ubiquitous computing, RFID, wireless sensor networks, security and privacy, information systems, and digital arithmetic. He is a member of IEEE Computer Society.

John D. Garofalakis (http://athos.cti.gr/garofalakis/) is associate professor at the Department of Computer Engineering and Informatics, University of Patras, Greece, and *Director of the applied research department "Telematics Center" of the Research Academic Computer Technology Institute (RACTI)*. He is responsible and scientific coordinator of several European and national IT and Telematics Projects (ICT, INTERREG, etc.). His publications include more than 100 articles in refereed International Journals and Conferences. His research interests include Web and Mobile Technologies, Performance Analysis of Computer Systems, Computer Networks and Telematics, Distributed Computer Systems, Queuing Theory.

Bryan Houliston has a bachelor's degree in commerce, a master's degree in Information Technology, and 13 years experience as a professional software developer. He's in his first year of a PhD researching RFID technology, its applications in health care, and in particular activity analysis. He's a member of the ACM, the NZ Computer Society, two book clubs, the Auckland Film Society, and Greenpeace.

Ric Jentzsch has over 30 years experience in the information technology industry. He has developed and delivered training courses for business and government in Australia, United States, Canada and throughout South East Asia. Ric has more than 60 published works in journals and international conferences. Ric has lectured at universities in Australia, United States, and Canada. His current research interests include: Technology diffusion and adoption - small to medium enterprises (SME) intelligent agents frameworks, models, and incorporation into business Security as a business enhancer Emerging and Developing technologies an SME perspective electronic content management methods, models, practical application Ric is currently on assignment to Compucat Research Pty Ltd as the documentation manager and a researcher.

Lena Mamykina (Siemens Corporate Research, Georgia Institute of Technology). Lena Mamykina is a PhD candidate in human-centered computing at the Georgia Institute of Technology. She investigates computing systems that help individuals with chronic diseases maintain their health and quality of life. She holds an MS degree in human- computer interaction from Georgia Tech and BS in Computer Science and Shipbuilding Engineering from the Ukrainian State Maritime Technical University.

Christos G. Mettouris is a graduate of the Computer Engineering & Informatics Department in the University of Patras. He holds a master's degree of the same department. He is a member of the e-learning sector of the Research Academic Computer Technology Institute *(RACTI). He has published his diploma thesis work in the 1st Hellenic Scientific Student Computing Conference, obtaining an award for presenting one the 3 top papers. His research interests include wireless technologies and mobile networks.*

Masoud Mohammadian research interests lie in adaptive self-learning systems, fuzzy logic, genetic algorithms, neural networks and their applications in industrial, financial and business problems. His current research concentrates on the application of computational intelligence techniques for learning and adaptation of intelligent agents. He has chaired over nine international conferences on computational intelligence and intelligent agents. He has published over ninety research papers in conferences, journal and books as well as editing fifteen books. Masoud has over fourteen years of academic experience and he has served as program committee member and/or co-chair of a large number of national and international conferences. He was the chair of IEEE ACT Section and he was the recipient of Awards from IEEE from USA and Ministry of Commerce from Austria.

Bartolomeo Montrucchio *received the MS degree in electronic engineering and the PhD degree in computer engineering both from Politecnico di Torino, Italy, in 1998, and 2002, respectively. He is currently an assistant professor of computer engineering at Department of Computer Engineering of Politecnico di Torino, Italy. His current research interests include image analysis and synthesis techniques, scientific visualization and sensor networks (also RFIDs). In these fields he is (co)-author of several scientific publications. Since 2002 he has been a member of IEEE Circuits and Systems Society and a member of Eurographics.*

Elizabeth D. Mynatt (Georgia Institute of Technology). Beth Mynatt, an associate professor in the College of Computing and director of the GVU Center, received a PhD degree in computer science from the Georgia Institute of Technology in 1995, where she was also a research scientist in the GVU Center. Her research centers around human computer interaction, ubiquitous computing, augmented reality, auditory interfaces, assistive technology and everyday computing.

Sarita Pais is currently doing her thesis on "Data Modelling for active RFID tags" at Auckland University of Technology, Auckland, New Zealand. Her supervisor is Dr. Judith Symonds. Sarita had done her bachelor's of science in computer science, mathematics and statistics in St. Aloysius College, Mangalore, India. She has 15 years of experience in the IT field. She has been teaching programming, database and system analysis and design. She is currently teaching in Whitireia Community Polytechnic, Auckland. She has also assisted in building some applications for in-house use.

Maryam Purvis, PhD, is a lecturer in information science at the University of Otago, Dunedin, New Zealand. Dr. Purvis obtained MA in Mathematics from University of Texas at Austin and PhD in information science from the University of Otago, Dunedin. Her research interests are in active learning, collaborative learning, distributed information systems and software engineering.

Maurizio Rebaudengo received the MS degree in electronics (1991), and the PhD degree in computer engineering (1995), both from Politecnico di Torino, Torino, Italy. Currently, he is an associate professor at the Department of Computer Engineering of the same Institution. His research interests include testing and dependability analysis of computer-based systems. In the field of RFIDs, his activity is mainly focused on the analysis of traceability systems based on RF devices for agri-food management.

Erwing R. Sanchez is a PhD student in the Department of Computer Engineering at the Politecnico di Torino. His research interests include ubiquitous technologies, RFID security, information theory and low-power wireless networks. Sanchez received his MS in electronic engineering from the Politecnico di Torino in 2005.

Bastin Tony Roy Savarimuthu, M.E., is a lecturer in information science at the University of Otago, Dunedin, New Zealand. His research interests are in the areas of distributed computing, agent based workflow systems, emergence of norms in agent societies and active learning.

Michele Ruta (m.ruta@poliba.it) received the master's degree in electronic engineering from Politecnico di Bari (Technical University of Bari) in 2002 and his PhD in Information Engineering from the same University in 2007. His research interests include pervasive computing and ubiquitous Web, mobile service discovery and composition, knowledge representation systems and applications for wireless ad-hoc contexts. On these topics he has co-authored various papers in international journals and conferences. He is involved in various research projects related to his research interests. He co-authored a paper which received the best paper award at the conference ICEC-2007.

Floriano Scioscia (f.scioscia@poliba.it) received the master's degree in information technology engineering from Politecnico di Bari (Technical University of Bari) in 2006. He is currently pursuing his PhD in Information Engineering at the same University. His research interests include pervasive computing, mobile service discovery and composition, knowledge representation systems and applications for wireless ad-hoc contexts. He co-authored a paper which received the best paper award at the conference ICEC-2007.

Bin SHEN received the BS degree from Department of Electronic Engineering, Tsinghua University, Beijing, China, in 2007. He is a master candidate in the same department in Tsinghua University now. His research interests include statistical learning, pattern recognition and computer vision. Currently, he is working on object tracking in video sequence.

Chin Boo Soon is a PhD candidate at The University of Auckland. He is an assistant lecturer in The Graduate School of Enterprise at The University of Auckland Business School. His current research topic is the adoption of radio frequency identification in the supply chains. Chin Boo has worked in the logistics industry for ten years including six years in military logistics. He received a bachelor's of commerce in information systems (first class honors, 2002) and a master's degree in information systems (2003) from The University of Auckland.

Ly-Fie Sugianto is an expert of international standing, appointed by the Australian Research Council College of Expert. Currently, she is a senior lecturer at the Faculty of Business and Economics, Monash University, Australia. She has published extensively (70+ refereed articles) in the fields of eCommerce, DSS, portals and optimization. Dr. Sugianto has also served as journal editorial board, referee for international journals, and program committee at international conferences.

Eufemia Tinelli (e.tinelli@poliba.it) has a master's degree in information technology engineering from the Technical University of Bari (Politecnico di Bari), Italy, and is currently pursuing her PhD in computer science at the University of Bari. Her research interests are in the areas of efficient storage and retrieval techniques for very large knowledge bases and applications of Semantic Web technologies to e-commerce.

David C. Wyld is the Robert Maurin Professor of Management at Southeastern Louisiana University, where he directs the College of Business' Strategic e-Commerce/e-Government Initiative. He is a noted RFID speaker/consultant/writer, being a frequent contributor to both academic and industry publications. He is a contributing editor to both RFID news and global identification. He is also the author of the recent research report, "RFID: The Right Frequency for Government," the most downloaded report in the history of the IBM Center for the Business of Government. In 2006, he was named a Rising Star in Government Information Technology by Federal Computer Week.

Yu-Jin Zhang is professor of image engineering with the Department of Electronic Engineering at Tsinghua University, Beijing, China, since 1997. His research interests include image processing, image analysis and image understanding, as well as their applications. He has published more than 300 research papers and 18 books, including two monographs: "Image Segmentation" and "Content-based Visual Information Retrieval" (Science Press), and two edited books: *Advances in Image and Video Segmentation* and *Semantic-Based Visual Information Retrieval* (IRM Press). He is vice president of China Society of Image and Graphics and the director of Academic Committee of the Society. He served the program chair of the First, Second, Fourth and Fifth International Conference on Image and Graphics (ICIG'2000, ICIG'2002, ICIG'2007, and ICIG'2007). http://www.ee.tsinghua.edu.cn/~zhangyujin/.

Index